The Hidden Language of
Computer Hardware and Software

C   O   D   E

Charles Petzold

PUBLISHED BY
Microsoft Press
A Division of Microsoft Corporation
One Microsoft Way
Redmond, Washington 98052-6399

Library of Congress Cataloging-in-Publication Data
Petzold, Charles, 1953–
    Code / Charles Petzold.
       p. cm.
    ISBN 0-7356-0505-X
    1. Computer programming. 2. Coding theory. I. Title.

    QA76.6 .P495 1999
    005.7'2 21--dc21   99-040198
                                                                 CIP

Printed and bound in the United States of America.

1 2 3 4 5 6 7 8 9   WCWC   4 3 2 1 0 9

Distributed in Canada by Penguin Books Canada Limited.

A CIP catalogue record for this book is available from the British Library.

Microsoft Press books are available through booksellers and distributors world-wide. For further information about international editions, contact your local Microsoft Corporation office or contact Microsoft Press International directly at fax (425) 936-7329. Visit our Web site at mspress.microsoft.com.

Images of Charles Babbage, George Boole, Louis Braille, Herman Hollerith, Samuel Morse, and John von Neumann appear courtesy of Corbis Images and were modified for this book by Joel Panchot. The January 1975 cover of *Popular Electronics* is reprinted by permission of Ziff-Davis and the Ziff family. All other illustrations in the book were produced by Joel Panchot.

Acquisitions Editor: Ben Ryan
Project Editor: Kathleen Atkins
Technical Editor: Jim Fuchs

Contents

code (kōd) ...

3.a. A system of signals used to represent letters or numbers in transmitting messages.

  b. A system of symbols, letters, or words given certain arbitrary meanings, used for transmitting messages requiring secrecy or brevity.

4. A system of symbols and rules used to represent instructions to a computer...

— The American Heritage Dictionary of the English Language

Chapter One

Best Friends

You're 10 years old. Your best friend lives across the street. In fact, the windows of your bedrooms face each other. Every night, after your parents have declared bedtime at the usual indecently early hour, you still need to exchange thoughts, observations, secrets, gossip, jokes, and dreams. No one can blame you. After all, the impulse to communicate is one of the most human of traits.

While the lights are still on in your bedrooms, you and your best friend can wave to each other from the windows and, using broad gestures and rudimentary body language, convey a thought or two. But sophisticated transactions seem difficult. And once the parents have decreed "Lights out!" the situation seems hopeless.

How to communicate? The telephone perhaps? Do you have a telephone in your room at the age of 10? Even so, wherever the phone is you'll be overheard. If your family personal computer is hooked into a phone line, it might offer soundless help, but again, it's not in your room.

What you and your best friend *do* own, however, are flashlights. Everyone knows that flashlights were invented to let kids read books under the bed covers; flashlights also seem perfect for the job of communicating after dark. They're certainly quiet enough, and the light is highly directional and probably won't seep out under the bedroom door to alert your suspicious folks.

Can flashlights be made to speak? It's certainly worth a try. You learned how to write letters and words on paper in first grade, so transferring that knowledge to the flashlight seems reasonable. All you have to do is stand at your window and draw the letters with light. For an O, you turn on the flashlight, sweep a circle in the air, and turn off the switch. For an I, you make a vertical stroke. But, as you discover quickly, this method simply doesn't work. As you watch your friend's flashlight making swoops and lines in the

3

air, you find that it's too hard to assemble the multiple strokes together in your head. These swirls and slashes of light are not *precise* enough.

You once saw a movie in which a couple of sailors signaled to each other across the sea with blinking lights. In another movie, a spy wiggled a mirror to reflect the sunlight into a room where another spy lay captive. Maybe that's the solution. So you first devise a simple technique. Each letter of the alphabet corresponds to a series of flashlight blinks. An A is 1 blink, a B is 2 blinks, a C is 3 blinks, and so on to 26 blinks for Z. The word BAD is 2 blinks, 1 blink, and 4 blinks with little pauses between the letters so you won't mistake the 7 blinks for a G. You'll pause a bit longer between words.

This seems promising. The good news is that you no longer have to wave the flashlight in the air; all you have to do is point and click. The bad news is that one of the first messages you try to send ("How are you?") turns out to require a grand total of 131 blinks of light! Moreover, you forgot about punctuation, so you don't know how many blinks correspond to a question mark.

But you're close. Surely, you think, somebody must have faced this problem before, and you're absolutely right. With daylight and a trip to the library for research, you discover a marvelous invention known as Morse code. It's *exactly* what you've been looking for, even though you must now relearn how to "write" all the letters of the alphabet.

Here's the difference: In the system you invented, every letter of the alphabet is a certain number of blinks, from 1 blink for A to 26 blinks for Z. In Morse code, you have two kinds of blinks—short blinks and long blinks. This makes Morse code more complicated, of course, but in actual use it turns out to be much more efficient. The sentence "How are you?" now requires only 32 blinks (some short, some long) rather than 131, and that's *including* a code for the question mark.

When discussing how Morse code works, people don't talk about "short blinks" and "long blinks." Instead, they refer to "dots" and "dashes" because that's a convenient way of showing the codes on the printed page. In Morse code, every letter of the alphabet corresponds to a short series of dots and dashes, as you can see in the following table.

A	•—	J	•———	S	•••
B	—•••	K	—•—	T	—
C	—•—•	L	•—••	U	••—
D	—••	M	——	V	•••—
E	•	N	—•	W	•——
F	••—•	O	———	X	—••—
G	——•	P	•——•	Y	—•——
H	••••	Q	——•—	Z	——••
I	••	R	•—•		

Although Morse code has absolutely nothing to do with computers, becoming familiar with the nature of codes is an essential preliminary to achieving a deep understanding of the hidden languages and inner structures of computer hardware and software.

In this book, the word *code* usually means a system for transferring information among people and machines. In other words, a code lets you communicate. Sometimes we think of codes as secret. But most codes are not. Indeed, most codes must be well understood because they're the basis of human communication.

In the beginning of *One Hundred Years of Solitude,* Gabriel Garcia Marquez recalls a time when "the world was so recent that many things lacked names, and in order to indicate them it was necessary to point." The names that we assign to things usually seem arbitrary. There seems to be no reason why cats aren't called "dogs" and dogs aren't called "cats." You could say English vocabulary is a type of code.

The sounds we make with our mouths to form words are a code intelligible to anyone who can hear our voices and understands the language that we speak. We call this code "the spoken word," or "speech." We have other code for words on paper (or on stone, on wood, or in the air, say, via skywriting). This code appears as handwritten characters or printed in newspapers, magazines, and books. We call it "the written word," or "text." In many languages, a strong correspondence exists between speech and text. In English, for example, letters and groups of letters correspond (more or less) to spoken sounds.

For people who can't hear or speak, another code has been devised to help in face-to-face communication. This is sign language, in which the hands and arms form movements and gestures that convey individual letters of words or whole words and concepts. For those who can't see, the written word can be replaced with Braille, which uses a system of raised dots that correspond to letters, groups of letters, and whole words. When spoken words must be transcribed into text very quickly, stenography or shorthand is useful.

We use a variety of different codes for communicating among ourselves because some codes are more convenient than others. For example, the code of the spoken word can't be stored on paper, so the code of the written word is used instead. Silently exchanging information across a distance in the dark isn't possible with speech or paper. Hence, Morse code is a convenient alternative. A code is useful if it serves a purpose that no other code can.

As we shall see, various types of codes are also used in computers to store and communicate numbers, sounds, music, pictures, and movies. Computers can't deal with human codes directly because computers can't duplicate the ways in which human beings use their eyes, ears, mouths, and fingers. Yet one of the recent trends in computer technology has been to enable our desktop personal computers to capture, store, manipulate, and render all types of information used in human communication, be it visual (text and pictures), aural (spoken words, sounds, and music), or a combination of both (animations and movies). All of these types of information require their own codes, just as speech requires one set of human organs (mouths and ears) while writing and reading require others (hands and eyes).

Even the table of Morse code shown on page 4 is itself a code of sorts. The table shows that each letter is represented by a series of dots and dashes. Yet we can't actually send dots and dashes. Instead, the dots and dashes correspond to blinks.

When sending Morse code with a flashlight, you turn the flashlight switch on and off very quickly (a fast blink) for a dot. You leave the flashlight turned on somewhat longer (a slower on-off blink) for a dash. To send an A, for example, you turn the flashlight on and off very quickly and then on and off at a lesser speed. You pause before sending the next character. By convention, the length of a dash should be about three times that of a dot. For example, if a dot is one second long, a dash is three seconds long. (In reality, Morse code is transmitted much faster than that.) The receiver sees the short blink and the long blink and knows it's an A.

Pauses between the dots and dashes of Morse code are crucial. When you send an A, for example, the flashlight should be off between the dot and the dash for a period of time equal to about one dot. (If the dot is one second long, the gap between dots and dashes is also a second.) Letters in the same word are separated by longer pauses equal to about the length of one dash (or three seconds if that's the length of a dash). For example, here's the Morse code for "hello," illustrating the pauses between the letters:

Words are separated by an off period of about two dashes (six seconds if a dash is three seconds long). Here's the code for "hi there":

The lengths of time that the flashlight remains on and off aren't fixed. They're all relative to the length of a dot, which depends on how fast the flashlight switch can be triggered and also how quickly a Morse code sender can remember the code for a particular letter. A fast sender's dash may be the same length as a slow sender's dot. This little problem could make reading a Morse code message tough, but after a letter or two, the receiver can usually figure out what's a dot and what's a dash.

At first, the definition of Morse code—and by *definition* I mean the correspondence of various sequences of dots and dashes to the letters of the alphabet—appears as random as the layout of a typewriter. On closer inspection, however, this is not entirely so. The simpler and shorter codes are assigned to the more frequently used letters of the alphabet, such as E and T. Scrabble players and *Wheel of Fortune* fans might notice this right away. The less common letters, such as Q and Z (which get you 10 points in Scrabble), have longer codes.

Almost everyone knows a little Morse code. Three dots, three dashes, and three dots represent SOS, the international distress signal. SOS isn't an abbreviation for anything—it's simply an easy-to-remember Morse code sequence. During the Second World War, the British Broadcasting Corporation prefaced some radio broadcasts with the beginning of Beethoven's Fifth Symphony—BAH, BAH, BAH, BAHMMMMM—which Ludwig didn't know at the time he composed the music is the Morse code V, for Victory.

One drawback of Morse code is that it makes no differentiation between uppercase and lowercase letters. But in addition to representing letters, Morse code also includes codes for numbers by using a series of five dots and dashes:

1	•————	6	—••••
2	••———	7	——•••
3	•••——	8	———••
4	••••—	9	————•
5	•••••	0	—————

These codes, at least, are a little more orderly than the letter codes. Most punctuation marks use five, six, or seven dots and dashes:

.	•—•—•—	'	•————•
,	——••——	(	—•——•
?	••——••	)	—•——•—
:	———•••	=	—•••—
;	—•—•—•	+	•—•—•
-	—••••—	$	•••—••—
/	—••—•	¶	•—•—••
"	•—••—•	_	•—•—•—

Additional codes are defined for accented letters of some European languages and as shorthand sequences for special purposes. The SOS code is one such shorthand sequence: It's supposed to be sent continuously with only a one-dot pause between the three letters.

You'll find that it's much easier for you and your friend to send Morse code if you have a flashlight made specifically for this purpose. In addition to the normal on-off slider switch, these flashlights also include a pushbutton switch that you simply press and release to turn the flashlight on and off. With some practice, you might be able to achieve a sending and receiving speed of 5 or 10 words per minute—still much slower than speech (which is somewhere in the 100-words-per-minute range), but surely adequate.

When finally you and your best friend memorize Morse code (for that's the only way you can become proficient at sending and receiving it), you can also use it vocally as a substitute for normal speech. For maximum speed, you pronounce a dot as *dih* (or *dit* for the last dot of a letter) and a dash as *dah*. In the same way that Morse code reduces written language to dots and dashes, the spoken version of the code reduces speech to just two vowel sounds.

The key word here is *two*. Two types of blinks, two vowel sounds, two different anything, really, can with suitable combinations convey all types of information.

Chapter Two

Codes and Combinations

᯲᯲᯲᯲᯲

Morse code was invented by Samuel Finley Breese Morse (1791–1872), whom we shall meet more properly later in this book. The invention of Morse code goes hand in hand with the invention of the telegraph, which we'll also examine in more detail. Just as Morse code provides a good introduction to the nature of codes, the telegraph provides a good introduction to the hardware of the computer.

Most people find Morse code easier to send than to receive. Even if you don't have Morse code memorized, you can simply use this table, conveniently arranged in alphabetical order:

A	•━	J	•━━━	S	•••
B	━•••	K	━•━	T	━
C	━•━•	L	•━••	U	••━
D	━••	M	━━	V	•••━
E	•	N	━•	W	•━━
F	••━•	O	━━━	X	━••━
G	━━•	P	•━━•	Y	━•━━
H	••••	Q	━━•━	Z	━━••
I	••	R	•━•		

Receiving Morse code and translating it back into words is considerably harder and more time consuming than sending because you must work backward to figure out the letter that corresponds to a particular coded sequence of dots and dashes. For example, if you receive a dash-dot-dash-dash, you have to scan through the table letter by letter before you finally discover that the code is the letter Y.

The problem is that we have a table that provides this translation:

Alphabetical letter → Morse code dots and dashes

But we *don't* have a table that lets us go backward:

Morse code dots and dashes → Alphabetical letter

In the early stages of learning Morse code, such a table would certainly be convenient. But it's not at all obvious how we could construct it. There's nothing in those dots and dashes that we can put into alphabetical order.

So let's forget about alphabetical order. Perhaps a better approach to organizing the codes might be to group them depending on how many dots and dashes they have. For example, a Morse code sequence that contains either one dot or one dash can represent only two letters, which are E and T:

•	E
—	T

A combination of exactly two dots or dashes gives us four more letters— I, A, N, and M:

••	I	—•	N
•—	A	——	M

A pattern of three dots or dashes gives us eight more letters:

•••	S	—••	D
••—	U	—•—	K
•—•	R	——•	G
•——	W	———	O

And finally (if we want to stop this exercise before dealing with numbers and punctuation marks), sequences of four dots and dashes give us 16 more characters:

••••	H	▬•••	B
•••▬	V	▬••▬	X
••▬•	F	▬•▬•	C
••▬▬	Ü	▬•▬▬	Y
•▬••	L	▬▬••	Z
•▬•▬	Ä	▬▬•▬	Q
•▬▬•	P	▬▬▬•	Ö
•▬▬▬	J	▬▬▬▬	Ş

Taken together, these four tables contain 2 plus 4 plus 8 plus 16 codes for a total of 30 letters, 4 more than are needed for the 26 letters of the Latin alphabet. For this reason, you'll notice that 4 of the codes in the last table are for accented letters.

These four tables might help you translate with greater ease when someone is sending you Morse code. After you receive a code for a particular letter, you know how many dots and dashes it has, and you can at least go to the right table to look it up. Each table is organized so that you find the all-dots code in the upper left and the all-dashes code in the lower right.

Can you see a pattern in the *size* of the four tables? Notice that each table has twice as many codes as the table before it. This makes sense: Each table has all the codes in the previous table followed by a dot, and all the codes in the previous table followed by a dash.

We can summarize this interesting trend this way:

Number of Dots and Dashes	Number of Codes
1	2
2	4
3	8
4	16

Each of the four tables has twice as many codes as the table before it, so if the first table has 2 codes, the second table has 2 × 2 codes, and the third table has 2 × 2 × 2 codes. Here's another way to show that:

Number of Dots and Dashes	Number of Codes
1	2
2	2 × 2
3	2 × 2 × 2
4	2 × 2 × 2 × 2

Of course, once we have a number multiplied by itself, we can start using exponents to show powers. For example, $2 \times 2 \times 2 \times 2$ can be written as 2^4 (*2 to the 4th power*). The numbers 2, 4, 8, and 16 are all powers of 2 because you can calculate them by multiplying 2 by itself. So our summary can also be shown like this:

Number of Dots and Dashes	Number of Codes
1	2^1
2	2^2
3	2^3
4	2^4

This table has become very simple. The number of codes is simply 2 to the power of the number of dots and dashes. We might summarize the table data in this simple formula:

$$\text{number of codes} = 2^{\text{number of dots and dashes}}$$

Powers of 2 tend to show up a lot in codes, and we'll see another example in the next chapter.

To make the process of decoding Morse code even easier, we might want to draw something like the big treelike table shown here.

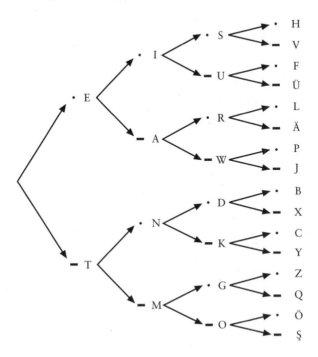

This table shows the letters that result from each particular consecutive sequence of dots and dashes. To decode a particular sequence, follow the arrows from left to right. For example, suppose you want to know which letter corresponds to the code dot-dash-dot. Begin at the left and choose the dot; then continue moving right along the arrows and choose the dash and then another dot. The letter is R, shown next to the last dot.

If you think about it, constructing such a table was probably necessary for defining Morse code in the first place. First, it ensures that you don't make the dumb mistake of using the same code for two different letters! Second, you're assured of using all the possible codes without making the sequences of dots and dashes unnecessarily long.

At the risk of extending this table beyond the limits of the printed page, we could continue it for codes of five dots and dashes and more. A sequence of exactly five dots and dashes gives us 32 (2×2×2×2×2, or 2^5) additional codes. Normally that would be enough for the 10 numbers and the 16 punctuation symbols defined in Morse code, and indeed the numbers are encoded with five dots and dashes. But many of the other codes that use a sequence of five dots and dashes represent accented letters rather than punctuation marks.

To include all the punctuation marks, the system must be expanded to six dots and dashes, which gives us 64 (2×2×2×2×2×2, or 2^6) additional codes for a grand total of 2+4+8+16+32+64, or 126, characters. That's overkill for Morse code, which leaves many of these longer codes "undefined." The word *undefined* used in this context refers to a code that doesn't stand for anything. If you were receiving Morse code and you got an undefined code, you could be pretty sure that somebody made a mistake.

Because we were clever enough to develop this little formula,

$$\text{number of codes} = 2^{\text{number of dots and dashes}}$$

we could continue figuring out how many codes we get from using longer sequences of dots and dashes:

Number of Dots and Dashes	Number of Codes
1	$2^1 = 2$
2	$2^2 = 4$
3	$2^3 = 8$
4	$2^4 = 16$
5	$2^5 = 32$
6	$2^6 = 64$
7	$2^7 = 128$
8	$2^8 = 256$
9	$2^9 = 512$
10	$2^{10} = 1024$

Fortunately, we don't have to actually write out all the possible codes to determine how many there would be. All we have to do is multiply 2 by itself over and over again.

Morse code is said to be a *binary* (literally meaning *two by two*) code because the components of the code consist of only two things—a dot and a dash. That's similar to a coin, which can land only on the head side or the tail side. Binary objects (such as coins) and binary codes (such as Morse code) are always described by powers of two.

What we're doing by analyzing binary codes is a simple exercise in the branch of mathematics known as *combinatorics* or *combinatorial analysis*. Traditionally, combinatorial analysis is used most often in the fields of probability and statistics because it involves determining the number of ways that things, like coins and dice, can be combined. But it also helps us understand how codes can be put together and taken apart.

Chapter Three

Braille and Binary Codes

Samuel Morse wasn't the first person to successfully translate the letters of written language to an interpretable code. Nor was he the first person to be remembered more as the name of his code than as himself. That honor must go to a blind French teenager born some 18 years after Samuel Morse but who made his mark much more precociously. Little is known of his life, but what is known makes a compelling story.

Louis Braille was born in 1809 in Coupvray, France, just 25 miles east of Paris. His father was a harness maker. At the age of three—an age when young boys shouldn't be playing in their fathers' workshops—he accidentally stuck a pointed tool in his eye. The wound became infected, and the infection spread to his other eye, leaving him totally blind. Normally he would have been doomed to a life of ignorance and poverty (as most blind people were in those days), but young Louis's intelligence and desire to learn were soon recognized. Through the intervention of the village priest and a schoolteacher, he first attended school in the village with the other children and at the age of 10 was sent to the Royal Institution for Blind Youth in Paris.

One major obstacle in the education of the blind is, of course, their inability to read printed books. Valentin Haüy (1745–1822), the founder of the Paris school, had invented a system of raised letters on paper that could be read by touch. But this system was very difficult to use, and only a few books had been produced using this method.

The sighted Haüy was stuck in a paradigm. To him, an A was an A was an A, and the letter A must look (or feel) like an A. (If given a flashlight to communicate, he might have tried drawing letters in the air as we did before we discovered it didn't work very well.) Haüy probably didn't realize that a type of code quite different from the printed alphabet might be more appropriate for sightless people.

The origins of an alternative type of code came from an unexpected source. Charles Barbier, a captain of the French army, had by 1819 devised a system of writing he called *écriture nocturne,* or "night writing." This system used a pattern of raised dots and dashes on heavy paper and was intended for use by soldiers in passing notes to each other in the dark when quiet was necessary. The soldiers were able to poke these dots and dashes into the back of the paper using an awl-like stylus. The raised dots could then be read with the fingers.

The problem with Barbier's system is that it was quite complex. Rather than using patterns of dots and dashes that corresponded to letters of the alphabet, Barbier devised patterns that corresponded to sounds, often requiring many codes for a single word. The system worked fine for short messages in the field but was distinctly inadequate for longer texts, let alone entire books.

Louis Braille became familiar with Barbier's system at the age of 12. He liked the use of raised dots, not only because it proved easy to read with the fingers but also because it was easy to *write*. A student in the classroom equipped with paper and a stylus could actually take notes and read them back. Louis Braille diligently tried to improve the system and within three years (at the age of 15) had come up with his own, the basics of which are still used today. For many years, the system was known only within the school, but it gradually made its way to the rest of the world. In 1835, Louis Braille contracted tuberculosis, which would eventually kill him shortly after his 43rd birthday in 1852.

Today, enhanced versions of the Braille system compete with tape-recorded books for providing the blind with access to the written word, but Braille still remains an invaluable system and the only way to read for people who are both blind and deaf. In recent years, Braille has become more familiar in the public arena as elevators and automatic teller machines are made more accessible to the blind.

What we're going to do in this chapter is dissect Braille code and see how it works. We don't have to actually *learn* Braille or memorize anything. We just want some insight into the nature of codes.

In Braille, every symbol used in normal written language—specifically, letters, numbers, and punctuation marks—is encoded as one or more raised dots within a two-by-three cell. The dots of the cell are commonly numbered 1 through 6:

In modern-day use, special typewriters or embossers punch the Braille dots into the paper.

Because embossing just a couple pages of this book in Braille would be prohibitively expensive, I've used a notation common for showing Braille on the printed page. In this notation, all six dots in the cell are shown. Large dots indicate the parts of the cell where the paper is raised. Small dots indicate the parts of the cell that are flat. For example, in the Braille character

dots 1, 3, and 5 are raised and dots 2, 4, and 6 are not.

What should be interesting to us at this point is that the dots are *binary*. A particular dot is either flat or raised. That means we can apply what we've learned about Morse code and combinatorial analysis to Braille. We know that there are 6 dots and that each dot can be either flat or raised, so the total number of combinations of 6 flat and raised dots is $2 \times 2 \times 2 \times 2 \times 2 \times 2$, or 2^6, or 64.

Thus, the system of Braille is capable of representing 64 unique codes. Here they are—all 64 possible Braille codes:

If we find fewer than 64 codes used in Braille, we should question why some of the 64 possible codes aren't being used. If we find *more* than 64 codes used in Braille, we should question either our sanity or fundamental truths of mathematics, such as 2 plus 2 equaling 4.

To begin dissecting the code of Braille, let's look at the basic lowercase alphabet:

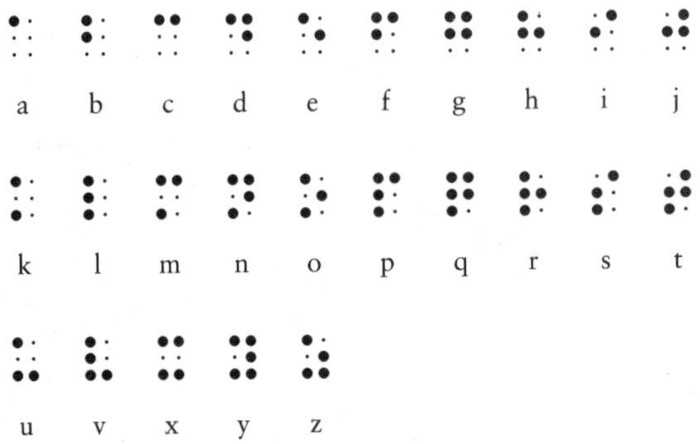

a   b   c   d   e   f   g   h   i   j

k   l   m   n   o   p   q   r   s   t

u   v   x   y   z

For example, the phrase "you and me" in Braille looks like this:

Notice that the cells for each letter within a word are separated by a little bit of space; a larger space (essentially a cell with no raised dots) is used between words.

This is the basis of Braille as Louis Braille devised it, or at least as it applies to the letters of the Latin alphabet. Louis Braille also devised codes for letters with accent marks, common in French. Notice that there's no code for *w*, which isn't used in classical French. (Don't worry. The letter will show up eventually.) At this point, only 25 of the 64 possible codes have been accounted for.

Upon close examination, you'll discover that the three rows of Braille illustrated above show a pattern. The first row (letters *a* through *j*) uses only the top four spots in the cell—dots 1, 2, 4, and 5. The second row duplicates the first row except that dot 3 is also raised. The third row is the same except that dots 3 and 6 are raised.

Since the days of Louis Braille, the Braille code has been expanded in various ways. Currently the system used most often in published material in English is called Grade 2 Braille. Grade 2 Braille uses many contractions in order to save trees and to speed reading. For example, if letter codes appear by themselves, they stand for common words. The following three rows (including a "completed" third row) show these word codes:

(none)	but	can	do	every	from	go	have	(none)	just

knowledge	like	more	not	(none)	people	quite	rather	so	that

us	very	it	you	as	and	for	of	the	with

Thus, the phrase "you and me" can be written in Grade 2 Braille as this:

So far, I've described 31 codes—the no-raised-dots space between words and the 3 rows of 10 codes for letters and words. We're still not close to the 64 codes that are theoretically available. In Grade 2 Braille, as we shall see, nothing is wasted.

First, we can use the codes for letters *a* through *j* combined with a raised dot 6. These are used mostly for contractions of letters within words and also include *w* and another word abbreviation:

ch	gh	sh	th	wh	ed	er	ou	ow	w
									(or "will")

For example, the word "about" can be written in Grade 2 Braille this way:

Second, we can take the codes for letters *a* through *j* and "lower" them to use only dots 2, 3, 5, and 6. These codes are used for some punctuation marks and contractions, depending on context:

ea	bb	cc	dis	en	to	gg	his	in	was
,	;	:	.		!	()	"	in	"

The first four of these codes are the comma, semicolon, colon, and period. Notice that the same code is used for both left and right parentheses but that two different codes are used for open and closed quotation marks.

We're up to 51 codes so far. The following 6 codes use various unused combinations of dots 3, 4, 5, and 6 to represent contractions and some additional punctuation:

st	ing	ble	ar	'	com
/		#			-

The code for "ble" is very important because when it's not part of a word, it means that the codes that follow should be interpreted as numbers. These number codes are the same as those for letters *a* through *j*:

| 1 | 2 | 3 | 4 | 5 | 6 | 7 | 8 | 9 | 0 |

Thus, this sequence of codes

means the number 256.

If you've been keeping track, we need 7 more codes to reach the maximum of 64. Here they are:

The first (a raised dot 4) is used as an accent indicator. The others are used as prefixes for some contractions and also for some other purposes: When dots 4 and 6 are raised (the fifth code in this row), the code is a decimal point in numbers or an emphasis indicator, depending on context. When dots 5 and 6 are raised, the code is a letter indicator that counterbalances a number indicator.

And finally (if you've been wondering how Braille encodes capital letters) we have dot 6—the capital indicator. This signals that the letter that follows is uppercase. For example, we can write the name of the original creator of this system as

This is a capital indicator, the letter l, the contraction ou, the letters i and s, a space, another capital indicator, and the letters b, r, a, i, l, l, and e. (In actual use, the name might be abbreviated even more by eliminating the last two letters, which aren't pronounced.)

In summary, we've seen how six binary elements (the dots) yield 64 possible codes and no more. It just so happens that many of these 64 codes perform double duty depending on their context. Of particular interest is the number indicator and the letter indicator that undoes the number indicator. These codes alter the meaning of the codes that follow them—from letters to numbers and from numbers back to letters. Codes such as these are often called *precedence,* or *shift,* codes. They alter the meaning of all subsequent codes until the shift is undone.

The capital indicator means that the following letter (and only the following letter) should be uppercase rather than lowercase. A code such as this is known as an *escape* code. Escape codes let you "escape" from the humdrum, routine interpretation of a sequence of codes and move to a new interpretation. As we'll see in later chapters, shift codes and escape codes are common when written languages are represented by binary codes.

Chapter Four

Anatomy
of a Flashlight

lashlights are useful for numerous tasks, of which reading under the covers and sending coded messages are only the two most obvious. The common household flashlight can also take center stage in an educational show-and-tell of the magical stuff known as electricity.

Electricity is an amazing phenomenon, managing to be pervasively useful while remaining largely mysterious, even to people who pretend to know how it works. But I'm afraid we must wrestle with electricity anyway. Fortunately, we need to understand only a few basic concepts to comprehend how it's used inside computers.

The flashlight is certainly one of the simpler electrical appliances found in most homes. Disassemble a typical flashlight, and you'll find it consists of a couple of batteries, a bulb, a switch, some metal pieces, and a plastic case to hold everything together.

You can make your own no-frills flashlight by disposing of everything except the batteries and the lightbulb. You'll also need some short pieces of insulated wire (with the insulation stripped from the ends) and enough hands to hold everything together.

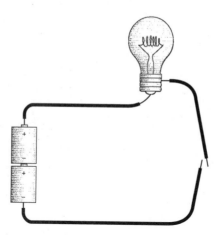

Notice the two loose ends of the wires at the right of the diagram. That's our switch. Assuming that the batteries are good and the bulb isn't burned out, touching these loose ends together will turn on the light.

What we've constructed here is a simple electrical circuit, and the first thing to notice is that a *circuit* is a *circle*. The lightbulb will be lit only if the path from the batteries to the wire to the bulb to the switch and back to the batteries is continuous. Any break in this circuit will cause the bulb to go out. The purpose of the switch is to control this process.

The circular nature of the electrical circuit suggests that something is moving around the circuit, perhaps like water flowing through pipes. The "water and pipes" analogy is quite common in explanations of how electricity works, but eventually it breaks down, as all analogies must. Electricity is like nothing else in this universe, and we must confront it on its own terms.

The prevailing scientific wisdom regarding the workings of electricity is called the *electron theory*, which says that electricity derives from the movement of electrons.

As we know, all matter—the stuff that we can see and feel (usually)—is made up of extremely small things called atoms. Every atom is composed of three types of particles; these are called neutrons, protons, and electrons. You can picture an atom as a little solar system, with the neutrons and protons bound into a nucleus and the electrons spinning around the nucleus like planets around a sun:

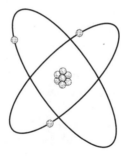

I should mention that this isn't exactly what you'd see if you were able to get a microscope powerful enough to see actual atoms, but it works as a convenient model.

The atom shown on the preceding page has 3 electrons, 3 protons, and 4 neutrons, which means that it's an atom of lithium. Lithium is one of 112 known *elements,* each of which has a particular *atomic number* ranging from 1 to 112. The atomic number of an element indicates the number of protons in the nucleus of each of the element's atoms and also (usually) the number of electrons in each atom. The atomic number of lithium is 3.

Atoms can chemically combine with other atoms to form *molecules.* Molecules usually have very different properties from the atoms they comprise. For example, water is composed of molecules that consist of two atoms of hydrogen and one atom of oxygen (hence, H_2O). Obviously water is appreciably different from either hydrogen or oxygen. Likewise, the molecules of table salt consist of an atom of sodium and an atom of chlorine, neither of which would be particularly appetizing on French fries.

Hydrogen, oxygen, sodium, and chlorine are all elements. Water and salt are called *compounds.* Salt water, however, is a *mixture* rather than a compound because the water and the salt maintain their own properties.

The number of electrons in an atom is usually the same as the number of protons. But in certain circumstances, electrons can be dislodged from atoms. That's how electricity happens.

The words *electron* and *electricity* both derive from the ancient Greek word ηλεκτρον (*elektron*), which you might expect means something like "little tiny invisible thing." But no—ηλεκτρον is actually the Greek word for "amber," which is the glasslike hardened sap of trees. The reason for this unlikely derivation is that the ancient Greeks experimented with rubbing amber with wool, which produces something we now call static electricity. Rubbing wool on amber causes the wool to pick up electrons from the amber. The wool winds up with more electrons than protons, and the amber ends up with fewer electrons than protons. In more modern experiments, carpeting picks up electrons from the soles of our shoes.

Protons and electrons have a characteristic called *charge.* Protons are said to have a positive (+) charge and electrons are said to have a negative (−) charge. Neutrons are neutral and have no charge. But even though we use plus and minus signs to denote protons and electrons, the symbols don't really mean plus and minus in the arithmetical sense or that protons have something that electrons don't. The use of these symbols just means that protons and electrons are opposite in some way. This opposite characteristic manifests itself in how protons and electrons relate to each other.

Protons and electrons are happiest and most stable when they exist together in equal numbers. An imbalance of protons and electrons will attempt to correct itself. When the carpet picks up electrons from your shoes, eventually everything gets evened out when you touch something and feel a spark. That spark of static electricity is the movement of electrons by a rather circuitous route from the carpet through your body back to your shoes.

Another way to describe the relationship between protons and electrons is to note that opposite charges attract and like charges repel. But this isn't what we might assume by looking at the diagram of the atom. It looks like the protons huddled together in the nucleus are attracting each other. The protons are held together by something stronger than the repulsion of like charges, and that something is called the *strong force*. Messing around with the strong force involves splitting the nucleus, which produces nuclear energy. In this chapter, we're merely fooling around with the electrons to get electricity.

Static electricity isn't limited to the little sparks produced by fingers touching doorknobs. During storms, the bottoms of clouds accumulate electrons while the tops of clouds lose electrons; eventually, the imbalance is evened out with a stroke of lightning. Lightning is a lot of electrons moving very quickly from one spot to another.

The electricity in the flashlight circuit is obviously much better mannered than a spark or a lightning bolt. The light burns steadily and continuously because the electrons aren't just jumping from one place to another. As one atom in the circuit loses an electron to another atom nearby, it grabs another electron from an adjacent atom, which grabs an electron from another adjacent atom, and so on. The electricity in the circuit is the passage of electrons from atom to atom.

This doesn't happen all by itself. We can't just wire up any old bunch of stuff and expect some electricity to happen. We need something to precipitate the movement of electrons around the circuit. Looking back at our diagram of the no-frills flashlight, we can safely assume that the thing that begins the movement of electricity is not the wires and not the lightbulb, so it's probably the batteries.

Almost everybody knows a few things about the types of batteries used in flashlights:

- They're tubular in shape and come in different sizes, such as D, C, A, AA, and AAA.
- Regardless of the battery's size, they're all labeled "1.5 volts."
- One end of the battery is flat and is labeled with a minus sign (–); the other end has a little protrusion and is labeled with a plus sign (+).
- If you want your appliance to work right, it's a good idea to install the batteries correctly with the plus signs facing the right way.
- Batteries wear out eventually. Sometimes they can be recharged, sometimes not.
- And finally, we suspect that in some weird way, batteries produce electricity.

In all batteries, chemical reactions take place, which means that some molecules break down into other molecules, or molecules combine to form new molecules. The chemicals in batteries are chosen so that the reactions between them generate spare electrons on the side of the battery marked with a minus sign (called the negative terminal, or *anode*) and demand extra electrons on the other side of the battery (the positive terminal, or *cathode*). In this way, chemical energy is converted to electrical energy.

The chemical reaction can't proceed unless there's some way that the extra electrons can be taken away from the negative terminal of the battery and delivered back to the positive terminal. So if the battery isn't connected to anything, nothing much happens. (Actually the chemical reactions still take place, but very slowly.) The reactions take place only if an electrical circuit is present to take electrons away from the negative side and supply electrons to the positive side. The electrons travel around this circuit in a counterclockwise direction:

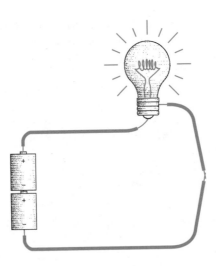

In this book, the color red is used to indicate that electricity is flowing through the wires.

Electrons from the chemicals in the batteries might not so freely mingle with the electrons in the copper wires if not for a simple fact: All electrons, wherever they're found, are identical. There's nothing that distinguishes a copper electron from any other electron.

Notice that both batteries are facing the same direction. The positive end of the bottom battery takes electrons from the negative end of the top battery. It's as if the two batteries have been combined into one bigger battery with a positive terminal at one end and a negative terminal at the other end. The combined battery is 3 volts rather than 1.5 volts.

If we turn one of the batteries upside down, the circuit won't work:

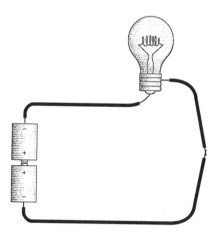

The two positive ends of the battery need electrons for the chemical reactions, but there's no way electrons can get to them because they're attached to each other. If the two positive ends of the battery are connected, the two negative ends should be also:

This works. The batteries are said to be connected *in parallel* rather than *in series* as shown earlier. The combined voltage is 1.5 volts, which is the same as the voltage of each of the batteries. The light will probably still glow, but not as brightly as with two batteries in series. But the batteries will last twice as long.

We normally like to think of a battery as providing electricity to a circuit. But we've seen that we can also think of a circuit as providing a way for a battery's chemical reactions to take place. The circuit takes electrons away from the negative end of the battery and delivers them to the positive end of the battery. The reactions in the battery proceed until all the chemicals are exhausted, at which time you throw away the battery or recharge it.

From the negative end of the battery to the positive end of the battery, the electrons flow through the wires and the lightbulb. But why do we need the wires? Can't the electricity just flow through the air? Well, yes and no. Yes, electricity can flow through air (particularly wet air), or else we wouldn't see lightning. But electricity doesn't flow through air very readily.

Some substances are significantly better than others for carrying electricity. The ability of an element to carry electricity is related to its subatomic structure. Electrons orbit the nucleus in various levels, called shells. An atom that has just one electron in its outer shell can readily give up that electron, which is what's necessary to carry electricity. These substances are conducive to carrying electricity and thus are said to be *conductors*. The best conductors are copper, silver, and gold. It's no coincidence that these three elements are found in the same column of the periodic table. Copper is the most common substance for making wires.

The opposite of conductance is *resistance*. Some substances are more resistant to the passage of electricity than others, and these are known as *resistors*. If a substance has a very high resistance—meaning that it doesn't conduct electricity much at all—it's known as an *insulator*. Rubber and plastic are good insulators, which is why these substances are often used to coat wires. Cloth and wood are also good insulators as is dry air. Just about anything will conduct electricity, however, if the voltage is high enough.

Copper has a very low resistance, but it still has *some* resistance. The longer a wire, the higher the resistance it has. If you tried wiring a flashlight with wires that were miles long, the resistance in the wires would be so high that the flashlight wouldn't work.

The thicker a wire, the lower the resistance it has. This may be somewhat counterintuitive. You might imagine that a thick wire requires much more electricity to "fill it up." But actually the thickness of the wire makes available many more electrons to move through the wire.

I've mentioned voltage but haven't defined it. What does it mean when a battery has 1.5 volts? Actually, voltage—named after Count Alessandro Volto (1745–1827), who invented the first battery in 1800—is one of the more difficult concepts of elementary electricity. Voltage refers to a *potential* for doing work. Voltage exists whether or not something is hooked up to a battery.

Consider a brick. Sitting on the floor, the brick has very little potential. Held in your hand four feet above the floor, the brick has more potential. All you need do to realize this potential is drop the brick. Held in your hand at the top of a tall building, the brick has much more potential. In all three cases, you're holding the brick and it's not doing anything, but the *potential* is different.

A much easier concept in electricity is the notion of *current*. Current is related to the number of electrons actually zipping around the circuit. Current is measured in *amperes*, named after André Marie Ampère (1775–1836), but everybody calls them *amps,* as in "a 10-amp fuse." To get one amp of current, you need 6,240,000,000,000,000,000 electrons flowing past a particular point per second.

The water-and-pipes analogy helps out here: Current is similar to the *amount* of water flowing through a pipe. Voltage is similar to the water *pressure.* Resistance is similar to the width of a pipe—the smaller the pipe, the larger the resistance. So the more water pressure you have, the more water that flows through the pipe. The smaller the pipe, the less water that flows through it. The amount of water flowing through a pipe (the current) is directly proportional to the water pressure (the voltage) and inversely pro-portional to the skinniness of the pipe (the resistance).

In electricity, you can calculate how much current is flowing through a circuit if you know the voltage and the resistance. Resistance—the tendency of a substance to impede the flow of electrons—is measured in *ohms,* named after Georg Simon Ohm (1789–1854), who also proposed the famous Ohm's Law. The law states

$$I = E / R$$

where I is traditionally used to represent current in amperes, E is used to represent voltage (it stands for *electromotive force*), and R is resistance.

For example, let's look at a battery that's just sitting around not connected to anything:

The voltage E is 1.5. That's a potential for doing work. But because the positive and negative terminals are connected solely by air, the resistance (the symbol R) is very, very, very high, which means the current (I) is 1.5 divided by a large number. This means that the current is just about zero.

Now let's connect the positive and negative terminals with a short piece of copper wire (and from here on, the insulation on the wires won't be shown):

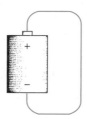

This is known as a *short circuit*. The voltage is still 1.5, but the resistance is now very, very low. The current is 1.5 volts divided by a very small number. This means that the current will be very, very high. Lots and lots of electrons will be flowing through the wire. In reality, the actual current will be limited by the physical size of the battery. The battery will probably not be able to deliver such a high current, and the voltage will drop below 1.5 volts. If the battery is big enough, the wire will get hot because the electrical energy is being converted to heat. If the wire gets very hot, it will actually glow and might even melt.

Most circuits are somewhere between these two extremes. We can symbolize them like so:

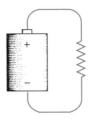

The squiggly line is recognizable to electrical engineers as the symbol for a resistor. Here it means that the circuit has a resistance that is neither very low nor very high.

If a wire has a low resistance, it can get hot and start to glow. This is how an incandescent lightbulb works. The lightbulb is commonly credited to America's most famous inventor, Thomas Alva Edison (1847–1931), but the concepts were well known at the time he patented the lightbulb (1879) and many other inventors also worked on the problem.

Inside a lightbulb is a thin wire called a filament, which is commonly made of tungsten. One end of the filament is connected to the tip at the bottom of the base; the other end of the filament is connected to the side of the metal base, separated from the tip by an insulator. The resistance of the wire causes it to heat up. In open air, the tungsten would get hot enough to burn, but in the vacuum of the lightbulb, the tungsten glows and gives off light.

Most common flashlights have two batteries connected in series. The total voltage is 3.0 volts. A lightbulb of the type commonly used in a flashlight has a resistance of about 4 ohms. Thus, the current is 3 volts divided by 4 ohms, or 0.75 ampere, which can also be expressed as 750 milliamperes. This means that 4,680,000,000,000,000,000 electrons are flowing through the lightbulb every second.

(A brief reality check: If you actually try to measure the resistance of a flashlight lightbulb with an ohmmeter, you'll get a reading much lower than 4 ohms. The resistance of tungsten is dependent upon its temperature, and the resistance gets higher as the bulb heats up.)

As you may know, lightbulbs you buy for your home are labeled with a certain wattage. The watt is named after James Watt (1736–1819), who is best known for his work on the steam engine. The watt is a measurement of power (P) and can be calculated as

$$P = E \times I$$

The 3 volts and 0.75 amp of our flashlight indicate that we're dealing with a 2.25-watt lightbulb.

Your home might be lit by 100-watt lightbulbs. These are designed for the 120 volts of your home. Thus, the current that flows through them is equal to 100 watts divided by 120 volts, or about 0.83 ampere. Hence, the resistance of a 100-watt lightbulb is 120 volts divided by 0.83 ampere, or 144 ohms.

So we've seemingly analyzed everything about the flashlight—the batteries, the wires, and the lightbulb. But we've forgotten the most important part!

Yes, the switch. The switch controls whether electricity is flowing in the circuit or not. When a switch allows electricity to flow, it is said to be *on*, or *closed*. An *off*, or *open*, switch doesn't allow electricity to flow. (The way we use the words *closed* and *open* for switches is opposite to the way we use them for a door. A closed door prevents anything from passing through it; a closed switch allows electricity to flow.)

Either the switched is closed or it's open. Either current flows or it doesn't. Either the lightbulb lights up or it doesn't. Like the binary codes invented by Morse and Braille, this simple flashlight is either on or off. There's no in-between. This similarity between binary codes and simple electrical circuits is going to prove very useful in the chapters ahead.

Chapter Five

Seeing
Around Corners

You're twelve years old. One horrible day your best friend's family moves to another town. You speak to your friend on the telephone now and then, but telephone conversations just aren't the same as those late-night sessions with the flashlights blinking out Morse code. Your second-best friend, who lives in the house next door to yours, eventually becomes your new best friend. It's time to teach your new best friend some Morse code and get the late-night flashlights blinking again.

The problem is, your new best friend's bedroom window doesn't face your bedroom window. The houses are side by side, but the bedroom windows face the same direction. Unless you figure out a way to rig up a few mirrors outside, the flashlights are now inadequate for after-dark communication.

Or are they?

Maybe you have learned something about electricity by this time, so you decide to make your own flashlights out of batteries, lightbulbs, switches, and wires. In the first experiment, you wire up the batteries and switch in your bedroom. Two wires go out your window, across a fence, and into your friend's bedroom, where they're connected to a lightbulb:

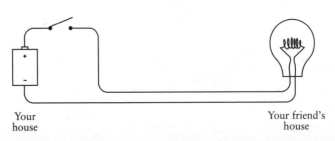

Your house   Your friend's house

Although I'm showing only one battery, you might actually be using two. In this and future diagrams, this will be an off (or open) switch:

and this will be the switch when it's on (or closed):

The flashlight in this chapter works the same way as the one illustrated in the previous chapter, although the wires connecting the components for this chapter's flashlight are a bit longer. When you close the switch at your end, the light goes on at your friend's end:

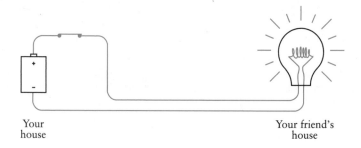

Your
house

Your friend's
house

Now you can send messages using Morse code.

Once you have one flashlight working, you can wire another long-distance flashlight so that your friend can send messages to you:

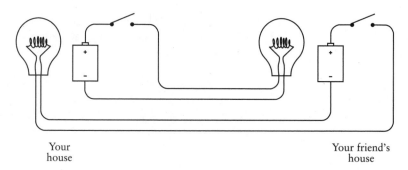

Your
house

Your friend's
house

Congratulations! You have just rigged up a bidirectional telegraph system. You'll notice that these are two identical circuits that are entirely independent of and unconnected to each other. In theory, you can be sending a message to your friend while your friend is sending a message to you (although it might be hard for your brain to read and send messages at the same time).

You also might be clever enough to discover that you can reduce your wire requirements by 25 percent by wiring the configuration this way:

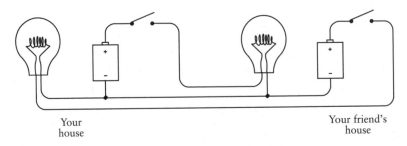

Your
house   Your friend's
house

Notice that the negative terminals of the two batteries are now connected. The two circular circuits (battery to switch to bulb to battery) still operate independently, even though they're now joined like Siamese twins.

This connection is called a *common*. In this circuit the common extends from the point where the leftmost lightbulb and battery are connected to the point where the rightmost lightbulb and battery are connected. These connections are indicated by dots.

Let's take a closer look to assure ourselves that nothing funny is going on. First, when you depress the switch on your side, the bulb in your friend's house lights up. The red wires show the flow of electricity in the circuit:

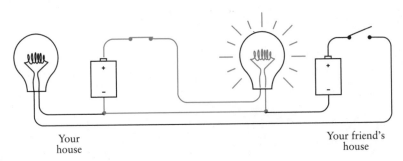

Your
house   Your friend's
house

No electricity flows in the other part of the circuit because there's no place for the electrons to go to complete a circuit.

When you're not sending but your friend is sending, the switch in your friend's house controls the lightbulb in your house. Once again, the red wires show how electricity flows in the circuit:

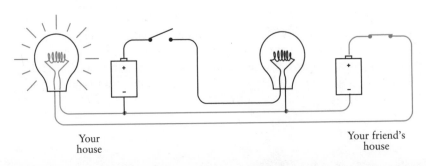

Your
house   Your friend's
house

When you and your friend both try to send at the same time, sometimes both switches are open, sometimes one switch is closed but the other is open, and sometimes both switches are depressed. In that case, the flow of electricity in the circuit looks like this:

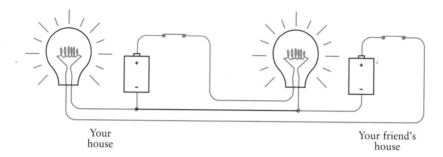

Your
house

Your friend's
house

No current flows through the common part of the circuit.

By using a common to join two separate circuits into one circuit, we've reduced the electrical connection between the two houses from four wires to three wires and reduced our wire expenses by 25 percent.

If we had to string the wires for a very long distance, we might be tempted to reduce our expenses even more by eliminating another wire. Unfortunately, this isn't feasible with 1.5-volt D cells and small lightbulbs. But if we were dealing with 100-volt batteries and much larger lightbulbs, it could certainly be done.

Here's the trick: Once you have established a common part of the circuit, you don't have to use wire for it. You can replace the wire with something else. And what you can replace it with is a giant sphere approximately 7900 miles in diameter made up of metal, rock, water, and organic material, most of which is dead. The giant sphere is known to us as Earth.

When I described good conductors in the last chapter, I mentioned silver, copper, and gold, but not gravel and mulch. In truth, the earth isn't such a hot conductor, although some kinds of earth (damp soil, for example) are better than others (such as dry sand). But one thing we learned about conductors is this: The larger the better. A very thick wire conducts much better than a very thin wire. That's where the earth excels. It's really, really, really big.

To use the earth as a conductor, you can't merely stick a little wire into the ground next to the tomato plants. You have to use something that maintains a substantial contact with the earth, and by that I mean a conductor with a large surface area. One good solution is a copper pole at least 8 feet long and ½ inch in diameter. That provides 150 square inches of contact with the earth. You can bury the pole into the ground with a sledgehammer and then connect a wire to it. Or, if the cold-water pipes in your home are made of copper and originate in the ground outside the house, you can connect a wire to the pipe.

An electrical contact with the earth is called an *earth* in Great Britain and a *ground* in America. A bit of confusion surrounds the word *ground* because it's also often used to refer to a part of a circuit we've been calling the *common*. In this chapter, and until I indicate otherwise, a ground is a physical connection with the earth.

When people draw electrical circuits, they use this symbol to represent a ground:

Electricians use this symbol because they don't like to take the time to draw an 8-foot copper pole buried in the ground.

Let's see how this works. We began this chapter by looking at a one-way configuration like this:

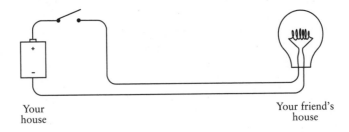

If you were using high-voltage batteries and lightbulbs, you would need only one wire between your house and your friend's house because you could use the earth as one of the connectors:

When you turn the switch on, electricity flows like this:

The electrons come out of the earth at your friend's house, go through the lightbulb and wire, the switch at your house, and then go into the positive terminal of the battery. Electrons from the negative terminal of the battery go into the earth.

You might also want to visualize electrons leaping from the 8-foot copper pole buried in the backyard of your house into the earth, then scurrying through the earth to get to the 8-foot copper pole buried in the backyard of your friend's house.

But if you consider that the earth is performing this same function for many thousands of electrical circuits around the world, you might ask: How do the electrons know where to go? Well, obviously they don't. A different image of the earth seems much more appropriate.

Yes, the earth is a massive conductor of electricity, but it can also be viewed as both a source of and a repository for electrons. *The earth is to electrons as an ocean is to drops of water.* The earth is a virtually limitless source of electrons and also a giant sink for electrons.

The earth, however, does have *some* resistance. That's why we can't use the earth ground to reduce our wiring needs if we're playing around with 1.5-volt D cells and flashlight bulbs. The earth simply has too much resistance for low-voltage batteries.

You'll notice that the previous two diagrams include a battery with the negative terminal connected to the ground:

I'm not going to draw this battery connected to the ground anymore. Instead, I'm going to use the capital letter V, which stands for *voltage*. The one-way lightbulb telegraph now looks like this:

The V stands for *voltage,* but it could also stand for *vacuum.* Think of the V as an electron vacuum and think of the ground as an ocean of electrons.

The electron vacuum pulls the electrons from the earth through the circuit, doing work along the way (such as lighting a lightbulb).

The ground is sometimes also known as the point of *zero potential*. This means that no voltage is present. A voltage—as I explained earlier—is a potential for doing work, much as a brick suspended in the air is a potential source of energy. Zero potential is like a brick sitting on the ground—there's no place left for it to fall.

In Chapter 4, one of the first things we noticed was that circuits were circles. Our new circuit doesn't look like a circle at all. It still is one, however. You could replace the V with a battery with the negative terminal connected to ground, and then you could draw a wire connecting all the places you see a ground symbol. You'd end up with the same diagram that we started with in this chapter.

So with the help of a couple of copper poles (or cold-water pipes), we can construct a two-way Morse code system with just two wires crossing the fence between your house and your friend's:

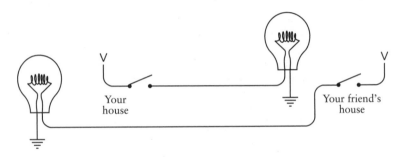

This circuit is functionally the same as the configuration shown previously, in which three wires crossed the fence between the houses.

In this chapter, we've taken an important step in the evolution of communications. Previously we had been able to communicate with Morse code but only in a straight line of sight and only as far as the beam from a flashlight would travel.

By using wires, not only have we constructed a system to communicate around corners beyond the line of sight, but we've freed ourselves of the limitation of distance. We can communicate over hundreds and thousands of miles just by stringing longer and longer wires.

Well, not exactly. Although copper is a very good conductor of electricity, it's not perfect. The longer the wires, the more resistance they have. The more resistance, the less current that flows. The less current, the dimmer the lightbulbs.

So how long exactly can we make the wires? That depends. Let's suppose you're using the original four-wire, bidirectional hookup without grounds and commons, and you're using flashlight batteries and lightbulbs. To keep your costs down, you may have initially purchased some 20-gauge speaker wire from Radio Shack at $9.99 per 100 feet. Speaker wire is normally used to connect your speakers to your stereo system. It has two conductors, so it's also a good choice for our telegraph system. If your bedroom and your friend's bedroom are less than 50 feet apart, this one roll of wire is all you need.

The thickness of wire is measured in *American Wire Gauge,* or *AWG.* The smaller the AWG number, the thicker the wire and also the less resistance it has. The 20-gauge speaker wire you bought has a diameter of about 0.032 inches and a resistance of about 10 ohms per 1000 feet, or 1 ohm for the 100-foot round-trip distance between the bedrooms.

That's not bad at all, but what if we strung the wire out for a mile? The total resistance of the wire would be more than 100 ohms. Recall from the last chapter that our lightbulb was only 4 ohms. From Ohm's Law, we can easily calculate that the current through the circuit will no longer be 0.75 amp (3 volts divided by 4 ohms) as before, but will now be less than 0.03 amp (3 volts divided by more than 100 ohms). Almost certainly, that won't be enough current to light the bulb.

Using thicker wire is a good solution, but that can be expensive. Ten-gauge wire (which Radio Shack sells as Automotive Hookup Wire at $11.99 for 35 feet, and you'd need twice as much because it has only one conductor rather than two) is about 0.1 inch thick but has a resistance of only 1 ohm per 1000 feet, or 5 ohms per mile.

Another solution is to increase the voltage and use lightbulbs with a much higher resistance. For example, a 100-watt lightbulb that lights a room in your house is designed to be used with 120 volts and has a resistance of about 144 ohms. The resistance of the wires will then affect the overall circuitry much less.

These are problems faced 150 years ago by the people who strung up the first telegraph systems across America and Europe. Regardless of the thickness of the wires and the high levels of voltage, telegraph wires simply couldn't be continued indefinitely. At most, the limit for a working system according to this scheme was a couple hundred miles. That's nowhere close to spanning the thousands of miles between New York and California.

The solution to this problem—not for flashlights but for the clicking and clacking telegraphs of yesteryear—turns out to be a simple and humble device, but one from which entire computers can be built.

Chapter Six

Telegraphs and Relays

~

S amuel Finley Breese Morse was born in 1791 in Charleston, Massachusetts, the town where the Battle of Bunker Hill was fought and which is now the northeast part of Boston. In the year of Morse's birth, the United States Constitution had been ratified just two years before and George Washington was serving his first term as president. Catherine the Great ruled Russia. Louis XVI and Marie Antoinette would lose their heads two years later in the French Revolution. And in 1791, Mozart completed *The Magic Flute,* his last opera, and died later that year at the age of 35.

Morse was educated at Yale and studied art in London. He became a successful portrait artist. His painting *General Lafayette* (1825) hangs in New York's City Hall. In 1836, he ran for mayor of New York City on an independent ticket and received 5.7 percent of the vote. He was also an early photography buff. Morse learned how to make daguerreotype photographs from Louis Daguerre himself and made some of the first daguerreotypes in America. In 1840, he taught the process to the 17-year-old Mathew Brady, who with his colleagues would be responsible for creating the most memorable photographs of the Civil War, Abraham Lincoln, and Samuel Morse himself.

But these are just footnotes to an eclectic career. Samuel F. B. Morse is best known these days for his invention of the telegraph and the code that bears his name.

The instantaneous worldwide communication we've become accustomed to is a relatively recent development. In the early 1800s, you could communicate instantly and you could communicate over long distances, but you couldn't do both at the same time. Instantaneous communication was limited to as far as your voice could carry (no amplification available) or as far as the eye could see (aided perhaps by a telescope). Communication over longer distances by letter took time and involved horses, trains, or ships.

For decades prior to Morse's invention, many attempts were made to speed long-distance communication. Technically simple methods employed a relay system of men standing on hills waving flags in semaphore codes. Technically more complex solutions used large structures with movable arms that did basically the same thing as men waving flags.

The idea of the telegraph (literally meaning "far writing") was certainly in the air in the early 1800s, and other inventors had taken a stab at it before Samuel Morse began experimenting in 1832. In principle, the idea behind an electrical telegraph was simple: You do something at one end of a wire that causes something to happen at the other end of the wire. This is exactly what we did in the last chapter when we made a long-distance flashlight. However, Morse couldn't use a lightbulb as his signaling device because a practical one wouldn't be invented until 1879. Instead, Morse relied upon the phenomenon of *electromagnetism*.

If you take an iron bar, wrap it with a couple hundred turns of thin wire, and then run a current through the wire, the iron bar becomes a magnet. It then attracts other pieces of iron and steel. (There's enough thin wire in the electromagnet to create a resistance great enough to prevent the electromagnet from constituting a short circuit.) Remove the current, and the iron bar loses its magnetism:

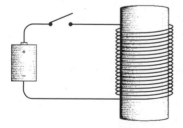

The electromagnet is the foundation of the telegraph. Turning the switch on and off at one end causes the electromagnet to do something at the other end.

Morse's first telegraphs were actually more complex than the ones that later evolved. Morse felt that a telegraph system should actually write something on paper, or as computer users would later phrase it, "produce a hard copy." This wouldn't necessarily be words, of course, because that would be too complex. But *something* should be written on paper, whether it be squiggles or dots and dashes. Notice that Morse was stuck in a paradigm that required paper and reading, much like Valentin Haüy's notion that books for the blind should use raised letters of the alphabet.

Although Samuel Morse notified the patent office in 1836 that he had invented a successful telegraph, it wasn't until 1843 that he was able to persuade Congress to fund a public demonstration of the device. The historic day was May 24, 1844, when a telegraph line rigged between Washington, D.C., and Baltimore, Maryland, successfully carried the biblical message: "What hath God wrought!"

The traditional telegraph "key" used for sending messages looked something like this:

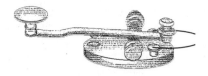

Despite the fancy appearance, this was just a switch designed for maximum speed. The most comfortable way to use the key for long periods of time was to hold the handle between thumb, forefinger, and middle finger, and tap it up and down. Holding the key down for a short period of time produced a Morse code dot. Holding it down longer produced a Morse code dash.

At the other end of the wire was a receiver that was basically an electromagnet pulling a metal lever. Originally, the electromagnet controlled a pen. While a mechanism using a wound-up spring slowly pulled a roll of paper through the gadget, an attached pen bounced up and down and drew dots and dashes on the paper. A person who could read Morse code would then transcribe the dots and dashes into letters and words.

Of course, we humans are a lazy species, and telegraph operators soon discovered that they could transcribe the code simply by listening to the pen bounce up and down. The pen mechanism was eventually eliminated in favor of the traditional telegraph "sounder," which looked something like this:

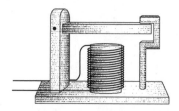

When the telegraph key was pressed, the electromagnet in the sounder pulled the movable bar down and it made a "click" noise. When the key was released, the bar sprang back to its normal position, making a "clack" noise. A fast "click-clack" was a dot; a slower "click...clack" was a dash.

The key, the sounder, a battery, and some wires can be connected just like the lightbulb telegraph in the preceding chapter:

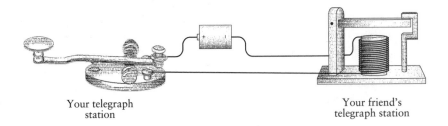

Your telegraph
station

Your friend's
telegraph station

As we discovered, you don't need two wires connecting the two telegraph stations. One wire will suffice if the earth provides the other half of the circuit.

As we did in the previous chapter, we can replace the battery connected to the ground with a capital V. So the complete one-way setup looks something like this:

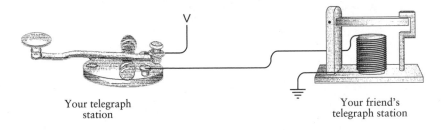

Your telegraph
station

Your friend's
telegraph station

Two-way communication simply requires another key and sender. This is similar to what we did in the preceding chapter.

The invention of the telegraph truly marks the beginning of modern communication. For the first time, people were able to communicate further than the eye could see or the ear could hear and faster than a horse could gallop. That this invention used a binary code is all the more intriguing. In later forms of electrical and wireless communication, including the telephone, radio, and television, binary codes were abandoned, only to later make an appearance in computers, compact discs, digital videodiscs, digital satellite television broadcasting, and high-definition TV.

Morse's telegraph triumphed over other designs in part because it was tolerant of bad line conditions. If you strung a wire between a key and a sounder, it usually worked. Other telegraph systems were not quite as forgiving. But as I mentioned in the last chapter, a big problem with the telegraph lay in the resistance of long lengths of wire. Although some telegraph lines used up to 300 volts and could work over a 300-mile length, wires couldn't be extended indefinitely.

One obvious solution is to have a relay system. Every couple hundred miles or so, a person equipped with a sounder and a key could receive a message and resend it.

Now imagine that you have been hired by the telegraph company to be part of this relay system. They have put you out in the middle of nowhere between New York and California in a little hut with a table and a chair. A wire coming through the east window is connected to a sounder. Your telegraph key is connected to a battery and wire going out the west window. Your job is to receive messages originating in New York and to resend them, eventually to reach California.

At first, you prefer to receive an entire message before resending it. You write down the letters that correspond to the clicks of the sounder, and when the message is finished, you start sending it using your key. Eventually you get the knack of sending the message as you're hearing it without having to write the whole thing down. This saves time.

One day while resending a message, you look at the bar on the sounder bouncing up and down, and you look at your fingers bouncing the key up and down. You look at the sounder again and you look at the key again, and you realize that the sounder is bouncing up and down the same way the key is bouncing up and down. So you go outside and pick up a little piece of wood and you use the wood and some string to physically connect the sounder and the key:

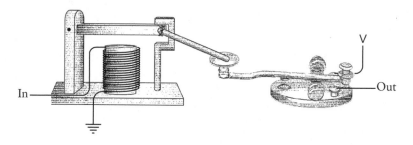

Now it works by itself, and you can take the rest of the afternoon off and go fishing.

It's an interesting fantasy, but in reality Samuel Morse had understood the concept of this device early on. The device we've invented is called a *repeater,* or a *relay*. A relay is like a sounder in that an incoming current is used to power an electromagnet that pulls down a metal lever. The lever, however, is used as part of a switch connecting a battery to an outgoing wire. In this way, a weak incoming current is "amplified" to make a stronger outgoing current.

Drawn rather schematically, the relay looks like this:

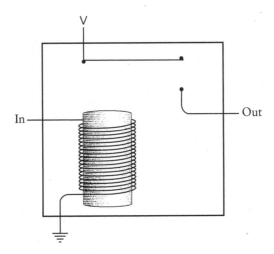

When an incoming current triggers the electromagnet, the electromagnet pulls down a flexible strip of metal that acts like a switch to turn on an outgoing current:

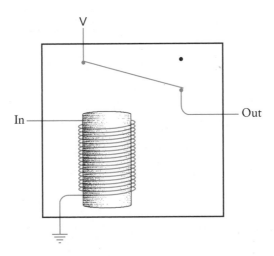

So a telegraph key, a relay, and a sounder are connected more or less like this:

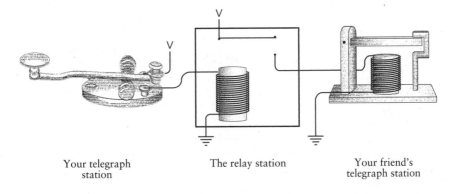

Your telegraph   The relay station   Your friend's
   station   telegraph station

The relay is a remarkable device. It's a switch, surely, but a switch that's turned on and off not by human hands but by a current. You could do amazing things with such devices. You could actually assemble much of a computer with them.

Yes, this relay thing is much too sweet an invention to leave sitting around the telegraphy museum. Let's grab one and stash it inside our jacket and walk quickly past the guards. This relay will come in very handy. But before we can use it, we're going to have to learn to count.

Chapter Seven

Our Ten Digits

T he idea that language is merely a code seems readily acceptable. Many of us at least attempted to learn a foreign language in high school, so we're willing to acknowledge that the animal we call a cat in English can also be a *gato, chat, Katze, КОШКа,* or *κάττα.*

Numbers, however, seem less culturally malleable. Regardless of the language we speak and the way we pronounce the numbers, just about everybody we're likely to come in contact with on this planet writes them the same way:

1 2 3 4 5 6 7 8 9 10

Isn't mathematics called "the universal language" for a reason?

Numbers are certainly the most abstract codes we deal with on a regular basis. When we see the number

3

we don't immediately need to relate it to anything. We might visualize 3 apples or 3 of something else, but we'd be just as comfortable learning from context that the number refers to a child's birthday, a television channel, a hockey score, or the number of cups of flour in a cake recipe. Because our numbers are so abstract to begin with, it's more difficult for us to understand that this number of apples

doesn't necessarily have to be denoted by the symbol

3

Much of this chapter and the next will be devoted to persuading ourselves that this many apples

can also be indicated by writing

11

Let's first dispense with the idea that there's something inherently special about the number ten. That most civilizations have based their number systems around ten (or sometimes five) isn't surprising. From the very beginning, people have used their fingers to count. Had our species developed possessing eight or twelve fingers, our ways of counting would be a little different. It's no coincidence that the word *digit* can refer to fingers or toes as well as numbers or that the words *five* and *fist* have similar roots.

So in that sense, using a *base-ten,* or *decimal* (from the Latin for *ten*), number system is completely arbitrary. Yet we endow numbers based on ten with an almost magical significance and give them special names. Ten years is a decade; ten decades is a century; ten centuries is a millennium. A thousand thousands is a million; a thousand millions is a billion. These numbers are all powers of ten:

$$10^1 = 10$$
$$10^2 = 100$$
$$10^3 = 1000 \text{ (thousand)}$$
$$10^4 = 10,000$$
$$10^5 = 100,000$$
$$10^6 = 1,000,000 \text{ (million)}$$
$$10^7 = 10,000,000$$
$$10^8 = 100,000,000$$
$$10^9 = 1,000,000,000 \text{ (billion)}$$

Most historians believe that numbers were originally invented to count things, such as people, possessions, and transactions in commerce. For example, if someone owned four ducks, that might be recorded with drawings of four ducks:

Eventually the person whose job it was to draw the ducks thought, "Why do I have to draw four ducks? Why can't I draw one duck and indicate that there are four of them with, I don't know, a scratch mark or something?"

And then there came the day when someone had 27 ducks, and the scratch marks got ridiculous:

Someone said, "There's got to be a better way," and a number system was born.

Of all the early number systems, only Roman numerals are still in common use. You find them on the faces of clocks and watches, used for dates on monuments and statues, for some page numbering in books, for some items in an outline, and—most annoyingly—for the copyright notice in movies. (The question "What year was this picture made?" can often be answered only if one is quick enough to decipher MCMLIII as the tail end of the credits goes by.)

Twenty-seven ducks in Roman numerals is

The concept here is easy enough: The X stands for 10 scratch marks and the V stands for 5 scratch marks.

The symbols of Roman numerals that survive today are

I V X L C D M

The I is a one. This could be derived from a scratch mark or a single raised finger. The V, which is probably a symbol for a hand, stands for five. Two V's make an X, which stands for ten. The L is a fifty. The letter C comes from the word *centum*, which is Latin for a hundred. D is five hundred. Finally, M comes from the Latin word *mille*, or a thousand.

Although we might not agree, for a long time Roman numerals were considered easy to add and subtract, and that's why they survived so long in Europe for bookkeeping. Indeed, when adding two Roman numerals, you simply combine all the symbols from both numbers and then simplify the result using just a few rules: Five I's make a V, two V's make an X, five X's make an L, and so forth.

But multiplying and dividing Roman numerals is difficult. Many other early number systems (such as that of the ancient Greeks) are similarly inadequate for working with numbers in a sophisticated manner. While the Greeks developed an extraordinary geometry still taught virtually unchanged in high schools today, the ancient Greeks aren't known for their algebra.

The number system we use today is known as the Hindu-Arabic or Indo-Arabic. It's of Indian origin but was brought to Europe by Arab mathematicians. Of particular renown is the Persian mathematician Muhammed ibn-Musa al-Khwarizmi (from whose name we have derived the word *algorithm*) who wrote a book on algebra around A.D. 825 that used the Hindu system of counting. A Latin translation dates from A.D. 1120 and was influential in hastening the transition throughout Europe from Roman numerals to our present Hindu-Arabic system.

The Hindu-Arabic number system was different from previous number systems in three ways:

- The Hindu-Arabic number system is said to be *positional,* which means that a particular digit represents a different quantity depending on where it is found in the number. Where digits appear in a number is just as significant (actually, more significant) than what the digits actually are. Both 100 and 1,000,000 have only a single 1 in them, yet we all know that a million is much larger than a hundred.

- Virtually all early number systems have something that the Hindu-Arabic system does *not* have, and that's a special symbol for the number ten. In our number system, there's *no* special symbol for ten.

- On the other hand, virtually all of the early number systems are missing something that the Hindu-Arabic system has, and which turns out to be much more important than a symbol for ten. And that's the zero.

Yes, the zero. The lowly zero is without a doubt one of the most important inventions in the history of numbers and mathematics. It supports positional notation because it allows differentiation of 25 from 205 and 250. The zero also eases many mathematical operations that are awkward in nonpositional systems, particularly multiplication and division.

The whole structure of Hindu-Arabic numbers is revealed in the way we pronounce them. Take 4825, for instance. We say "four thousand, eight hundred, twenty-five." That means

> four thousands
> eight hundreds
> two tens and
> five.

Or we can write the components like this:

$$4825 = 4000 + 800 + 20 + 5$$

Or breaking it down even further, we can write the number this way:

$$4825 = 4 \times 1000 +$$
$$8 \times 100 +$$
$$2 \times 10 +$$
$$5 \times 1$$

Or, using powers of ten, the number can be rewritten like this:

$$4825 = 4 \times 10^3 +$$
$$8 \times 10^2 +$$
$$2 \times 10^1 +$$
$$5 \times 10^0$$

Remember that any number to the 0 power equals 1.

Each position in a multidigit number has a particular meaning, as shown in the following diagram. The seven boxes shown here let us represent any number from 0 through 9,999,999:

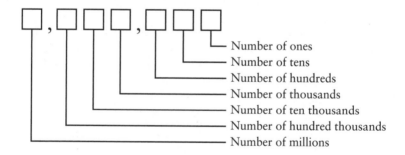

Each position corresponds to a power of ten. We don't need a special symbol for ten because we set the 1 in a different position and we use the 0 as a placeholder.

What's also really nice is that fractional quantities shown as digits to the right of a decimal point follow this same pattern. The number 42,705.684 is

$$4 \times 10,000 +$$
$$2 \times 1000 +$$
$$7 \times 100 +$$
$$0 \times 10 +$$
$$5 \times 1 +$$
$$6 \div 10 +$$
$$8 \div 100 +$$
$$4 \div 1000$$

This number can also be written without any division, like this:

$$4 \times 10{,}000 +$$
$$2 \times 1000 +$$
$$7 \times 100 +$$
$$0 \times 10 +$$
$$5 \times 1 +$$
$$6 \times 0.1 +$$
$$8 \times 0.01 +$$
$$4 \times 0.001$$

Or, using powers of ten, the number is

$$4 \times 10^4 +$$
$$2 \times 10^3 +$$
$$7 \times 10^2 +$$
$$0 \times 10^1 +$$
$$5 \times 10^0 +$$
$$6 \times 10^{-1} +$$
$$8 \times 10^{-2} +$$
$$4 \times 10^{-3}$$

Notice how the exponents go down to zero and then become negative numbers.

We know that 3 plus 4 equals 7. Similarly, 30 plus 40 equals 70, 300 plus 400 equals 700, and 3000 plus 4000 equals 7000. This is the beauty of the Hindu-Arabic system. When you add decimal numbers of any length, you follow a procedure that breaks down the problem into steps. Each step involves nothing more complicated than adding pairs of single-digit numbers. That's why someone a long time ago forced you to memorize an addition table:

+	0	1	2	3	4	5	6	7	8	9
0	0	1	2	3	4	5	6	7	8	9
1	1	2	3	4	5	6	7	8	9	10
2	2	3	4	5	6	7	8	9	10	11
3	3	4	5	6	7	8	9	10	11	12
4	4	5	6	7	8	9	10	11	12	13
5	5	6	7	8	9	10	11	12	13	14
6	6	7	8	9	10	11	12	13	14	15
7	7	8	9	10	11	12	13	14	15	16
8	8	9	10	11	12	13	14	15	16	17
9	9	10	11	12	13	14	15	16	17	18

Find the two numbers you wish to add in the top row and the left column. Follow down and across the get the sum. For example, 4 plus 6 equals 10.

Similarly, when you need to multiply two decimal numbers, you follow a somewhat more complicated procedure but still one that breaks down the problem so that you need do nothing more complex than adding or multiplying single-digit decimal numbers. Your early schooling probably also entailed memorizing a multiplication table:

x	0	1	2	3	4	5	6	7	8	9
0	0	0	0	0	0	0	0	0	0	0
1	0	1	2	3	4	5	6	7	8	9
2	0	2	4	6	8	10	12	14	16	18
3	0	3	6	9	12	15	18	21	24	27
4	0	4	8	12	16	20	24	28	32	36
5	0	5	10	15	20	25	30	35	40	45
6	0	6	12	18	24	30	36	42	48	54
7	0	7	14	21	28	35	42	49	56	63
8	0	8	16	24	32	40	48	56	64	72
9	0	9	18	27	36	45	54	63	72	81

What's best about the positional system of notation isn't how well it works, but how well it works for counting systems *not* based on ten. Our number system isn't necessarily appropriate for everyone. One big problem with our base-ten system of numbers is that it doesn't have any relevance for cartoon characters. Most cartoon characters have only four fingers on each hand (or paw), so they prefer a number system that's based on eight. Interestingly enough, much of what we know about decimal numbering can be applied to a numbering system more appropriate for our friends in cartoons.

Chapter Eight

Alternatives to Ten

Ten is an exceptionally important number to us humans. Ten is the number of fingers and toes most of us have, and we certainly prefer to have all ten of each. Because our fingers are convenient for counting, we humans have adapted an entire number system that's based on the number 10.

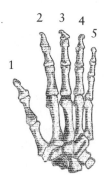

As I mentioned in the previous chapter, the number system that we use is called *base ten*, or *decimal*. The number system seems so natural to us that it's difficult at first to conceive of alternatives. Indeed, when we see the number *10* we can't help but think that this number refers to this many ducks:

10 =

But the only reason that the number 10 refers to this many ducks is that this many ducks is the same as the number of fingers we have. If human beings had a different number of fingers, the way we counted would be different, and 10 would mean something else. That same number 10 could refer to this many ducks:

$$10 = $$

or this many ducks:

$$10 = $$

or even this many ducks:

$$10 = $$

When we get to the point where 10 means just two ducks, we'll be ready to examine how switches, wires, lightbulbs, and relays (and by extension, computers) can represent numbers.

What if human beings had only four fingers on each hand, like cartoon characters? We probably never would have thought to develop a number system based on ten. Instead, we would have considered it normal and natural and sensible and inevitable and incontrovertible and undeniably proper to base our number system on eight. We wouldn't call this a *decimal* number system. We'd call it an *octal* number system, or *base eight*.

If our number system were organized around eight rather than ten, we wouldn't need the symbol that looks like this:

$$9$$

Show this symbol to any cartoon character and you'll get the response, "What's that? What's it for?" And if you think about it a moment, we also wouldn't need the symbol that looks like this:

$$8$$

In the decimal number system, there's no special symbol for ten, so in the octal number system there's no special symbol for eight.

The way we count in the decimal number system is 0, 1, 2, 3, 4, 5, 6, 7, 8, 9, and then 10. The way we count in the octal number system is 0, 1, 2, 3, 4, 5, 6, 7, and then what? We've run out of symbols. The only thing that makes sense is 10, and that's correct. In octal, the next number after 7 is 10. But this 10 doesn't mean the number of fingers that humans have. In octal, 10 refers to the number of fingers that cartoon characters have.

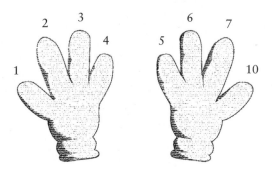

We can continue counting on our four-toed feet:

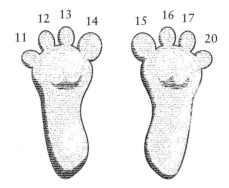

When you're working with number systems other than decimal, you can avoid some confusion if you pronounce a number like 10 as *one zero*. Similarly, 13 is pronounced *one three* and 20 is pronounced *two zero*. To *really* avoid confusion, we can say *two zero base eight* or *two zero octal*.

Even though we've run out of fingers and toes, we can still continue counting in octal. It's basically the same as counting in decimal except that we skip every number that has an 8 or a 9 in it. And of course, the actual numbers refer to different quantities:

0, 1, 2, 3, 4, 5, 6, 7, 10, 11, 12, 13, 14, 15, 16, 17, 20, 21, 22, 23, 24, 25, 26, 27, 30, 31, 32, 33, 34, 35, 36, 37, 40, 41, 42, 43, 44, 45, 46, 47, 50, 51, 52, 53, 54, 55, 56, 57, 60, 61, 62, 63, 64, 65, 66, 67, 70, 71, 72, 73, 74, 75, 76, 77, 100...

That last number is pronounced *one zero zero*. It's the number of fingers that cartoon characters have, multiplied by itself.

When writing decimal and octal numbers, we can avoid confusion and denote which is which by using a subscript to indicate the numbering system. The subscript TEN means base ten or decimal, and EIGHT means base eight or octal.

Thus, the number of dwarfs that Snow White meets is 7_{TEN} or 7_{EIGHT}

The number of fingers that cartoon characters have is 8_{TEN} or 10_{EIGHT}

The number of symphonies that Beethoven wrote is 9_{TEN} or 11_{EIGHT}

The number of fingers that humans have is 10_{TEN} or 12_{EIGHT}

The number of months in a year is 12_{TEN} or 14_{EIGHT}

The number of days in a fortnight is 14_{TEN} or 16_{EIGHT}

The "sweet" birthday celebration is 16_{TEN} or 20_{EIGHT}

The number of hours in a day is 24_{TEN} or 30_{EIGHT}

The number of letters in the Latin alphabet is 26_{TEN} or 32_{EIGHT}

The number of fluid ounces in a quart is 32_{TEN} or 40_{EIGHT}

The number of cards in a deck is 52_{TEN} or 64_{EIGHT}

The number of squares on a chessboard is 64_{TEN} or 100_{EIGHT}

The most famous address on Sunset Strip is 77_{TEN} or 115_{EIGHT}

The number of yards in an American football field is 100_{TEN} or 144_{EIGHT}

The number of starting women singles players at Wimbledon is 128_{TEN} or 200_{EIGHT}

The number of square miles in Memphis is 256_{TEN} or 400_{EIGHT}

Notice that there are a few nice round octal numbers in this list, such as 100_{EIGHT} and 200_{EIGHT} and 400_{EIGHT}. By the term *nice round number* we usually mean a number that has some zeros at the end. Two zeros on the end of a decimal number means that the number is a multiple of 100_{TEN}, which is 10_{TEN} times 10_{TEN}. With octal numbers, two zeros on the end means that the number is a multiple of 100_{EIGHT}, which is 10_{EIGHT} times 10_{EIGHT} (or 8_{TEN} times 8_{TEN}, which is 64_{TEN}).

You might also notice that these nice round octal numbers 100_{EIGHT} and 200_{EIGHT} and 400_{EIGHT} have the decimal equivalents 64_{TEN}, 128_{TEN}, and 256_{TEN}, all of which are powers of two. This makes sense. The number 400_{EIGHT} (for example) is 4_{EIGHT} times 10_{EIGHT} times 10_{EIGHT}, all of which are powers of two. And anytime we multiply a power of two by a power of two, we get another power of two.

The following table shows some powers of two with the decimal and octal representations:

Power of Two	Decimal	Octal
2^0	1	1
2^1	2	2
2^2	4	4
2^3	8	10
2^4	16	20
2^5	32	40
2^6	64	100
2^7	128	200
2^8	256	400
2^9	512	1000
2^{10}	1024	2000
2^{11}	2048	4000
2^{12}	4096	10000

The nice round numbers in the rightmost column are a hint that number systems other than decimal might help in working with binary codes.

The octal system isn't different from the decimal system in any structural way. It just differs in details. For example, each position in an octal number is a digit that's multiplied by a power of eight:

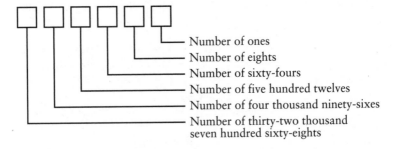

Number of ones
Number of eights
Number of sixty-fours
Number of five hundred twelves
Number of four thousand ninety-sixes
Number of thirty-two thousand seven hundred sixty-eights

Thus, an octal number such as 3725_{EIGHT} can be broken down like so:

$$3725_{EIGHT} = 3000_{EIGHT} + 700_{EIGHT} + 20_{EIGHT} + 5_{EIGHT}$$

This can be rewritten in any of several ways. Here's one way, using the powers of eight in their decimal forms:

$$3725_{EIGHT} = 3 \times 512_{TEN} +$$
$$7 \times 64_{TEN} +$$
$$2 \times 8_{TEN} +$$
$$5 \times 1$$

This is the same thing with the powers of eight shown in their octal form:

$$3725_{EIGHT} = 3 \times 1000_{EIGHT} +$$
$$7 \times 100_{EIGHT} +$$
$$2 \times 10_{EIGHT} +$$
$$5 \times 1$$

Here's another way of doing it:

$$3725_{EIGHT} = 3 \times 8^3 +$$
$$7 \times 8^2 +$$
$$2 \times 8^1 +$$
$$5 \times 8^0$$

If you work out this calculation in decimal, you'll get 2005_{TEN}. This is how you can convert octal numbers to decimal numbers.

We can add and multiply octal numbers the same way we add and multiply decimal numbers. The only real difference is that we use different tables for adding and multiplying the individual digits. Here's the addition table for octal numbers:

+	0	1	2	3	4	5	6	7
0	0	1	2	3	4	5	6	7
1	1	2	3	4	5	6	7	10
2	2	3	4	5	6	7	10	11
3	3	4	5	6	7	10	11	12
4	4	5	6	7	10	11	12	13
5	5	6	7	10	11	12	13	14
6	6	7	10	11	12	13	14	15
7	7	10	11	12	13	14	15	16

For example, $5_{EIGHT} + 7_{EIGHT} = 14_{EIGHT}$. So we can add two longer octal numbers the same way we add decimal numbers:

$$
\begin{array}{r}
135 \\
+\ 643 \\
\hline
1000
\end{array}
$$

To begin with the right column, 5 plus 3 equals 10. Put down the 0, carry the 1. One plus 3 plus 4 equals 10. Put down the 0, carry the 1. One plus 1 plus 6 equals 10.

Similarly, 2 times 2 is still 4 in octal. But 3 times 3 isn't 9. How could it be? Instead 3 times 3 is 11_{EIGHT}, which is the same amount as 9_{TEN}. You can see the entire octal multiplication table at the top of the following page.

x	0	1	2	3	4	5	6	7
0	0	0	0	0	0	0	0	0
1	0	1	2	3	4	5	6	7
2	0	2	4	6	10	12	14	16
3	0	3	6	11	14	17	22	25
4	0	4	10	14	20	24	30	34
5	0	5	12	17	24	31	36	43
6	0	6	14	22	30	36	44	52
7	0	7	16	25	34	43	52	61

Here we have 4 × 6 equaling 30_{EIGHT}, but 30_{EIGHT} is the same as 24_{TEN}, which is what 4 × 6 equals in decimal.

Octal is as valid a number system as decimal. But let's go further. Now that we've developed a numbering system for cartoon characters, let's develop something that's appropriate for lobsters. Lobsters don't have fingers exactly, but they do have pincers at the ends of their two front legs. An appropriate number system for lobsters is the *quaternary* system, or base four:

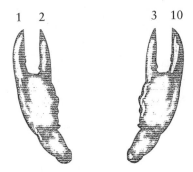

Counting in quaternary goes like this: 0, 1, 2, 3, 10, 11, 12, 13, 20, 21, 22, 23, 30, 31, 32, 33, 100, 101, 102, 103, 110, and so forth.

I'm not going to spend much time with the quaternary system because we'll be moving on shortly to something much more important. But we can see how each position in a quaternary number corresponds this time to a power of *four*:

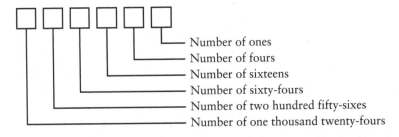

The quaternary number 31232 can be written like this:

$$31232_{FOUR} = 3 \times 256_{TEN} +$$
$$1 \times 64_{TEN} +$$
$$2 \times 16_{TEN} +$$
$$3 \times 4_{TEN} +$$
$$2 \times 1_{TEN}$$

which is the same as

$$31232_{FOUR} = 3 \times 10000_{FOUR} +$$
$$1 \times 1000_{FOUR} +$$
$$2 \times 100_{FOUR} +$$
$$3 \times 10_{FOUR} +$$
$$2 \times 1_{FOUR}$$

And it's also the same as

$$31232_{FOUR} = 3 \times 4^4 +$$
$$1 \times 4^3 +$$
$$2 \times 4^2 +$$
$$3 \times 4^1 +$$
$$2 \times 4^0$$

If we do the calculations in decimal, we'll find that 31232_{FOUR} equals 878_{TEN}.

Now we're going to make another leap, and this one is extreme. Suppose we were dolphins and must resort to using our two flippers for counting. This is the number system known as base two, or *binary* (from the Latin for *two by two*). It seems likely that we'd have only two digits, and these two digits would be 0 and 1.

Now, 0 and 1 isn't a whole lot to work with, and it takes some practice to get accustomed to binary numbers. The big problem is that you run out of digits very quickly. For example, here's how a dolphin counts using its flippers:

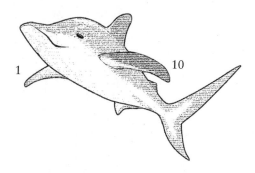

Yes, in binary the next number after 1 is 10. This is startling, but it shouldn't really be a surprise. No matter what number system we use, whenever we run out of single digits, the first two-digit number is always 10. In binary we count like this:

0, 1, 10, 11, 100, 101, 110, 111, 1000, 1001, 1010, 1011, 1100,
1101, 1110, 1111, 10000, 10001…

These numbers might look large, but they're really not. It's more accurate to say that binary numbers get *long* very quickly rather than large:

The number of heads that humans have is 1_{TEN} or 1_{TWO}

The number of flippers that dolphins have is 2_{TEN} or 10_{TWO}

The number of teaspoons in a tablespoon is 3_{TEN} or 11_{TWO}

The number of sides to a square is 4_{TEN} or 100_{TWO}

The number of fingers on one human hand is 5_{TEN} or 101_{TWO}

The number of legs on an insect is 6_{TEN} or 110_{TWO}

The number of days in a week is 7_{TEN} or 111_{TWO}

The number of musicians in an octet is 8_{TEN} or 1000_{TWO}

The number of planets in our solar system (including Pluto) is 9_{TEN} or 1001_{TWO}

The number of gallons in a cowboy hat is 10_{TEN} or 1010_{TWO}

and so forth.

In a multidigit binary number, the positions of the digits correspond to powers of two:

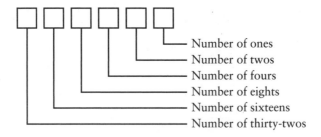

Number of ones
Number of twos
Number of fours
Number of eights
Number of sixteens
Number of thirty-twos

So anytime we have a binary number composed of a 1 followed by all zeros, that number is a power of two. The power is the same as the number of zeros in the binary number. Here's our expanded table of the powers of two demonstrating this rule:

Power of Two	Decimal	Octal	Quaternary	Binary
2^0	1	1	1	1
2^1	2	2	2	10
2^2	4	4	10	100
2^3	8	10	20	1000
2^4	16	20	100	10000
2^5	32	40	200	100000
2^6	64	100	1000	1000000
2^7	128	200	2000	10000000
2^8	256	400	10000	100000000
2^9	512	1000	20000	1000000000
2^{10}	1024	2000	100000	10000000000
2^{11}	2048	4000	.200000	100000000000
2^{12}	4096	10000	1000000	1000000000000

Let's say we have the binary number 101101011010. This can be written as

$$101101011010_{TWO} = 1 \times 2048_{TEN} +$$
$$0 \times 1024_{TEN} +$$
$$1 \times 512_{TEN} +$$
$$1 \times 256_{TEN} +$$
$$0 \times 128_{TEN} +$$
$$1 \times 64_{TEN} +$$
$$0 \times 32_{TEN} +$$
$$1 \times 16_{TEN} +$$
$$1 \times 8_{TEN} +$$
$$0 \times 4_{TEN} +$$
$$1 \times 2_{TEN} +$$
$$0 \times 1_{TEN}$$

The same number can be written this way:

$$101101011010_{TWO} = 1 \times 2^{11} +$$
$$0 \times 2^{10} +$$
$$1 \times 2^9 +$$
$$1 \times 2^8 +$$
$$0 \times 2^7 +$$
$$1 \times 2^6 +$$
$$0 \times 2^5 +$$
$$1 \times 2^4 +$$
$$1 \times 2^3 +$$
$$0 \times 2^2 +$$
$$1 \times 2^1 +$$
$$0 \times 2^0 +$$

If we just add up the parts in decimal, we get 2048 + 512 + 256 + 64 + 16 + 8 + 2, which is 2,906$_{TEN}$.

To convert binary numbers to decimal more concisely, you might prefer a method that uses a template I've prepared:

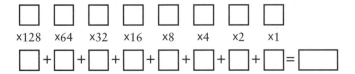

This template allows you to convert numbers up to eight binary digits in length, but it could easily be extended. To use it, put up to eight binary digits in the 8 boxes at the top, one digit to a box. Do the eight multiplications and put the products in the 8 lower boxes. Add these eight boxes for the final result. This example shows how to find the decimal equivalent of 10010110:

1	0	0	1	0	1	1	0
×128	×64	×32	×16	×8	×4	×2	×1

128 + 0 + 0 + 16 + 0 + 4 + 2 + 0 = 150

Converting from decimal to binary isn't quite as straightforward, but here's a template that let's you convert decimal numbers from 0 through 255 to binary:

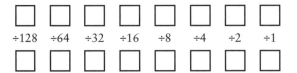

The conversion is actually trickier than it appears, so follow the directions carefully. Put the entire decimal number (less than or equal to 255) in the box in the upper left corner. Divide that number (the dividend) by the first divisor (128), as indicated. Put the quotient in the box below (the box at the lower left corner), and the remainder in the box to the right (the second box on the top row). That first remainder is the dividend for the next calculation, which uses a divisor of 64. Continue in the same manner through the template.

Keep in mind that each quotient will be either 0 or 1. If the dividend is less than the divisor, the quotient is 0 and the remainder is simply the dividend. If the dividend is greater than or equal to the divisor, the quotient is 1 and the remainder is the dividend minus the divisor. Here's how it's done with 150:

150	22	22	22	6	6	2	0
÷128	÷64	÷32	÷16	÷8	÷4	÷2	÷1
1	0	0	1	0	1	1	0

If you need to add or multiply two binary numbers, it's probably easier to do the calculation in binary rather than convert to decimal. This is the part you're *really* going to like. Imagine how quickly you could have mastered addition if the only thing you had to memorize was this:

+	0	1
0	0	1
1	1	10

Let's use this table to add two binary numbers:

$$\begin{array}{r} 1100101 \\ + \ 0110110 \\ \hline 10011011 \end{array}$$

Starting at the right column: 1 plus 0 equals 1. Second column from right: 0 plus 1 equals 1. Third column: 1 plus 1 equals 0, carry the 1. Fourth column: 1 (carried) plus 0 plus 0 equals 1. Fifth column: 0 plus 1 equals 1. Sixth column: 1 plus 1 equals 0, carry the 1. Seventh column: 1 (carried) plus 1 plus 0 equals 10.

The multiplication table is even simpler than the addition table because it can be entirely derived by using two of the very basic rules of multiplication: Multiplying anything by 0 gets you 0, and multiplying any number by 1 has no effect on the number.

x	0	1
0	0	0
1	0	1

Here's a multiplication of 13_{TEN} by 11_{TEN} in binary:

$$\begin{array}{r} 1101 \\ \times \ 1011 \\ \hline 1101 \\ 1101 \\ 0000 \\ 1101 \\ \hline 10001111 \end{array}$$

The result is 143_{TEN}.

People who work with binary numbers often write them with leading zeros (that is, zeros to the left of the first 1)—for example, 0011 rather than just 11. This doesn't change the value of the number at all; it's just for cosmetic purposes. For example, here are the first sixteen binary numbers with their decimal equivalents:

Binary	Decimal
0000	0
0001	1
0010	2
0011	3
0100	4
0101	5
0110	6
0111	7
1000	8
1001	9
1010	10
1011	11
1100	12
1101	13
1110	14
1111	15

Let's take a look at this list of binary numbers for a moment. Consider each of the four vertical columns of zeros and ones, and notice how the digits alternate going down the column:

- The rightmost digit alternates between 0 and 1.
- The next digit from the right alternates between two 0s and two 1s.
- The next digit alternates between four 0s and four 1s.
- The next digit alternates between eight 0s and eight 1s.

This is *very* methodical, wouldn't you say? Indeed, you can easily write the next sixteen binary numbers by just repeating the first sixteen and putting a 1 in front:

Binary	Decimal
10000	16
10001	17
10010	18
10011	19
10100	20
10101	21
10110	22
10111	23
11000	24
11001	25
11010	26
11011	27
11100	28
11101	29
11110	30
11111	31

Here's another way of looking at it: When you count in binary, the rightmost digit (also called the least significant digit), alternates between 0 and 1. Every time it changes from a 1 to a 0, the digit second to right (that is, the next most significant digit) also changes, either from 0 to 1 or from 1 to 0. So every time a binary digit changes from a 1 to a 0, the next most significant digit also changes, either from a 0 to a 1 or from a 1 to a 0.

When we're writing large decimal numbers, we use commas every three places so that we can more easily know what the number means at a glance. For example, if you see 12000000, you probably have to count digits, but if you see 12,000,000, you know that means twelve million.

Binary numbers can get very long very quickly. For example, twelve million in binary is 101101110001101100000000. To make this a *little* more readable, it's customary to separate every four binary digits with a dash, for example 1011-0111-0001-1011-0000-0000 or with spaces: 1011 0111 0001 1011 0000 0000. Later on in this book, we'll look at a more concise way of expressing binary numbers.

By reducing our number system to just the binary digits 0 and 1, we've gone as far as we can go. We can't get any simpler. Moreover, the binary number system bridges the gap between arithmetic and electricity. In previous chapters, we've been looking at switches and wires and lightbulbs and relays, and any of these objects can represent the binary digits 0 and 1:

A wire can be a binary digit. If current is flowing through the wire, the binary digit is 1. If not, the binary digit is 0.

A switch can be a binary digit. If the switch is on, or closed, the binary digit is 1. If the switch is off, or open, the binary digit is 0.

A lightbulb can be a binary digit. If the lightbulb is lit, the binary digit is 1. If the lightbulb is not lit, the binary digit is 0.

A telegraph relay can be a binary digit. If the relay is closed, the binary digit is 1. If the relay is at rest, the binary digit is 0.

Binary numbers have a whole *lot* to do with computers.

Sometime around 1948, the American mathematician John Wilder Tukey (born 1915) realized that the words *binary digit* were likely to assume a much greater importance in the years ahead as computers became more prevalent. He decided to coin a new, shorter word to replace the unwieldy five syllables of *binary digit*. He considered *bigit* and *binit* but settled instead on the short, simple, elegant, and perfectly lovely word *bit*.

Chapter Nine

Bit by Bit by Bit

When Tony Orlando requested in a 1973 song that his beloved "Tie a Yellow Ribbon Round the Ole Oak Tree," he wasn't asking for elaborate explanations or extended discussion. He didn't want any ifs, ands, or buts. Despite the complex feelings and emotional histories that would have been at play in the real-life situation the song was based on, all the man really wanted was a simple yes or no. He wanted a yellow ribbon tied around the tree to mean "Yes, even though you messed up big time and you've been in prison for three years, I still want you back with me under my roof." And he wanted the absence of a yellow ribbon to mean "Don't even *think* about stopping here."

These are two clear-cut, mutually exclusive alternatives. Tony Orlando did *not* sing, "Tie half of a yellow ribbon if you want to think about it for a while" or "Tie a blue ribbon if you don't love me anymore but you'd still like to be friends." Instead, he made it very, very simple.

Equally effective as the absence or presence of a yellow ribbon (but perhaps more awkward to put into verse) would be a choice of traffic signs in the front yard: Perhaps "Merge" or "Wrong Way."

Or a sign hung on the door: "Closed" or "Open."

Or a flashlight in the window, turned on or off.

You can choose from lots of ways to say yes or no if that's all you need to say. You don't need a sentence to say yes or no; you don't need a word, and you don't even need a letter. All you need is a *bit,* and by that I mean all you need is a 0 or a 1.

As we discovered in the previous chapters, there's nothing really all that special about the decimal number system that we normally use for counting. It's pretty clear that we base our number system on ten because that's the number of fingers we have. We could just as reasonably base our number system on eight (if we were cartoon characters) or four (if we were lobsters) or even two (if we were dolphins).

But there *is* something special about the binary number system. What's special about binary is that it's the *simplest* number system possible. There are only two binary digits—0 and 1. If we want something simpler than binary, we'll have to get rid of the 1, and then we'll be left with just a 0. We can't do much of anything with just a 0.

The word *bit,* coined to mean *binary digit,* is surely one of the loveliest words invented in connection with computers. Of course, the word has the normal meaning, "a small portion, degree, or amount," and that normal meaning is perfect because a bit—one binary digit—is a very small quantity indeed.

Sometimes when a new word is invented, it also assumes a new meaning. That's certainly true in this case. A *bit* has a meaning beyond the *binary digits* used by dolphins for counting. In the computer age, the bit has come to be regarded as *the basic building block of information.*

Now that's a bold statement, and of course, bits aren't the only things that convey information. Letters and words and Morse code and Braille and decimal digits convey information as well. The thing about the bit is that it conveys very *little* information. A bit of information is the tiniest amount of information possible. Anything less than a bit is no information at all. But because a bit represents the smallest amount of information possible, more complex information can be conveyed with multiple bits. (By saying that a bit conveys a "small" amount of information, I surely don't mean that the information borders on the unimportant. Indeed, the yellow ribbon is a *very* important bit to the two people concerned with it.)

"Listen, my children, and you shall hear / Of the midnight ride of Paul Revere," wrote Henry Wadsworth Longfellow, and while he might not have been historically accurate when describing how Paul Revere alerted the American colonies that the British had invaded, he did provide a thought-provoking example of the use of bits to communicate important information:

> He said to his friend "If the British march
> By land or sea from the town to-night,
> Hang a lantern aloft in the belfry arch
> Of the North Church tower as a special light,—
> One, if by land, and two, if by sea..."

To summarize, Paul Revere's friend has two lanterns. If the British are invading by land, he will put just one lantern in the church tower. If the British are coming by sea, he will put both lanterns in the church tower.

However, Longfellow isn't explicitly mentioning all the possibilities. He left unspoken a *third* possibility, which is that the British aren't invading just yet. Longfellow implies that this possibility will be conveyed by the *absence* of lanterns in the church tower.

Let's assume that the two lanterns are actually permanent fixtures in the church tower. Normally they aren't lit:

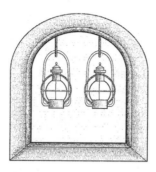

This means that the British aren't yet invading. If one of the lanterns is lit,

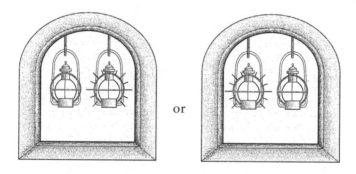

or

the British are coming by land. If both lanterns are lit,

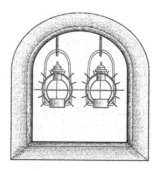

the British are coming by sea.

Each lantern is a bit. A lit lantern is a 1 bit and an unlit lantern is a 0 bit. Tony Orlando demonstrated to us that only one bit is necessary to convey one of two possibilities. If Paul Revere needed only to be alerted that the

British were invading (and not where they were coming from), one lantern would have been sufficient. The lantern would have been lit for an invasion and unlit for another evening of peace.

Conveying one of three possibilities requires another lantern. Once that second lantern is present, however, the two bits allows communicating one of four possibilities:

> 00 = The British aren't invading tonight.
> 01 = They're coming by land.
> 10 = They're coming by land.
> 11 = They're coming by sea.

What Paul Revere did by sticking to just three possibilities was actually quite sophisticated. In the lingo of communication theory, he used *redundancy* to counteract the effect of *noise*. The word *noise* is used in communication theory to refer to anything that interferes with communication. Static on a telephone line is an obvious example of noise that interferes with a telephone communication. Communication over the telephone is usually successful, nevertheless, even in the presence of noise because spoken language is heavily redundant. We don't need to hear every syllable of every word in order to understand what's being said.

In the case of the lanterns in the church tower, noise can refer to the darkness of the night and the distance of Paul Revere from the tower, both of which might prevent him from distinguishing one lantern from the other. Here's the crucial passage in Longfellow's poem:

> *And lo! As he looks, on the belfry's height*
> *A glimmer, and then a gleam of light!*
> *He springs to the saddle, the bridle he turns,*
> *But lingers and gazes, till full on his sight*
> *A second lamp in the belfry burns!*

It certainly doesn't sound as if Paul Revere was in a position to figure out exactly which one of the two lanterns was first lit.

The essential concept here is that *information represents a choice among two or more possibilities.* For example, when we talk to another person, every word we speak is a choice among all the words in the dictionary. If we numbered all the words in the dictionary from 1 through 351,482, we could just as accurately carry on conversations using the numbers rather than words. (Of course, both participants would need dictionaries where the words are numbered identically, as well as plenty of patience.)

The flip side of this is that *any information that can be reduced to a choice among two or more possibilities can be expressed using bits.* Needless to say, there are plenty of forms of human communication that do *not* represent choices among discrete possibilities and that are also vital to our existence. This is why people don't form romantic relationships with computers. (Let's hope they don't, anyway.) If you can't express something in words, pictures, or sounds, you're not going to be able to encode the information in bits. Nor would you want to.

A thumb up or a thumb down is one bit of information. And two thumbs up or down—such as the thumbs of film critics Roger Ebert and the late Gene Siskel when they rendered their final verdicts on the latest movies—convey two bits of information. (We'll ignore what they actually had to *say* about the movies; all we care about here are their thumbs.) Here we have four possibilities that can be represented with a pair of bits:

> 00 = They both hated it.
> 01 = Siskel hated it; Ebert loved it.
> 10 = Siskel loved it; Ebert hated it.
> 11 = They both loved it.

The first bit is the Siskel bit, which is 0 if Siskel hated the movie and 1 if he liked it. Similarly, the second bit is the Ebert bit.

So if your friend asked you, "What was the verdict from Siskel and Ebert about that movie *Impolite Encounter*?" instead of answering, "Siskel gave it a thumbs up and Ebert gave it a thumbs down" or even "Siskel liked it; Ebert didn't," you could have simply said, "One zero." As long as your friend knew which was the Siskel bit and which was the Ebert bit, and that a 1 bit meant thumbs up and a 0 bit meant thumbs down, your answer would be perfectly understandable. But you and your friend have to know the code.

We could have declared initially that a 1 bit meant a thumbs down and a 0 bit meant a thumbs up. That might seem counterintuitive. Naturally, we like to think of a 1 bit as representing something affirmative and a 0 bit as the opposite, but it's really just an arbitrary assignment. The only requirement is that everyone who uses the code must know what the 0 and 1 bits mean.

The meaning of a particular bit or collection of bits is always understood contextually. The meaning of a yellow ribbon around a particular oak tree is probably known only to the person who put it there and the person who's supposed to see it. Change the color, the tree, or the date, and it's just a meaningless scrap of cloth. Similarly, to get some useful information out of Siskel and Ebert's hand gestures, at the very least we need to know what movie is under discussion.

If you maintained a list of the movies that Siskel and Ebert reviewed and how they voted with their thumbs, you could add another bit to the mix to include your own opinion. Adding this third bit increases the number of different possibilities to eight:

> 000 = Siskel hated it; Ebert hated it; I hated it.
> 001 = Siskel hated it; Ebert hated it; I loved it.
> 010 = Siskel hated it; Ebert loved it; I hated it.
> 011 = Siskel hated it; Ebert loved it; I loved it.
> 100 = Siskel loved it; Ebert hated it; I hated it.
> 101 = Siskel loved it; Ebert hated it; I loved it.
> 110 = Siskel loved it; Ebert loved it; I hated it.
> 111 = Siskel loved it; Ebert loved it; I loved it.

One bonus of using bits to represent this information is that we know that we've accounted for all the possibilities. We know there can be eight and only eight possibilities and no more or fewer. With 3 bits, we can count only from zero to seven. There are no more 3-digit binary numbers.

Now, during this description of the Siskel and Ebert bits, you might have been considering a very serious and disturbing question, and that question is this: What do we do about *Leonard Maltin's Movie & Video Guide*? After all, Leonard Maltin doesn't do the thumbs up and thumbs down thing. Leonard Maltin rates the movies using the more traditional star system.

To determine how many Maltin bits we need, we must first know a few things about his system. Maltin gives a movie anything from 1 star to 4 stars, with half stars in between. (Just to make this interesting, he doesn't actually award a single star; instead, the movie is rated as a BOMB.) There are seven possibilities, which means that we can represent a particular rating using just 3 bits:

$$000 = BOMB$$
$$001 = \star \tfrac{1}{2}$$
$$010 = \star \star$$
$$011 = \star \star \tfrac{1}{2}$$
$$100 = \star \star \star$$
$$101 = \star \star \star \tfrac{1}{2}$$
$$110 = \star \star \star \star$$

"What about 111?" you may ask. Well, that code doesn't mean anything. It's not defined. If the binary code 111 were used to represent a Maltin rating, you'd know that a mistake was made. (Probably a computer made the mistake because people never do.)

You'll recall that when we had two bits to represent the Siskel and Ebert ratings, the leftmost bit was the Siskel bit and the rightmost bit was the Ebert bit. Do the individual bits mean anything here? Well, sort of. If you take the numeric value of the bit code, add 2, and then divide by 2, that will give you the number of stars. But that's only because we defined the codes in a reasonable and consistent manner. We could just as well have defined the codes this way:

$$000 = \star \star \star$$
$$001 = \star \tfrac{1}{2}$$
$$010 = \star \star \tfrac{1}{2}$$
$$011 = \star \star \star \star$$
$$101 = \star \star \star \ \tfrac{1}{2}$$
$$110 = \star \star$$
$$111 = BOMB$$

This code is just as legitimate as the preceding code so long as everybody knows what it means.

If Maltin ever encountered a movie undeserving of even a single full star, he could award a half star. He would certainly have enough codes for the half-star option. The codes could be redefined like so:

```
000 = MAJOR BOMB
001 = BOMB
010 = ★½
011 = ★★
100 = ★★½
101 = ★★★
110 = ★★★½
111 = ★★★★
```

But if he then encountered a movie not even worthy of a half star and decided to award no stars (ATOMIC BOMB?), he'd need another bit. No more 3-bit codes are available.

The magazine *Entertainment Weekly* gives grades, not only for movies but for television shows, CDs, books, CD-ROMs, Web sites, and much else. The grades range from A+ straight down to F (although it seems that only Pauly Shore movies are worthy of that honor). If you count them, you see 13 possible grades. We would need 4 bits to represent these grades:

```
0000 = F
0001 = D−
0010 = D
0011 = D+
0100 = C−
0101 = C
0110 = C+
0111 = B−
1000 = B
1001 = B+
1010 = A−
1011 = A
1100 = A+
```

We have three unused codes: 1101, 1110, and 1111, for a grand total of 16.

Whenever we talk about bits, we often talk about a certain *number* of bits. The more bits we have, the greater the number of different possibilities we can convey.

It's the same situation with decimal numbers, of course. For example, how many telephone area codes are there? The area code is three decimal digits long, and if all of them are used (which they aren't, but we'll ignore that), there are 10^3, or 1000, codes, ranging from 000 through 999. How many

7-digit phone numbers are possible within the 212 area code? That's 10^7, or 10,000,000. How many phone numbers can you have with a 212 area code and a 260 prefix? That's 10^4, or 10,000.

Similarly, in binary the number of possible codes is always equal to 2 to the power of the number of bits:

Number of Bits	Number of Codes
1	$2^1 = 2$
2	$2^2 = 4$
3	$2^3 = 8$
4	$2^4 = 16$
5	$2^5 = 32$
6	$2^6 = 64$
7	$2^7 = 128$
8	$2^8 = 256$
9	$2^9 = 512$
10	$2^{10} = 1024$

Every additional bit doubles the number of codes.

If you know how many codes you need, how can you calculate how many bits you need? In other words, how do you go backward in the preceding table?

The method you use is something called the *base two logarithm*. The logarithm is the opposite of the power. We know that 2 to the 7th power equals 128. The base two logarithm of 128 equals 7. To use more mathematical notation, this statement

$$2^7 = 128$$

is equivalent to this statement:

$$\log_2 128 = 7$$

So if the base two logarithm of 128 is 7, and the base two logarithm of 256 is 8, then what's the base two logarithm of 200? It's actually about 7.64, but we really don't have to know that. If we needed to represent 200 different things with bits, we'd need 8 bits.

Bits are often hidden from casual observation deep within our electronic appliances. We can't see the bits encoded in our compact discs or in our digital watches or inside our computers. But sometimes the bits are in clear view.

Here's one example. If you own a camera that uses 35-millimeter film, take a look at a roll of film. Hold it this way:

You'll see a checkerboard-like grid of silver and black squares that I've numbered 1 through 12 in the diagram. This is called *DX-encoding*. These 12 squares are actually 12 bits. A silver square means a 1 bit and a black square means a 0 bit. Square 1 and square 7 are always silver (1).

What do the bits mean? You might be aware that some films are more sensitive to light than others. This sensitivity to light is often called the film *speed*. A film that's very sensitive to light is said to be *fast* because it can be exposed very quickly. The speed of the film is indicated by the film's ASA (American Standards Association) rating, the most popular being 100, 200, and 400. This ASA rating isn't only printed on the box and the film's cassette but is also encoded in bits.

There are 24 standard ASA ratings for photographic film. Here they are:

25	32	40
50	64	80
100	125	160
200	250	320
400	500	640
800	1000	1250
1600	2000	2500
3200	4000	5000

How many bits are required to encode the ASA rating? The answer is 5. We know that 2^4 equals 16, so that's too few. But 2^5 equals 32, which is more than sufficient.

The bits that correspond to the film speed are shown in the following table:

Square 2	Square 3	Square 4	Square 5	Square 6	Film Speed
0	0	0	1	0	25
0	0	0	0	1	32
0	0	0	1	1	40
1	0	0	1	0	50
1	0	0	0	1	64
1	0	0	1	1	80
0	1	0	1	0	100
0	1	0	0	1	125
0	1	0	1	1	160
1	1	0	1	0	200
1	1	0	0	1	250
1	1	0	1	1	320
0	0	1	1	0	400
0	0	1	0	1	500
0	0	1	1	1	640
1	0	1	1	0	800
1	0	1	0	1	1000
1	0	1	1	1	1250
0	1	1	1	0	1600
0	1	1	0	1	2000
0	1	1	1	1	2500
1	1	1	1	0	3200
1	1	1	0	1	4000
1	1	1	1	1	5000

Most modern 35-millimeter cameras use these codes. (Exceptions are cameras on which you must set the exposure manually and cameras that have built-in light meters but require you to set the film speed manually.) If you take a look inside the camera where you put the film, you should see six metal contacts that correspond to squares 1 through 6 on the film canister. The silver squares are actually the metal of the film cassette, which is a conductor. The black squares are paint, which is an insulator.

The electronic circuitry of the camera runs a current into square 1, which is always silver. This current will be picked up (or not picked up) by the five contacts on squares 2 through 6, depending on whether the squares are bare silver or are painted over. Thus, if the camera senses a current on contacts 4 and 5 but not on contacts 2, 3, and 6, the film speed is 400 ASA. The camera can then adjust film exposure accordingly.

Inexpensive cameras need read only squares 2 and 3 and assume that the film speed is 50, 100, 200, or 400 ASA.

Most cameras don't read or use squares 8 through 12. Squares 8, 9, and 10 encode the number of exposures on the roll of film, and squares 11 and 12 refer to the *exposure latitude,* which depends on whether the film is for black-and-white prints, for color prints, or for color slides.

Perhaps the most common visual display of binary digits is the ubiquitous Universal Product Code (UPC), that little bar code symbol that appears on virtually every packaged item that we purchase these days. The UPC has come to symbolize one of the ways computers have crept into our lives.

Although the UPC often inspires fits of paranoia, it's really an innocent little thing, invented for the purpose of automating retail checkout and inventory, which it does fairly successfully. When it's used with a well-designed checkout system, the consumer can have an itemized sales receipt, which isn't possible with conventional cash registers.

Of interest to us here is that the UPC is a binary code, although it might not seem like one at first. So it will be instructive to decode the UPC and examine how it works.

In its most common form, the UPC is a collection of 30 vertical black bars of various widths, divided by gaps of various widths, along with some digits. For example, this is the UPC that appears on the 10 ¾-ounce can of Campbell's Chicken Noodle Soup:

We're tempted to try to visually interpret the UPC in terms of thin bars and black bars, narrow gaps and wide gaps, and indeed, that's one way to look at it. The black bars in the UPC can have four different widths, with the thicker bars being two, three, and four times the width of the thinnest bar. Similarly, the wider gaps between the bars are two, three, and four times the width of the thinnest gap.

But another way to look at the UPC is as a series of bits. Keep in mind that the whole bar code symbol isn't exactly what the scanning wand "sees" at the checkout counter. The wand doesn't try to interpret the numbers at the bottom, for example, because that would require a more sophisticated computing technique known as *optical character recognition,* or OCR. Instead, the scanner sees just a thin slice of this whole block. The UPC is as large as it is to give the checkout person something to aim the scanner at. The slice that the scanner sees can be represented like this:

I I ▪ I ▪ I ▪ I ▪ I ▪ I ▪ I I I I ▪ I ▪ ▪ ▪ ▪ I ▪ ▪ ▪ I I I II

This looks almost like Morse code, doesn't it?

As the computer scans this information from left to right, it assigns a 1 bit to the first black bar it encounters, a 0 bit to the next white gap. The subsequent gaps and bars are read as series of bits 1, 2, 3, or 4 bits in a row, depending on the width of the gap or the bar. The correspondence of the scanned bar code to bits is simply:

I I ▪ I ▪ I ▪ I ▪ I ▪ I ▪ I I I I ▪ I ▪ ▪ ▪ ▪ I ▪ ▪ ▪ I I I II
10100011010110001001100100011010001101000110101010111001011001101101100100111011001101000100101

So the entire UPC is simply a series of 95 bits. In this particular example, the bits can be grouped as follows:

Bits	Meaning
101	Left-hand guard pattern
0001101 ⎤	
0110001 ⎥	
0011001 ⎥	Left-side digits
0001101 ⎥	
0001101 ⎥	
0001101 ⎦	
01010	Center guard pattern
1110010 ⎤	
1100110 ⎥	
1101100 ⎥	Right-side digits
1001110 ⎥	
1100110 ⎥	
1000100 ⎦	
101	Right-hand guard pattern

The first 3 bits are always 101. This is known as the *left-hand guard pattern,* and it allows the computer-scanning device to get oriented. From the guard pattern, the scanner can determine the width of the bars and gaps that correspond to single bits. Otherwise, the UPC would have to be a specific size on all packages.

The left-hand guard pattern is followed by six groups of 7 bits each. Each of these is a code for a numeric digit 0 through 9, as I'll demonstrate shortly. A 5-bit center guard pattern follows. The presence of this fixed pattern (always 01010) is a form of built-in error checking. If the computer scanner doesn't find the center guard pattern where it's supposed to be, it won't acknowledge that it has interpreted the UPC. This center guard pattern is one of several precautions against a code that has been tampered with or badly printed.

The center guard pattern is followed by another six groups of 7 bits each, which are then followed by a right-hand guard pattern, which is always 101. As I'll explain later, the presence of a guard pattern at the end allows the UPC code to be scanned backward (that is, right to left) as well as forward.

So the entire UPC encodes 12 numeric digits. The left side of the UPC encodes 6 digits, each requiring 7 bits. You can use the following table to decode these bits:

Left-Side Codes

0001101 = 0	0110001 = 5
0011001 = 1	0101111 = 6
0010011 = 2	0111011 = 7
0111101 = 3	0110111 = 8
0100011 = 4	0001011 = 9

Notice that each 7-bit code begins with a 0 and ends with a 1. If the scanner encounters a 7-bit code on the left side that begins with a 1 or ends with a 0, it knows either that it hasn't correctly read the UPC code or that the code has been tampered with. Notice also that each code has only two groups of consecutive 1 bits. This implies that each digit corresponds to two vertical bars in the UPC code.

You'll see that each code in this table has an odd number of 1 bits. This is another form of error and consistency checking known as *parity*. A group of bits has *even parity* if it has an even number of 1 bits and *odd parity* if it has an odd number of 1 bits. Thus, all of these codes have odd parity.

To interpret the six 7-bit codes on the right side of the UPC, use the following table:

Right-Side Codes

1110010 = 0	1001110 = 5
1100110 = 1	1010000 = 6
1101100 = 2	1000100 = 7
1000010 = 3	1001000 = 8
1011100 = 4	1110100 = 9

These codes are the complements of the earlier codes: Wherever a 0 appeared is now a 1, and vice versa. These codes always begin with a 1 and end with a 0. In addition, they have an even number of 1 bits, which is even parity.

So now we're equipped to decipher the UPC. Using the two preceding tables, we can determine that the 12 digits encoded in the 10¾-ounce can of Campbell's Chicken Noodle Soup are

0 51000 01251 7

This is *very* disappointing. As you can see, these are precisely the same numbers that are conveniently printed at the bottom of the UPC. (This makes a lot of sense because if the scanner can't read the code for some reason, the person at the register can manually enter the numbers. Indeed, you've undoubtedly seen this happen.) We didn't have to go through all that work to decode them, and moreover, we haven't come close to decoding any secret information. Yet there isn't anything left in the UPC to decode. Those 30 vertical lines resolve to just 12 digits.

The first digit (a 0 in this case) is known as the *number system character*. A 0 means that this is a regular UPC code. If the UPC appeared on variable-weight grocery items such as meat or produce, the code would be a 2. Coupons are coded with a 5.

The next five digits make up the manufacturer code. In this case, 51000 is the code for the Campbell Soup Company. All Campbell products have this code. The five digits that follow (01251) are the code for a particular product of that company, in this case, the code for a 10¾-ounce can of chicken noodle soup. This product code has meaning only when combined with the manufacturer's code. Another company's chicken noodle soup might have a different product code, and a product code of 01251 might mean something totally different from another manufacturer.

Contrary to popular belief, the UPC doesn't include the price of the item. That information has to be retrieved from the computer that the store uses in conjunction with the checkout scanners.

The final digit (a 7 in this case) is called the *modulo check character*. This character enables yet another form of error checking. To examine how this works, let's assign each of the first 11 digits (0 51000 01251 in our example) a letter:

A BCDEF GHIJK

Now calculate the following:

$$3 \times (A + C + E + G + I + K) + (B + D + F + H + J)$$

and subtract that from the next highest multiple of 10. That's called the *modulo check character*. In the case of Campbell's Chicken Noodle Soup, we have

$$3 \times (0 + 1 + 0 + 0 + 2 + 1) + (5 + 0 + 0 + 1 + 5) = 3 \times 4 + 11 = 23$$

The next highest multiple of 10 is 30, so

$$30 - 23 = 7$$

and that's the modulo check character printed and encoded in the UPC. This is a form of redundancy. If the computer controlling the scanner doesn't calculate the same modulo check character as the one encoded in the UPC, the computer won't accept the UPC as valid.

Normally, only 4 bits would be required to specify a decimal digit from 0 through 9. The UPC uses 7 bits per digit. Overall, the UPC uses 95 bits to encode only 11 useful decimal digits. Actually, the UPC includes blank space (equivalent to nine 0 bits) at both the left and the right side of the guard pattern. That means the entire UPC requires 113 bits to encode 11 decimal digits, or over 10 bits per decimal digit!

Part of this overkill is necessary for error checking, as we've seen. A product code such as this wouldn't be very useful if it could be easily altered by a customer wielding a felt-tip pen.

The UPC also benefits by being readable in both directions. If the first digits that the scanning device decodes have even parity (that is, an even number of 1 bits in each 7-bit code), the scanner knows that it's interpreting the UPC code from right to left. The computer system then uses this table to decode the right-side digits:

Right-Side Codes in Reverse

0100111 = 0	0111001 = 5
0110011 = 1	0000101 = 6
0011011 = 2	0010001 = 7
0100001 = 3	0001001 = 8
0011101 = 4	0010111 = 9

and this table for the left-side digits:

Left-Side Codes in Reverse

1011000 = 0	1000110 = 5
1001100 = 1	1111010 = 6
1100100 = 2	1101110 = 7
1011110 = 3	1110110 = 8
1100010 = 4	1101000 = 9

These 7-bit codes are all different from the codes read when the UPC is scanned from left to right. There's no ambiguity.

We began looking at codes in this book with Morse code, composed of dots, dashes, and pauses between the dots and dashes. Morse code doesn't immediately seem like it's equivalent to zeros and ones, yet it is.

Recall the rules of Morse code: A dash is three times as long as a dot. The dots and dashes of a single letter are separated by a pause the length of a dot. Letters within a word are separated by pauses equal in length to a dash. Words are separated by pauses equal in length to two dashes.

Just to simplify this analysis a bit, let's assume that a dash is twice the length of a dot rather than three times. That means that a dot can be a 1 bit and a dash can be two 1 bits. Pauses are 0 bits.

Here's the basic table of Morse code from Chapter 2:

A	·—	J	·———	S	···
B	—···	K	—·—	T	—
C	—·—·	L	·—··	U	··—
D	—··	M	——	V	···—
E	·	N	—·	W	·——
F	··—·	O	———	X	—··—
G	——·	P	·——·	Y	—·——
H	····	Q	——·—	Z	——··
I	··	R	·—·		

Here's the table converted to bits:

A	101100	J	101101101100	S	1010100
B	1101010100	K	110101100	T	1100
C	11010110100	L	1011010100	U	10101100
D	11010100	M	1101100	V	1010101100
E	100	N	110100	W	101101100
F	1010110100	O	1101101100	X	11010101100
G	110110100	P	10110110100	Y	110101101100
H	101010100	Q	110110101100	Z	11011010100
I	10100	R	10110100		

Notice that all the codes begin with a 1 bit and end with a pair of 0 bits. The pair of 0 bits represents the pause between letters in the same word. The code for the space between words is another pair of 0 bits. So the Morse code for "hi there" is normally given as

····   ··   —   ····   ·   ·—·   ·

but Morse code using bits can look like the cross section of the UPC code:

1010101001010000110010101010010010110100010000

In terms of bits, Braille is much simpler than Morse code. Braille is a 6-bit code. Each character is represented by an array of six dots, and each of the six dots can be either raised or not raised. As I explained in Chapter 3, the dots are commonly numbered 1 through 6:

1 ◯ ◯ 4
2 ◯ ◯ 5
3 ◯ ◯ 6

The word "code" (for example) is represented by the Braille symbols:

If a raised dot is 1 and a flat dot is 0, each of the characters in Braille can be represented by a 6-bit binary number. The four Braille symbols for the letters in the word "code" are then simply:

100100 101010 100110 100010

where the leftmost bit corresponds to the 1 position in the grid, and the rightmost bit corresponds to the 6 position.

As we shall see later in this book, bits can represent words, pictures, sounds, music, and movies as well as product codes, film speeds, movie ratings, an invasion of the British army, and the intentions of one's beloved. But most fundamentally, bits are numbers. All that needs to be done when bits represent other information is to count the number of possibilities. This determines the number of bits that are needed so that each possibility can be assigned a number.

Bits also play a part in *logic*, that strange blend of philosophy and mathematics for which a primary goal is to determine whether certain statements are true or false. True and false can also be 1 and 0.

Chapter Ten

Logic and Switches

What is truth? Aristotle thought that logic had something to do with it. The collection of his teachings known as the *Organon* (which dates from the fourth century B.C.E.) is the earliest extensive writing on the subject of logic. To the ancient Greeks, logic was a means of analyzing language in the search for truth and thus was considered a form of philosophy. The basis of Aristotle's logic was the *syllogism*. The most famous syllogism (which isn't actually found in the works of Aristotle) is

> *All men are mortal;*
> *Socrates is a man;*
> *Hence, Socrates is mortal.*

In a syllogism, two premises are assumed to be correct, and from these a conclusion is deduced.

The mortality of Socrates might seem straightforward enough, but there are many varieties of syllogisms. For example, consider the following two premises, proposed by the nineteenth-century mathematician Charles Dodgson (also known as Lewis Carroll):

> *All philosophers are logical;*
> *An illogical man is always obstinate.*

The conclusion isn't obvious at all. (It's "Some obstinate persons are not philosophers." Notice the unexpected and disturbing appearance of the word "some.")

For over two thousand years, mathematicians wrestled with Aristotle's logic, attempting to corral it using mathematical symbols and operators. Prior to the nineteenth century, the only person to come close was Gottfried Wilhelm von Leibniz (1648–1716), who dabbled with logic early in life but then went on to other interests (such as independently inventing calculus at the same time as Isaac Newton).

And then came George Boole.

George Boole was born in England in 1815 to a world where the odds were certainly stacked against him. Because he was the son of a shoemaker and a former maid, Britain's rigid class structure would normally have prevented Boole from achieving anything much different from his ancestors. But aided by an inquisitive mind and his helpful father (who had strong interests in science, mathematics, and literature), young George gave himself the type of education normally the privilege of upper-class boys; his studies included Latin, Greek, and mathematics. As a result of his early papers on mathematics, in 1849 Boole was appointed the first Professor of Mathematics at Queen's College, Cork, in Ireland.

Several mathematicians in the mid-1800s had been working on a mathematical definition of logic (most notably Augustus De Morgan), but it was Boole who had the real conceptual breakthrough, first in the short book *The Mathematical Analysis of Logic, Being an Essay Towards a Calculus of Deductive Reasoning* (1847) and then in a much longer and more ambitious text, *An Investigation of the Laws of Thought on Which Are Founded the Mathematical Theories of Logic and Probabilities* (1854), more conveniently referred to as *The Laws of Thought*. Boole died in 1864 at the age of 49 after hurrying to class in the rain and contracting pneumonia.

The title of Boole's 1854 book suggests an ambitious motivation: Because the rational human brain uses logic to think, if we were to find a way in which logic can be represented by mathematics, we would also have a mathematical description of how the brain works. Of course, nowadays this view of the mind seems to us quite naive. (Either that or it's way ahead of its time.)

Boole invented a kind of algebra that looks and acts very much like conventional algebra. In conventional algebra, the *operands* (which are usually letters) stand for numbers, and the *operators* (most often + and ×) indicate how these numbers are to be combined. Often we use conventional algebra to solve problems such as this: Anya has 3 pounds of tofu. Betty has twice as much tofu as Anya. Carmen has 5 pounds more tofu than Betty. Deirdre has three times the tofu that Carmen has. How much tofu does Deirdre have?

To solve this problem, we first convert the English to arithmetical statements, using four letters to stand for the pounds of tofu that each of the four women has:

$$A = 3$$
$$B = 2 \times A$$
$$C = B + 5$$
$$D = 3 \times C$$

We can combine these four statements into one statement by substitution and then finally perform the additions and multiplications:

$$D = 3 \times C$$
$$D = 3 \times (B + 5)$$
$$D = 3 \times ((2 \times A) + 5)$$
$$D = 3 \times ((2 \times 3) + 5)$$
$$D = 33$$

When we do conventional algebra, we follow certain rules. These rules have probably become so ingrained in our practice that we no longer think of them as rules and might even forget their names. But rules indeed underlie all the workings of any form of mathematics.

The first rule is that addition and multiplication are *commutative*. That means we can switch around the symbols on each side of the operations:

$$A + B = B + A$$
$$A \times B = B \times A$$

By contrast, subtraction and division are *not* commutative.

Addition and multiplication are also *associative*, that is

$$A + (B + C) = (A + B) + C$$
$$A \times (B \times C) = (A \times B) \times C$$

And finally, multiplication is said to be *distributive* over addition:

$$A \times (B + C) = (A \times B) + (A \times C)$$

Another characteristic of conventional algebra is that it always deals with numbers, such as pounds of tofu or numbers of ducks or distances that a train travels or the ages of family members. It was Boole's genius to make algebra more abstract by divorcing it from concepts of number. In Boolean algebra (as Boole's algebra was eventually called), the operands refer not to numbers but instead to *classes*. A class is simply a group of things, what in later times came to be known as a *set*.

Let's talk about cats. Cats can be either male or female. For convenience, we can use the letter M to refer to the class of male cats and F to refer to the class of female cats. Keep in mind that these two symbols do *not* represent numbers of cats. The number of male and female cats can change by the minute as new cats are born and old cats (regrettably) pass away. The letters stand for classes of cats—cats with specific characteristics. Instead of referring to male cats, we can just say "M."

We can also use other letters to represent the color of the cats: For example, T can refer to the class of tan cats, B can be the class of black cats, W the class of white cats, and O the class of cats of all "other" colors—all cats not in the class T, B, or W.

Finally (at least as far as this example goes), cats can be either neutered or unneutered. Let's use the letter N to refer to the class of neutered cats and U for the class of unneutered cats.

In conventional (numeric) algebra, the operators + and × are used to indicate addition and multiplication. In Boolean algebra, the same + and × symbols are used, and here's where things might get confusing. Everybody knows how to add and multiply numbers in conventional algebra, but how do we add and multiply *classes*?

Well, we don't actually add and multiply in Boolean algebra. Instead, the + and × symbols mean something else entirely.

The + symbol in Boolean algebra means a *union* of two classes. A union of two classes is everything in the first class combined with everything in the second class. For example, B + W represents the class of all cats that are either black or white.

The × symbol in Boolean algebra means an *intersection* of two classes. An intersection of two classes is everything that is in *both* the first class *and* the second class. For example, F × T represents the class of all cats that are both female and tan. As in conventional algebra, we can write F × T as F·T or simply FT (which is what Boole preferred). You can think of the two letters as two adjectives strung together: "female tan" cats.

To avoid confusion between conventional algebra and Boolean algebra, sometimes the symbols ∪ and ∩ are used for union and intersection instead of + and ×. But part of Boole's liberating influence on mathematics was to make the use of familiar operators more abstract, so I've decided to stick with his decision not to introduce new symbols into his algebra.

The commutative, associative, and distributive rules all hold for Boolean algebra. What's more, in Boolean algebra the + operator is distributive over the × operator. This isn't true of conventional algebra:

$$W + (B \times F) = (W + B) \times (W + F)$$

The union of white cats and black female cats is the same as the intersection of two unions: the union of white cats and black cats, and the union of white cats and female cats. This is somewhat difficult to grasp, but it works.

Two more symbols are necessary to complete Boolean algebra. These two symbols might look like numbers, but they're really not because they're sometimes treated a little differently than numbers. The symbol 1 in Boolean algebra means "the universe"—that is, everything we're talking about. In this example, the symbol 1 means "the class of all cats." Thus,

$$M + F = 1$$

This means that the union of male cats and female cats is the class of all cats. Similarly, the union of tan cats and black cats and white cats and other colored cats is also the class of all cats:

$$T + B + W + O = 1$$

And you achieve the class of all cats this way, too:

$$N + U = 1$$

The 1 symbol can be used with a minus sign to indicate the universe *excluding* something. For example,

$$1 - M$$

is the class of all cats except the male cats. The universe excluding all male cats is the same as the class of female cats:

$$1 - M = F$$

The other symbol that we need is the 0, and in Boolean algebra the 0 means an empty class—a class of nothing. The empty class results when we take an intersection of two mutually exclusive classes, for example, cats that are both male and female:

$$F \times M = 0$$

Notice that the 1 and 0 symbols sometimes work the same way in Boolean algebra as in conventional algebra. For example, the intersection of all cats and female cats is the class of female cats:

$$1 \times F = F$$

The intersection of no cats and female cats is the class of no cats:

$$0 \times F = 0$$

The union of no cats and all female cats is the class of female cats:

$$0 + F = F$$

But sometimes the result doesn't look the same as in conventional algebra. For example, the union of all cats and female cats is the class of all cats:

$$1 + F = 1$$

This doesn't make much sense in conventional algebra.

Because F is the class of all female cats, and $(1 - F)$ is the class of all cats that aren't female, the union of these two classes is 1:

$$F + (1 - F) = 1$$

and the intersection of the two classes is 0:

$$F \times (1 - F) = 0$$

Historically, this formulation represents an important concept in logic: It's called the Law of Contradiction and indicates that something can't be both itself and the opposite of itself.

Where Boolean algebra really looks different from conventional algebra is in a statement like this:

$$F \times F = F$$

The statement makes perfect sense in Boolean algebra: The intersection of female cats and female cats is still the class of female cats. But it sure wouldn't look quite right if F referred to a number. Boole considered

$$X^2 = X$$

to be the single statement that differentiates his algebra from conventional algebra. Another Boolean statement that looks funny in terms of conventional algebra is this:

$$F + F = F$$

The union of female cats and female cats is still the class of female cats.

Boolean algebra provides a mathematical method for solving the syllogisms of Aristotle. Let's look at the first two-thirds of that famous syllogism again, but now using gender-neutral language:

> *All persons are mortal;*
> *Socrates is a person.*

We'll use P to represent the class of all persons, M to represent the class of mortal things, and S to represent the class of Socrates. What does it mean to say that "all persons are mortal"? It means that the intersection of the class of all persons and the class of all mortal things is the class of all persons:

$$P \times M = P$$

It would be wrong to say that $P \times M = M$, because the class of all mortal things includes cats, dogs, and elm trees.

To say, "Socrates is a person," means that the intersection of the class containing Socrates (a very small class) and the class of all persons (a much larger class) is the class containing Socrates:

$$S \times P = S$$

Because we know from the first equation that P equals (P × M) we can substitute that into the second equation:

$$S \times (P \times M) = S$$

By the associative law, this is the same as

$$(S \times P) \times M = S$$

But we already know that (S × P) equals S, so we can simplify by using this substitution:

$$S \times M = S$$

And now we're finished. This formula tells us that the intersection of Socrates and the class of all mortal things is S, which means that Socrates is mortal. If we found instead that (S × M) equaled 0, we'd conclude that Socrates wasn't mortal. If we found that (S × M) equaled M, the conclusion would have to be that Socrates was the only mortal thing and everything else was immortal!

Using Boolean algebra might seem like overkill for proving the obvious fact (particularly considering that Socrates proved himself mortal 2400 years ago), but Boolean algebra can also be used to determine whether something satisfies a certain set of criteria. Perhaps one day you walk into a pet shop and say to the salesperson, "I want a male cat, neutered, either white or tan; or a female cat, neutered, any color but white; or I'll take any cat you have as long as it's black." And the salesperson says to you, "So you want a cat from the class of cats represented by the following expression:

$$(M \times N \times (W + T)) + (F \times N \times (1 - W)) + B$$

Right?" And you say, "Yes! Exactly!"

In verifying that the salesperson is correct, you might want to forgo the concepts of union and intersection and instead switch to the words OR and AND. I'm capitalizing these words because the words normally represent concepts in English, but they can also represent operations in Boolean algebra. When you form a union of two classes, you're actually accepting things from the first class OR the second class. And when you form an intersection, you're accepting only those things in both the first class AND the second class. In addition, you can use the word NOT wherever you see a 1 followed by a minus sign. In summary,

- The + (previously known as a union) now means OR.
- The × (previously known as an intersection) now means AND.
- The 1 – (previously the universe without something) now means NOT.

So the expression can also be written like this:

(M AND N AND (W OR T)) OR (F AND N AND (NOT W)) OR B

This is very nearly what you said. Notice how the parentheses clarify your intentions. You want a cat from one of three classes:

(M AND N AND (W OR T))
OR
(F AND N AND (NOT W))
OR
B

With this formula written down, the salesperson can perform something called a *Boolean test*. Without making a big fuss about it, I've subtly shifted to a somewhat different form of Boolean algebra. In this form of Boolean algebra, letters no longer refer to classes. Instead, the letters can now be assigned numbers. The catch is that they can be assigned only the number 0 or 1. The numeral 1 means Yes, True, this particular cat satisfies these criteria. The numeral 0 means No, False, this cat doesn't satisfy these criteria.

First the salesperson brings out an unneutered tan male. Here's the expression of acceptable cats:

$$(M \times N \times (W + T)) + (F \times N \times (1 - W)) + B$$

and here's how it looks with 0s and 1s substituted:

$$(1 \times 0 \times (0 + 1)) + (0 \times 0 \times (1 - 0)) + 0$$

Notice that the only symbols assigned 1s are M and T because the cat is male and tan.

What we must do now is simplify this expression. If it simplifies to 1, the cat satisfies your criteria; if it simplifies to 0, the cat doesn't. While we're simplifying the expression, keep in mind that we're not really adding and multiplying, although generally we can pretend that we are. Most of the same rules apply when + means OR and × means AND. (Sometimes in modern texts the symbols $\land$ and $\lor$ are used for AND and OR instead of × and +. But here's where the + and × signs perhaps make the most sense.)

When the × sign means AND, the possible results are

$$0 \times 0 = 0$$
$$0 \times 1 = 0$$
$$1 \times 0 = 0$$
$$1 \times 1 = 1$$

In other words, the result is 1 only if both the left operand AND the right operand are 1. This operation works exactly the same way as regular multiplication, and it can be summarized in a little table, similar to the way the addition and multiplication tables were shown in Chapter 8:

AND	0	1
0	0	0
1	0	1

When the + sign means OR, the possible results are

$$0 + 0 = 0$$
$$0 + 1 = 1$$
$$1 + 0 = 1$$
$$1 + 1 = 1$$

The result is 1 if either the left operand OR the right operand is 1. This operation produces results very similar to those of regular addition, except that in this case 1 + 1 equals 1. The OR operation can be summarized in another little table:

OR	0	1
0	0	1
1	1	1

We're ready to use these tables to calculate the result of the expression

$$(1 \times 0 \times 1) + (0 \times 0 \times 1) + 0 = 0 + 0 + 0 = 0$$

The result 0 means No, False, this kitty won't do.

Next the salesperson brings out a neutered white female. The original expression was

$$(M \times N \times (W + T)) + (F \times N \times (1 - W)) + B$$

Substitute the 0s and 1s again:

$$(0 \times 1 \times (1 + 0)) + (1 \times 1 \times (1 - 1)) + 0$$

And simplify it:

$$(0 \times 1 \times 1) + (1 \times 1 \times 0) + 0 = 0 + 0 + 0 = 0$$

And another poor kitten must be rejected.

Next the salesperson brings out a neutered gray female. (Gray qualifies as an "other" color—not white or black or tan.) Here's the expression:

$$(0 \times 1 \times (0 + 0)) + (1 \times 1 \times (1 - 0)) + 0$$

Now simplify it:

$$(0 \times 1 \times 0) + (1 \times 1 \times 1) + 0 = 0 + 1 + 0 = 1$$

The final result 1 means Yes, True, a kitten has found a home. (And it was the cutest one too!)

Later that evening, when the kitten is curled up sleeping in your lap, you wonder whether you could have wired some switches and a lightbulb to help you determine whether particular kittens satisfied your criteria. (Yes, you are a strange kid.) Little do you realize that you're about to make a crucial conceptual breakthrough. You're about to perform some experiments that will unite the algebra of George Boole with electrical circuitry and thus make possible the design and construction of computers that work with binary numbers. But don't let that intimidate you.

To begin your experiment, you connect a lightbulb and battery as you would normally, but you use two switches instead of one:

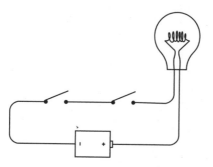

Switches connected in this way—one right after the other—are said to be wired *in series*. If you close the left switch, nothing happens:

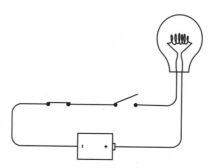

Similarly, if you leave the left switch open and close the right switch, nothing happens. The lightbulb lights up only if both the left switch and the right switch are closed, as shown on the next page.

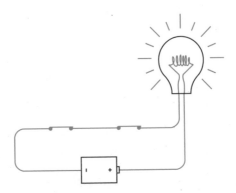

The key word here is *and*. Both the left switch *and* the right switch must be closed for the current to flow through the circuit.

This circuit is performing a little exercise in logic. In effect, the lightbulb is answering the question "Are both switches closed?" We can summarize the workings of this circuit in the following table:

Left Switch	Right Switch	Lightbulb
Open	Open	Not lit
Open	Closed	Not lit
Closed	Open	Not lit
Closed	Closed	Lit

In the preceding chapter, we saw how binary digits, or bits, can represent information—everything from numbers to the direction of Roger Ebert's thumb. We were able to say that a 0 bit means "Ebert's thumb points down" and a 1 bit means "Ebert's thumb points up." A switch has two positions, so it can represent a bit. We can say that a 0 means "switch is open" and a 1 means "switch is closed." A lightbulb has two states; hence it too can represent a bit. We can say that a 0 means "lightbulb is not lit" and a 1 means "lightbulb is lit." Now we simply rewrite the table:

Left Switch	Right Switch	Lightbulb
0	0	0
0	1	0
1	0	0
1	1	1

Notice that if we swap the left switch and the right switch, the results are the same. We really don't have to identify which switch is which. So the table can be rewritten to resemble the AND and OR tables that were shown earlier:

Switches in Series	0	1
0	0	0
1	0	1

And indeed, this is the *same* as the AND table. Check it out:

AND	0	1
0	0	0
1	0	1

This simple circuit is actually performing an AND operation in Boolean algebra.

Now try connecting the two switches a little differently:

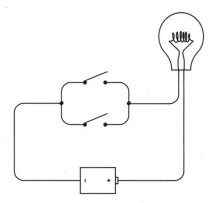

These switches are said to be connected *in parallel*. The difference between this and the preceding connection is that this lightbulb will light if you close the top switch:

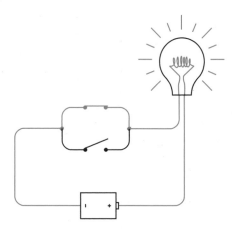

or close the bottom switch:

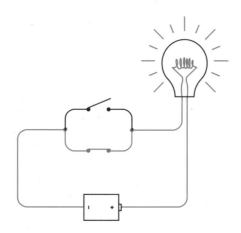

or close both switches:

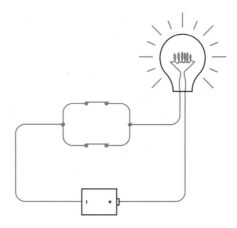

The lightbulb lights if the top switch *or* the bottom switch is closed. The key word here is *or*.

Again, the circuit is performing an exercise in logic. The lightbulb answers the question, "Is either switch closed?" The following table summarizes how this circuit works:

Left Switch	Right Switch	Lightbulb
Open	Open	Not lit
Open	Closed	Lit
Closed	Open	Lit
Closed	Closed	Lit

Again, using 0 to mean an open switch or an unlit lightbulb and 1 to mean a closed switch or a lit lightbulb, this table can be rewritten this way:

Left Switch	Right Switch	Lightbulb
0	0	0
0	1	1
1	0	1
1	1	1

Again it doesn't matter if the two switches are swapped, so the table can also be rewritten like this:

Switches in Parallel	0	1
0	0	1
1	1	1

And you've probably already guessed that this is the same as the Boolean OR:

OR	0	1
0	0	1
1	1	1

which means that two switches in parallel are performing the equivalent of a Boolean OR operation.

When you originally entered the pet shop, you told the salesperson, "I want a male cat, neutered, either white or tan; or a female cat, neutered, any color but white; or I'll take any cat you have as long as it's black," and the salesperson developed this expression:

$$(M \times N \times (W + T)) + (F \times N \times (1 - W)) + B$$

Now that you know that two switches wired in series perform a logical AND (which is represented by a × sign) and two switches in parallel perform a logical OR (which is represented by the + sign), you can wire up eight switches like so:

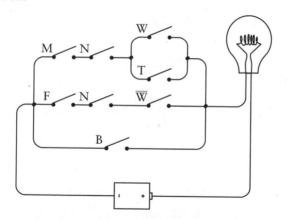

Each switch in this circuit is labeled with a letter—the same letters as in the Boolean expression. ($\overline{W}$ means NOT W and is an alternative way to write $1 - W$). Indeed, if you go through the wiring diagram from left to right starting at the top and moving from top to bottom, you'll encounter the letters in the same order that they appear in the expression. Each × sign in the expression corresponds to a point in the circuit where two switches (or groups of switches) are connected in series. Each + sign in the expression corresponds to a place in the circuit where two switches (or groups of switches) are connected in parallel.

As you'll recall, the salesperson first brought out an unneutered tan male. Close the appropriate switches:

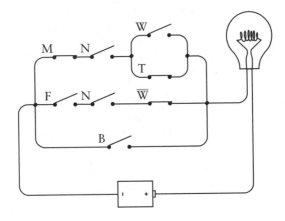

Although the M, T, and NOT W switches are closed, we don't have a complete circuit to light up the lightbulb. Next the salesperson brought out a neutered white female:

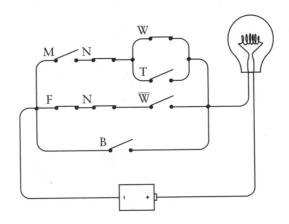

Again, the right switches aren't closed to complete a circuit. But finally, the salesperson brought out a neutered gray female:

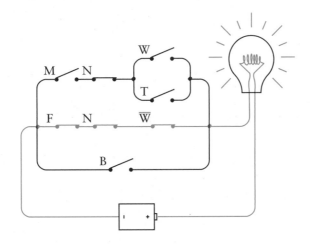

And that's enough to complete the circuit, light up the lightbulb, and indicate that the kitten satisfies all your criteria.

George Boole never wired such a circuit. He never had the thrill of seeing a Boolean expression realized in switches, wires, and lightbulbs. One obstacle, of course, was that the incandescent lightbulb wasn't invented until 15 years after Boole's death. But Samuel Morse had demonstrated his telegraph in 1844—ten years before the publication of Boole's *The Laws of Thought*—and it would be simple to substitute a telegraph sounder for the lightbulb in the circuit shown above.

But nobody in the nineteenth century made the connection between the ANDs and ORs of Boolean algebra and the wiring of simple switches in series and in parallel. No mathematician, no electrician, no telegraph operator, nobody. Not even that icon of the computer revolution Charles Babbage (1792–1871), who had corresponded with Boole and knew his work, and who struggled for much of his life designing first a Difference Engine and then an Analytical Engine that a century later would be regarded as the precursors to modern computers. What might have helped Babbage, we know now, was the realization that perhaps instead of gears and levers to perform calculations, a computer might better be built out of telegraph relays.

Yes, telegraph relays.

Chapter Eleven

Gates (Not Bill)

I n some far-off distant time, when the twentieth century history of primitive computing is just a murky memory, someone is likely to suppose that devices known as *logic gates* were named after the famous cofounder of Microsoft Corporation. Not quite. As we'll soon see, logic gates bear a much greater resemblance to those ordinary gates through which pass water or people. Logic gates perform simple tasks in logic by blocking or letting through the flow of electrical current.

You'll recall how in the last chapter you went into a pet shop and announced, "I want a male cat, neutered, either white or tan; or a female cat, neutered, any color but white; or I'll take any cat you have as long as it's black." This is summarized by the following Boolean expression:

$$(M \times N \times (W + T)) + (F \times N \times (1 - W)) + B$$

and also by this circuit made up of switches and a lightbulb:

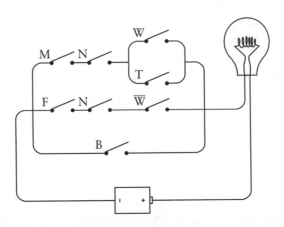

Such a circuit is sometimes called a *network,* except that nowadays that word is used much more often to refer to connected computers rather than an assemblage of mere switches.

Although this circuit contains nothing that wasn't invented in the nineteenth century, nobody in that century ever realized that Boolean expressions could be directly realized in electrical circuits. This equivalence wasn't discovered until the 1930s, most notably by Claude Elwood Shannon (born 1916), whose famous 1938 M.I.T. master's thesis was entitled "A Symbolic Analysis of Relay and Switching Circuits." (Ten years later, Shannon's article "The Mathematical Theory of Communication" was the first publication that used the word *bit* to mean *binary digit.*)

Prior to 1938, people knew that when you wired two switches in series, both switches had to be closed for current to flow, and when you wired two switches in parallel, one or the other had to be closed. But nobody had shown with Shannon's clarity and rigor that electrical engineers could use all the tools of Boolean algebra to design circuits with switches. In particular, if you can simplify a Boolean expression that describes a network, you can simplify the network accordingly.

For example, the expression that indicates the characteristics you want in a cat looks like this:

$$(M \times N \times (W + T)) + (F \times N \times (1 - W)) + B$$

Using the associative law, we can reorder the variables that are combined with the AND ($\times$) signs and rewrite the expression this way:

$$(N \times M \times (W + T)) + (N \times F \times (1 - W)) + B$$

In an attempt to clarify what I'm going to do here, I'll define two new symbols named X and Y:

$$X = M \times (W + T)$$
$$Y = F \times (1 - W)$$

Now the expression for the cat you want can be written like this:

$$(N \times X) + (N \times Y) + B$$

After we're finished, we can put the X and Y expressions back in.

Notice that the N variable appears twice in the expression. Using the distributive law, the expression can be rewritten like this, with only one N:

$$(N \times (X + Y)) + B$$

Now let's put the X and Y expressions back in:

$$(N \times ((M \times (W + T)) + (F \times (1 - W)))) + B$$

Due to the plethora of parentheses, this expression hardly looks simplified. But there's one less variable in this expression, which means there's one less switch in the network. Here's the revised version:

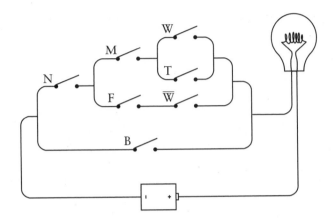

Indeed, it's probably easier to see that this network is equivalent to the earlier one than to verify that the expressions are the same.

Actually, there are still three too many switches in this network. In theory, you need only four switches to define your perfect cat. Why four? Each switch is a bit. You should be able to get by with one switch for the sex (off for male, on for female), another switch that's on for neutered, off for unneutered, and two more switches for the color. There are four possible colors (white, black, tan, and "other"), and we know that four choices can be defined with 2 bits, so all you need are two color switches. For example, both switches can be off for white, one switch on for black, the other switch on for tan, and both switches on for other colors.

Let's make a control panel right now for choosing a cat. The control panel is simply four switches (much like the on/off switches you have on your walls for controlling your lights) and a lightbulb mounted in a panel:

The switches are on (closed) when they're up, and off (open) when they're down. The two switches for the cat's color are labeled somewhat obscurely, I'm afraid, but that's a drawback of reducing this panel to the bare minimum: The left switch of the pair is labeled B; that means that the left switch on by itself (as shown) indicates the color black. The right switch of the pair is labeled T; that switch on by itself means the color tan. Both switches up means other colors; this choice is labeled O. Both switches down means the color white, indicated by W, the letter at the bottom.

In computer terminology, the switches are an *input device*. Input is information that controls how a circuit behaves. In this case, the input switches correspond to 4 bits of information that describe a cat. The *output device* is the lightbulb. This bulb lights up if the switches describe a satisfactory cat. The switches shown in the control panel on page 104 are set for a female unneutered black cat. This satisfies your criteria, so the lightbulb is lit.

Now all we have to do is design a circuit that makes this control panel work.

You'll recall that Claude Shannon's thesis was entitled "A Symbolic Analysis of Relay and Switching Circuits." The relays he was referring to were quite similar to the telegraph relays that we encountered in Chapter 6. By the time of Shannon's paper, however, relays were being used for other purposes and, in particular, in the vast network of the telephone system.

Like switches, relays can be connected in series and in parallel to perform simple tasks in logic. These combinations of relays are called *logic gates*. When I say that these logic gates perform *simple* tasks in logic, I mean as simple as possible. Relays have an advantage over switches in that relays can be switched on and off by other relays rather than by fingers. This means that logic gates can be combined to perform more complex tasks, such as simple functions in arithmetic. Indeed, the next chapter will demonstrate how to wire switches, lightbulbs, a battery, and telegraph relays to make an adding machine (albeit one that works solely with binary numbers).

As you recall, relays were crucial to the workings of the telegraph system. Over long distances, the wires connecting telegraph stations had a very high resistance. Some method was needed to receive a weak signal and send an identical strong signal. The relay did this by using an electromagnet to control a switch. In effect, the relay *amplified* a weak signal to create a strong signal.

For our purposes, we're not interested in using the relay to amplify a weak signal. We're interested only in the idea of a relay being a switch that can be controlled by electricity rather than by fingers. We can wire a relay with a switch, a lightbulb, and a couple of batteries like this:

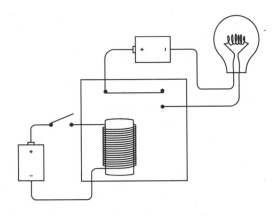

Notice that the switch at the left is open and the lightbulb is off. When you close the switch, the battery at the left causes current to flow through the many turns of wire around the iron bar. The iron bar becomes magnetic and pulls down a flexible metal contact that connects the circuit to turn on the lightbulb:

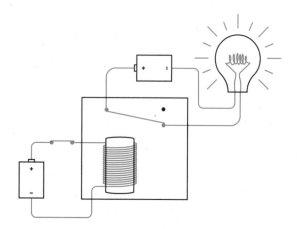

When the electromagnet pulls the metal contact, the relay is said to be *trig-gered*. When the switch is turned off, the iron bar stops being magnetic, and the metal contact returns to its normal position.

This seems like a rather indirect route to light the bulb, and indeed it is. If we were interested only in lighting the bulb, we could dispense with the relay entirely. But we're not interested in lighting bulbs. We have a much more ambitious goal.

We're going to be using relays a lot in this chapter (and then hardly at all after the logic gates have been built), so I want to simplify the diagram. We can eliminate some of the wires by using a ground. In this case, the grounds simply represent a common connection; they don't need to be connected to the physical earth:

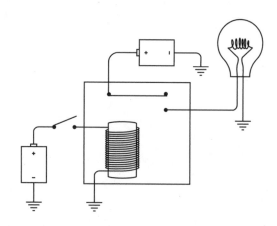

I know this doesn't look like a simplification, but we're not done yet. Notice that the negative terminals of both batteries are connected to ground. So anywhere we see something like this:

let's replace it with the capital letter V (which stands for *voltage*), as we did in Chapters 5 and 6. Now our relay looks like this:

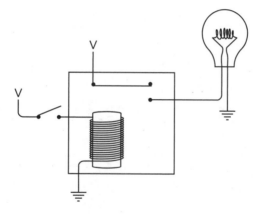

When the switch is closed, a current flows between V and ground through the coils of the electromagnet. This causes the electromagnet to pull the flexible metal contact. That connects the circuit between V, the lightbulb, and ground. The bulb lights up:

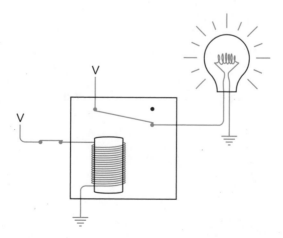

These diagrams of the relay show two voltage sources and two grounds, but in all the diagrams in this chapter, all the V's can be connected to one another and all the grounds can be connected to one another. All the networks of relays and logic gates in this chapter and the next will require only one battery, although it might need to be a big battery. For example, the preceding diagram can be redrawn with only one battery like this:

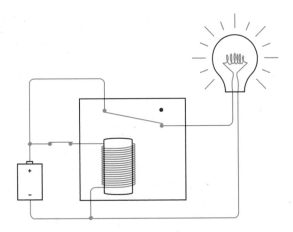

But for what we need to do with relays, this diagram isn't very clear. It's better to avoid the circular circuits and look at the relay—like the control panel earlier—in terms of *inputs* and *outputs:*

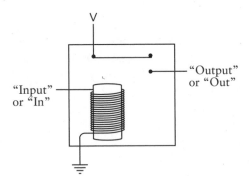

If a current is flowing through the input (for example, if a switch connects the input to V), the electromagnet is triggered and the output has a voltage.

The input of a relay need not be a switch, and the output of a relay need not be a lightbulb. The output of one relay can be connected to the input of another relay, for example, like this:

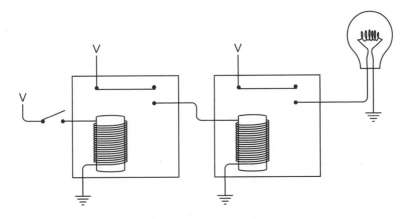

When you turn the switch on, the first relay is triggered, which then provides a voltage to the second relay. The second relay is triggered and the light goes on:

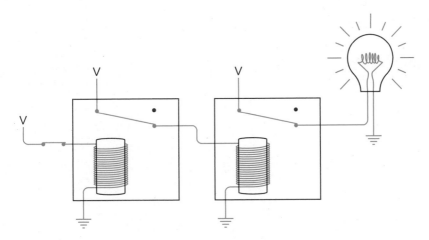

Connecting relays is the key to building logic gates.

Actually, the lightbulb can be connected to the relay in two ways. Notice the flexible metal piece that's pulled by the electromagnet. At rest, it's touching one contact; when the electromagnet pulls it, it hits another contact. We've been using that lower contact as the output of the relay, but we could just as well use the upper contact. When we use this contact, the output of the relay is reversed and the lightbulb is on when the input switch is open:

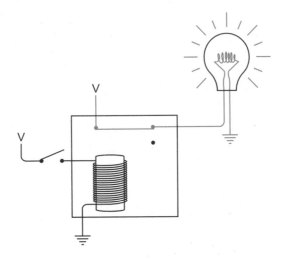

And when the input switch is closed, the bulb goes out:

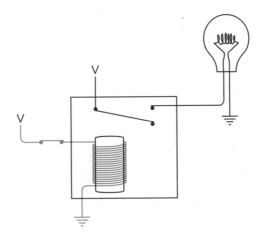

Using the terminology of switches, this type of relay is called a *double-throw* relay. It has two outputs that are electrically opposite—when one has a voltage, the other doesn't.

By the way, if you're having a tough time visualizing what modern relays look like, you can see a few in conveniently transparent packaging at your local Radio Shack. Some, like the heavy-duty relays with Radio Shack part numbers 275-206 and 275-214, are about the size of ice cubes. The insides are encased in a clear plastic shell, so you can see the electromagnet and the metal contacts. The circuits I'll be describing in this chapter and the next could be built using Radio Shack part number 275-240 relays, which are smaller (about the size of a Chiclet) and cheaper ($2.99 apiece).

Just as two switches can be connected in series, two relays can be connected in series:

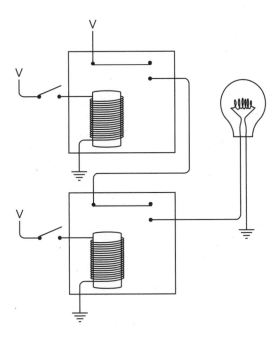

The output of the top relay supplies a voltage to the second relay. As you can see, when both switches are open, the lightbulb isn't lit. We can try closing the top switch:

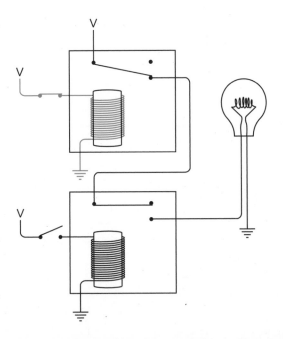

Still the lightbulb doesn't light because the bottom switch is still open and that relay isn't triggered. We can try opening the top switch and closing the bottom switch:

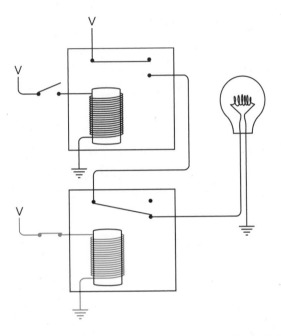

The lightbulb is still not lit. The current can't reach the lightbulb because the first relay isn't triggered. The only way to get the bulb to light up is to close both switches:

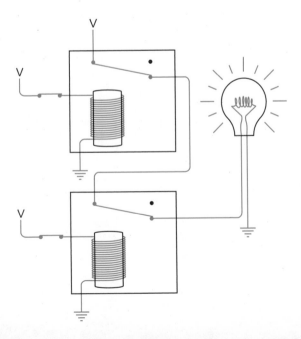

Now both relays are triggered, and current can flow between V, the lightbulb, and ground.

Like the two switches wired in series, these two relays are performing a little exercise in logic. The bulb lights up only if both relays are triggered. These two relays wired in series are known as an *AND gate*. To avoid excessive drawing, electrical engineers have a special symbol for an AND gate. That symbol looks like this:

This is the first of four basic logic gates. The AND gate has two inputs (at the left in this diagram) and one output (at the right). You'll often see the AND gate drawn as this one is with the inputs at the left and the output at the right. That's because people who are accustomed to reading from left to right also like to read electrical diagrams from left to right. But the AND gate can just as well be drawn with the inputs at the top, the right, or the bottom.

The original circuit with the two relays wired in series with two switches and a lightbulb looked like this:

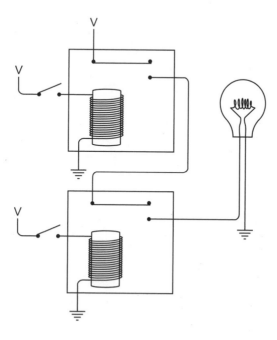

Using the symbol for the AND gate, this same circuit looks like this:

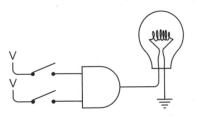

Notice that this symbol for the AND gate not only takes the place of two relays wired in series, but it also implies that the top relay is connected to a voltage, and both relays are connected to ground. Again, the lightbulb lights up only if both the top switch *and* the bottom switch are closed. That's why it's called an *AND gate*.

The inputs of the AND gate don't necessarily have to be connected to switches, and the output doesn't necessarily have to be connected to a lightbulb. What we're really dealing with here are voltages at the inputs and a voltage at the output. For example, the output of one AND gate can be an input to a second AND gate, like this:

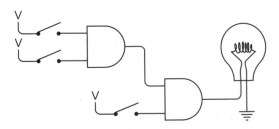

This bulb will light up only if all three switches are closed. Only if the top two switches are closed will the output of the first AND gate trigger the first relay in the second AND gate. The bottom switch triggers the second relay in the second AND gate.

If we think of the absence of a voltage as a 0, and the presence of a voltage as a 1, the output of the AND gate is dependent on inputs like this:

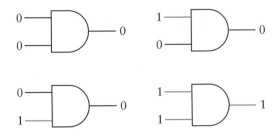

As with the two switches wired in series, the AND gate can also be described in this little table:

AND	0	1
0	0	0
1	0	1

It's also possible to make AND gates with more than two inputs. For example, suppose you connect three relays in series:

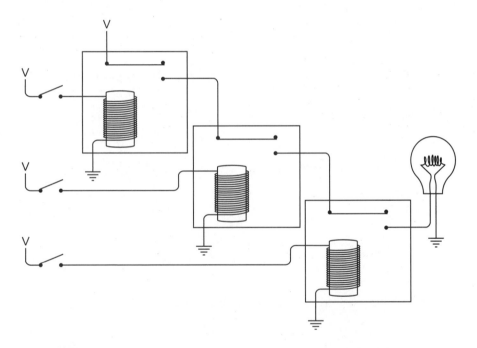

The lightbulb lights up only if all three switches are closed. This configuration is expressed by this symbol:

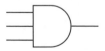

It's called a 3-input AND gate.

The next logic gate involves two relays that are wired in parallel like this:

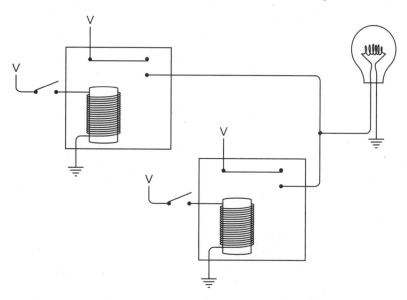

Notice that the outputs of the two relays are connected to each other. This connected output then provides power for the lightbulb. Either one of the two relays is enough to light the bulb. For example, if we close the top switch, the bulb lights up. The bulb is getting power from the left relay.

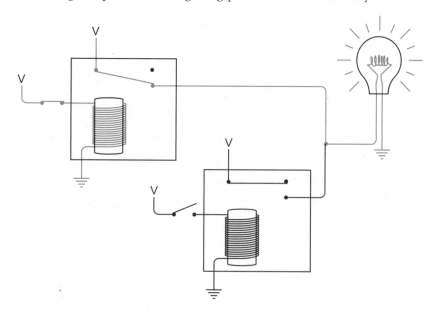

Similarly, if we leave the top switch open but close the bottom switch, the bulb lights up:

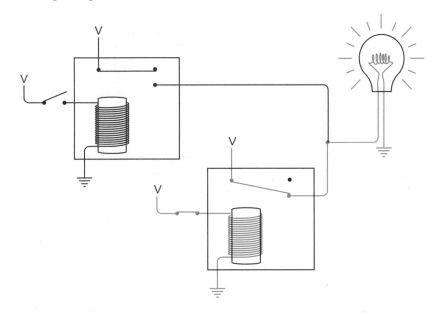

The bulb also lights if both switches are closed:

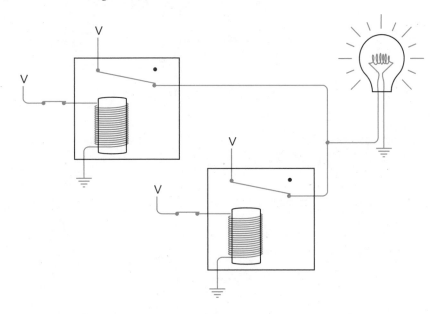

What we have here is a situation in which the bulb lights up if the top switch
or the bottom switch is closed. The key word here is *or,* so this is called the
OR gate. Electrical engineers use a symbol for the OR gate that looks like this:

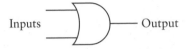

It's somewhat similar to the symbol for the AND gate except that the input
side is rounded, much like the O in OR. (That might help you to keep them
straight.)

   The output of the OR gate supplies a voltage if either of the two inputs
has a voltage. Again, if we say that the absence of a voltage is 0 and the presence of a voltage is 1, the OR gate has four possible states:

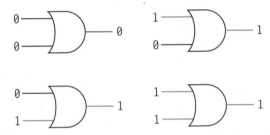

In the same way that we summarized the output of the AND gate, we can
summarize the output of the OR gate:

OR	0	1
0	0	1
1	1	1

OR gates can also have more than two inputs. (The output of such a gate is
1 if any of the inputs are 1; the output is 0 only if all the outputs are 0.)

   Earlier I explained how the relays that we're using are called *double-throw*
relays because an output can be connected two different ways. Normally,
the bulb isn't lit when the switch is open:

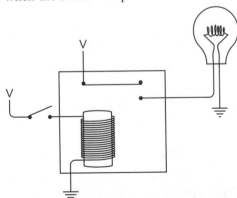

When the switch is closed, the bulb lights up.

Alternatively, you can use the other contact so that the bulb is lit when the switch is *open:*

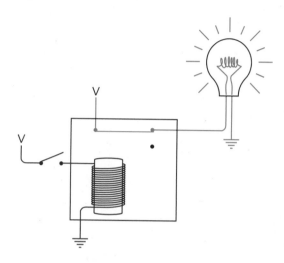

In this case, the lightbulb goes out when you close the switch. A single relay wired in this way is called an *inverter*. An inverter isn't a logic gate (logic gates always have two or more inputs), but it's often very useful nonetheless. It's represented by a special symbol that looks like this:

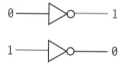

It's called an inverter because it inverts 0 (no voltage) to 1 (voltage) and vice versa:

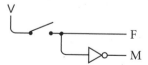

With the inverter, the AND gate, and the OR gate, we can start wiring the control panel to automate a choice of the ideal kitty. Let's begin with the switches. The first switch is closed for female and open for male. Thus we can generate two signals that we'll call F and M, like this:

When F is 1, M will be 0 and vice versa. Similarly, the second switch is closed
for a neutered cat and open for an unneutered cat:

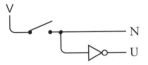

The next two switches are more complicated. In various combinations,
these switches must indicate four different colors. Here are the two switches,
both wired to a voltage:

When both switches are open (as shown), they indicate the color white.
Here's how to use two inverters and one AND gate to generate a signal I'll
call W, which is a voltage (1) if you select a white cat and not a voltage (0)
if not:

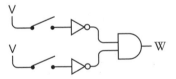

When the switches are open, the inputs to both inverters are 0. The outputs
of the inverters (which are inputs to the AND gate) are thus both 1. That
means the output of the AND gate is 1. If either of the switches is closed,
the output of the AND gate will be a 0.

To indicate a black cat, we close the first switch. This can be realized using
one inverter and an AND gate:

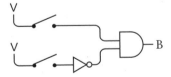

The output of the AND gate will be 1 only if the first switch is closed and
the second switch is open.

Similarly, if the second switch is closed, we want a tan cat:

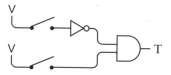

And if both switches are closed, we want a cat of an "other" color:

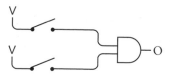

Now let's combine all four little circuits into one big circuit. (As usual, the black dots indicate connections between wires in the circuit; wires that cross without black dots *are not connected*.)

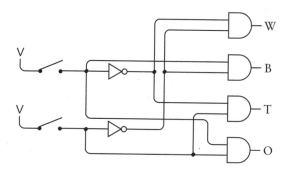

Yes, I know this set of connections now looks very complicated. But if you trace through very carefully—if you look at the two inputs to each AND gate to see where they're coming from and try to ignore where they're also going— you'll see that the circuit works. If both switches are off, the W output will be 1 and the rest will be 0. If the first switch is closed, the B output will be 1 and the rest will be 0, and so forth.

Some simple rules govern how you can connect gates and inverters: The output of one gate (or inverter) can be the input to one or more other gates (or inverters). But the outputs of two or more gates (or inverters) are never connected to one another.

This circuit of four AND gates and two inverters is called a *2-Line-to-4-Line Decoder*. The input is two bits that in various combinations can represent four different values. The output is four signals, only one of which is 1 at any time, depending on the two input values. On similar principles, you can make a 3-Line-to-8-Line Decoder or a 4-Line-to-16-Line Decoder, and so forth.

The simplified version of the cat-selection expression was

$$(N \times ((M \times (W + T)) + (F \times (1 - W)))) + B$$

For every + sign in this expression, there must be an OR gate in the circuit. For every × sign, there must be an AND gate.

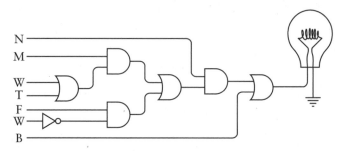

The symbols down the left side of the circuit diagram are in the same order as they appear in the expression. These signals come from the switches wired with inverters and the 2-line-to-4-line decoder. Notice the use of the inverter for the (1 − W) part of the expression.

Now you might say, "That's a heck of a lot of relays," and yes, that's true. There are two relays in every AND gate and OR gate, and one relay for each inverter. I'd say the only realistic response is, "Get used to it." We'll be using a lot more relays in the chapters ahead. Just be thankful you don't actually have to buy them and wire them at home.

We'll look at two more logic gates in this chapter. Both use the output of the relay that normally has a voltage present when the relay is untriggered. (This is the output used in the inverter.) For example, in this configuration the output from one relay supplies power to a second relay. With both inputs off, the lightbulb is on:

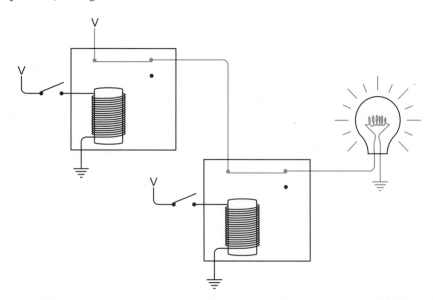

If the top switch is closed, the bulb goes off:

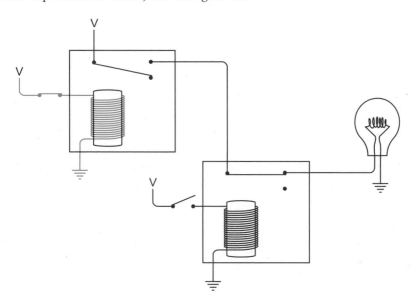

The light goes off because power is no longer being supplied to the second relay. Similarly, if the bottom switch is closed, the light is also off:

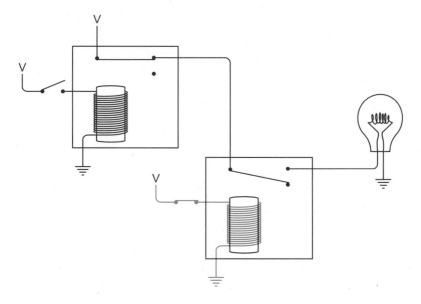

And if both switches are closed, the lightbulb is off:

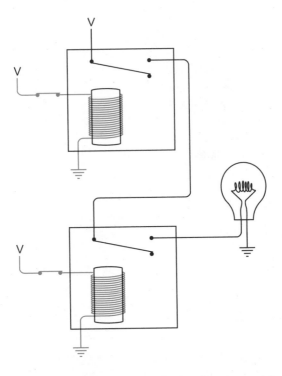

This behavior is precisely the opposite of what happens with the OR gate. It's called *NOT OR* or, more concisely, *NOR*. This is the symbol for the NOR gate:

It's the same as the symbol for the OR except with a little circle at the output. The circle means *invert*. The NOR is the same as

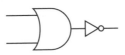

The output of the NOR gate is shown in the following table:

NOR	0	1
0	1	0
1	0	0

This table shows results opposite those of the OR gate, which are 1 if either of the two inputs is 1 and 0 only if both inputs are 0.

And yet another way to wire two relays is shown here:

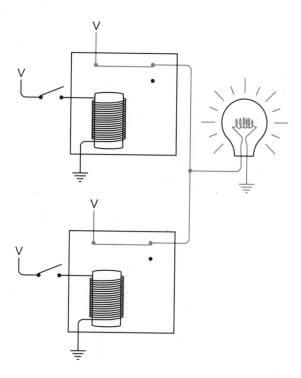

In this case, the two outputs are connected, which is similar to the OR configuration but using the other contacts. The lightbulb is on when both switches are open.

The lightbulb remains on when the top switch is closed:

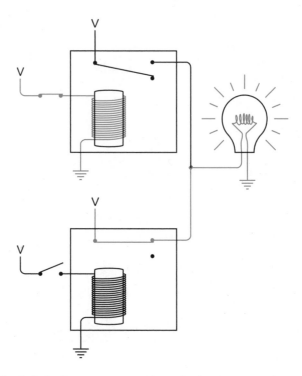

Similarly, the lightbulb remains on when the bottom switch is closed:

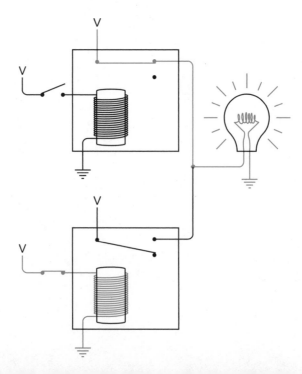

Only when both switches are closed does the lightbulb go off:

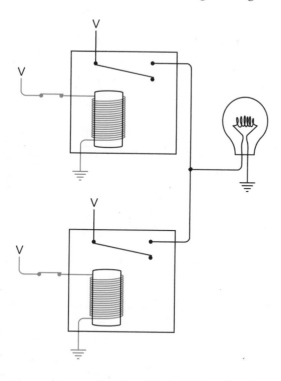

This behavior is exactly opposite that of the AND gate. This is called *NOT AND* or, more concisely, *NAND*. The NAND gate is drawn just like the AND gate but with a circle at the output, meaning the output is the inverse of the AND gate:

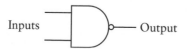

The NAND gate has the following behavior:

NAND	0	1
0	1	1
1	1	0

Notice that the output of the NAND gate is opposite the AND gate. The output of the AND gate is 1 only if both inputs are 1; otherwise, the output is 0.

At this point, we've looked at four different ways of wiring relays that have two inputs and one output. Each configuration behaves in a slightly different way. To avoid drawing and redrawing the relays, we've called them logic gates and decided to use the same symbols to represent them that are used by electrical engineers. The output of the particular logic gate depends on the input, which is summarized here:

AND	0	1
0	0	0
1	0	1

OR	0	1
0	0	1
1	1	1

NAND	0	1
0	1	1
1	1	0

NOR	0	1
0	1	0
1	0	0

So now we have four logic gates and the inverter. Completing this array of tools is just a regular old relay:

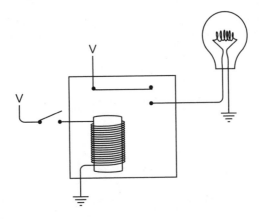

This is called a *buffer,* and this is the symbol for it:

It's the same symbol as the inverter but without the little circle. The buffer is remarkable for not doing much. The output of the buffer is the same as the input:

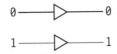

But you can use a buffer when an input signal is weak. You'll recall that this was the reason relays were used with the telegraph many years ago. Or a buffer can be used to slightly delay a signal. This works because the relay requires a little time—some fraction of a second—to be triggered.

From here on in the book, you'll see very few drawings of relays. Instead, the circuits that follow will be built from buffers, inverters, the four basic logic gates, and more sophisticated circuits (like the 2-Line-to-4-Line Decoder) built from these logic gates. All these other components are made from relays, of course, but we don't actually have to look at the relays.

Earlier, when building the 2-Line-to-4-Line Decoder, we saw a little circuit that looked like this:

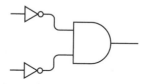

Two inputs are inverted and become inputs to an AND gate. Sometimes a configuration like this is drawn without the inverters:

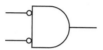

Notice the little circles at the input to the AND gate. Those little circles mean that the signals are inverted at that point—a 0 (no voltage) becomes a 1 (voltage) and vice versa.

An AND gate with two inverted inputs does exactly the same thing as a NOR gate:

The output is 1 only if both inputs are 0.

Similarly, an OR gate with the two inputs inverted is equivalent to a NAND gate:

The output is 0 only if both inputs are 1.

These two pairs of equivalent circuits represent an electrical implementation of *De Morgan's Laws*. Augustus De Morgan was another Victorian-era mathematician, nine years older than Boole, whose book *Formal Logic* was published in 1847, the very same day (the story goes) as Boole's *The Mathematical Analysis of Logic*. Indeed, Boole had been inspired to investigate logic by a very public feud that was being waged between De Morgan and another British mathematician involving accusations of plagiarism. (De Morgan has been exonerated by history.) Very early on, De Morgan recognized the importance of Boole's insights. He unselfishly encouraged Boole and helped him along the way, and is today sadly almost forgotten except for his famous laws.

De Morgan's Laws are most simply expressed this way:

$$\overline{A} \times \overline{B} = \overline{A + B}$$
$$\overline{A} + \overline{B} = \overline{A \times B}$$

A and B are two Boolean operands. In the first expression, they're inverted and then combined with the Boolean AND operator. This is the same as combining the two operands with the Boolean OR operator and then inverting the result (which is the NOR). In the second expression, the two operands are inverted and then combined with the Boolean OR operator. This is the same as combining the operands with the Boolean AND operator and then inverting (which is the NAND).

De Morgan's Laws are an important tool for simplifying Boolean expressions and hence, for simplifying circuits. Historically, this was what Claude Shannon's paper really meant for electrical engineers. But obsessively simplifying circuits won't be a major concern in this book. It's preferable to get things working rather than to get things working as simply as possible. And what we're going to get working next is nothing less than an adding machine.

Chapter Twelve

A Binary
Adding Machine

A ddition is the most basic of arithmetic operations, so if we want to build a computer (and that is my hidden agenda in this book), we must first know how to build something that adds two numbers together. When you come right down to it, addition is just about the *only* thing that computers do. If we can build something that adds, we're well on our way to building something that uses addition to also subtract, multiply, divide, calculate mortgage payments, guide rockets to Mars, play chess, and foul up our phone bills.

The adding machine that we'll build in this chapter will be big, clunky, slow, and noisy, at least compared to the calculators and computers of modern life. What's most interesting is that we're going to build this adding machine entirely out of simple electrical devices that we've learned about in previous chapters—switches, lightbulbs, wires, a battery, and relays that have been prewired into various logic gates. This adding machine will contain nothing that wasn't invented at least 120 years ago. And what's really nice is that we don't have to actually build anything in our living rooms; instead, we can build this adding machine on paper and in our minds.

This adding machine will work entirely with binary numbers and will lack some modern amenities. You won't be able to use a keyboard to indicate the numbers you want to add; instead you'll use a row of switches. Rather than a numeric display to show the results, this adding machine will have a row of lightbulbs.

But this machine will definitely add two numbers together, and it will do so in a way that's very much like the way that computers add numbers.

Adding binary numbers is a lot like adding decimal numbers. When you want to add two decimal numbers such as 245 and 673, you break the problem into simpler steps. Each step requires only that you add a pair of decimal digits. In this example, you begin with 5 plus 3. The problem goes a lot faster if you memorized an addition table sometime during your life.

The big difference between adding decimal and binary numbers is that you use a much simpler table for binary numbers:

+	0	1
0	0	1
1	1	10

If you actually grew up with a community of whales and memorized this table in school, you might have chanted aloud:

0 plus 0 equals 0.
0 plus 1 equals 1.
1 plus 0 equals 1.
1 plus 1 equals 0, carry the 1.

You can rewrite the addition table with leading zeros so that each result is a 2-bit value:

+	0	1
0	00	01
1	01	10

Viewed like this, the result of adding a pair of binary numbers is 2 bits, which are called the *sum* bit and the *carry* bit (as in "1 plus 1 equals 0, *carry* the 1"). Now we can divide the binary addition table into two tables, the first one for the sum bit:

+ sum	0	1
0	0	1
1	1	0

and the second one for the carry bit:

+ carry	0	1
0	0	0
1	0	1

It's convenient to look at binary addition in this way because our adding machine will do sums and carries separately. Building a binary adding machine requires that we design a circuit that performs these operations. Working solely in binary simplifies the problem immensely because all the parts of a circuit—switches, lightbulbs, and wires—can be binary digits.

As in decimal addition, we add two binary numbers column by column beginning with the rightmost column:

$$\begin{array}{r} 01100101 \\ + \ 10110110 \\ \hline 100011011 \end{array}$$

Notice that when we add the third column from the right, a 1 is carried over to the next column. This happens again in the sixth, seventh, and eighth columns from the right.

What size binary numbers do we want to add? Since we're building our adding machine only in our minds, we could build one to add very long numbers. But let's be reasonable and decide to add binary numbers up to 8 bits long. That is, we want to add binary numbers that can range from 0000-0000 through 1111-1111, or decimal 0 through 255. The sum of two 8-bit numbers can be as high as 1-1111-1110, or 510.

The control panel for our binary adding machine can look like this:

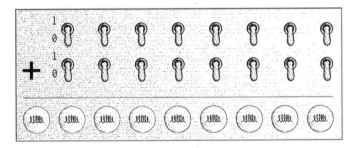

We have on this panel two rows of eight switches. This collection of switches is the input device, and we'll use it to "key in" the two 8-bit numbers. In this input device, a switch is off (down) for 0 and on (up) for 1, just like the wall switches in your home. The output device at the bottom of the panel is a row of nine lightbulbs. These bulbs will indicate the answer. An unlit bulb is a 0 and a lit bulb is a 1. We need nine bulbs because the sum of the two 8-bit numbers can be a 9-bit number.

The rest of the adding machine will consist of logic gates wired together in various ways. The switches will trigger the relays in the logic gates, which will then turn on the correct lights. For example, if we want to add 0110-0101 and 1011-0110 (the two numbers shown in the preceding example), we throw the appropriate switches as shown on the following page.

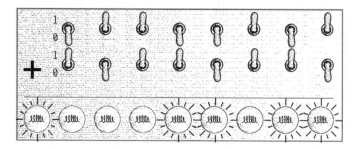

The bulbs light up to indicate the answer of 1-0001-1011. (Well, let's hope so, anyway. We haven't built it yet!)

I mentioned in the last chapter that I'll be using lots of relays in this book. The 8-bit adding machine we're building in this chapter requires no fewer than 144 relays—18 for each of the 8 pairs of bits we're adding together. If I showed you the completed circuit in its entirety, you'd definitely freak. There's no way that anyone could make sense of 144 relays wired together in strange ways. Instead, we're going to approach this problem in stages using logic gates.

Maybe you saw right away a connection between logic gates and binary addition when you looked at the table of the carry bit that results from adding two 1-bit numbers together:

+ carry	0	1
0	0	0
1	0	1

You might have realized that this was identical to the output of the AND gate shown in the last chapter:

AND	0	1
0	0	0
1	0	1

So the AND gate calculates a carry bit for the addition of two binary digits.

Aha! We're definitely making progress. Our next step seems to be to persuade some relays to behave like this:

+ sum	0	1
0	0	1
1	1	0

This is the other half of the problem in adding a pair of binary digits. The sum bit turns out to be not quite as straightforward as the carry bit, but we'll get there.

The first thing to realize is that the OR gate is close to what we want except for the case in the lower right corner:

OR	0	1
0	0	1
1	1	1

The NAND gate is also close to what we want except for the case in the upper left corner:

NAND	0	1
0	1	1
1	1	0

So let's connect both an OR gate and a NAND gate to the same inputs:

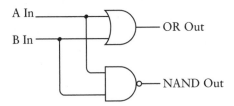

The following table summarizes the outputs of these OR and NAND gates and compares that to what we want for the adding machine:

A In	B In	OR Out	NAND Out	What we want
0	0	0	1	0
0	1	1	1	1
1	0	1	1	1
1	1	1	0	0

Notice that what we want is 1 only if the output from the OR gate *and* the NAND gate are both 1. This suggests that these two outputs can be an input to an AND gate:

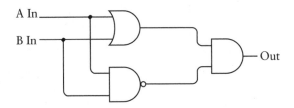

And that's it.

Notice that there are still only two inputs and one output to this entire circuit. The two inputs go into both the OR gate and the NAND gate. The outputs from the OR and NAND gates go into the AND gate, and that gives us exactly what we want:

A In	B In	OR Out	NAND Out	AND Out
0	0	0	1	0
0	1	1	1	1
1	0	1	1	1
1	1	1	0	0

There's actually a name for what this circuit does. It's called the *Exclusive OR gate* or, more briefly, the XOR gate. It's called the Exclusive OR gate because the output is 1 if the A input is 1 *or* the B input is 1, but not both. So, instead of drawing an OR gate, NAND gate, and AND gate, we can use the symbol that electrical engineers use for the XOR gate:

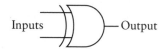

Inputs   Output

It looks very much like the OR gate except that it has another curved line at the input side. The behavior of the XOR gate is shown here:

XOR	0	1
0	0	1
1	1	0

The XOR gate is the final logic gate I describe in detail in this book. (A sixth gate sometimes shows up in electrical engineering. It's called the *coincidence* or *equivalence gate* because the output is 1 only if the two inputs are the same. The coincidence gate describes an output opposite that of the XOR gate, so this gate's symbol is the same as the XOR gate but with a little circle at the output end.)

Let's review what we know so far. Adding two binary numbers produces a sum bit and a carry bit:

+ sum	0	1
0	0	1
1	1	0

+ carry	0	1
0	0	0
1	0	1

You can use the following two logic gates to get these results:

XOR	0	1
0	0	1
1	1	0

AND	0	1
0	0	0
1	0	1

The sum of two binary numbers is given by the output of an XOR gate, and the carry bit is given by the output of an AND gate. So we can combine an AND gate and an XOR gate to add two binary digits called A and B:

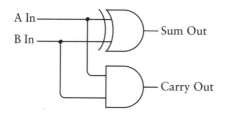

And instead of drawing and redrawing an AND gate and an XOR gate, you can simply draw a box like this:

A In —— A   Half Adder   S —— Sum Out
B In —— B   CO —— Carry Out

This box is labeled *Half Adder* for a reason. Certainly it adds two binary digits and gives you a sum bit and a carry bit. But the vast majority of binary numbers are longer than 1 bit. What the Half Adder fails to do is add a possible carry bit from a previous addition. For example, suppose we're adding two binary numbers like these:

$$
\begin{array}{r}
1111 \\
+\ 1111 \\
\hline
11110
\end{array}
$$

We can use the Half Adder only for the addition of the rightmost column: 1 plus 1 equals 0, carry the 1. For the second column from the right, we really need to add *three* binary numbers because of the carry. And that goes for all subsequent columns. Each subsequent addition of two binary numbers can include a carry bit from the previous column.

To add three binary numbers, we need two Half Adders and an OR gate, wired this way:

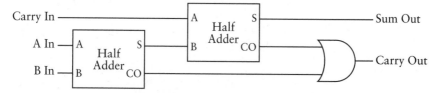

To understand this, begin with the A and B inputs to the first Half Adder at the left. The output is a sum and a carry. That sum must be added to the carry from the previous column, so they're inputs to the second Half Adder. The sum from the second Half Adder is the final sum. The two Carry Outs from the Half Adders are inputs to an OR gate. You might think another Half Adder is called for here, and that would certainly work. But if you go through all the possibilities, you'll find that the Carry Outs from the two Half Adders are never *both* equal to 1. The OR gate is sufficient for adding them because the OR gate is the same as the XOR gate if the inputs are never both 1.

Instead of drawing and redrawing that diagram, we can just call it a *Full Adder*:

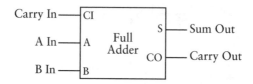

The following table summarizes all the possible combinations of inputs to the Full Adder and the resultant outputs:

A In	B In	Carry In	Sum Out	Carry Out
0	0	0	0	0
0	1	0	1	0
1	0	0	1	0
1	1	0	0	1
0	0	1	1	0
0	1	1	0	1
1	0	1	0	1
1	1	1	1	1

I said early on in this chapter that we would need 144 relays for our adding machine. Here's how I figured that out: Each AND, OR, and NAND gate requires 2 relays. So an XOR gate comprises 6 relays. A Half Adder is an XOR gate and an AND gate, so a Half Adder requires 8 relays. Each Full Adder is two Half Adders and an OR gate, or 18 relays. We need 8 Full Adders for our 8-bit adding machine. That's 144 relays.

Recall our original control panel with the switches and lightbulbs:

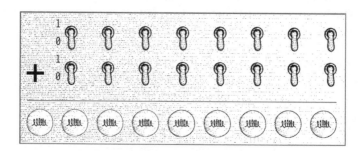

We can now start wiring the switches and lightbulbs to the Full Adder.

First connect the two rightmost switches and the rightmost lightbulb to a Full Adder:

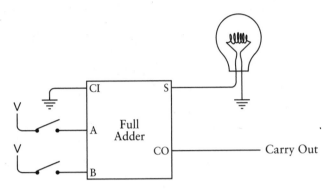

When you begin adding two binary numbers, the first column of digits that you add is different. It's different because every subsequent column might include a carry bit from the previous column. The first column doesn't include a carry bit, which is why the carry input to the Full Adder is connected to ground. That means a 0 bit. The addition of the first pair of binary digits could, of course, *result* in a carry bit. That carry output is an input to the next column.

For the next two digits and the next lightbulb, you use a Full Adder wired this way:

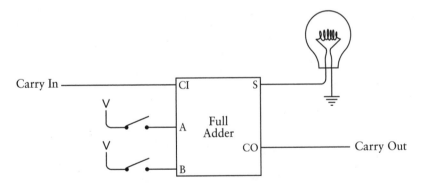

The carry output from the first Full Adder is an input to this second Full Adder. Each subsequent column of digits is wired the same way. Each carry output from one column is a carry input to the next column.

Finally the eighth and last pair of switches are wired to the last Full Adder:

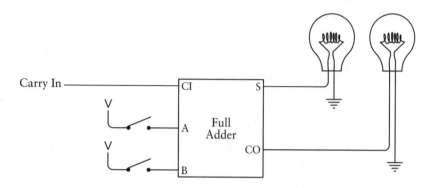

Here the final carry output goes to the ninth lightbulb.

We're done.

Here's another way to look at this assemblage of eight Full Adders, with each Carry Out serving as input to the next Carry In:

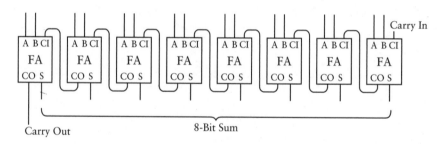

Here's the complete 8-Bit Adder drawn as one box. The inputs are labeled A_0 through A_7 and B_0 through B_7. The outputs are labeled S_0 through S_7 (for sum):

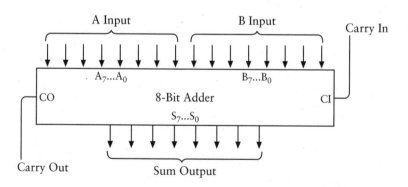

This is a common way to label the separate bits of a multibit number. The bits A_0, B_0, and S_0 are the *least-significant,* or rightmost, bits. The bits A_7, B_7, and S_7 are the *most-significant,* or leftmost, bits. For example, here's how these subscripted letters would apply to the binary number 0110-1001:

$$A_7 \quad A_6 \quad A_5 \quad A_4 \quad A_3 \quad A_2 \quad A_1 \quad A_0$$
$$0 \quad 1 \quad 1 \quad 0 \quad 1 \quad 0 \quad 0 \quad 1$$

The subscripts start at 0 and get higher for more significant digits because they correspond to the exponents of powers of two:

$$2^7 \quad 2^6 \quad 2^5 \quad 2^4 \quad 2^3 \quad 2^2 \quad 2^1 \quad 2^0$$
$$0 \quad 1 \quad 1 \quad 0 \quad 1 \quad 0 \quad 0 \quad 1$$

If you multiply each power of two by the digit below it and add, you'll get the decimal equivalent of 0110-1001, which is 64 + 32 + 8 + 1, or 105.

Another way an 8-Bit Adder might be drawn is like this:

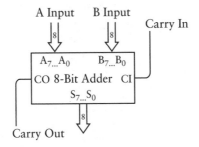

The double-line arrows have an 8 inside to indicate that each represents a group of eight separate signals. They are labeled $A_7...A_0$, $B_7...B_0$, and $S_7...S_0$ also to indicate 8-bit numbers.

Once you build one 8-Bit Adder, you can build another. It then becomes easy to *cascade* them to add two 16-bit numbers:

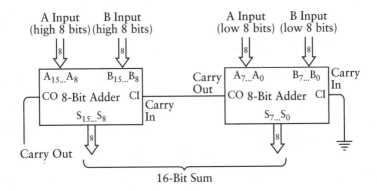

The Carry Out of the adder on the right is connected to the Carry In of the adder on the left. The adder on the left has as input the most-significant eight digits of the two numbers to be added and creates as output the most-significant eight digits of the result.

And now you might ask, "Is this *really* the way that computers add numbers together?"

Basically, yes. But not exactly.

First, adders can be made faster than this one. If you look at how this circuit works, a carry output from the least-significant pair of numbers is required for the next pair to be added, and a carry output from the second pair is required for the third pair to be added, and so forth. The total speed of the adder is equal to the number of bits times the speed of the Full Adder component. This is called a *ripple carry*. Faster adders use additional circuitry called a *look-ahead carry* that speeds up this process.

Second (and most important), computers don't use relays any more! They did at one time, however. The first digital computers built beginning in the 1930s used relays and later vacuum tubes. Today's computers use transistors. When used in computers, transistors basically function the same way relays do, but (as we'll see) they're much faster and much smaller and much quieter and use much less power and are much cheaper. Building an 8-Bit Adder still requires 144 transistors (more if you replace the ripple carry with a look-ahead carry), but the circuit is microscopic.

Chapter Thirteen

But What About Subtraction?

After you've convinced yourself that relays can indeed be wired to-gether to add binary numbers, you might ask, "But what about subtraction?" Rest assured that you're not making a nuisance of yourself by asking questions like this; you're actually being quite perceptive. Addition and subtraction complement each other in some ways, but the mechanics of the two operations are different. An addition marches consis-tently from the rightmost column of digits to the leftmost column. Each carry from one column is added to the next column. We don't *carry* in subtrac-tion, however; we *borrow*, and that involves an intrinsically different mecha-nism—a messy back-and-forth kind of thing.

For example, let's look at a typical borrow-laden subtraction problem:

$$
\begin{array}{r}
253 \\
-\ 176 \\
\hline
??? \\
\end{array}
$$

To do this, we start with the rightmost column. First we see that 6 is bigger than 3, so we have to borrow 1 from the 5, and then subtract 6 from 13, which is 7. Then we have to remember that we borrowed 1 from the 5, so it's really a 4, and this 4 is smaller than 7, so we borrow 1 from the 2 and subtract 7 from 14, which is 7. Then we have to remember that we borrowed 1 from the 2, so it's really a 1, and then we subtract 1 from it to get 0. Our answer is 77:

$$
\begin{array}{r}
253 \\
-\ 176 \\
\hline
77 \\
\end{array}
$$

Now how are we ever going to persuade a bunch of logic gates to go through such perverse logic?

Well, we're not going to try. Instead, we're going to use a little trick that lets us subtract *without* borrowing. This will please Polonius ("Neither a borrower nor a lender be") and the rest of us as well. Moreover, examining subtraction in detail is useful because it directly relates to the way in which binary codes are used for storing negative numbers in computers.

For this explanation, I need to refer to the two numbers being subtracted. Their proper names are the *minuend* and the *subtrahend*. The subtrahend is subtracted from the minuend, and the result is the *difference*:

$$
\begin{array}{r}
\text{Minuend} \\
- \text{Subtrahend} \\
\hline
\text{Difference}
\end{array}
$$

To subtract without borrowing, you first subtract the subtrahend *not* from the minuend but from 999:

$$
\begin{array}{r}
999 \\
- 176 \\
\hline
823
\end{array}
$$

You use 999 here because the numbers have 3 digits. If the numbers had 4 digits, you would use 9999. Subtracting a number from a string of 9s results in a number called the *nines' complement*. The nines' complement of 176 is 823. And it works in reverse: The nines' complement of 823 is 176. What's nice is this: No matter what the subtrahend is, calculating the nines' complement *never requires a borrow*.

After you've calculated the nines' complement of the subtrahend, you add it to the original minuend:

$$
\begin{array}{r}
253 \\
+ 823 \\
\hline
1076
\end{array}
$$

And finally you add 1 and subtract 1000:

$$
\begin{array}{r}
1076 \\
+ 1 \\
- 1000 \\
\hline
77
\end{array}
$$

You're finished. The result is the same as before, and never once did you borrow.

Why does this work? The original subtraction problem is

$$253 - 176$$

If any number is both added to and subtracted from this expression, the result will be the same. So let's add 1000 and subtract 1000:

$$253 - 176 + 1000 - 1000$$

This expression is equivalent to

$$253 - 176 + 999 + 1 - 1000$$

Now the various numbers can be regrouped, this way:

$$253 + (999 - 176) + 1 - 1000$$

And this is identical to the calculation I demonstrated using the nines' complement. We replaced the one subtraction with two subtractions and two additions, but in the process we got rid of all the nasty borrows.

What if the subtrahend is larger than the minuend? For example, the subtraction problem could be

$$\begin{array}{r} 176 \\ - 253 \\ \hline ??? \end{array}$$

Normally, you would look at this and say, "Hmmm. I see that the subtrahend is larger than the minuend, so I have to switch the two numbers around, perform the subtraction, and remember that the result is really a negative number." You might be able to switch them around in your head and write the answer this way:

$$\begin{array}{r} 176 \\ - 253 \\ \hline 77 \end{array}$$

Doing this calculation without borrowing is a little different from the earlier example. You begin as you did before by subtracting the subtrahend (253) from 999 to get the nines' complement:

$$\begin{array}{r} 999 \\ - 253 \\ \hline 746 \end{array}$$

Now add the nines' complement to the original minuend:

$$\begin{array}{r} 176 \\ + 746 \\ \hline 922 \end{array}$$

At this point in the earlier problem, you were able to add 1 and subtract 1000 to get the final result. But in this case, that strategy isn't going to work well. You would need to subtract 1000 from 923, and that really means subtracting 923 from 1000, and that requires borrowing.

Instead, since we effectively added 999 earlier, let's subtract 999 now:

$$
\begin{array}{r}
922 \\
- \ 999 \\
\hline
??? \\
\end{array}
$$

When we see this, we realize that our answer will be a negative number and that we really need to switch around the two numbers by subtracting 922 from 999. This again involves no borrowing, and the answer is as we expect:

$$
\begin{array}{r}
922 \\
- \ 999 \\
\hline
- \ 77 \\
\end{array}
$$

This same technique can also be used with binary numbers and is actually simpler than with decimal numbers. Let's see how it works.

The original subtraction problem was

$$
\begin{array}{r}
253 \\
- \ 176 \\
\hline
??? \\
\end{array}
$$

When these numbers are converted to binary, the problem becomes

$$
\begin{array}{r}
11111101 \\
- \ 10110000 \\
\hline
???????? \\
\end{array}
$$

Step 1. Subtract the subtrahend from 11111111 (which equals 255):

$$
\begin{array}{r}
11111101 \\
- \ 10110000 \\
\hline
01001111 \\
\end{array}
$$

When we were working with decimal numbers, the subtrahend was subtracted from a string of nines, and the result was called the nines' complement. With binary numbers, the subtrahend is subtracted from a string of ones and the result is called the *ones' complement*. But notice that we don't really have to do a subtraction to calculate the ones' complement. That's because every 0 bit in the original number becomes a 1 bit in the ones' complement, and every 1 bit becomes a 0 bit. For this reason, the ones' complement is also sometimes called the *negation,* or the *inverse.* (At this point, you might recall from Chapter 11 that we built something called an inverter that changed a 0 to a 1 and a 1 to a 0.)

Step 2. Add the ones' complement of the subtrahend to the minuend:

$$
\begin{array}{r}
11111101 \\
+ \ 01001111 \\
\hline
101001100 \\
\end{array}
$$

Step 3. Add 1 to the result:

$$
\begin{array}{r}
101001100 \\
+\qquad 1 \\
\hline
101001101
\end{array}
$$

Step 4. Subtract 100000000 (which equals 256):

$$
\begin{array}{r}
101001101 \\
-\ 100000000 \\
\hline
1001101
\end{array}
$$

The result is equivalent to 77 in decimal.

Let's try it again with the two numbers reversed. In decimal, the subtraction problem is

$$
\begin{array}{r}
176 \\
-\ 253 \\
\hline
???
\end{array}
$$

and in binary it looks like this:

$$
\begin{array}{r}
10110000 \\
-\ 11111101 \\
\hline
?????????
\end{array}
$$

Step 1. Subtract the subtrahend from 11111111. You get the ones' complement:

$$
\begin{array}{r}
11111111 \\
-\ 11111101 \\
\hline
00000010
\end{array}
$$

Step 2. Add the ones' complement of the subtrahend to the minuend:

$$
\begin{array}{r}
10110000 \\
+\ 00000010 \\
\hline
10110010
\end{array}
$$

Now 11111111 must be subtracted from the result in some way. When the original subtrahend is smaller than the minuend, you accomplish this task by adding 1 and subtracting 100000000. But you can't subtract this way without borrowing. So instead, we subtract this result from 11111111:

$$
\begin{array}{r}
11111111 \\
-\ 10110010 \\
\hline
01001101
\end{array}
$$

Again, this strategy really means that we're just inverting all the bits to get the result. The answer again is 77, but really –77.

At this point, we have all the knowledge we need to modify the adding machine developed in the last chapter so that it can perform subtraction as well as addition. So that this doesn't become *too* complex, this new adding and subtracting machine will perform subtractions only when the subtrahend is less than the minuend, that is, when the result is a positive number.

The core of the adding machine was an 8-Bit Adder assembled from logic gates:

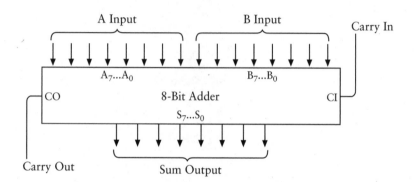

As you probably recall, the inputs A0 through A7 and B0 through B7 were connected to switches that indicated two 8-bit values to be added. The Carry In input was connected to ground. The S0 through S7 outputs were connected to eight lightbulbs that displayed the result of the addition. Because the addition could result in a 9-bit value, the Carry Out output was also connected to a ninth lightbulb.

The control panel looked like this:

In this diagram, the switches are set to add 183 (or 10110111) and 22 (00010110), producing the result of 205, or 11001101 as shown in the row of lightbulbs.

The new control panel for adding and subtracting two 8-bit numbers is just slightly modified. It includes an extra switch to indicate whether we want to add or subtract.

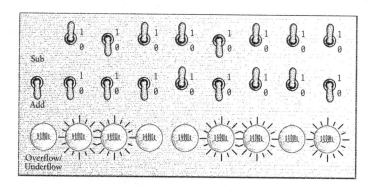

You turn this switch off for addition and on for subtraction, as labeled. Also, only the rightmost eight lightbulbs are used to display results. The ninth lightbulb is now labeled "Overflow/Underflow." This lightbulb indicates that a number is being calculated that can't be represented by the eight lightbulbs. This will happen if an addition produces a number greater than 255 (that's called an overflow) or if a subtraction produces a negative number (an underflow). A subtraction will produce a negative number if the subtrahend is larger than the minuend.

The major addition to the adding machine is some circuitry that calculates a ones' complement of an 8-bit number. Recall that the ones' complement is equivalent to inverting bits, so something to calculate the ones' complement of an 8-bit number might look as simple as eight inverters:

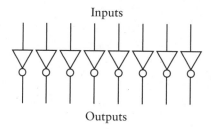

The problem with this circuit is that it *always* inverts the bits that enter into it. We're trying to create a machine that does both addition and subtraction, so the circuitry needs to invert the bits only if a subtraction is being performed. A better circuit looks like this:

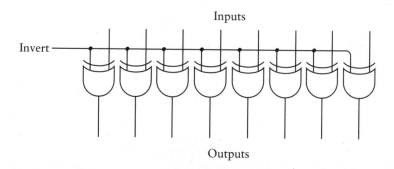

A single signal labeled *Invert* is input to each of eight XOR (exclusive OR) gates. Recall that the XOR exhibits the following behavior:

XOR	0	1
0	0	1
1	1	0

So if the Invert signal is 0, the eight outputs of the XOR gates are the same as the eight inputs. For example, if 01100001 is input, then 01100001 is output. If the Invert signal is 1, the eight input signals are inverted. If 01100001 is input, 10011110 is output.

Let's package these eight XOR gates in a box labeled *Ones' Complement*:

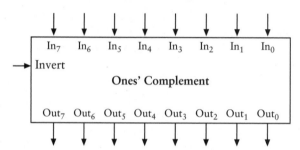

The Ones' Complement box, the 8-Bit Adder box, and a final exclusive OR gate can now be wired together like this:

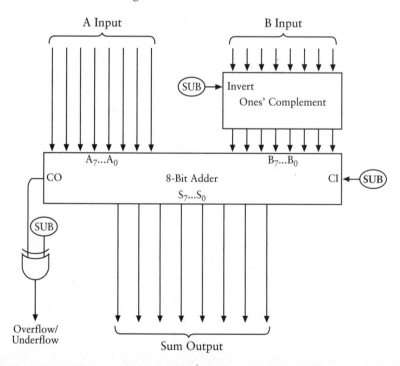

Notice the three signals all labeled *SUB*. This is the Add/Subtract switch. This signal is 0 if an addition is to be performed and 1 if a subtraction is to be performed. For a subtraction, the B inputs (the second row of switches) are all inverted by the Ones' Complement circuit before entering the adder. Also for a subtraction, you add 1 to the result of the addition by setting the CI (Carry In) input of the adder to 1. For an addition, the Ones' Complement circuit has no effect and the CI input is 0.

The SUB signal and the CO (Carry Out) output of the adder also go into an XOR gate that's used to light up the Overflow/Underflow lamp. If the SUB signal is 0 (which means an addition is being performed), the lightbulb will be lit if the CO output of the adder is 1. This means that the result of the addition is greater than 255.

If a subtraction is being performed and if the subtrahend (the B switches) is less than the minuend (the A switches), it's normal that the CO output from the adder is 1. This represents the 100000000 that must be subtracted in the final step. So the Overflow/Underflow lamp is lit only if the CO output from the adder is 0. This means that the subtrahend is greater than the minuend and the result is negative. The machine shown above isn't designed to display negative numbers.

You must surely be glad you asked, "But what about subtraction?"

I've been talking about negative numbers in this chapter, but I haven't yet indicated what negative binary numbers look like. You might assume that the traditional negative sign is used with binary just as it is in decimal. For example, −77 is written in binary as −1001101. You can certainly do that, but one of the goals in using binary numbers is to represent *everything* using 0s and 1s—even tiny symbols such as the negative sign.

Of course, you could simply use another bit for the negative sign. You could make that extra bit 1 for a negative number and 0 for a positive number, which would work, although it doesn't go quite far enough. There's another solution for representing negative numbers that also provides a hassle-free method for adding negative and positive numbers together. The drawback of this other method is that you must decide ahead of time how many digits are required for all the numbers you might encounter.

Let's think about this for a moment. The advantage of writing positive and negative numbers the way we normally do is that they can go on forever. We imagine 0 as the middle of an infinite stream of positive numbers going off in one direction and an infinite stream of negative numbers going off in another:

... −1,000,000 −999,999 ... −3 −2 −1 0 1 2 3 ... 999,999 1,000,000 ...

But suppose we don't need an infinite number of numbers. Suppose we know at the outset that every number we come across will be within a particular range.

Let's look at a checking account, which is one place people sometimes see negative numbers. Let's assume that we never have as much as $500 in our checking account and that the bank has given us a no-bounce checking limit of $500. This means that the balance in our checking account is always a number somewhere between $499 and –$500. Let's also assume that we never deposit as much as $500, we never write a check for more than $500, and we deal only in dollars and don't care about cents.

This set of conditions means that the range of numbers we deal with in using our checking account include –500 through 499. That's a total of 1000 numbers. This restriction implies that we can use just three decimal digits and no negative sign to represent *all* the numbers we need. The trick is that we really don't need positive numbers ranging from 500 through 999. That's because we've already established that the maximum positive number we need is 499. So the three-digit numbers from 500 through 999 can actually represent negative numbers. Here's how it works:

To mean –500, we use 500.

To mean –499, we use 501.

To mean –498, we use 502.

(yada, yada, yada)

To mean –2, we use 998.

To mean –1, we use 999.

To mean 0, we use 000.

To mean 1, we use 001.

To mean 2, we use 002.

(yada, yada, yada)

To mean 497, we use 497.

To mean 498, we use 498.

To mean 499, we use 499.

In other words, every 3-digit number that begins with a 5, 6, 7, 8, or 9 is actually a negative number. Instead of writing the numbers like this:

–500 –499 –498 ... –4 –3 –2 –1 0 1 2 3 4 ... 497 498 499

we write them this way:

500 501 502 ... 996 997 998 999 000 001 002 003 004 ... 497 498 499

Notice that this forms a circle of sorts. The lowest negative number (500) looks as if it continues from the highest positive number (499). And the number 999 (which is actually –1) is one less than zero. If we add 1 to 999, we'd normally get 1000. But since we're only dealing with three digits, it's actually 000.

This type of notation is called *ten's complement*. To convert a 3-digit negative number to ten's complement, we subtract it from 999 and add 1. In other words, the ten's complement is the nines' complement plus one. For example, to write –255 in ten's complement, subtract it from 999 to get 744 and then add 1 to get 745.

You've probably heard it said that "Subtraction is merely addition using negative numbers." To which you've probably replied, "Yeah, but you still have to *subtract* them." Well, using the ten's complement, you don't subtract numbers at all. Everything is addition.

Suppose you have a checking account balance of $143. You write a check for $78. That means you have to add a negative $78 to $143. In ten's complement, −78 is written as 999 − 078 + 1, or 922. So, our new balance is $143 + $922, which equals (ignoring the overflow), $65. If we then write a check for $150 dollars, we have to add −150, which in ten's complement equals 850. So our previous balance of 065 plus 850 equals 915, our new balance. This is actually equivalent to −$85.

The equivalent system in binary is called *two's complement*. Let's assume that we're working with 8-bit numbers. These range from 00000000 to 11111111, which normally correspond to decimal numbers 0 through 255. But if you also want to express negative numbers, every 8-bit number that begins with a 1 will actually represent a negative number, as shown in the following table:

Binary	Decimal
10000000	−128
10000001	−127
10000010	−126
10000011	−125
⋮	
11111101	−3
11111110	−2
11111111	−1
00000000	0
00000001	1
00000010	2
⋮	
01111100	124
01111101	125
01111110	126
01111111	127

The range of numbers that you can represent is now limited to −128 through +127. The most significant (leftmost) bit is known as the *sign bit*. The sign bit is 1 for negative numbers and 0 for positive numbers.

To calculate the two's complement, first calculate the ones' complement and then add 1. This is equivalent to inverting all the digits and adding 1. For example, the decimal number 125 is 01111101. To express −125 in two's complement, first invert the digits of 01111101 to get 10000010, and then add 1 to get 10000011. You can verify the result using the preceding table. To go backward, do the same thing—invert all the bits and add 1.

This system gives us a way to express positive and negative numbers without using negative signs. It also lets us freely add positive and negative numbers using only the rules of addition. For example, let's add the binary equivalents of −127 and 124. Using the preceding table as a cheat sheet, this is simply

$$
\begin{array}{r}
10000001 \\
+\ 01111100 \\
\hline
11111101
\end{array}
$$

The result is equivalent to −3 in decimal.

What you need to watch out for here is overflow and underflow conditions. That's when the result of an addition is greater than 127 or less than −128. For example, suppose you add 125 to itself:

$$
\begin{array}{r}
01111101 \\
+\ 01111101 \\
\hline
11111010
\end{array}
$$

Because the high bit is set to 1, the result must be interpreted as a negative number, specifically the binary equivalent of −6. Something similar happens when −125 is added to itself:

$$
\begin{array}{r}
10000011 \\
+\ 10000011 \\
\hline
100000110
\end{array}
$$

We decided at the outset that we're restricting ourselves to 8-bit numbers, so the leftmost digit of the result must be ignored. The rightmost 8 bits are equivalent to +6.

In general, the result of an addition involving positive and negative numbers is invalid if the sign bits of the two operands are the same but the sign bit of the result is different.

Now we have two different ways of using binary numbers. Binary numbers can be either *signed* or *unsigned*. Unsigned 8-bit numbers range from 0 through 255. Signed 8-bit numbers range from −128 through 127. Nothing about the numbers themselves will tell you whether they're signed or unsigned. For example, suppose someone says, "I have an 8-bit binary number and the value is 10110110. What's the decimal equivalent?" You must first inquire, "Is that a signed or an unsigned number? It could be −74 or 182."

That's the trouble with bits: They're just zeros and ones and don't tell you anything *about* themselves.

Chapter Fourteen

Feedback
and Flip-Flops

Everybody knows that electricity makes things move. A brief glance around the average home reveals electric motors in appliances as diverse as clocks, fans, food processors, and compact disc players. Electricity also makes the cones in loudspeakers vibrate, bringing forth sounds, speech, and music from the stereo system and the television set. But perhaps the simplest and most elegant way that electricity makes things move is illustrated by a class of devices that are quickly disappearing as electronic counterparts replace them. I refer to the marvelously retro electric buzzers and bells.

Consider a relay wired this way with a switch and battery:

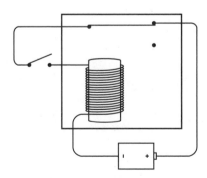

If this looks a little odd to you, you're not imagining things. We haven't seen a relay wired quite like this yet. Usually a relay is wired so that the input is separate from the output. Here it's all one big circle. If you close the switch, a circuit is completed:

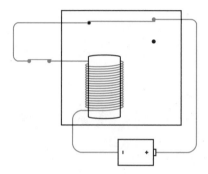

The completed circuit causes the electromagnet to pull down the flexible contact:

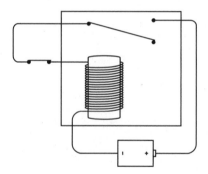

But when the contact changes position, the circuit is no longer complete, so the electromagnet loses its magnetism and the flexible contact flips back up:

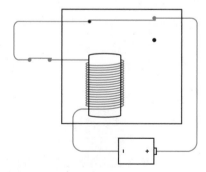

which, of course, completes the circuit again. What happens is this: As long as the switch is closed, the metal contact goes back and forth—alternately closing the circuit and opening it—most likely making a sound. If the contact makes a rasping sound, it's a buzzer. If you attach a hammer to it and provide a metal gong, you'll have the makings of an electric bell.

You can choose from a couple of ways to wire this relay to make a buzzer. Here's another way to do it using the conventional voltage and ground symbols:

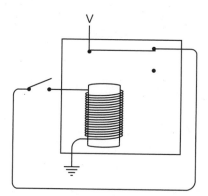

You might recognize in this diagram the inverter from Chapter 11. The circuit can be drawn more simply this way:

As you'll recall, the output of an inverter is 1 if the input is 0, and 0 if the input is 1. Closing the switch on this circuit causes the relay in the inverter to alternately open and close. You can also wire the inverter without a switch to go continuously:

This drawing might seem to be illustrating a logical contradiction because the output of an inverter is supposed to be opposite the input, but here the output *is* the input! Keep in mind, however, that the inverter is actually just a relay, and the relay requires a little bit of time to change from one state to another. So even if the input is the same as the output, the output will soon change, becoming the inverse of the input (which, of course, changes the input, and so forth and so on).

What is the output of this circuit? Well, the output quickly alternates between providing a voltage and not providing a voltage. Or, we can say, *the output quickly alternates between 0 and 1.*

This circuit is called an *oscillator*. It's intrinsically different from everything else we've looked at so far. All the previous circuits have changed their state only with the intervention of a human being who closes or opens a switch. The oscillator, however, doesn't require a human being; it basically runs by itself.

Of course, the oscillator in isolation doesn't seem to be very useful. We'll see later in this chapter and in the next few chapters that such a circuit connected to other circuits is an essential part of automation. All computers have some kind of oscillator that makes everything else move in synchronicity.

The output of the oscillator alternates between 0 and 1. A common way to symbolize that fact is with a diagram that looks like this:

This is understood to be a type of graph. The horizontal axis represents time, and the vertical axis indicates whether the output is 0 or 1:

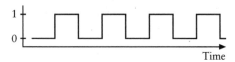

All this is really saying that as time passes, the output of the oscillator alternates between 0 and 1 on a regular basis. For that reason, an oscillator is sometimes often referred to as a *clock* because by counting the number of oscillations you can tell time (kind of).

How fast will the oscillator run? That is, how quickly will the metal contact of the relay vibrate back and forth? How many times a second? That obviously depends on how the relay is built. One can easily imagine a big, sturdy relay that clunks back and forth slowly and a small, light relay that buzzes rapidly.

A *cycle* of an oscillator is defined as the interval during which the output of the oscillator changes and then comes back again to where it started:

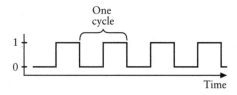

The time required for one cycle is called the *period* of the oscillator. Let's assume that we're looking at a particular oscillator that has a period of 0.05 second. We can then label the horizontal axis in seconds beginning from some arbitrary time we denote as 0:

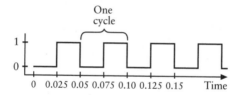

The *frequency* of the oscillator is 1 divided by the period. In this example, if the period of the oscillator is 0.05 second, the frequency of the oscillator is 1 ÷ 0.05, or 20 *cycles per second*. Twenty times per second, the output of the oscillator changes and changes back.

Cycles per second is a fairly self-explanatory term, much like *miles per hour* or *pounds per square inch* or *calories per serving*. But *cycles per second* isn't used much any more. In commemoration of Heinrich Rudolph Hertz (1857–1894), who was the first person to transmit and receive radio waves, the word *hertz* is now used instead. This usage started first in Germany in the 1920s and then expanded into other countries over the decades.

Thus, we can say that our oscillator has a frequency of 20 hertz, or (to abbreviate) 20 Hz.

Of course, we just guessed at the actual speed of one particular oscillator. By the end of this chapter, we'll be able to build something that lets us actually measure the speed of an oscillator.

To begin this endeavor, let's look at a pair of NOR gates wired a particular way. You'll recall that the output of a NOR gate is a voltage only if both inputs aren't voltages:

NOR	0	1
0	1	0
1	0	0

Here's a circuit with two NOR gates, two switches, and a lightbulb:

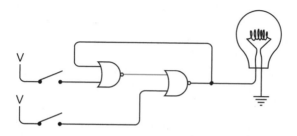

Notice the oddly contorted wiring: The output of the NOR gate on the left is an input to the NOR gate on the right, and the output of the right NOR gate is an input to the left NOR gate. This is a type of *feedback*. Indeed, just as in the oscillator, an output circles back to become an input. This idiosyncrasy will be a characteristic of most of the circuits in this chapter.

At the outset, the only current flowing in this circuit is from the output of the left NOR gate. That's because both inputs to that gate are 0. Now close the upper switch. The output from the left NOR gate becomes 0, which means the output from the right NOR gate becomes 1 and the lightbulb goes on:

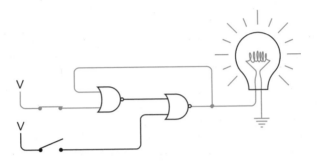

The magic occurs when you now open the upper switch. Because the output of a NOR gate is 0 if either input is 1, the output of the left NOR gate remains the same and the light remains lit:

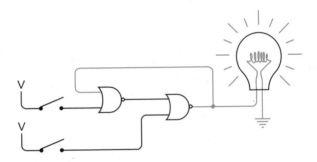

Now this is odd, wouldn't you say? Both switches are open—the same as in the first drawing—yet now the lightbulb is on. This situation is certainly different from anything we've seen before. Usually the output of a circuit is dependent solely upon the inputs. That doesn't seem to be the case here. Moreover, at this point you can close and open that upper switch and the light remains lit. That switch has no further effect on the circuit because the output of the left NOR gate remains 0.

Now close the lower switch. Because one of the inputs to the right NOR gate is now 1, the output becomes 0 and the lightbulb goes out. The output of the left NOR gate becomes 1:

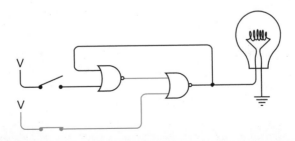

Now you can open the bottom switch and the lightbulb stays off:

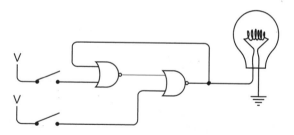

We're back where we started. At this time, you can close and open the bottom switch with no further effect on the lightbulb. In summary

- Closing the top switch causes the lightbulb to go on, and it stays on when the top switch is opened.
- Closing the bottom switch causes the lightbulb to go off, and it stays off when the bottom switch is opened.

The strangeness of this circuit is that sometimes when both switches are open the light is on, and sometimes when both switches are open, the light is off. We can say that this circuit has two *stable states* when both switches are open. Such a circuit is called a *flip-flop,* a word also used for beach sandals and the tactics of politicians. The flip-flop dates from 1918 with the work of English radio physicist William Henry Eccles (1875–1966) and F.W. Jordan (about whom not much seems to be known).

A flip-flop circuit *retains information.* It "remembers." In particular, the flip-flop shown previously remembers which switch was most recently closed. If you happen to come upon such a flip-flop in your travels and you see that the light is on, you can surmise that it was the upper switch that was most recently closed; if the light is off, the lower switch was most recently closed.

A flip-flop is very much like a seesaw. A seesaw has two stable states, never staying long in that precarious middle position. You can always tell from looking at a seesaw which side was pushed down most recently.

Although it might not be apparent yet, flip-flops are essential tools. They add memory to a circuit to give it a history of what's gone on before. Imagine trying to count if you couldn't remember anything. You wouldn't know what number you were up to and what number comes next! Similarly, a *circuit* that counts (which I'll show you later in this chapter) needs flip-flops.

There are a couple of different types of flip-flops. What I've just shown is the simplest and is called an R-S (or Reset-Set) flip-flop. The two NOR gates are more commonly drawn and labeled as in the diagram at the top of the next page to give it a symmetrical look.

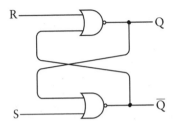

The output that we used for the lightbulb is traditionally called Q. In addition, there's a second output called $\overline{Q}$ (pronounced Q *bar*) that's the opposite of Q. If Q is 0, then $\overline{Q}$ is 1, and vice versa. The two inputs are called S for *set* and R for *reset*. You can think of these verbs as meaning "set Q to 1" and "reset Q to 0." When S is 1 (which corresponds to closing the top switch in the earlier diagram), Q becomes 1 and $\overline{Q}$ becomes 0. When R is 1 (corresponding to closing the bottom switch in the earlier diagram), Q becomes 0 and $\overline{Q}$ becomes 1. When both inputs are 0, the output indicates whether Q was last set or reset. These results are summed up in the following table:

Inputs		Outputs	
S	R	Q	$\overline{Q}$
1	0	1	0
0	1	0	1
0	0	Q	$\overline{Q}$
1	1	Disallowed	

This is called a *function table* or a *logic table* or a *truth table*. It shows the outputs that result from particular combinations of inputs. Because there are only two inputs to the R-S flip-flop, the number of combinations of inputs is four. These correspond to the four rows of the table under the headings.

Notice the row second from the bottom when S and R are both 0: The outputs are indicated as Q and $\overline{Q}$. This means that the Q and $\overline{Q}$ outputs remain what they were before both the S and R inputs became 0. The final row of the table indicates that a situation in which the S and R inputs are both 1 is *disallowed* or *illegal*. This doesn't mean you'll get arrested for doing it, but if both inputs are 1 in this circuit, both outputs are 0, which violates the notion of $\overline{Q}$ being the opposite of Q. So when you're designing circuitry that uses the R-S flip-flop, avoid situations in which the S and R inputs are both 1.

The R-S flip-flop is often drawn as a little box with the two inputs and two outputs labeled like this:

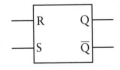

The R-S flip-flop is certainly interesting as a first example of a circuit that seems to "remember" which of two inputs was last a voltage. What turns out to be much more useful, however, is a circuit that remembers whether a particular signal was 0 or 1 *at a particular point in time.*

Let's think about how such a circuit should behave before we actually try to build it. It would have two inputs. Let's call one of them *Data.* Like all digital signals, the Data input can be 0 or 1. Let's call the other one *Hold That Bit,* which is the digital equivalent of a person saying "Hold that thought." Normally the Hold That Bit signal is 0, in which case the Data signal has no effect on the circuit. When Hold That Bit is 1, the circuit reflects the value of the Data signal. The Hold That Bit signal can then go back to being 0, at which time the circuit remembers the last value of the Data signal. Any changes in the Data signal have no further effect.

In other words, we want something that has the following function table:

Inputs		Outputs
Data	Hold That Bit	Q
0	1	0
1	1	1
0	0	Q
1	0	Q

In the first two cases, when the Hold That Bit signal is 1, the output Q is the same as the Data input. In the second two cases, when the Hold That Bit signal is 0, the Q output is the same as it was before. Notice in the second two cases that when Hold That Bit is 0, the Q output is the same regardless of what the Data input is. The function table can be simplified a little, like this:

Inputs		Outputs
Data	Hold That Bit	Q
0	1	0
1	1	1
X	0	Q

The X means "don't care." It doesn't matter what the Data input is because if the Hold That Bit input is 0, the output Q is the same as it was before.

Implementing a Hold That Bit signal based on our existing R-S flip-flop requires that we add two AND gates at the input end, as in the diagram at the top of the following page.

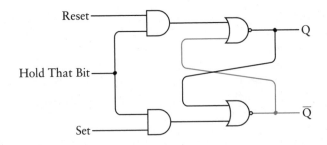

Recall that the output of an AND gate is 1 only if both inputs are 1. In this diagram, the Q output is 0 and the $\overline{Q}$ output is 1.

As long as the Hold That Bit signal is 0, the Set signal has no effect on the outputs:

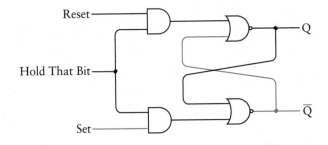

Similarly, the Reset signal has no effect:

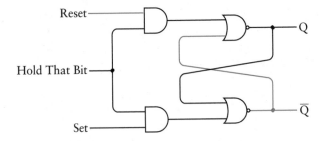

Only when the Hold That Bit signal is 1 will this circuit function the same way as the normal R-S flip-flop shown earlier:

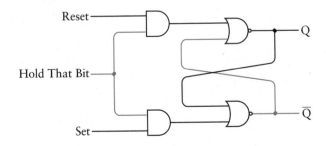

It behaves like a normal R-S flip-flop because now the output of the upper AND gate is the same as the Reset signal, and the output of the lower AND gate is the same as the Set signal.

But we haven't yet achieved our goal. We want only two inputs, not three. How is this done? If you recall the original function table of the R-S flip-flop, the case in which Set and Reset were both 1 was disallowed, so we want to avoid that. And it doesn't make much sense for the Set and Reset signals to now both be 0 because that's simply the case in which the output didn't change. We can accomplish the same thing in this circuit by setting Hold That Bit to 0.

So it makes sense that if Set is 1, Reset is 0; and if Set is 0, Reset is 1. A signal called Data can be equivalent to a Set, and the Data signal inverted can be the Reset signal:

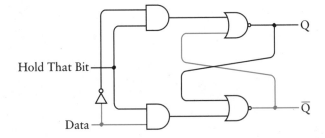

In this case, both inputs are 0 and the output Q is 0 (which means that $\overline{Q}$ is 1). As long as Hold That Bit is 0, the Data input has no effect on the circuit:

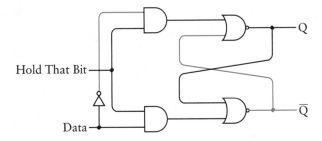

But when Hold That Bit is 1, the circuit reflects the value of the Data input:

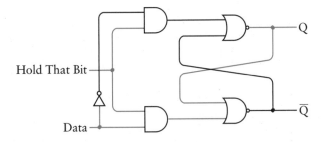

The Q output is now the same as the Data input, and $\overline{Q}$ is the opposite. Now Hold That Bit can go back to being 0:

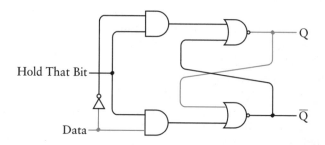

The circuit now remembers the value of Data when Hold That Bit was last 1, regardless of how Data changes. The Data signal could, for example, go back to 0 with no effect on the output:

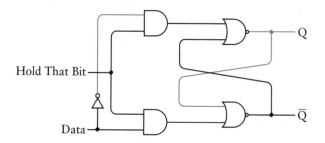

This circuit is called a *level-triggered D-type flip-flop*. The D stands for *Data*. *Level-triggered* means that the flip-flop saves the value of the Data input when the Hold That Bit input is at a particular *level,* in this case 1. (We'll look at an alternative to level-triggered flip-flops shortly.)

Usually when a circuit like this appears in a book, the input isn't labeled Hold That Bit. It's usually labeled *Clock.* Of course, this signal isn't a *real* clock, but it might sometimes have clocklike attributes, which means that it might tick back and forth between 0 and 1 on a regular basis. But for now, the Clock input simply indicates when the Data input is to be saved:

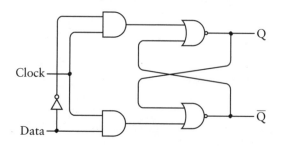

And usually when the function table is shown, Data is abbreviated as *D* and Clock is abbreviated as *Clk*:

Inputs		Outputs
D	Clk	Q
0	1	0
1	1	1
X	0	$\overline{Q}$

This circuit is also known as a level-triggered D-type *latch,* and that term simply means that the circuit *latches onto* one bit of data and keeps it around for further use. The circuit can also be referred to as a 1-bit *memory.* I'll demonstrate in Chapter 16 how very many of these flip-flops can be wired together to provide many bits of memory.

Saving a multibit value in latches is often useful. Suppose you want to use the adding machine in Chapter 12 to add three 8-bit numbers together. You'd key in the first number on the first set of switches and the second number on the second set of switches as usual, but then you'd have to write down the result. You'd then have to key in that result on one set of switches and key in the third number on the other set of switches. You really shouldn't have to key in an intermediate result. You should be able to use it directly from the first calculation.

Let's solve this problem using latches. Let's assemble eight latches in a box. Each of the eight latches uses two NOR gates and two AND gates and one inverter, as shown previously. The Clock inputs are all connected. Here's the resultant package:

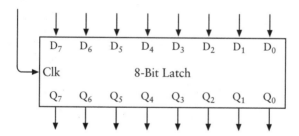

This latch is capable of saving 8 bits at once. The eight inputs on the top are labeled D_0 through D_7, and the eight outputs on the bottom are labeled Q_0 through Q_7. The input at the left is the Clock. The Clock signal is normally 0. When the Clock signal is 1, the 8-bit value on the D inputs is transferred to the Q outputs. When the Clock signal goes back to 0, that 8-bit value stays there until the next time the Clock signal is 1.

The 8-Bit Latch can also be drawn with the eight Data inputs and eight Q outputs grouped together as you see on the following page.

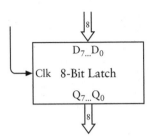

Here's the 8-Bit Adder:

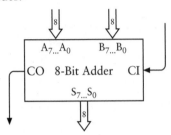

Normally (ignoring what we did with subtraction in the last chapter), the eight A inputs and eight B inputs are connected to switches, the CI (Carry In) input is connected to ground, and the eight S (Sum) outputs and CO (Carry Out) are connected to lightbulbs.

In this revised version, the eight S outputs of the 8-Bit Adder can be connected to both the lightbulbs *and* the D inputs of the 8-Bit Latch. A switch labeled *Save* can be the Clock input of the latches to save a result from the adder:

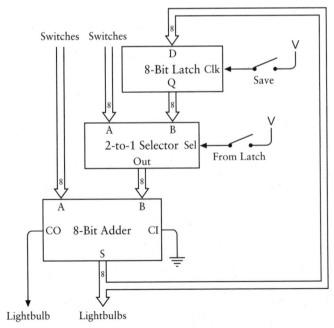

The box labeled *2-Line-to-1-Line Selector* lets you choose with a switch whether you want the B inputs to the adder to come from the second row of switches or from the Q outputs of the latches. You close the switch to select the outputs from the 8-Bit Latch. The 2-Line-to-1-Line Selector uses eight of the following circuits:

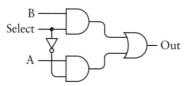

If the Select input is 1, the output of the OR gate is the same as the B input. That's because the output of the top AND gate is the same as the B input, and the output of the bottom AND gate is 0. Similarly, if the Select input is 0, the output is the same as the A input. This is summed up in the following function table:

Inputs			Outputs
Select	A	B	Q
0	0	X	0
0	1	X	1
1	X	0	0
1	X	1	1

The box shown in the revised adding machine comprises eight of these 1-bit selectors. All the Select inputs are wired together.

This revised adding machine isn't handling the Carry Out signal very well. If the addition of two numbers causes the Carry Out signal to be 1, the signal is ignored when the next number is added in. One possible solution is to make the Adder, the Latch, and the Selector all 16 bits wide, or at least wider than the largest sum you'll encounter. I won't really be solving this problem until Chapter 17.

A more interesting approach to the adding machine eliminates an entire row of eight switches. But first we need to modify the D-type flip-flop slightly by adding an OR gate and an input signal called *Clear*. The Clear input is normally 0. But when it's 1, the Q output becomes 0, as shown here:

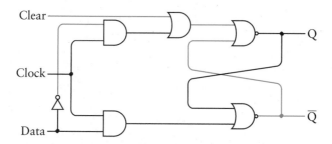

This signal forces Q to be 0 regardless of the other input signals, in effect clearing the flip-flop.

Why do we need this, you might ask? Why can't we clear the flip-flop by setting the Data input to 0 and the Clock input to 1? Well, maybe we can't control exactly what's going into the Data input. Maybe we have a set of eight of these latches wired to the outputs of an 8-Bit Adder, like so:

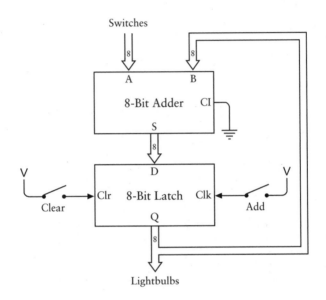

Notice that the switch labeled *Add* now controls the Clock input of the latch.

You might find this adder easier to use than the previous one, particularly if you need to add a long list of numbers. You begin by pressing the Clear switch. That action causes the output of the latches to be 0, turning off all the lights and also setting the second set of inputs to the 8-Bit Adder to all 0s. You key in the first number and press the Add button. That number appears on the lights. You then key in the second number and again press the Add button. The number set up by the switches is added to the previous total, and it appears on the lights. Just continue keying in more numbers and pressing the Add switch.

I mentioned earlier that the D-type flip-flop we designed was *level-triggered*. This means that the Clock input must change its *level* from 0 to 1 in order for the value of the Data input to be stored in the latch. But during the time that the Clock input is 1, the Data input can change; any changes in the Data input while the Clock input is 1 will be reflected in the values of the Q and Q̄ outputs.

For some applications, a level-triggered Clock input is quite sufficient. But for other applications, an *edge-triggered* Clock input is preferred. An edge trigger causes the outputs to change *only when the Clock makes a transition from 0 to 1*. As with the level-triggered flip-flop, when the Clock input is 0, any changes to the Data input don't affect the outputs. The difference in an edge-triggered flip-flop is that changes to the Data input also don't affect the outputs when the Clock input is 1. The Data input affects the outputs only at the instant that the Clock changes from 0 to 1.

An edge-triggered D-type flip-flop is constructed from two stages of R-S flip-flops, wired together this way:

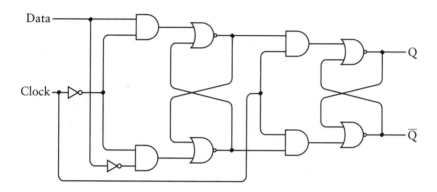

The idea here is that the Clock input controls both the first stage and the second stage. But notice that the clock is inverted in the first stage. This means that the first stage works exactly like a D-type flip-flop except that the Data input is stored when the Clock is 0. The outputs of the second stage are inputs to the first stage, and these are saved when the Clock is 1. The overall result is that the Data input is saved when the Clock changes from 0 to 1.

Let's take a closer look. Here's the flip-flop at rest with both the Data and Clock inputs at 0 and the Q output at 0:

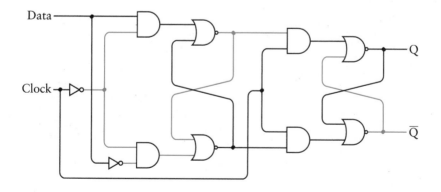

Now change the Data input to 1:

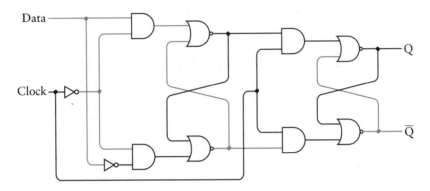

This changes the first flip-flop stage because the inverted Clock input is 1. But the second stage remains unchanged because the uninverted Clock input is 0. Now change the Clock input to 1:

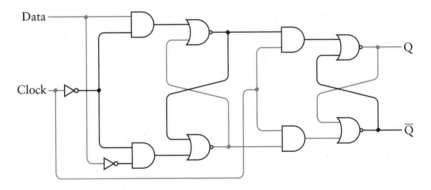

This causes the second stage to change, and the Q output goes to 1. The difference is that the Data input can now change (for example, back to 0) without affecting the Q output:

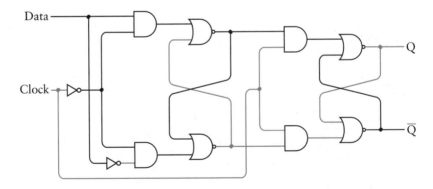

The Q and $\overline{Q}$ outputs can change only at the instant that the Clock input changes from 0 to 1.

The function table of the edge-triggered D-type flip-flop requires a new symbol, which is an arrow pointing up (↑). This symbol indicates a signal making a transition from a 0 to a 1:

Inputs		Outputs	
D	Clk	Q	$\overline{Q}$
0	↑	0	1
1	↑	1	0
X	0	Q	$\overline{Q}$

The arrow indicates that the output Q becomes the same as the Data input when the Clock makes a transition from 0 to 1. This is known as a *positive transition* of the Clock signal. (A *negative transition* is the transition from 1 to 0.) The flip-flop has a diagram like this:

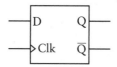

The little angle bracket indicates that the flip-flop is edge triggered.

Now I want to show you a circuit using the edge-triggered D-type flip-flop that you can't duplicate with the level-triggered version. You'll recall the oscillator that we constructed at the beginning of this chapter. The output of the oscillator alternates between 0 and 1:

Let's connect the output of the oscillator to the Clock input of the edge-triggered D-type flip-flop. And let's connect the $\overline{Q}$ output to the D input:

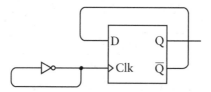

The output of the flip-flop is itself an input to the flip-flop. It's feedback upon feedback! (In practice, this could present a problem. The oscillator is constructed out of a relay that's flipping back and forth as fast as it can. The output of the oscillator is connected to the relays that make up the flip-flop. These other relays might not be able to keep up with the speed of the oscillator. To avoid these problems, let's assume that the relay used in the oscillator is much slower than the relays used elsewhere in these circuits.)

To see what happens in this circuit, let's look at a function table that illustrates the various changes. At the start, let's say that the Clock input is 0 and the Q output is 0. That means that the $\overline{Q}$ output is 1, which is connected to the D input:

Inputs		Outputs	
D	Clk	Q	$\overline{Q}$
1	0	0	1

When the Clock input changes from 0 to 1, the Q output will become the same as the D input:

Inputs		Outputs	
D	Clk	Q	$\overline{Q}$
1	0	0	1
1	↑	1	0

But because the $\overline{Q}$ output changes to 0, the D input will also change to 0. The Clock input is now 1:

Inputs		Outputs	
D	Clk	Q	$\overline{Q}$
1	0	0	1
1	↑	1	0
0	1	1	0

The Clock input changes to back to 0 without affecting the outputs:

Inputs		Outputs	
D	Clk	Q	$\overline{Q}$
1	0	0	1
1	↑	1	0
0	1	1	0
0	0	1	0

Now the Clock input changes to 1 again. Because the D input is 0, the Q output becomes 0 and the $\overline{Q}$ output becomes 1:

Inputs		Outputs	
D	Clk	Q	$\overline{Q}$
1	0	0	1
1	↑	1	0
0	1	1	0
0	0	1	0
0	↑	0	1

So the D input also becomes 1:

Inputs		Outputs	
D	Clk	Q	$\overline{Q}$
1	0	0	1
1	↑	1	0
0	1	1	0
0	0	1	0
0	↑	0	1
1	1	0	1

What's happening here can be summed up very simply: Every time the Clock input changes from 0 to 1, the Q output changes, either from 0 to 1 or from 1 to 0. The situation is clearer if we look at the timing diagram:

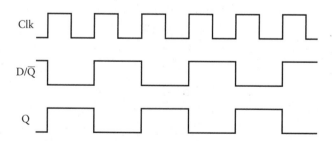

When the Clock input goes from 0 to 1, the value of D (which is the same as $\overline{Q}$) is transferred to Q, thus also changing $\overline{Q}$ and D for the next transition of the Clock input from 0 to 1.

If the frequency of the oscillator is 20 Hz (which means 20 cycles per second), the frequency of the Q output is half that, or 10 Hz. For this reason, such a circuit—in which the $\overline{Q}$ output is routed back to the Data input of a flip-flop—is also known as a *frequency divider*.

Of course, the output from the frequency divider can be the Clock input of another frequency divider to divide the frequency once again. Here's an arrangement of three of them:

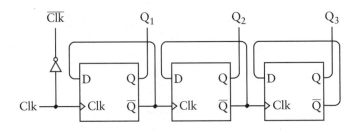

Let's look at the four signals I've labeled at the top of that diagram:

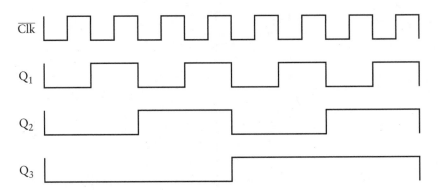

I'll admit that I've started and ended this diagram at an opportune spot, but there's nothing dishonest about it: The circuit will repeat this pattern over and over again. But do you recognize anything familiar about it?

I'll give you a hint. Let's label these signals with 0s and 1s:

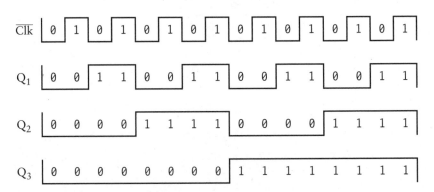

Do you see it yet? Try turning the diagram 90 degrees clockwise, and read the 4-bit numbers going across. Each of them corresponds to a decimal number from 0 through 15:

Binary	Decimal
0000	0
0001	1
0010	2
0011	3
0100	4
0101	5
0110	6
0111	7
1000	8
1001	9
1010	10
1011	11
1100	12
1101	13
1110	14
1111	15

Thus, this circuit is doing nothing less than *counting in binary numbers,* and the more flip-flops we add to the circuit, the higher it will count. I pointed out in Chapter 8 that in a sequence of increasing binary numbers, each column of digits alternates between 0 and 1 at half the frequency of the column to the right. The counter mimics this. At each positive transition of the Clock signal, the outputs of the counter are said to *increment,* that is, to increase by 1.

Let's string eight flip-flops together and put them in a box:

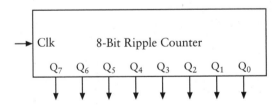

This is called a *ripple* counter because the output of each flip-flop becomes the Clock input of the next flip-flop. Changes ripple through the stages sequentially, and the flip-flops at the end might be delayed a little in changing. More sophisticated counters are *synchronous,* in which all the outputs change at the same time.

I've labeled the outputs Q_0 through Q_7. These are arranged so that the output from the first flip-flop in the chain (Q_0) is at the far right. Thus, if you connected lightbulbs to these outputs, you could read an 8-bit number.

A timing diagram of such a counter could show all eight outputs separately, or it could show them together, like this:

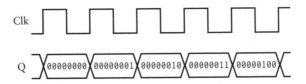

At each positive transition of the Clock, some Q outputs might change and some might not, but together they reflect increasing binary numbers.

I said earlier in this chapter that we'd discover some way to determine the frequency of an oscillator. This is it. If you connect an oscillator to the Clock input of the 8-Bit Counter, the counter will show you how many cycles the oscillator has gone through. When the total reaches 11111111 (255 in decimal), it goes back to 00000000. Probably the easiest way to use this counter to determine the frequency of an oscillator is to connect eight lightbulbs to the outputs of the 8-Bit Counter. Now wait until all the outputs are 0 (that is, when none of the lightbulbs are lit) and start a stopwatch. Stop the stopwatch when all the lights go out again. That's the time required for 256 cycles of the oscillator. Say it's 10 seconds. The frequency of the oscillator is thus $256 \div 10$, or 25.6 Hz.

As flip-flops gain features, they also gain in complexity. This one is called an *edge-triggered D-type flip-flop with preset and clear*:

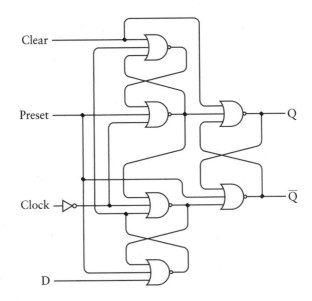

The Preset and Clear inputs override the Clock and Data inputs. Normally these two inputs are 0. When the Preset input is 1, Q becomes 1 and $\overline{Q}$ becomes 0. When the Clear input is 1, Q becomes 0 and $\overline{Q}$ becomes 1. (Like the Set and Reset inputs of an R-S flip-flop, Preset and Clear shouldn't be 1 at the same time.) Otherwise, this behaves like a normal edge-triggered D-type flip-flop:

Inputs				Outputs	
Pre	Clr	D	Clk	Q	$\overline{Q}$
1	0	X	X	1	0
0	1	X	X	0	1
0	0	0	↑	0	1
0	0	1	↑	1	0
0	0	X	0	Q	$\overline{Q}$

The diagram for the edge-triggered D-type flip-flop with preset and clear looks like this:

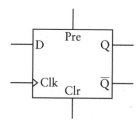

We have now persuaded telegraph relays to add, subtract, and count in binary numbers. This is quite an accomplishment, particularly considering that all the hardware we've been using was available more than a hundred years ago. We have still more to discover. But let's now take a short break from building things and have another look at number bases.

Chapter Fifteen

Bytes and Hex

The two improved adding machines of the last chapter illustrate clearly the concept of *data paths*. Throughout the circuitry, 8-bit values move from one component to another. Eight-bit values are inputs to the adders, latches, and data selectors, and also outputs from these units. Eight-bit values are also defined by switches and displayed by lightbulbs. The data path in these circuits is thus said to be *8 bits wide*. But why 8 bits? Why not 6 or 7 or 9 or 10?

The simple answer is that these improved adding machines were based on the original adding machine in Chapter 12, which worked with 8-bit values. But there's really no reason why it had to be built that way. Eight bits just seemed at the time to be a convenient amount—a nice *biteful* of bits, if you will. And perhaps I was being just a little bit sneaky, for I now confess that I knew all along (and perhaps you did as well) that 8 bits of data are known as a *byte*.

The word *byte* originated at IBM, probably around 1956. The word had its origins in the word *bite* but was spelled with a *y* so that nobody would mistake the word for *bit*. For a while, a byte meant simply the number of bits in a particular data path. But by the mid-1960s, in connection with the development of IBM's System/360 (their large complex of business computers), the word came to mean a group of 8 bits.

As an 8-bit quantity, a byte can take on values from 00000000 through 11111111. These values can represent positive integers from 0 through 255, or if two's complements are used to represent negative numbers, they can represent both positive and negative integers in the range –128 through 127. Or a particular byte can simply represent one of 2^8, or 256, different things.

It turns out that 8 is, indeed, a nice bite size of bits. The byte is right, in more ways than one. One reason that IBM gravitated toward 8-bit bytes was the ease in storing numbers in a format known as BCD (which I'll describe in Chapter 23). But as we'll see in the chapters ahead, quite by coincidence a byte is ideal for storing text because most written languages around the world (with the exception of the ideographs used in Chinese, Japanese, and Korean) can be represented with fewer than 256 characters. A byte is also ideal for representing gray shades in black-and-white photographs because the human eye can differentiate approximately 256 shades of gray. And where 1 byte is inadequate (for representing, for example, the aforementioned ideographs of Chinese, Japanese, and Korean), 2 bytes—which allow the representation of 2^{16}, or 65,536, things—usually works just fine.

Half a byte—that is, 4 bits—is sometimes referred to as a *nibble* (and is sometimes spelled *nybble*), but this word doesn't come up in conversation nearly as often as *byte*.

Because bytes show up a lot in the internals of computers, it's convenient to be able to refer to their values in as succinct a manner as possible. The eight binary digits 10110110, for example, are certainly explicit but hardly succinct.

We could always refer to bytes by their decimal equivalents, of course, but that requires converting from binary to decimal—not a particularly nasty calculation, but certainly a nuisance. I showed one approach in Chapter 8 that's fairly straightforward. Because each binary digit corresponds to a power of 2, we can simply write down the digits of the binary number and the powers of 2 underneath. Multiply each column and add up the products. Here's the conversion of 10110110:

1	0	1	1	0	1	1	0
×128	×64	×32	×16	×8	×4	×2	×1

$$128 + 0 + 32 + 16 + 0 + 4 + 2 + 0 = 182$$

Converting a decimal number to binary is a bit more awkward. You start with the decimal number and divide by decreasing powers of 2. For each division, the quotient is a binary digit and the remainder is divided by the next smallest power of 2. Here's the conversion of 182 back to binary:

182	54	54	22	6	6	2	0
÷128	÷64	÷32	÷16	÷8	÷4	÷2	÷1
1	0	1	1	0	1	1	0

Chapter 8 has a more extensive description of this technique. Regardless, converting between binary and decimal is usually not something that can be done without a paper and pencil or lots of practice.

In Chapter 8, we also learned about the octal, or base-8, number system. Octal uses only the digits 0, 1, 2, 3, 4, 5, 6, and 7. Converting between octal and binary is a snap. All you need remember is the 3-bit equivalent of each octal digit, as shown in the table on the next page.

Binary	Octal
000	0
001	1
010	2
011	3
100	4
101	5
110	6
111	7

If you have a binary number (such as 10110110), start at the rightmost digits. Each group of 3 bits is an octal digit:

$$10\underbrace{110}\,\underbrace{110}$$
$$2 \quad 6 \quad 6$$

So the byte 10110110 can be expressed as the octal digits 266. This is certainly more succinct, and octal is indeed one good method for representing bytes. But octal has a little problem.

The binary representations of bytes range from 00000000 through 11111111. The octal representations of bytes range from 000 through 377. As is clear in the preceding example, 3 bits correspond to the middle and rightmost octal digits, but only 2 bits correspond to the leftmost octal digit. This means that an octal representation of a 16-bit number

$$1\underbrace{011}\,\underbrace{001}\,\underbrace{111}\,\underbrace{000}\,\underbrace{101}$$
$$1 \quad 3 \quad 1 \quad 7 \quad 0 \quad 5$$

isn't the same as the octal representations of the 2 bytes that compose the 16-bit number

$$10\underbrace{110}\,\underbrace{011} \qquad 11\underbrace{000}\,\underbrace{101}$$
$$2 \quad 6 \quad 3 \qquad 3 \quad 0 \quad 5$$

In order for the representations of multibyte values to be consistent with the representations of the individual bytes, we need to use a system in which each byte is divided into equal numbers of bits. That means that we need to divide each byte into four values of 2 bits each (that would be base 4) or two values of 4 bits each (base 16).

Base 16. Now that's something we haven't looked at yet, and for good reason. The base-16 number system is called *hexadecimal,* and even the word itself is a mess. Most words that begin with the *hexa-* prefix (such as hexagon or hexapod or hexameter) refer to six of something. Hexadecimal is supposed to mean *sixteen.* And even though *The Microsoft Manual of Style for Technical Publications* clearly states, "Do not abbreviate as *hex,*" everyone always does and I will too.

That's not the only peculiarity of hexadecimal. In decimal, we count like this:

0 1 2 3 4 5 6 7 8 9 10 11 12...

In octal, you'll recall, we no longer need digits 8 and 9:

0 1 2 3 4 5 6 7 10 11 12...

Similarly, the base-4 number system also doesn't need 4, 5, 6, or 7:

0 1 2 3 10 11 12...

And binary, of course, needs only 0 and 1:

0 1 10 11 100...

But hexadecimal is different because it requires *more* digits than decimal. Counting in hexadecimal goes something like this:

0 1 2 3 4 5 6 7 8 9 ? ? ? ? ? ? 10 11 12...

where 10 (pronounced *one-zero*) is actually 16_{TEN}. The question marks indicate that we need six more symbols to display hexadecimal numbers. What are these symbols? Where do they come from? Well, they weren't handed down to us in tradition like the rest of our number symbols, so the rational thing to do is make up six new symbols, for example:

Unlike the symbols used for most of our numbers, these have the benefit of being easy to remember and identify with the actual quantities they represent. There's a 10-gallon cowboy hat, a football (11 players on a team), a dozen donuts, a black cat (associated with unlucky 13), a full moon that occurs about a fortnight (14 days) after the new moon, and a knife that reminds us of the assassination of Julius Caesar on the ides (the 15th day) of March.

Each byte can be expressed as two hexadecimal digits. In other words, a hexadecimal digit is equivalent to 4 bits, or 1 nibble. The table on the next page shows how to convert between binary, hexadecimal, and decimal.

Binary	Hexadecimal	Decimal	Binary	Hexadecimal	Decimal
0000	0	0	1000	8	8
0001	1	1	1001	9	9
0010	2	2	1010		10
0011	3	3	1011		11
0100	4	4	1100		12
0101	5	5	1101		13
0110	6	6	1110		14
0111	7	7	1111		15

Here's how to represent the byte 10110110 in hexadecimal:

$$10110110$$

And it doesn't matter if we're dealing with multibyte numbers:

$$10110110 \qquad 11000101$$

One byte is always represented by a pair of hexadecimal digits.

Unfortunately (or perhaps, much to your relief), we really aren't going to be using footballs and donuts to write hexadecimal numbers. It could have been done that way, but it wasn't. Instead, the hexadecimal system ensures that everybody gets really confused and stays that way. Those six missing hexadecimal digits are actually represented by the first six letters of the Latin alphabet, like this:

0 1 2 3 4 5 6 7 8 9 A B C D E F 10 11 12...

The following table shows the *real* conversion between binary, hexadecimal, and decimal:

Binary	Hexadecimal	Decimal
0000	0	0
0001	1	1
0010	2	2
0011	3	3
0100	4	4
0101	5	5
0110	6	6
0111	7	7
1000	8	8
1001	9	9
1010	A	10
1011	B	11
1100	C	12
1101	D	13
1110	E	14
1111	F	15

The byte 10110110 can thus be represented by the hexadecimal number B6 without your drawing a football. As you'll recall from previous chapters, I've been indicating number bases by subscripts, such as

10110110_{TWO}

for binary, and

2312_{FOUR}

for quaternary, and

266_{EIGHT}

for octal, and

182_{TEN}

for decimal. To continue the same system, we can use

$B6_{SIXTEEN}$

for hexadecimal. But that's clearly excessive. Fortunately, several other, terser, methods of denoting hexadecimal numbers are common. You can indicate the numbers this way:

$B6_{HEX}$

In this book, I'll be using mostly a very common approach, which is a lowercase *h* following the number, like so:

B6h

In a hexadecimal number, the positions of each digit correspond to powers of 16:

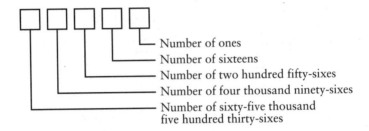

The hexadecimal number 9A48Ch is

$$9A48Ch = 9 \times 10000h +$$
$$A \times 1000h +$$
$$4 \times 100h +$$
$$8 \times 10h +$$
$$C \times 1h$$

This can be written using powers of 16:

$$9A48Ch = 9 \times 16^4 +$$
$$A \times 16^3 +$$
$$4 \times 16^2 +$$
$$8 \times 16^1 +$$
$$C \times 16^0$$

Or using the decimal equivalents of those powers:

$$9A48Ch = 9 \times 65,536 +$$
$$A \times 4096 +$$
$$4 \times 256 +$$
$$8 \times 16 +$$
$$C \times 1$$

Notice that there's no ambiguity in writing the single digits of the number (9, A, 4, 8, and C) without a subscript to indicate the number base. A 9 is a 9 whether it's decimal or hexadecimal. And an A is obviously hexadecimal—equivalent to 10 in decimal.

Converting all the digits to decimal lets us actually do the calculation:

$$9A48Ch = \quad 9 \times 65{,}536 +$$
$$10 \times 4096 +$$
$$4 \times 256 +$$
$$8 \times 16 +$$
$$12 \times 1$$

And the answer is 631,948. This is how hexadecimal numbers are converted to decimal.

Here's a template for converting any 4-digit hexadecimal number to decimal:

```
┌─────┐   ┌─────┐   ┌─────┐   ┌─────┐
│     │   │     │   │     │   │     │
└─────┘   └─────┘   └─────┘   └─────┘
 ×4096     ×256      ×16        ×1
┌─────┐ + ┌─────┐ + ┌─────┐ + ┌─────┐ = ┌─────┐
│     │   │     │   │     │   │     │   │     │
└─────┘   └─────┘   └─────┘   └─────┘   └─────┘
```

For example, here's the conversion of 79ACh. Keep in mind that the hexadecimal digits A and C are decimal 10 and 12, respectively:

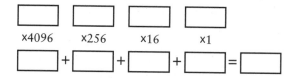

```
┌─────┐   ┌─────┐   ┌─────┐   ┌─────┐
│  7  │   │  9  │   │  A  │   │  C  │
└─────┘   └─────┘   └─────┘   └─────┘
 ×4096     ×256      ×16        ×1
┌──────┐+ ┌─────┐ + ┌─────┐ + ┌─────┐ = ┌──────┐
│28,672│  │2304 │   │ 160 │   │ 12  │   │31,148│
└──────┘  └─────┘   └─────┘   └─────┘   └──────┘
```

Converting decimal numbers to hexadecimal generally requires divisions. If the number is 255 or smaller, you know that it can be represented by 1 byte, which is two hexadecimal digits. To calculate those two digits, divide the number by 16 to get the quotient and the remainder. Let's use an earlier example—the decimal number 182. Divide 182 by 16 to get 11 (which is a B in hexadecimal) with a remainder of 6. The hexadecimal equivalent is B6h.

If the decimal number you want to convert is smaller than 65,536, the hexadecimal equivalent will have four digits or fewer. Here's a template for converting such a number to hexadecimal:

```
┌─────┐   ┌─────┐   ┌─────┐   ┌─────┐
│     │   │     │   │     │   │     │
└─────┘   └─────┘   └─────┘   └─────┘
 ÷4096     ÷256      ÷16        ÷1
┌─────┐   ┌─────┐   ┌─────┐   ┌─────┐
│     │   │     │   │     │   │     │
└─────┘   └─────┘   └─────┘   └─────┘
```

You start by putting the entire decimal number in the box in the upper left corner. That's your first dividend. Divide by 4096, the first divisor. The quotient goes in the box below the dividend, and the remainder goes in the box to the right of the dividend. That remainder is the new dividend that you divide by 256. Here's the conversion of 31,148 back to hexadecimal:

31,148	2476	172	12
÷4096	÷256	÷16	÷1
7	9	10	12

Of course, decimal numbers 10 and 12 correspond to hexadecimal A and C. The result is 79ACh.

One problem with this technique is that you probably want to use a calculator for the divisions, but calculators don't show remainders. If you divide 31,148 by 4096 on a calculator, you'll get 7.6044921875. To calculate the remainder, you need to multiply 4096 by 7 (to get 28,672) and subtract that from 31,148. Or multiply 4096 by 0.6044921875, the fractional part of the quotient. (On the other hand, some calculators can convert between decimal and hexadecimal.)

Another approach to converting decimal numbers through 65,535 to hex involves first separating the number into 2 bytes by dividing by 256. Then for each byte, divide by 16. Here's a template for doing it:

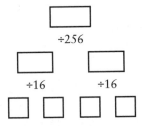

Start at the top. With each division, the quotient goes in the box to the left below the divisor, and the remainder goes in the box to the right. For example, here's the conversion of 51,966:

51,966			
÷256			
202		254	
÷16		÷16	
12	10	15	14

The hexadecimal digits are 12, 10, 15, and 14, or CAFE, which looks more like a word than a number! (And if you go there, you may want to order your coffee 56,495.)

As for every other number base, there's an addition table associated with hexadecimal:

+	0	1	2	3	4	5	6	7	8	9	A	B	C	D	E	F
0	0	1	2	3	4	5	6	7	8	9	A	B	C	D	E	F
1	1	2	3	4	5	6	7	8	9	A	B	C	D	E	F	10
2	2	3	4	5	6	7	8	9	A	B	C	D	E	F	10	11
3	3	4	5	6	7	8	9	A	B	C	D	E	F	10	11	12
4	4	5	6	7	8	9	A	B	C	D	E	F	10	11	12	13
5	5	6	7	8	9	A	B	C	D	E	F	10	11	12	13	14
6	6	7	8	9	A	B	C	D	E	F	10	11	12	13	14	15
7	7	8	9	A	B	C	D	E	F	10	11	12	13	14	15	16
8	8	9	A	B	C	D	E	F	10	11	12	13	14	15	16	17
9	9	A	B	C	D	E	F	10	11	12	13	14	15	16	17	18
A	A	B	C	D	E	F	10	11	12	13	14	15	16	17	18	19
B	B	C	D	E	F	10	11	12	13	14	15	16	17	18	19	1A
C	C	D	E	F	10	11	12	13	14	15	16	17	18	19	1A	1B
D	D	E	F	10	11	12	13	14	15	16	17	18	19	1A	1B	1C
E	E	F	10	11	12	13	14	15	16	17	18	19	1A	1B	1C	1D
F	F	10	11	12	13	14	15	16	17	18	19	1A	1B	1C	1D	1E

You can use the table and normal carry rules to add hexadecimal numbers:

$$\begin{array}{r} 4A3378E2 \\ + \ 877AB982 \\ \hline D1AE3264 \end{array}$$

You'll recall from Chapter 13 that you can use two's complements to represent negative numbers. If you're dealing with 8-bit signed values in binary, the negative numbers all begin with 1. In hexadecimal, 2-digit signed numbers are negative if they begin with 8, 9, A, B, C, D, E, or F because the binary representations of these hexadecimal digits all begin with 1. For example, 99h could represent either decimal 153 (if you know you're dealing with 1-byte unsigned numbers) or decimal −103 (if you're dealing with signed numbers).

Or the byte 99h could actually be the number 99 in decimal! This has a certain appeal to it, of course, but it seems to violate everything we've learned so far. I'll explain how it works in Chapter 23. But next I must talk about memory.

Chapter Sixteen

An Assemblage of Memory

A s we rouse ourselves from sleep every morning, memory fills in the blanks. We remember where we are, what we did the day before, and what we plan to do today. These memories might come in a rush or a dribble, and maybe after some minutes a few lapses might persist ("Funny, I don't remember wearing my socks to bed"), but all in all we can usually reassemble our lives and achieve enough continuity to commence living another day.

Of course, human memory isn't very orderly. Try to remember something about high school geometry, and you're likely to start thinking about the kid who sat in front of you or the day there was a fire drill just as the teacher was about to explain what QED meant.

Nor is human memory foolproof. Indeed, writing was probably invented specifically to compensate for the failings of human memory. Perhaps last night you suddenly woke up at 3:00 A.M. with a great idea for a screenplay. You grabbed the pen and paper you keep by your bed specifically for that purpose, and you wrote it down so you wouldn't forget. The next morning you can read the brilliant idea and start work on the screenplay. ("Boy meets girl w. car chase & explosions"? That's it?) Or maybe not.

We *write* and we later *read*. We *save* and we later *retrieve*. We *store* and we later *access*. The function of memory is to keep the information intact between those two events. Anytime we store information, we're making use of different types of memory. Paper is a good medium for storing textual information, and magnetic tape works well for music and movies.

Telegraph relays too—when assembled into logic gates and then flip-flops—can store information. As we've seen, a flip-flop is capable of storing 1 bit. This isn't a whole lot of information, but it's a start. For once we know how to store 1 bit, we can easily store 2, or 3, or more.

In Chapter 14, we encountered the level-triggered D-type flip-flop, which is made out of an inverter, two AND gates, and two NOR gates:

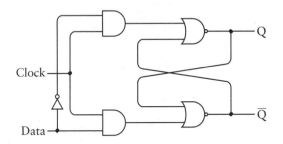

When the Clock input is 1, the Q output is the same as the Data input. But when the Clock input goes to 0, the Q output holds the last value of the Data input. Further changes to the Data input don't affect the outputs until the Clock input goes to 1 again. The logic table of the flip-flop is the following:

Inputs		Outputs
D	Clk	Q
0	1	0
1	1	1
X	0	Q

In Chapter 14, this flip-flop was featured in a couple of different circuits, but in this chapter it will be used in only one way—to store 1 bit of information. For that reason, I'm going to rename the inputs and outputs so that they'll be more in accordance with that purpose:

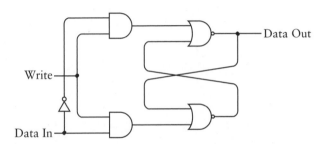

This is the same flip-flop, but now the Q output is named Data Out, and the Clock input (which started out in Chapter 14 as *Hold That Bit*) is named

Write. Just as we might write down some information on paper, the Write signal causes the Data In signal to be *written into* or *stored* in the circuit. Normally, the Write input is 0 and the Data In signal has no effect on the output. But whenever we want to store the Data In signal in the flip-flop, we make the Write input 1 and then 0 again. As I mentioned in Chapter 14, this type of circuit is also called a *latch* because it latches onto data. Here's how we might represent a 1-bit latch without drawing all of the individual components:

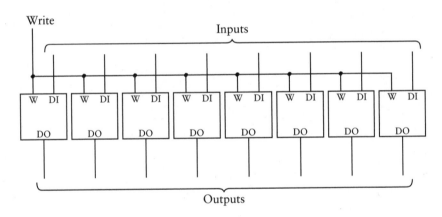

It's fairly easy to assemble multiple 1-bit latches into a multibit latch. All you have to do is connect the Write signals:

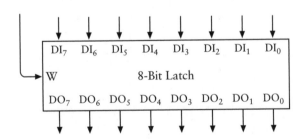

This 8-bit latch has eight inputs and eight outputs. In addition, the latch has a single input named Write that's normally 0. To save an 8-bit value in this latch, make the Write input 1 and then 0 again. This latch can also be drawn as a single box, like so:

Or to be more consistent with the 1-bit latch, it can be drawn this way:

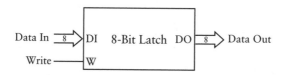

Another way of assembling eight 1-bit latches isn't quite as straightforward as this. Suppose we want only one Data In signal and one Data Out signal. But we want the ability to save the value of the Data In signal at eight different times during the day, or maybe eight different times during the next minute. And we also want the ability to later check those eight values by looking at just one Data Out signal.

In other words, rather than saving one 8-bit value as in the 8-bit latch, we want to save eight separate 1-bit values.

Why do we want to do it this way? Well, maybe because we have only one lightbulb.

We know we need eight 1-bit latches. Let's not worry right now about how data actually gets stored in these latches. Let's focus first on checking the Data Out signals of these eight latches using only one lightbulb. Of course, we could always test the output of each latch by *manually* moving the lightbulb from latch to latch, but we'd prefer something a bit more automated than that. In fact, we'd like to use switches to select which of the eight 1-bit latches we want to look at.

How many switches do we need? If we want to select something from eight items, we need three switches. Three switches can represent eight different values: 000, 001, 010, 011, 100, 101, 110, and 111.

So here are our eight 1-bit latches, three switches, a lightbulb, and something else that we need in between the switches and the lightbulb:

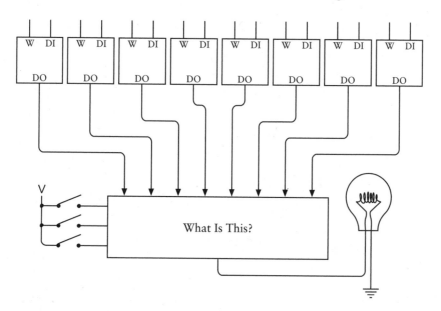

The "something else" is that mysterious box with eight inputs on top and three inputs on the left. By closing and opening the three switches, we can select which of the eight inputs is routed to the output at the bottom of the box. This output lights up the lightbulb.

So what exactly is "What Is This?"? We've encountered something like it before, although not with so many inputs. It's similar to a circuit we used in Chapter 14 in the first revised adding machine. At that time, we needed something that let us select whether a row of switches or the output from a latch was used as an input to the adder. In that chapter, it was called a 2-Line-to-1-Line Selector. Here we need an *8-Line-to-1-Line Data Selector*:

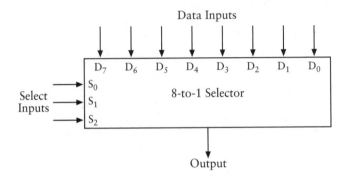

The 8-to-1 Selector has eight Data inputs (shown at the top) and three Select inputs (shown at the left). The Select inputs choose which of the Data inputs appears at the Output. For example, if the Select inputs are 000, the Output is the same as D_0. If the Select inputs are 111, the Output is the same as D_7. If the Select inputs are 101, the Output is the same as D_5. Here's the logic table:

Inputs			Outputs
S_2	S_1	S_0	Q
0	0	0	D_0
0	0	1	D_1
0	1	0	D_2
0	1	1	D_3
1	0	0	D_4
1	0	1	D_5
1	1	0	D_6
1	1	1	D_7

The 8-to-1 Selector is built from three inverters, eight 4-input AND gates, and an 8-input OR gate, like this:

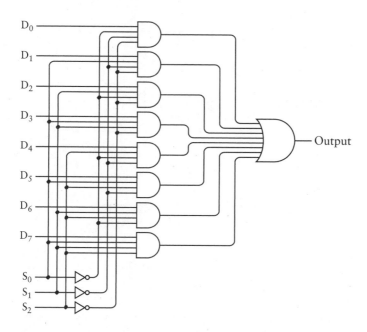

Now, this is a fairly hairy circuit, but perhaps just one example will convince you that it works. Suppose S_2 is 1, S_1 is 0, and S_0 is 1. The inputs to the sixth AND gate from the top include S_0, $\overline{S}_1$, S_2, all of which are 1. No other AND gate has these three inputs, so all the other AND gates will have an output of 0. The sixth AND gate from the top will possibly have an output of 0 if D_5 is 0. Or it will have an output of 1 if D_5 is 1. The same goes for the OR gate at the far right. Thus, if the Select inputs are 101, the Output is the same as D_5.

Let's recap what we're trying to do here. We're trying to wire eight 1-bit latches so that they can be individually written to using a single Data In signal and individually examined using a single Data Out signal. We've already established that we can choose a Data Output signal from one of the eight latches by using an 8-to-1 Selector, as shown on the following page.

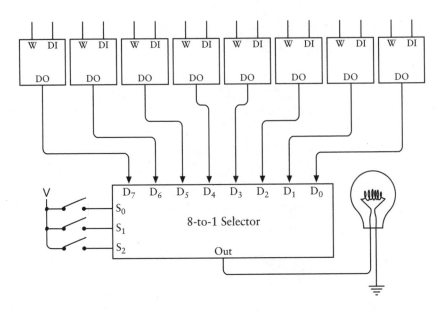

We're halfway finished. Now that we've established what we need for the output side, let's look at the input side.

The input side involves the Data input signals and the Write signal. On the input side of the latches, we can connect all the Data input signals together. But we can't connect the eight Write signals together because we want to be able to write into each latch individually. We have a single Write signal that must be routed to one (and only one) of the latches:

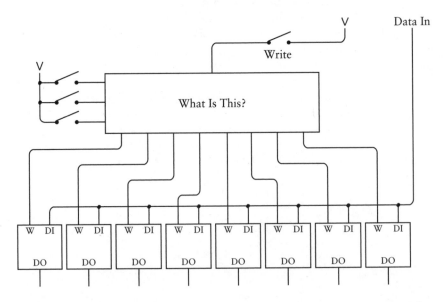

To accomplish this task, we need another circuit that looks somewhat similar to the 8-to-1 Selector but actually does the opposite. This is the

3-to-8 Decoder. We've also seen a simple Data Decoder before—when wiring the switches to select the color of our ideal cat in Chapter 11.

The 3-to-8 Decoder has eight Outputs. At any time, all but one of the Outputs are 0. The exception is the Output that's selected by the S_0, S_1, and S_2 inputs. This Output is the same as the Data Input.

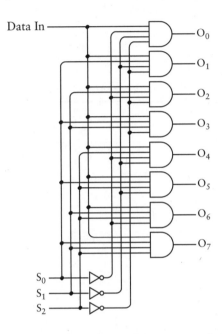

Again, notice that the inputs to the sixth AND gate from the top include S_0, S_1, S_2. No other AND gate has these three inputs. So if the Select inputs are 101, then all the other AND gates will have an output of 0. The sixth AND gate from the top will possibly have an output of 0 if the Data Input is 0 or an output of 1 if the Data Input is 1. Here's the complete logic table:

Inputs			Outputs							
S_2	S_1	S_0	O_7	O_6	O_5	O_4	O_4	O_2	O_1	O_0
0	0	0	0	0	0	0	0	0	0	Data
0	0	1	0	0	0	0	0	0	Data	0
0	1	0	0	0	0	0	0	Data	0	0
0	1	1	0	0	0	0	Data	0	0	0
1	0	0	0	0	0	Data	0	0	0	0
1	0	1	0	0	Data	0	0	0	0	0
1	1	0	0	Data	0	0	0	0	0	0
1	1	1	Data	0	0	0	0	0	0	0

And here's the complete circuit with the 8 latches:

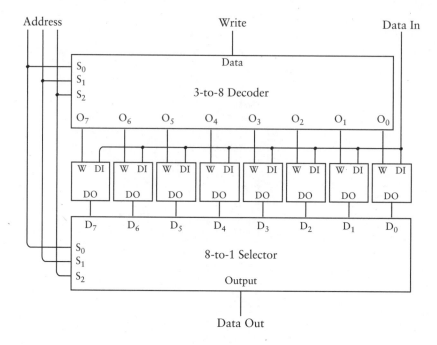

Notice that the three Select signals to the Decoder and the Selector are the same and that I've also labeled those three signals the *Address*. Like a post office box number, this 3-bit address determines which of the eight 1-bit latches is being referenced. On the input side, the Address input determines which latch the Write signal will trigger to store the Data input. On the output side (at the bottom of the figure), the Address input controls the 8-to-1 Selector to select the output of one of the eight latches.

This configuration of latches is sometimes known as *read/write memory*, but more commonly as *random access memory*, or RAM (pronounced the same as the animal). This particular RAM configuration stores eight separate 1-bit values. It can be represented this way:

It's called *memory* because it retains information. It's called *read/write* memory because you can store a new value in each latch (that is, *write* the value) and because you can determine what's stored in each latch (that is, you can later *read* the value). It's called *random access* memory because each of the eight latches can be read from or written to simply by changing the Address inputs. In contrast, some other types of memory have to be read sequentially—that is, you'd have to read the value stored at address 100 before you could read the value stored at address 101.

A particular configuration of RAM is often referred to as a RAM *array*. This particular RAM array is organized in a manner called in abbreviated form *8 × 1* (pronounced *eight by one*). Each of the eight values in the array is 1 bit. Multiply the two values to get the total number of bits that can be stored in the RAM array.

RAM arrays can be combined in various ways. For example, you can take two 8 × 1 RAM arrays and arrange them so that they are addressed in the same way:

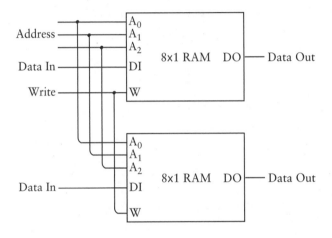

The Address and Write inputs of the two 8 × 1 RAM arrays are connected, so the result is an 8 × 2 RAM array:

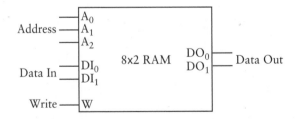

This RAM array stores eight values, but each of them is 2 bits in size.

Or the two 8 × 1 RAM arrays can be combined in much the same way that the individual latches were combined—by using a 2-to-1 Selector and a 1-to-2 Decoder, as shown on the next page.

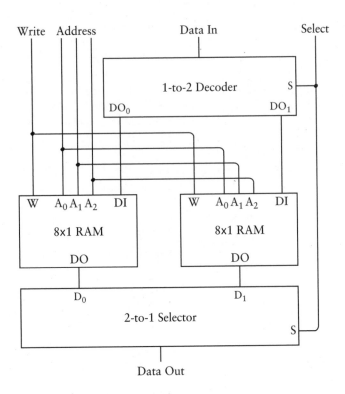

The Select input that goes to both the Decoder and the Selector essentially selects between the two 8 × 1 RAM arrays. It's really a fourth address line. So this is actually a 16 × 1 RAM array:

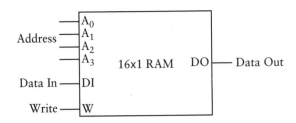

This RAM array stores 16 values, each of which is 1 bit.

The number of values that a RAM array stores is directly related to the number of Address inputs. With no Address inputs (which is the case with the 1-bit latch and the 8-bit latch), only one value can be stored. With one Address input, two values are possible. With two Address inputs, four values are stored. With three Address inputs, eight values, and with four Address inputs, sixteen values. The relationship is summed up by this equation:

$$\text{Number of values in RAM array} = 2^{\text{Number of Address inputs}}$$

I've demonstrated how small RAM arrays can be constructed, and it shouldn't be difficult to imagine much larger ones. For example

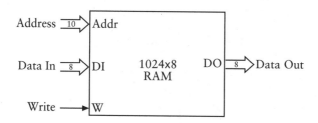

This RAM array stores a total of 8196 bits, organized as 1024 values of eight bits each. There are ten Address inputs because 2^{10} equals 1024. There are eight Data inputs and eight Data outputs.

In other words, this RAM array stores 1024 bytes. It's like a post office with 1024 post office boxes. Each one has a different 1-byte value inside (which may or may not be better than junk mail).

One thousand twenty-four bytes is known as a *kilobyte,* and herein lies much confusion. The prefix *kilo* (from the Greek *khilioi,* meaning a thousand) is most often used in the metric system. For example, a kilogram is 1000 grams and a kilometer is 1000 meters. But here I'm saying that a kilobyte is 1024 bytes—*not* 1000 bytes.

The problem is that the metric system is based on powers of 10, and binary numbers are based on powers of 2, and never the twain shall meet. Powers of 10 are 10, 100, 1000, 10000, 100000, and so on. Powers of 2 are 2, 4, 8, 16, 32, 64, and so on. There is no integral power of 10 that equals some integral power of 2.

But every once in a while they do come close. Yes, 1000 is fairly close to 1024, or to put it more mathematically using an "approximately equal to" sign:

$$2^{10} \approx 10^3$$

Nothing is magical about this relationship. All it implies is that a particular power of 2 is approximately equal to a particular power of 10. This little quirk allows people to conveniently refer to a kilobyte of memory when they really mean 1024 bytes.

Kilobyte is abbreviated K or KB. The RAM array shown above can be said to store 1024 bytes or 1 kilobyte or 1K or 1 KB.

What you *don't* say is that a 1-KB RAM array stores 1000 bytes, or (in English) "one thousand bytes." It's *more* than a thousand—it's 1024. To sound like you know what you're talking about, you say either "1K" or "one kilobyte."

One kilobyte of memory has eight Data inputs, eight Data outputs, and ten Address inputs. Because the bytes are accessed by ten Address inputs, the RAM array stores 2^{10} bytes. Whenever we add another address input, we double the amount of memory. Each line of the following sequence represents a doubling of memory:

1 kilobyte = 1024 bytes = 2^{10} bytes ≈ 10^3 bytes
2 kilobytes = 2048 bytes = 2^{11} bytes
4 kilobytes = 4096 bytes = 2^{12} bytes
8 kilobytes = 8192 bytes = 2^{13} bytes
16 kilobytes = 16,384 bytes = 2^{14} bytes
32 kilobytes = 32,768 bytes = 2^{15} bytes
64 kilobytes = 65,536 bytes = 2^{16} bytes
128 kilobytes = 131,072 bytes = 2^{17} bytes
256 kilobytes = 262,144 bytes = 2^{18} bytes
512 kilobytes = 524,288 bytes = 2^{19} bytes
1,024 kilobytes = 1,048,576 bytes = 2^{20} bytes ≈ 10^6 bytes

Note that the numbers of kilobytes shown on the left are also powers of 2.

With the same logic that lets us call 1024 bytes a kilobyte, we can also refer to 1024 kilobytes as a *megabyte*. (The Greek word *megas* means *great*.) Megabyte is abbreviated MB. And the memory doubling continues:

1 megabyte = 1,048,576 bytes = 2^{20} bytes ≈ 10^6 bytes
2 megabytes = 2,097,152 bytes = 2^{21} bytes
4 megabytes = 4,194,304 bytes = 2^{22} bytes
8 megabytes = 8,388,608 bytes = 2^{23} bytes
16 megabytes = 16,777,216 bytes = 2^{24} bytes
32 megabytes = 33,554,432 bytes = 2^{25} bytes
64 megabytes = 67,108,864 bytes = 2^{26} bytes
128 megabytes = 134,217,728 bytes = 2^{27} bytes
256 megabytes = 268,435,456 bytes = 2^{28} bytes
512 megabytes = 536,870,912 bytes = 2^{29} bytes
1,024 megabytes = 1,073,741,824 bytes = 2^{30} bytes ≈ 10^9 bytes

The Greek work *gigas* means *giant*, so 1024 megabytes are called a *gigabyte*, which is abbreviated GB.

Similarly, a *terabyte* (*teras* means *monster*) equals 2^{40} bytes (approximately 10^{12}) or 1,099,511,627,776 bytes. Terabyte is abbreviated TB.

A kilobyte is approximately a thousand bytes, a megabyte is approximately a million bytes, a gigabyte is approximately a billion bytes, and a terabyte is approximately a trillion bytes.

Ascending into regions that few have traveled, a *petabyte* equals 2^{50} bytes or 1,125,899,906,842,624 bytes, which is approximately 10^{15} or a quadrillion. An *exabyte* equals 2^{60} bytes or 1,152,921,504,606,846,976 bytes, approximately 10^{18} or a quintillion.

Just to provide you with a little grounding here, home computers purchased at the time this book was written (1999) commonly have 32 MB or 64 MB or sometimes 128 MB of random access memory. (And don't get too confused just yet—I haven't mentioned anything about hard drives; I'm talking only about RAM.) That's 33,554,432 bytes or 67,108,864 bytes or 134,217,728 bytes.

People, of course, speak in shorthand. Somebody who has 65,536 bytes of memory will say, "I have 64K (and I'm a visitor from the year 1980)." Somebody who has 33,554,432 bytes will say, "I have 32 megs." That rare person who has 1,073,741,824 bytes of memory will say, "I've got a gig (and I'm not talking music)."

Sometimes people will refer to *kilobits* or *megabits* (notice *bits* rather than *bytes*), but this is rare. Almost always when people talk about memory, they're talking number of bytes, not bits. (Of course, to convert bytes to bits, multiply by 8.) Usually when kilobits or megabits come up in conversation, it will be in connection with data being transmitted over a wire and will occur in such phrases as "kilobits per second" or "megabits per second." For example, a 56K modem refers to 56 kilobits per second, not kilobytes.

Now that we know how to construct RAM in any array size we want, let's not get too out of control. For now, let's simply assume that we have assembled 65,536 bytes of memory:

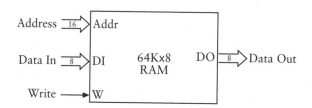

Why 64 KB? Why not 32 KB or 128 KB? *Because 65,536 is a nice round number.* It's 2^{16}. This RAM array has a 16-bit address. In other words, the address is 2 bytes exactly. In hexadecimal, the address ranges from 0000h through FFFFh.

As I implied earlier, 64 KB was a common amount of memory in personal computers purchased around 1980, although it wasn't constructed from telegraph relays. But could you really build such a thing using relays? I trust you won't consider it. Our design requires nine relays for each bit of memory, so the total 64K × 8 RAM array requires almost 5 million of them!

It will be advantageous for us to have a control panel that lets us manage all this memory—to write values into memory or examine them. Such a control panel has 16 switches to indicate an address, 8 switches to define an 8-bit value that we want to write into memory, another switch for the Write signal itself, and 8 lightbulbs to display a particular 8-bit value, as shown on the following page.

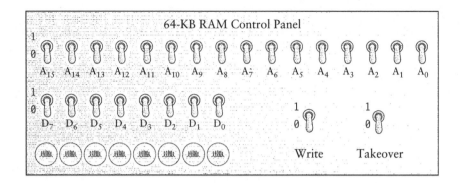

All the switches are shown in their off (0) positions. I've also included a switch labeled *Takeover*. The purpose of this switch is to let other circuits use the same memory that the control panel is connected to. When the switch is set to 0 (as shown), the rest of the switches on the control panel don't do anything. When the switch is set to 1, however, the control panel has exclusive control over the memory.

This is a job for a bunch of 2-to-1 Selectors. In fact, we need 25 of them—16 for the Address signals, 8 for the Data input switches, and another for the Write switch. Here's the circuit:

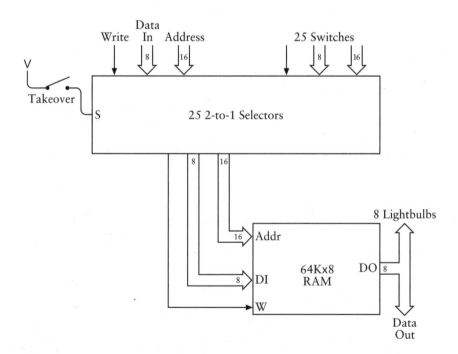

When the Takeover switch is open (as shown), the Address, Data input, and Write inputs to the 64K × 8 RAM array come from external signals shown at the top left of the 2-to-1 Selectors. When the Takeover switch is closed, the Address, Data input, and Write signals to the RAM array come from the switches on the control panel. In either case, the Data Out signals from the RAM array go to the eight lightbulbs and possibly someplace else.

I'll draw a 64K × 8 RAM array with such a control panel this way:

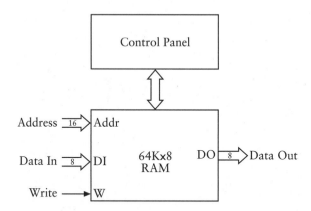

When the Takeover switch is closed, you can use the 16 Address switches to select any of 65,536 addresses. The lightbulbs show you the 8-bit value currently stored in memory at that address. You can use the 8 Data switches to define a new value, and you can write that value into memory using the Write switch.

The 64K × 8 RAM array and control panel can certainly help you keep track of any 65,536 8-bit values you may need to have handy. But we have also left open the opportunity for something else—some other circuitry perhaps—to use the values we have stored in memory and to write other ones in as well.

There's one more thing you have to remember about memory, and it's *very* important: When I introduced the concept of logic gates in Chapter 11, I stopped drawing the individual relays that compose these gates. In particular, I no longer indicated that every relay is connected to some kind of supply of electricity. Whenever a relay is triggered, electricity is flowing through the coils of the electromagnet and holding a metal contact in place.

So if you have a 64K × 8 RAM array filled to the brim with 65,536 of your favorite bytes and you turn off the power to it, what happens? All the electromagnets lose their magnetism and with a loud *thunk,* all the relay contacts return to their untriggered states. And the contents of this RAM? They all go POOF! Gone forever.

This is why random access memory is also called *volatile* memory. It requires a constant supply of electricity to retain its contents.

Chapter Seventeen

Automation

T he human species is often amazingly inventive and industrious but at the same time profoundly lazy. It's very clear that we humans don't like to work. This aversion to work is so extreme—and our ingenuity so acute—that we're eager to devote countless hours designing and building devices that might shave a few minutes off our workday. Few fantasies tickle the human pleasure center more than a vision of relaxing in a hammock watching some newfangled contraption we just built mow the lawn.

I'm afraid I won't be showing plans for an automatic lawn-mowing machine in these pages. But in this chapter, through a progression of ever more sophisticated machines, I *will* automate the process of adding and subtracting numbers. This hardly sounds earth-shattering, I know. But the final machine in this chapter will be so versatile that it will be able to solve virtually any problem that makes use of addition and subtraction, and that includes a great many problems indeed.

Of course, with sophistication comes complexity, so some of this might be rough going. No one will blame you if you skim over the excruciating details. At times, you might rebel and promise that you'll never seek electrical or mechanical assistance for a math problem ever again. But stick with me because by the end of this chapter we'll have invented a machine we can legitimately call a *computer*.

The last adder we looked at was in Chapter 14. That version included an 8-bit latch that accumulated a running total entered on one set of eight switches:

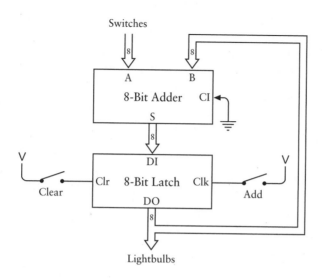

Lightbulbs

As you'll recall, an 8-bit latch uses flip-flops to store an 8-bit value. To use this device, you first momentarily press the Clear switch to set the stored contents of the latch to all zeros. Then you use the switches to enter your first number. The adder simply adds this number to the zero output of the latch, so the result is the number you entered. Pressing the Add switch stores that number in the latch and turns on some lightbulbs to display it. Now you set up the second number on the switches. The adder adds this one to the number stored in the latch. Pressing the Add button again stores the total in the latch and displays it using the lightbulbs. In this way, you can add a whole string of numbers and display the running total. The limitation, of course, is that the eight lightbulbs can't display a total greater than 255.

At the time I showed this circuit to you in Chapter 14, the only latches that I had introduced so far were *level triggered*. In a level-triggered latch, the Clock input has to go to 1 and then back to 0 in order for the latch to store something. During the time the Clock input is 1, the data inputs of the latch can change and these changes will affect the stored output. Later in that chapter, I introduced *edge-triggered* latches. These latches save their values in the brief moment that the Clock input goes from 0 to 1. Edge-triggered latches are often somewhat easier to use, so I want to assume that all the latches in this chapter are edge triggered.

A latch used to accumulate a running total of numbers is called an *accumulator*. But we'll see later in this chapter that an accumulator need not simply accumulate. An accumulator is often a latch that holds first one number and then that number plus or minus another number.

The big problem with the adding machine shown above is fairly obvious: Say you have a list of 100 binary numbers you want to add together. You sit down at the adding machine and doggedly enter each and every number and accumulate the sum. But when you're finished, you discover that a couple of the numbers on the list were incorrect. Now you have to do the whole thing over again.

But maybe not. In the preceding chapter, we used almost 5 million relays to build a RAM array containing 64 KB of memory. We also wired a control panel (shown on page 204) that let us close a switch labeled *Takeover* and literally take over all the writing and reading of this RAM array using switches.

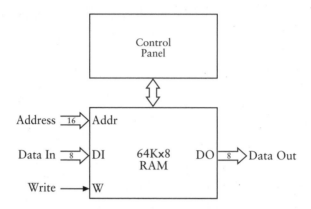

If you had typed all 100 binary numbers into this RAM array rather than directly into the adding machine, making a few corrections would be a lot easier.

So now we face the challenge of connecting the RAM array to the accumulating adder. It's pretty obvious that the RAM Data Out signals replace the switches to the adder, but it's perhaps not so obvious that a 16-bit counter (such as we built in Chapter 14) can control the address signals of the RAM array. The Data Input and Write signals to the RAM aren't needed in this circuit:

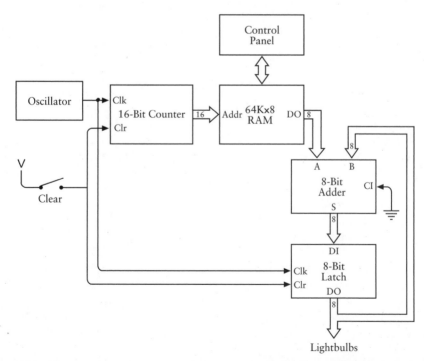

This is certainly not the easiest piece of calculating equipment ever invented. To use it, you first must close the switch labeled Clear. This clears the contents of the latch and sets the output of the 16-bit counter to 0000h. Then you close the Takeover switch on the RAM control panel. You can then enter a set of 8-bit numbers that you want to add beginning at RAM address 0000h. If you have 100 numbers, you'll store these numbers at addresses 0000h through 0063h. (You should also set all the unused entries in the RAM array to 00h.) You can then open the Takeover switch of the RAM control panel (so that the control panel no longer has control over the RAM array) and open the Clear switch. Then just sit back and watch the flashing lightbulbs.

Here's how it works: When the Clear switch is first opened, the address of the RAM array is 0000h. The 8-bit value stored in the RAM array at that address is an input to the adder. The other input to the adder is 00h because the latch is also cleared.

The oscillator provides a clock signal—a signal that alternates between 0 and 1 very quickly. After the Clear switch is opened, whenever the clock changes from a 0 to a 1, two things happen simultaneously: The latch stores the sum from the adder, and the 16-bit counter increments, thus addressing the next value in the RAM array. The first time the clock changes from 0 to 1 after the Clear switch is opened, the latch stores the first value and the counter increments to 0001h. The second time, the latch stores the sum of the first and second values, and the counter increments to 0002h. And so on.

Of course, I'm making some assumptions here. Above all, I'm assuming that the oscillator is slow enough to allow all the rest of the circuitry to work. With each stroke of the clock, a lot of relays must trigger other relays before a valid sum shows up at the output of the adder.

One problem with this circuit is that we have no way of stopping it! At some point, the lightbulbs will stop flashing because all the rest of the numbers in the RAM array will be 00h. At that time, you can read the binary sum. But when the counter eventually reaches FFFFh, it will *roll over* (just like a car odometer) to 0000h and this automated adder will begin adding the numbers again to the sum that was already calculated.

This adding machine has other problems as well. All it does is add, and all it adds are 8-bit numbers. Not only is each number in the RAM array limited to 255, but the sum is limited to 255 as well. The adder also has no way to subtract numbers, although it's possible that you're using negative numbers in two's complements, in which case this machine is limited to handling numbers from −128 through 127. One obvious way to make it add larger numbers (for example, 16-bit values) is to double the width of the RAM array, the adder, and the latch, as well as provide eight more lightbulbs. But you might not be willing to make that investment quite yet.

Of course, I wouldn't even mention these problems unless I knew we were going to solve them eventually. But the problem I want to focus on first is yet another. What if you didn't need to add 100 numbers together in one big sum? What if instead you wanted to use an automated adder to add 50 pairs of numbers to get 50 different sums? Or maybe you'd like a machine versatile enough to add pairs of numbers together, or 10 numbers together, or 100. And you want all the results to be available for your convenient perusal.

The automated adder shown previously displays the running total on a set of lightbulbs attached to the latch. This approach is no good if you want to add 50 pairs of numbers together to get 50 different sums. Instead, you probably want the results to be stored back in the RAM array. That way, you can use the RAM control panel to examine the results at your convenience. That control panel has its own lightbulbs specifically for this purpose.

What this means is that we can get rid of the lightbulbs connected to the latch. But instead, the output from the latch must be connected to the data input of the RAM array so that the sums can be written into the RAM:

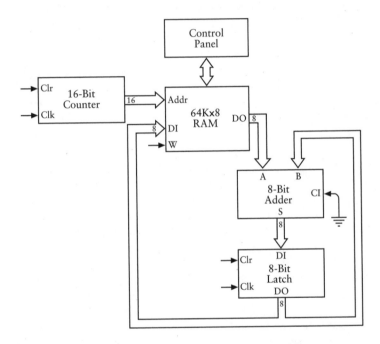

I've eliminated some other parts of the automated adder in this diagram as well, specifically the oscillator and the Clear switch. I removed them because it's no longer at all obvious where the Clear and Clock inputs to the counter and the latch will come from. Moreover, now that we've made use of the RAM data inputs, we need a way to control the RAM Write signal.

So let's not worry about the circuit for a moment and instead focus on the problem we're trying to solve. What we're trying to do here is configure an automated adder so that it's not restricted merely to accumulating a running total of a bunch of numbers. We want to have complete freedom in how many numbers we add and how many different sums are saved in RAM for later examination.

For example, suppose we want to add three numbers together and then add two numbers together and then add another three numbers together. We might imagine typing these numbers into the RAM array beginning at address 0000h so that the contents of the memory look like this:

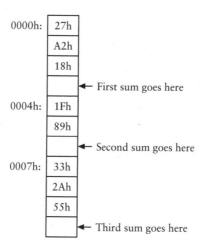

This is how I'll be showing a section of memory in this book. The boxes represent the contents of the memory. Each byte of memory is in a box. The address of that box is at the left. Not every address needs to be indicated because the addresses are sequential and you can always figure out what address applies to a particular box. At the right are some comments about this memory. These particular comments indicate that we want the automated adder to store the three sums in the empty boxes. (Although these boxes are empty, the memory isn't necessarily empty. Memory always contains *something,* even if it's just random data. But right now it doesn't contain anything useful.)

Now I know you're tempted to practice your hexadecimal arithmetic and fill in the little boxes yourself. But that's not the point of this demonstration. We want the automated adder to do the additions for us.

Instead of making the automated adder do just one thing—which in the first version involved adding the contents of a RAM address to the 8-bit latch that I've called the accumulator—we actually want it now to do *four different things.* To begin an addition, we want it to transfer a byte from memory into the accumulator. I'll call this operation *Load.* The second operation we need to perform is to *Add* a byte in memory to the contents of the accumulator. Third, we need to take a sum in the accumulator and *Store* it in memory. Finally, we need some way to *Halt* the automated adder.

In gory detail, what we want the automated adder to do in this particular example is this:

- *Load* the value at address 0000h into the accumulator.
- *Add* the value at address 0001h to the accumulator.
- *Add* the value at address 0002h to the accumulator.
- *Store* the contents of the accumulator at address 0003h.
- *Load* the value at address 0004h into the accumulator.

- *Add* the value at address 0005h to the accumulator.
- *Store* the contents of the accumulator at address 0006h.
- *Load* the value at address 0007h into the accumulator.
- *Add* the value at address 0008h to the accumulator.
- *Add* the value at address 0009h to the accumulator.
- *Store* the contents of the accumulator at address 000Ah.
- *Halt* the workings of the automated adder.

Notice that just as in the original automated adder, each byte of memory is still being addressed sequentially beginning at 0000h. The original automated adder simply added the contents of the memory at that address to the contents of the accumulator. In some cases, we still want to do that. But we also sometimes want to *Load* the accumulator directly with a value in memory or to *Store* the contents of the accumulator in memory. And after everything is done, we want the automated adder to simply stop so that the contents of the RAM array can be examined.

How can we accomplish this? Well, it's not sufficient to simply key in a bunch of numbers in RAM and expect the automated adder to do the right thing. For each number in RAM, we also need some kind of numeric code that indicates what the automated adder is to do: *Load*, *Add*, *Store*, or *Halt*.

Perhaps the easiest (but certainly not the cheapest) way to store these codes is in a whole separate RAM array. This second RAM array is accessed at the same time as the original RAM array. But instead of containing numbers to be added, it contains the codes that indicate what the automated adder is supposed to do with the corresponding address in the original RAM array. These two RAM arrays can be labeled *Data* (the original RAM array) and *Code* (the new one):

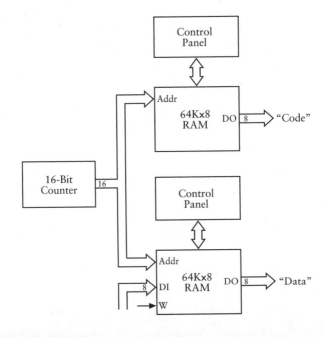

We've already established that our new automated adder needs to be able to write sums into the original RAM array (labeled *Data*). But the new RAM array (labeled *Code*) will be written to solely through the control panel.

We need four codes for the four actions we want the new automated adder to do. These codes can be anything we want to assign. Here are four possibilities:

Operation	Code
Load	10h
Store	11h
Add	20h
Halt	FFh

So to perform the three sets of addition in the example I just outlined, you'll need to use the control panel to store the following values in the Code RAM array:

0000h:	10h	Load
	20h	Add
	20h	Add
	11h	Store
0004h:	10h	Load
	20h	Add
	11h	Store
0007h:	10h	Load
	20h	Add
	20h	Add
	11h	Store
000Bh:	FFh	Halt

You might want to compare the contents of this RAM array with the RAM array containing the data we want to add (shown on page 211). You'll notice that each code in the Code RAM corresponds to a value in the Data RAM that is to be loaded into or added to the accumulator, or the code indicates that a value is to be stored back in memory. Numeric codes used in such a manner are often called *instruction codes*, or *operation codes*, or (most concisely) *opcodes*. They "instruct" circuitry to perform a certain "operation."

As I mentioned earlier, the output of the 8-bit latch in the original automated adder needs to be an input to the Data RAM array. That's how the *Store* instruction works. Another change is necessary: Originally, the output of the 8-Bit Adder was the input to the 8-bit latch. But now, to carry out the *Load* instruction, the output of the Data RAM array must sometimes be the input to the 8-bit latch. What's needed is a 2-Line-to-1-Line Data Selector. The revised automated adder looks like the illustration on the next page.

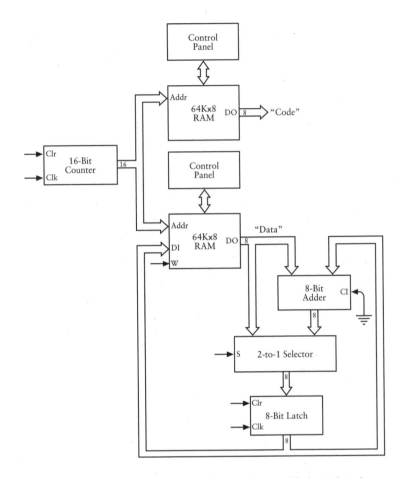

This diagram is missing a few pieces, but it shows all the 8-bit data paths between the various components. The 16-bit counter provides an address for the two RAM arrays. The output of the Data RAM array goes into the 8-Bit Adder, as usual, to perform the *Add* instruction. But the input to the 8-bit latch can be either the output of the Data RAM array (in the case of a *Load* instruction) or the output of the adder (in the case of an *Add* instruction). This situation requires a 2-to-1 Selector. The output of the latch circles back to the adder, as usual, but it's also the data input of the Data RAM array for a *Store* instruction.

What this diagram is missing are all the little signals that control these components, known collectively as the *control* signals. These include the Clock and Clear inputs to the 16-bit counter, the Clock and Clear inputs to the 8-bit latch, the Write input to the Data RAM array, and the Select input to the 2-to-1 Selector. Some of these signals will obviously be based on the output of the Code RAM array. For example, the Select input to the 2-to-1 Selector must be 0 (selecting the Data RAM output) if the output of the Code RAM array indicates a *Load* instruction. The Write input to the Data RAM array must be 1 only when the opcode is a *Store* instruction. These control signals can be generated by various combinations of logic gates.

With a minimal amount of extra hardware and the addition of a new opcode, we can also persuade this circuit to subtract a number from the value in the accumulator. The first step is to expand the table of operation codes:

Operation	Code
Load	10h
Store	11h
Add	20h
Subtract	21h
Halt	FFh

The codes for *Add* and *Subtract* differ only by the least-significant bit of the code value, which we'll call C_0. If the operation code is 21h, the circuit should do the same thing it does for an *Add* instruction, except that the data out from the Data RAM array is inverted before it goes into the adder, and the carry input to the adder is set to 1. The C_0 signal can perform both those tasks in this revised automated adder that includes an inverter:

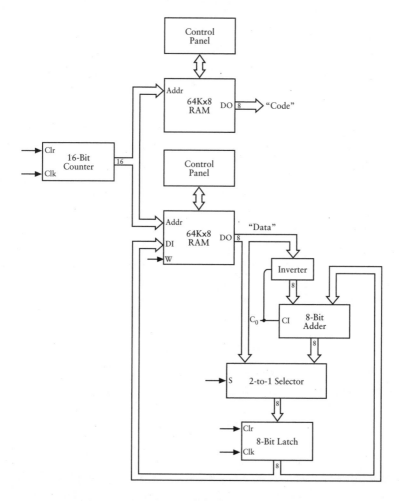

Now suppose we wish to add 56h and 2Ah together and then subtract 38h from the sum. You can do it with the following codes and data stored in the two RAM arrays:

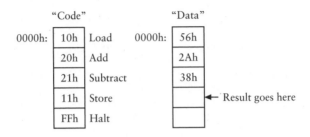

After the *Load* operation, the accumulator contains the value 56h. After the *Add* operation, the accumulator contains the sum of 56h and 2Ah, or 80h. The *Subtract* operation causes the bits of the next value in the Data RAM array (38h) to be inverted. The inverted value C7h is added to 80h with the carry input of the adder set to 1:

$$\begin{array}{r} \text{C7h} \\ +\ \text{80h} \\ +\ \ \ \text{1h} \\ \hline \text{48h} \end{array}$$

The result is 48h. (In decimal, 86 plus 42 minus 56 equals 72.)

One persistent problem that hasn't yet been adequately addressed is the meager 8-bit data width of the adder and everything else that's attached to it. In the past, the only solution I've offered is to connect two 8-Bit Adders (and two of mostly everything else) together to get 16-bit devices.

But a much less expensive solution is possible. Suppose you want to add two 16-bit numbers, for example:

$$\begin{array}{r} \text{76ABh} \\ +\ \text{232Ch} \end{array}$$

This 16-bit addition is the same as separately adding this rightmost byte (often called the *low-order* byte):

$$\begin{array}{r} \text{ABh} \\ +\ \text{2Ch} \\ \hline \text{D7h} \end{array}$$

and then the leftmost, or *high-order,* byte:

$$\begin{array}{r} \text{76h} \\ +\ \text{23h} \\ \hline \text{99h} \end{array}$$

for a result of 99D7h. So if we store the two 16-bit numbers in memory like this:

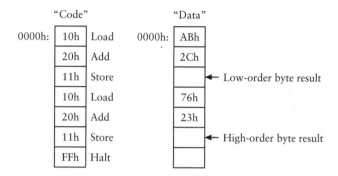

the result D7h will be stored at address 0002h, and the result 99h will be stored at address 0005h.

Of course, this won't work all the time. It works for the numbers I've chosen as an example, but what if the two 16-bit numbers to be added were 76ABh and 236Ch? In that case, adding the 2 low-order bytes results in a carry:

$$\begin{array}{r} \text{ABh} \\ +\ \text{6Ch} \\ \hline \text{117h} \end{array}$$

This carry must be added to the sum of the 2 high-order bytes:

$$\begin{array}{r} \text{1h} \\ +\ \text{76h} \\ +\ \text{23h} \\ \hline \text{9Ah} \end{array}$$

for a final result of 9A17h.

Can we enhance the circuitry of our automated adding machine to add two 16-bit numbers correctly? Yes, we can. All we need do is *save the Carry Out bit* from the 8-Bit Adder when the first addition is performed and then use that Carry Out bit as the Carry Input bit to the next addition. How can a bit be saved? By a 1-bit latch, of course; this time, the latch is known as the *Carry latch*.

To use the Carry latch, another operation code is needed. Let's call it *Add with Carry*. When you're adding 8-bit numbers together, you use the regular old *Add* instruction. The carry input to the adder is 0, and the carry output from the adder is latched in the Carry latch (although it need not be used at all).

If you want to add two 16-bit numbers together, you use the regular *Add* instruction for adding the low-order bytes. The carry input to the adder is 0 and the carry output is latched in the Carry latch. To add the 2 high-order bytes, you use the new *Add with Carry* instruction. In this case, the two numbers are added using the output of the Carry latch as the carry input to the adder. So if the first addition resulted in a carry, that carry bit is used in the second addition. If no carry resulted, the output from the Carry latch is 0.

If you're subtracting one 16-bit number from another, you need another new instruction; this one is called *Subtract with Borrow*. Normally, a *Subtract* instruction requires that you invert the subtrahend and set the carry input of the adder to 1. A carry out of 1 is normal and should usually be ignored. If you're subtracting a 16-bit number, however, that carry output should be saved in the Carry latch. In the second subtraction, the carry input to the adder should be set to the result of the Carry latch.

With the new *Add with Carry* and *Subtract with Borrow* operations, we have a total of seven opcodes so far:

Operation	Code
Load	10h
Store	11h
Add	20h
Subtract	21h
Add with Carry	22h
Subtract with Borrow	23h
Halt	FFh

The number sent to the adder is inverted for a *Subtract* or a *Subtract with Borrow* operation. The carry output of the adder is the data input to the Carry latch. The latch is clocked whenever an *Add, Subtract, Add with Carry,* or *Subtract with Borrow* operation is being performed. The carry input of the 8-Bit Adder is set to 1 when a *Subtract* operation is performed or when the data output of the Carry latch is 1 and an *Add with Carry* or *Subtract with Borrow* operation is being performed.

Keep in mind that the *Add with Carry* instruction causes the carry input of the 8-Bit Adder to be set to 1 only if the previous *Add* or *Add with Carry* instruction resulted in a carry output from the adder. Thus you use the *Add with Carry* instruction whenever you're adding multibyte numbers whether or not the operation is actually needed. To properly code the 16-bit addition shown earlier, you use

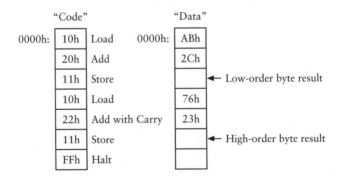

This works correctly regardless of what the numbers are.

With these two new opcodes, we've greatly expanded the scope of the machine. No longer are we restricted to adding 8-bit values. By repeated use of the *Add with Carry* instruction, we can now add 16-bit values, 24-bit values, 32-bit values, 40-bit values, and so on. Suppose we want to add the 32-bit values 7A892BCDh and 65A872FFh. We need one *Add* instruction and three *Add with Carry* instructions:

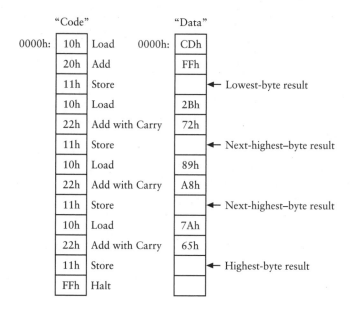

Of course, actually keying these numbers into memory isn't the most rewarding job around. Not only do you have to use switches to represent binary numbers, but the numbers aren't stored in consecutive addresses. For example, the number 7A892BCDh goes into addresses 0000h, 0003h, 0006h, and 0009h starting with the least-significant byte. To get the final result, you have to examine the values located at addresses 0002h, 0005h, 0008h, and 000Bh.

Moreover, the current design of our automated adder doesn't allow the reuse of results in subsequent calculations. Suppose we want to add three 8-bit numbers together and then subtract an 8-bit number from that sum and store the result. That would require a *Load* instruction, two *Add* instructions, a *Subtract*, and a *Store*. But what if we also wanted to subtract other numbers from that original sum? That sum isn't accessible. We'd have to recalculate it every time we needed it.

The problem is that we've built an automated adder that addresses the *Code* memory and the *Data* memory simultaneously and sequentially beginning at address 0000h. Each instruction in the Code memory corresponds to a location in the Data memory at the same address. Once a *Store* instruction causes something to be stored in the Data memory, that value can't later be loaded back into the accumulator.

To fix this problem, I'm going to make a fundamental and excruciating change to the automated adder that will at first seem insanely complicated. But in time, you'll see (I hope) that it opens a wide door of flexibility.

Here we go. We currently have seven opcodes:

Operation	Code
Load	10h
Store	11h
Add	20h
Subtract	21h
Add with Carry	22h
Subtract with Borrow	23h
Halt	FFh

Each of these codes occupies 1 byte in memory. With the exception of the *Halt* code, I now want each of these instructions to require 3 bytes of memory. The first byte will be the code itself, and the next 2 bytes will be a 16-bit memory location. For the *Load* instruction, that address indicates a location in the Data RAM array that contains the byte to be loaded into the accumulator. For the *Add, Subtract, Add with Carry,* and *Subtract with Borrow* instructions, that address indicates the location of the byte that's to be added to or subtracted from the accumulator. For the *Store* instruction, the address indicates where the contents of the accumulator are to be stored.

For example, just about the simplest chore that the current automated adder can do is add two numbers together. To do this, you set up the Code and Data RAM arrays this way:

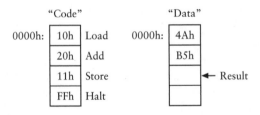

In the revised automated adder, each instruction (except *Halt*) requires 3 bytes:

"Code"

0000h:	10h	Load byte at address 0000h into accumulator
	00h	
	00h	
0003h:	20h	Add byte at address 0001h to accumulator
	00h	
	01h	
0006h:	11h	Store contents of accumulator at address 0002h
	00h	
	02h	
0009h:	FFh	Halt

Each of the instruction codes (except *Halt*) is followed by 2 bytes that indicate a 16-bit address in the Data RAM array. These three addresses happen to be 0000h, 0001h, and 0002h, but they could be anything.

Earlier I showed how to add a pair of 16-bit numbers—specifically 76ABh and 232Ch—using the *Add* and *Add with Carry* instructions. But we had to store the 2 low-order bytes of these numbers at memory locations 0000h and 0001h, and the 2 high-order bytes at 0003h and 0004h. The result of the addition was stored at 0002h and 0005h.

With this change, we can store the two numbers and the result in a more rational manner, and perhaps in an area of memory that we've never used before:

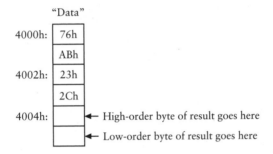

These six locations don't have to be all together like this. They can be scattered anywhere throughout the whole 64-KB Data RAM array. To add these values at these memory locations, you must set up the instructions in the Code RAM array, like this:

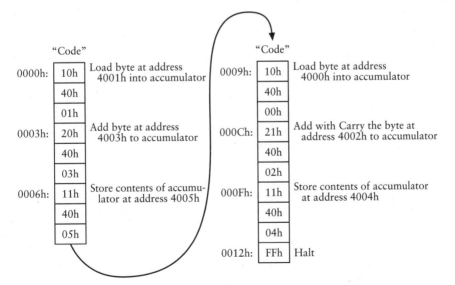

Notice that the 2 low-order bytes located at addresses 4001h and 4003h are added first, with the result stored at address 4005h. The 2 high-order bytes (at addresses 4000h and 4002h) are added with the *Add with Carry* instruction, and the result is stored at address 4004h. And if we were to remove the *Halt* instruction and add more instructions to the Code memory, a subsequent calculation could later make use of the original numbers and the sum of them simply by referring to these memory addresses.

The key to implementing this design is to have the data output of the Code RAM array go into three 8-bit latches. Each of these latches stores one of the bytes of the 3-byte instruction. The first latch stores the instruction code, the second latch stores the high-order byte of the address, and the third latch stores the low-order address byte. The output of the second and third latches becomes the 16-bit address of the Data RAM array:

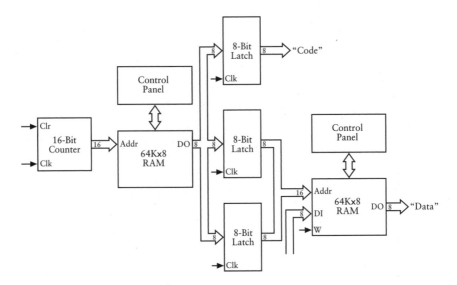

The process of retrieving an instruction from memory is known as the *instruction fetch*. In our machine, each instruction is 3 bytes in length, and it's retrieved from memory 1 byte at a time; the instruction fetch requires three cycles of the Clock signal. The entire *instruction cycle* requires a fourth cycle of the Clock signal. These changes certainly complicate the control signals.

The machine is said to *execute* an instruction when it does a series of actions in response to the instruction code. But it's not as if the machine is *alive* or anything. It's not analyzing the machine code and deciding what to do. Each machine code is just triggering various control signals in a unique way that causes the machine to do various things.

Notice that by making this machine more versatile, we've also slowed it down. Using the same oscillator, it adds numbers at only one-fourth the speed of the first automated adder I showed in this chapter. This is the result of an engineering principle known as TANSTAAFL (pronounced *tans toffle*), which means "There Ain't No Such Thing As A Free Lunch." Usually, whenever you make a machine better in one way, something else tends to suffer as a result.

If you were actually building such a machine out of relays, the bulk of the circuit would obviously be the two 64-KB RAM arrays. Indeed, much earlier you might have skimped on these components and decided that initially you would need only 1 KB of memory. If you made sure you stored everything in addresses 0000h through 03FFh, using less memory than 64 KB would work out just fine.

Still, however, you probably weren't thrilled that you needed *two* RAM arrays. And in fact, you don't. I originally introduced two RAM arrays— one for code and one for data—so that the architecture of the automated adder would be as clear and simple as possible. But now that we've decided to make each instruction 3 bytes long—with the second and third bytes indicating an address where the data is located—it's no longer necessary to have two separate RAM arrays. Both code and data can be stored in the *same* RAM array.

To accomplish this, we need to have a 2-to-1 Selector to determine how the RAM array is addressed. Usually, the address is the 16-bit counter, as before. The RAM Data Out is still connected to three latches that latch the instruction code and the 2 address bytes that accompany each instruction. But the 16-bit address is the second input to the 2-to-1 Selector. After the address is latched, this selector allows the latched address to be the address input to the RAM array:

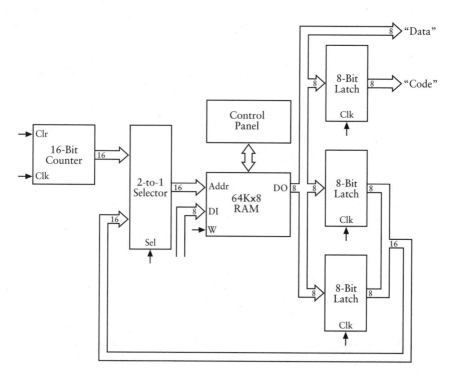

We've made a lot of progress. Now it's possible to enter the instructions and the data in a single RAM array. For example, the diagram on the next page shows how to add two 8-bit numbers together and subtract a third.

0000h:	10h	Load byte at address 0010h into accumulator
	00h	
	10h	
	20h	Add byte at address 0011h to accumulator
	00h	
	11h	
	21h	Subtract byte at address 0012h from accumulator
	00h	
	12h	
	11h	Store byte in accumulator at address 0013h
	00h	
	13h	
000Ch:	FFh	Halt
	⋮	
0010h:	45h	
	A9h	
	8Eh	
		← Final result goes here

As usual, the instructions begin at 0000h because that's where the counter starts accessing the RAM array after it has been reset. The final *Halt* instruction is stored at address 000Ch. We could have stored the three numbers and the results anywhere in the RAM array (except in the first 13 bytes, of course, because those memory locations are occupied by instructions), but we chose to store the data starting at address 0010h.

Now suppose you discover that you need to add two more numbers to that result. Well, you can replace all the instructions you just entered with some new instructions, but maybe you don't want to do that. Maybe you'd prefer to just continue with the new instructions starting at the end of these instructions, first replacing the *Halt* instruction with a new *Load* instruction at address 000Ch. But you also need two new *Add* instructions, a *Store* instruction, and a new *Halt* instruction. Your only problem is that you have some data stored at address 0010h. You have to move that data someplace at a higher memory address. And you then have to change the instructions that refer to those memory instructions.

Hmmm, you think. Maybe combining Code and Data into a single RAM array wasn't such a hot idea after all. But I assure you, a problem such as this would have come up sooner or later. So let's solve it. In this case, maybe what you'd like to do is enter the new instructions beginning at address 0020h and the new data at address 0030h:

0020h:	10h	Load byte at address 0013h into accumulator
	00h	
	13h	
	20h	Add byte at address 0030h to accumulator
	00h	
	30h	
	20h	Add byte at address 0031h to accumulator
	00h	
	31h	
	11h	Store byte in accumulator at address 0032h
	00h	
	32h	
	FFh	Halt
	⋮	
0030h:	43h	
	2Fh	
		← Final result goes here

Notice that the first *Load* instruction refers to the memory location 0013h, which is where the result of the first calculation was stored.

So now we have some instructions starting at address 0000h, some data starting at 0010h, some more instructions at 0020h, and some more data at 0030h. We want to let the automated adding machine start at 0000h and execute all the instructions.

We know we must remove that *Halt* instruction at address 000Ch, and by *remove* I really mean replace it with something else. But is that sufficient? The problem is that whatever we replace the *Halt* instruction with is going to be interpreted as an instruction byte. And so will the bytes stored every 3 bytes after that—at 000Fh, and 0012h, and 0015h, and 0018h, and 001Bh, and 001Eh. What if one of these bytes just happens to be an 11h? That's a *Store* instruction. And what if the 2 bytes following that *Store* instruction happened to refer to address 0023h? That would cause the machine to write the contents of the accumulator to that address. But that address contains something important already! And even if nothing like this happened, the next instruction byte that the adder retrieves from memory after the one at 001Eh will be at address 0021h, not 0020h, which is where our next real instruction happens to be.

Are we all in agreement that we can't just remove the *Halt* instruction at address 000Ch and hope for the best?

But what we *can* replace it with is a new instruction called *Jump*. Let's add that to our repertoire.

Operation	Code
Load	10h
Store	11h
Add	20h
Subtract	21h
Add with Carry	22h
Subtract with Borrow	23h
Jump	30h
Halt	FFh

Normally, this automated adder addresses the RAM array sequentially. A *Jump* instruction causes the machine to alter that pattern. Instead, it begins addressing the RAM array at a different specified address. Such an instruction is sometimes also called a *Branch* instruction, or *Goto*, as in "go to another place."

In the preceding example, we can replace the *Halt* instruction at address 000Ch with a *Jump* instruction:

000Ch: | 30h | Jump to instruction at address 0020h
|---|
| 00h |
| 20h |

The 30h byte is the code for a *Jump* instruction. The 16-bit address that follows indicates the address of the next instruction that the automated adder is to read.

So in the preceding example, the automated adder begins at 0000h, as usual, and does a *Load* instruction, an *Add*, a *Subtract*, and a *Store*. It then does the *Jump* instruction and continues at address 0020h with a *Load*, two *Add* instructions, a *Store*, and finally *Halt*.

The *Jump* instruction affects the 16-bit counter. Whenever the automated adder encounters a *Jump* instruction, the counter must somehow be forced to output that new address that follows the *Jump* instruction code. This is implemented by using the Preset and Clear inputs of the edge-triggered D-type flip-flops that make up the 16-bit counter:

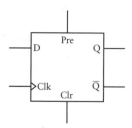

You'll recall that the Preset and Clear inputs should both be 0 for normal operation. But if Preset is 1, Q becomes 1. And if Clear is 1, Q becomes 0.

If you want to load a single flip-flop with a new value (which I'll call *A* for address), you can wire it like this:

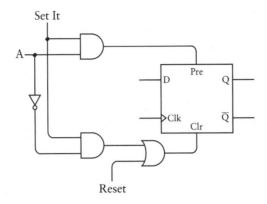

Normally the Set It signal is 0. In that case, the Preset input to the flip-flop is 0. The Clear input is also 0 unless the Reset signal is 1. This allows the flip-flop to be cleared independently of the Set It signal. When the Set It signal is 1, the Preset input will be 1 and the Clear input will be 0 if A is 1. If A is 0, the Preset input will be 0 and the Clear input will be 1. This means that Q will be set to the value of A.

We need one of these for each bit of the 16-bit counter. Once loaded with a particular value, the counter will continue counting from that value on.

Otherwise, the changes aren't severe. The 16-bit address that's latched from the RAM array is an input to both the 2-to-1 Selector (which allows this address to be an address input to the RAM array) and the 16-bit counter for the Set It function:

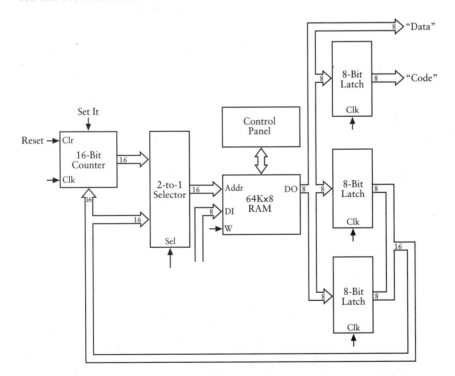

Obviously, we must ensure that the Set It signal is 1 only if the instruction code is 30h and the address has been latched.

The *Jump* instruction is certainly useful. But it's not nearly as useful as an instruction that jumps sometimes but not all the time. Such an instruction is known as a *conditional jump,* and perhaps the best way to show how useful such an instruction can be is to pose a question: How can we persuade our automated adder to *multiply* two 8-bit numbers? For example, how do we get the result for something as simple as A7h times 1Ch?

Easy, right? The result of multiplying two 8-bit values is a 16-bit product. For convenience, all three numbers involved in the multiplication are expressed as 16-bit values. The first job is to decide where you want to put the numbers and the product:

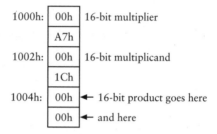

Everyone knows that multiplying A7h and 1Ch (which is 28 in decimal) is the same as 28 additions of A7h. So the 16-bit location at addresses 1004h and 1005h will actually be an accumulated summation. Here's the code for adding A7h to that location once:

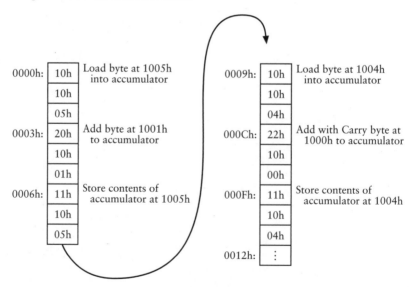

At the completion of these six instructions, the 16-bit value at memory locations 1004h and 1005h will equal A7h times 1. Therefore, these six instructions have to be repeated 27 more times in order for that 16-bit value to equal A7h times 1Ch. You can achieve this by typing in these six instructions 27 more times beginning at address 0012h. Or you can put a *Halt* instruction at 0012h and press the Reset button 28 times to get the final answer.

Of course, neither of these two options is ideal. They both require that you do something—type in a bunch of instructions or press the Reset button—a number of times that's proportional to one of the numbers being multiplied. Surely you wouldn't want to generalize this process for 16-bit values that you want to multiply.

But what if you put a *Jump* instruction at 0012h? This instruction causes the counter to start from 0000h again:

0012h: | 30h | Jump to the instruction at 0000h
       | 00h |
       | 00h |

This certainly does the trick (sort of). The first time through, the 16-bit value at memory locations 1004h and 1005h will equal A7h times 1. Then the *Jump* instruction will go back up to the top. At the end of the second time through, the 16-bit result will equal A7h times 2. Eventually, it will equal A7h times 1Ch, but there's no stopping it. It just keeps going and going and going.

What we want is a *Jump* instruction that starts the process over again only as many times as are needed. That's the conditional jump. And it's really not that hard to implement. The first thing we'll want to add is a 1-bit latch similar to the Carry latch. This will be called the *Zero latch* because it will latch a value of 1 only if the output of the 8-Bit Adder is all zeros:

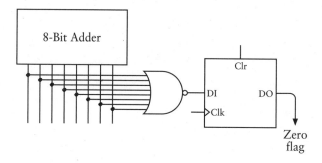

The output of that 8-bit NOR gate is 1 only if all the inputs are 0. Like the Clock input of the Carry latch, the Clock input of the Zero latch latches a value only when an *Add, Subtract, Add with Carry,* or *Subtract with Borrow* instruction is being performed. This latched value is known as the *Zero flag*. Watch out because it could seem as if it's working backward: The Zero flag is 1 if the output of the adder is all zeros, and the Zero flag is 0 if output of the adder is not all zeros.

With the Carry latch and the Zero latch, we can expand our repertoire of instructions by four:

Operation	Code
Load	10h
Store	11h
Add	20h
Subtract	21h
Add with Carry	22h
Subtract with Borrow	23h
Jump	30h
Jump If Zero	31h
Jump If Carry	32h
Jump If Not Zero	33h
Jump If Not Carry	34h
Halt	FFh

For example, the *Jump If Not Zero* instruction jumps to the specified address only if the output of the Zero latch is 0. In other words, there will be *no* jump if the last *Add, Subtract, Add with Carry,* or *Subtract with Borrow* instruction resulted in 0. Implementing this design is just an add-on to the control signals that implement the regular *Jump* command: If the instruction is *Jump If Not Zero*, the Set It signal on the 16-bit counter is triggered only if the Zero flag is 0.

Now all that's necessary to make the code shown above multiply two numbers are the following instructions starting at address 0012h:

0012h:	10h	Load byte at address 1003h into accumulator
	10h	
	03h	
0015h:	20h	Add byte at address 001Eh to accumulator
	00h	
	1Eh	
0018h:	11h	Store byte in accumulator at address 1003h
	10h	
	03h	
001Bh:	33h	Jump to 0000h if the zero flag is not 1
	00h	
	00h	
001Eh:	FFh	Halt

The first time through, the 16-bit location at 0004h and 0005h contains A7h times 1, as we've already established. The instructions here load the byte from location 1003h into the accumulator. This is 1Ch. This byte is added to the value at location 001Eh. This happens to be the *Halt* instruction, but of course it's also a valid number. Adding FFh to 1Ch is the same as subtracting 1 from 1Ch, so the result is 1Bh. This isn't 0, so the Zero flag is 0. The 1Bh byte is stored back at address 1003h. Next is a *Jump If Not Zero* instruction. The Zero flag isn't set to 1, so the jump occurs. The next instruction is the one located at address 0000h.

Keep in mind that the *Store* instruction doesn't affect the Zero flag. The Zero flag is affected only by the *Add, Subtract, Add with Carry,* or *Subtract with Borrow* instruction, so it will remain the same value that was set the last time one of these instructions occurred.

The second time through, the 16-bit location at 1004h and 1005h will contain the value A7h times 2. The value 1Bh is added to FFh to get the result 1Ah. That's not 0, so back to the top.

On the twenty-eighth time through, the 16-bit location at 1004h and 1005h will contain the value A7h times 1Ch. At location 1003h will be the value 1. This will be added to FFh and the result will be zero. The Zero flag will be set! So the *Jump If Not Zero* instruction will *not* jump back to 0000h. Instead, the next instruction is a *Halt*. We're done.

I now assert that at long last we've assembled a piece of hardware that we can honestly call a *computer*. To be sure, it's a primitive computer, but it's a computer nonetheless. What makes the difference is the conditional jump. Controlled repetition or *looping* is what separates computers from calculators. I've just demonstrated how a conditional jump instruction allows this machine to multiply two numbers. In a similar way, it can also divide two numbers. Moreover, it's not limited to 8-bit values. It can add, subtract, multiply, and divide 16-bit, 24-bit, 32-bit, or even larger numbers. And if it can do this, it can calculate square roots, logarithms, and trigonometric functions.

Now that we've assembled a computer, we can start using words that sound like we're talking about computers.

The particular computer that we've assembled is classified as a *digital* computer because it works with discrete numbers. At one time, there were also *analog* computers that are now largely extinct. (Digital data is *discrete* data—data that has certain specific distinct values. Analog information is *continuous* and varies throughout an entire range.)

A digital computer has four main parts: a *processor, memory,* at least one *input* device, and least one *output* device. In our machine, the memory is the 64-KB RAM array. The input and output devices are the rows of switches and lightbulbs on the RAM array control panel. These switches and lightbulbs let us (the human beings in this show) put numbers into memory and examine the results.

The processor is everything else. A processor is also called a *central processing unit,* or CPU. More casually, the processor is sometimes called the *brain* of the computer, but I'd like to avoid using such terminology, mainly because what we designed in this chapter hardly seems anything like a brain to me. (The word *microprocessor* is very common these days. A microprocessor is just a processor that—through use of technology I'll describe in Chapter 18—is very small. What we've built out of relays in this chapter could hardly be defined as a *micro* anything!)

The processor that we've built is an *8-bit* processor. The accumulator is 8 bits wide and most of the data paths are 8 bits wide. The only 16-bit data path is the address to the RAM array. If we used 8 bits for that, we'd be limited to 256 bytes of memory rather than 65,536 bytes, and that would be quite restrictive.

A processor has several components. I've already identified the *accumulator,* which is simply a latch that holds a number inside the processor. In our computer, the 8-bit inverter and the 8-Bit Adder together can be termed the *Arithmetic Logic Unit,* or ALU. Our ALU performs only arithmetic, specifically addition and subtraction. In slightly more sophisticated computers (as we'll see), the ALU can also perform logical functions, such as AND, OR, and XOR. The 16-bit counter is called a *Program Counter.*

The computer that we've built is constructed from relays, wires, switches, and lightbulbs. All of these things are *hardware.* In contrast, the instructions and other numbers that we enter into memory are called *software.* It's "soft" because it can be changed much more easily than the hardware can.

When we speak of computers, the word *software* is almost synonymous with the term *computer program,* or, more simply, *program.* Writing software is known as *computer programming.* Computer programming is what I was doing when I determined the series of instructions that would allow our computer to multiply two numbers together.

Generally, in computer programs, we can distinquish between *code* (which refers to the instructions themselves) and *data,* which are the numbers that the code manipulates. Sometimes the distinction isn't so obvious, as when the *Halt* instruction served double duty as the number −1.

Computer programming is sometimes also referred to as *writing code,* or *coding,* as in, "I spent my vacation coding" or "I was up until seven this morning banging out some code." Sometimes computer programmers are known as *coders,* although some might consider this a derogatory term. Such programmers might prefer to be called *software engineers.*

The operation codes that a processor responds to (such as 10h and 11h for *Load* and *Store*) are known as *machine codes,* or *machine language.* The term *language* is used because it's akin to a spoken or written human language in that a machine "understands" it and responds to it.

I've been referring to the instructions that our machine carries out by rather long phrases, such as *Add with Carry.* Commonly, machine codes are assigned short mnemonics that are written with uppercase letters.

These mnemonics can be as short as 2 or 3 letters. Here's a set of possible mnemonics for the machine codes that our computer recognizes:

Operation	Code	Mnemonic
Load	10h	LOD
Store	11h	STO
Add	20h	ADD
Subtract	21h	SUB
Add with Carry	22h	ADC
Subtract with Borrow	23h	SBB
Jump	30h	JMP
Jump If Zero	31h	JZ
Jump If Carry	32h	JC
Jump If Not Zero	33h	JNZ
Jump If Not Carry	34h	JNC
Halt	FFh	HLT

These mnemonics are particularly useful when combined with a couple of other shortcuts. For example, instead of saying something long-winded like, "Load byte at address 1003h into accumulator," we can instead write the statement:

```
LOD A,[1003h]
```

The *A* and the *[1003]* that appear to the right of the mnemonic are called *arguments* that indicate what's going on with this particular *Load* instruction. The arguments are written with a *destination* on the left (the A stands for accumulator) and a *source* on the right. The brackets indicate that the accumulator should be loaded not with the value 1003h but with the value stored in memory at address 1003h.

Similarly, the instruction "Add byte at address 001Eh to accumulator" can be shortened to

```
ADD A,[001Eh]
```

and "Store contents of accumulator at address 1003h" is

```
STO [1003h],A
```

Notice that the destination (a memory location for the *Store* instruction) is still on the left and the source is on the right. The contents of the accumulator must be stored in memory at address 1003h. The wordy "Jump to 0000h if the Zero flag is not 1" is more concisely written as

```
JNZ 0000h
```

The brackets aren't used in this instruction because the instruction jumps to address 0000h, not to the value that might be stored at address 0000h.

It's convenient to write these instructions in this type of shorthand because the instructions can be listed sequentially in a readable way that doesn't require us to draw boxes of memory locations. To indicate that a particular instruction is stored at a particular address, you can use the hexadecimal address followed by a colon, such as

```
0000h:    LOD A,[1005h]
```

And here's how we can indicate some data stored at a particular address:

```
1000h:    00h, A7h
1002h:    00h, 1Ch
1004h:    00h, 00h
```

The 2 bytes separated by commas indicate that the first byte is stored at the address on the left and the second byte is stored at the next address. These three lines are equivalent to

```
1000h:    00h, A7h, 00h, 1Ch, 00h, 00h
```

So the entire multiplication program can be written as a series of statements like this:

```
0000h:    LOD A,[1005h]
          ADD A,[1001h]
          STO [1005h],A

          LOD A,[1004h]
          ADC A,[1000h]
          STO [1004h],A

          LOD A,[1003h]
          ADD A,[001Eh]
          STO [1003h],A

          JNZ 0000h

001Eh:    HLT

1000h:    00h, A7h
1002h:    00h, 1Ch
1004h:    00h, 00h
```

The judicious use of blank lines and other *white space* is simply to make the whole program more readable for human beings like you and me.

It's better not to use actual numeric addresses when writing code because they can change. For example, if you decided to store the numbers at memory locations 2000h through 20005h, you'd need to rewrite many of the statements as well. It's better to use *labels* to refer to locations in memory. These labels are simply words, or they look almost like words, like this:

```
BEGIN:      LOD A,[RESULT + 1]
            ADD A,[NUM1 + 1]
            STO [RESULT + 1],A

            LOD A,[RESULT]
            ADC A,[NUM1]
            STO [RESULT],A

            LOD A,[NUM2 + 1]
            ADD A,[NEG1]
            STO [NUM2 + 1],A

            JNZ BEGIN

NEG1:       HLT

NUM1:       00h, A7h
NUM2:       00h, 1Ch
RESULT:     00h, 00h
```

Notice that the labels *NUM1*, *NUM2*, and *RESULT* all refer to memory locations where 2 bytes are stored. In these statements, the labels *NUM1 + 1*, *NUM2 + 1*, and *RESULT + 1* refer to the second byte after the particular label. Notice the *NEG1* (*negative one*) label on the *HLT* instruction.

Finally, if there's a chance that you'll forget what these statements do, you can add little *comments,* which are in English and are separated from the actual statements by a semicolon:

```
BEGIN:      LOD A,[RESULT + 1]
            ADD A,[NUM1 + 1]       ; Add low-order byte
            STO [RESULT + 1],A

            LOD A,[RESULT]
            ADC A,[NUM1]           ; Add high-order byte
            STO [RESULT],A

            LOD A,[NUM2 + 1]
            ADD A,[NEG1]           ; Decrement second number
            STO [NUM2 + 1],A

            JNZ BEGIN

NEG1:       HLT

NUM1:       00h, A7h
NUM2:       00h, 1Ch
RESULT:     00h, 00h
```

I'm showing you here a type of computer programming language known as *assembly language*. It's something of a compromise between the naked numbers of machine code and the wordiness of our English descriptions of the instructions, coupled with symbolic representations of memory addresses. People are sometimes confused about the difference between machine code and assembly language because they're really just two different ways of looking at the same thing. Every statement in assembly language corresponds to certain specific bytes of machine code.

If you were to write a program for the computer that we've built in this chapter, you'd probably want to write it first (on paper) in assembly language. Then, once you were satisfied that it was mostly correct and ready to be tested, you would *hand assemble* it: This means that you would manually convert each assembly-language statement to machine code, still on paper. At that point, you can use the switches to enter the machine code into the RAM array and *run the program,* which means to let the machine execute the instructions.

When you're learning the concepts of computer programming, it's never too early to get acquainted with *bugs*. When you're coding—particularly in machine code—it's very easy to make mistakes. It's bad enough to enter a number incorrectly, but what happens when you enter an instruction code incorrectly? If you enter a 11h (the *Store* instruction) when you really meant to enter a 10h (the *Load* instruction), not only will the machine not load in the number it's supposed to, but that number will be overwritten by whatever happens to be in the accumulator.

Some bugs can have unpredictable results. Suppose you use the *Jump* instruction to jump to a location that doesn't contain a valid instruction code. Or suppose you accidentally use the *Store* instruction to write over instructions. Anything can happen (and often does).

There's even a bug in my multiplication program. If you run it twice, the second time through it will multiply A7h by 256 and add that result to the result already calculated. This is because after you run the program once, the number at address 1003h will be 0. When you run it the second time, FFh will be added to that value. The result won't be 0, so the program will keep running until it is.

We've seen that this machine can do multiplication, and in a similar way it can also do division. I've also asserted that this machine can use these primitive functions to do square roots, logarithms, and trigonometric functions. All a machine needs is the hardware to add and subtract and some way to use conditional jump instructions to execute the proper code. As a programmer might say, "I can do the rest in software."

Of course, this software might be quite complex. Many whole books have been written that describe the *algorithms* that programmers use to solve specific problems. We're not yet ready for that. We've been thinking about whole numbers and haven't taken a crack at how to represent decimal fractions in the computer. I'll get to that in Chapter 23.

I've mentioned several times that all the hardware to build these devices was available over a hundred years ago. But it's unlikely that the computer shown in this chapter could have been built at that time. Many of the concepts implicit in its design weren't apparent when relay computers were first built in the mid-1930s and only started to be understood around 1945 or so. Until that time, for example, people were still trying to build computers that internally used decimal numbers rather than binary. And computer programs weren't always stored in memory but instead were sometimes coded on paper tape. In particular, in the early days of computers, memory was expensive and bulky. Building a 64-KB RAM array from five million telegraph relays would have been as absurd one hundred years ago as it is now.

It's time to put what we've done in perspective and to review the history of calculation and computing devices and machines. Perhaps we shall find that we don't have to build this elaborate relay computer after all. As I mentioned in Chapter 12, relays were eventually replaced with electronic devices such as vacuum tubes and transistors. Perhaps we shall also find that someone else has built something that's equivalent to the processor and the memory we designed but that can fit in the palm of your hand.

Chapter Eighteen

From Abaci to Chips

T hroughout recorded history, people have invented numerous clever gadgets and machines in a universal quest to make mathematical calculations just a little bit easier. While the human species seemingly has an innate numerical ability, we also require frequent assistance. We can often conceive of problems that we can't easily solve ourselves.

The development of number systems can be seen as an early tool to help people keep track of commodities and property. Many cultures, including the ancient Greeks and native Americans, seem to have counted with the assistance also of pebbles or kernels of grain. In Europe, this led to counting boards, and in the Middle East to the familiar frame-and-bead abacus:

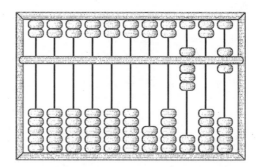

Although commonly associated with Asian cultures, the abacus seems to have been introduced to China by traders around 1200 CE.

No one has ever really enjoyed multiplication and division, but few people have done anything about it. The Scottish mathematician John Napier (1550–1617) was one of those few. He invented logarithms for the specific purpose of simplifying these operations. The product of two numbers is simply the sum of their logarithms. So if you need to multiply two numbers, you look them up in a table of logarithms, add the numbers from the table, and then use the table in reverse to find the actual product.

The construction of tables of logarithms occupied some of the greatest minds of the subsequent 400 years while others designed little gadgets to use in place of these tables. The slide rule has a long history beginning with a logarithmic scale made by Edmund Gunter (1581–1626) and refined by William Oughtred (1574–1660). The history of the slide rule effectively ended in 1976, when the Keuffel & Esser Company presented its last manufactured slide rule to the Smithsonian Institution in Washington D.C. The cause of death was the hand-held calculator.

Napier also invented another multiplication aid, which is composed of strips of numbers usually inscribed on bone, horn, or ivory and hence referred to as *Napier's Bones*. The earliest mechanical calculator was a somewhat automated version of Napier's bones built around 1620 by Wilhelm Schickard (1592–1635). Other calculators based on interlocking wheels, gears, and levers are almost as old. Two of the more significant builders of mechanical calculators were the mathematicians and philosophers Blaise Pascal (1623–1662) and Gottfried Wilhelm von Leibniz (1646–1716).

You'll no doubt recall what a nuisance the carry bit was in both the original 8-Bit Adder and the computer that (among other things) automated the addition of numbers wider than 8 bits. The carry seems at first to be just a little quirk of addition, but in adding machines, the carry is really the central problem. If you've designed an adding machine that does everything except the carry, you're nowhere close to being finished!

How successfully the carry is dealt with is a key to the evaluation of old calculating machines. For example, Pascal's design of the carry mechanism prohibited the machine from subtracting. To subtract, the nines' complement had to be added the way that I demonstrated in Chapter 13. Successful mechanical calculators that real people could use weren't available until the late nineteenth century.

One curious invention that was to have a later influence on the history of computing—as well as a profound influence on the textile industry—was an automated loom developed by Joseph Marie Jacquard (1752–1834). The Jacquard loom (circa 1801) used metal cards with holes punched in them (much like those of a player piano) to control the weaving of patterns in fabrics. Jacquard's own tour de force was a self-portrait in black and white silk that required about 10,000 cards.

In the eighteenth century (and indeed up to the 1940s), a *computer* was a person who calculated numbers for hire. Tables of logarithms were always needed, and trigonometric tables were essential for nautical navigation using the stars and planets. If you wanted to publish a new set of tables, you would hire a bunch of computers, set them to work, and then assemble all the results. Errors could creep in at any stage of this process, of course, from the initial calculation to setting up the type to print the final pages.

The desire to eliminate errors from mathematical tables motivated the work of Charles Babbage (1791–1871), a British mathematician and economist who was almost an exact contemporary of Samuel Morse.

At the time, mathematical tables (of logarithms, for example) were *not* created by calculating an actual logarithm for each and every entry in the table. This would have taken far too long. Instead, the logarithms were calculated for select numbers, and then numbers in between were calculated by interpolation, using what are called *differences* in relatively simple calculations.

Beginning about 1820, Babbage believed that he could design and build a machine that would automate the process of constructing a table, even to the point of setting up type for printing. This would eliminate errors. He conceived the Difference Engine, and basically it was a big mechanical adding machine. Multidigit decimal numbers were represented by geared wheels that could be in any of 10 positions. Negatives were handled using the ten's complement. Despite some early models that showed Babbage's design to be sound and some grants from the British government (never enough, of course), the Difference Engine was never completed. Babbage abandoned work on it in 1833.

By that time, however, Babbage had an even better idea. It was called the Analytical Engine, and through repeated design and redesign (with a few small models and parts of it actually built) it consumed Babbage off and on until his death. The Analytical Engine is the closest thing to a computer that the nineteenth century has to offer. In Babbage's design, it had a *store* (comparable to our concept of memory) and a *mill* (the arithmetic unit). Multiplication could be handled by repeated addition, and division by repeated subtraction.

What's most intriguing about the Analytical Engine is that it could be programmed using cards that were adapted from the cards used in the Jacquard pattern-weaving loom. As Augusta Ada Byron, Countess of Lovelace (1815–1852), put it (in notes to her translation of an article written by an Italian mathematician about Babbage's Analytical Engine), "We may say that the Analytical Engine weaves algebraical patterns just as the Jacquard-loom weaves flowers and leaves."

Babbage seems to be the first person to understand the importance of a conditional jump in computers. Here's Ada Byron again: "A *cycle* of operations, then, must be understood to signify any *set of operations* which is repeated *more than once*. It is equally a *cycle*, whether it be repeated *twice* only, or an indefinite number of times; for it is the fact of a *repetition occurring at all* that constitutes it such. In many cases of analysis there is a *recurring group* of one or more cycles; that is, a *cycle of cycle*, or a *cycle of cycles*."

Although a difference engine was eventually built by father-and-son team Georg and Edvard Scheutz in 1853, Babbage's engines were forgotten for many years, only to be resurrected in the 1930s when people began searching for the roots of twentieth century computing. By that time, everything Babbage had done had already been surpassed by later technology, and he had little to offer the twentieth century computer engineer except a precocious vision of automation.

Another milestone in the history of computing resulted from Article I, Section 2, of the Constitution of the United States of America. Among other things, this section calls for a census to be taken every ten years. By the time of the 1880 census, information was accumulated on age, sex, and national origin. The data amassed took about seven years to process.

Fearing that the 1890 census would take longer than a decade to process, the Census Office explored the possibility of automating the system and chose machinery developed by Herman Hollerith (1860–1929), who had worked as a statistician for the 1880 census.

Hollerith's plan involved manila punch cards 6 ⅝ × 3 ¼ inches in size. (It's unlikely that Hollerith knew about Charles Babbage's use of cards to program his Analytical Engine, but he was almost certainly familiar with the use of cards in the Jacquard loom.) The holes in these cards were organized into 24 columns of 12 positions each, for a total of 288 positions. These positions represented certain characteristics of a person being tallied in the census. The census taker indicated these characteristics by punching ¼-inch square holes into the appropriate positions on the card.

This book has probably so accustomed you to thinking in terms of binary codes that you might immediately assume that a card with 288 possible punches is capable of storing 288 bits of information. But the cards weren't used that way.

For example, a census card used in a purely binary system would have one position for sex. It would be either punched for male or unpunched for female (or the other way around). But Hollerith's cards had two positions for sex. One position was punched for male, the other for female. Likewise, the census taker indicated a subject's age by making two punches. The first punch designated a five-year age range: 0 through 4, 5 through 9, 10 through 14, and so forth. The second punch was in one of five positions to indicate the precise age within that range. Coding the age required a total of 28 positions on the card. A pure binary system would require just 7 positions to code any age from 0 through 127.

We should forgive Hollerith for not implementing a binary system for recording census information: Converting an age to binary numbers was a little too much to ask of the 1890 census takers. There's also a practical reason why a system of punched cards can't be entirely binary. A binary system would produce cases in which *all* the holes (or nearly all) were punched, rendering the card very fragile and structurally unsound.

Census data is collected so that it can be counted, or *tabulated*. You want to know how many people live in each census district, of course, but it's also interesting to obtain information about the age distribution of the population. For this, Hollerith created a tabulating machine that combined hand operation and automation. An operator pressed a board containing 288 spring-loaded pins on each card. Pins corresponding to punched holes in the cards came into contact with a pool of mercury that completed an electrical circuit that triggered an electromagnet that incremented a decimal counter.

Hollerith also used electromagnets in a machine that sorted cards. For example, you might want to accumulate separate age statistics for each occupation that you've tallied. You first need to sort the cards by occupation and then accumulate the age statistics separately for each. The sorting machine used the same hand press as the tabulator, but the sorter had electromagnets to open a hatch to one of 26 separate compartments. The operator dropped the card into the compartment and manually closed the hatch.

This experiment in automating the 1890 census was a resounding success. All told, over 62 million cards were processed. They contained twice as much data as was accumulated in the 1880 census, and the data was processed in about one-third the time. Hollerith and his inventions became known around the world. In 1895, he even traveled to Moscow and succeeded in selling his equipment for use in the very first Russian census, which occurred in 1897.

Herman Hollerith also set in motion a long trail of events. In 1896, he founded the Tabulating Machine Company to lease and sell the punch-card equipment. By 1911, with the help of a couple of mergers, it had become the Computing-Tabulating-Recording Company, or C-T-R. By 1915, the president of C-T-R was Thomas J. Watson (1874–1956), who in 1924 changed the name of the company to International Business Machines Corporation, or IBM.

By 1928, the original 1890 census cards had evolved into the famous "do not spindle, fold, or mutilate" IBM cards, with 80 columns and 12 rows. They remained in active use for over 50 years, and even in their later years were sometimes referred to as *Hollerith cards*. I'll describe the legacy of these cards more in Chapters 20, 21, and 24.

Before we move on to the twentieth century, let's not leave the nineteenth century with too warped a view about that era. For obvious reasons, in this book I've been focusing most closely on inventions that are digital in nature. These include the telegraph, Braille, Babbage's engines, and the Hollerith card. When working with digital concepts and devices, you might find it easy to think that the whole world must be digital. But the nineteenth century is characterized more by discoveries and inventions that were decidedly *not* digital. Indeed, very little of the natural world that we experience through our senses is digital. It's instead mostly a continuum that can't be so easily quantified.

Although Hollerith used relays in his card tabulators and sorters, people didn't really begin building computers using relays—*electromechanical* computers, as they were eventually called—until the mid 1930s. The relays used in these machines were generally not telegraph relays, but instead were relays developed for the telephone system to control the routing of calls.

Those early relay computers were *not* like the relay computer that we built in the last chapter. (As we'll see, I based the design of that computer on microprocessors from the 1970s.) In particular, while it's obvious to us today that computers internally should use binary numbers, that wasn't always the case.

Another difference between our relay computer and the early real ones is that nobody in the 1930s was crazy enough to construct 524,288 bits of memory out of relays! The cost and space and power requirements would have made so much memory impossible. The scant memory available was used only for storing intermediate results. The programs themselves were on a physical medium such as a paper tape with punched holes. Indeed, our process of putting code and data into memory is a more modern concept.

Chronologically, the first relay computer seems to have been constructed by Conrad Zuse (1910–1995), who as an engineering student in 1935 began building a machine in his parents' apartment in Berlin. It used binary numbers but in the early versions used a mechanical memory scheme rather than relays. Zuse punched holes in old 35mm movie film to program his computers.

In 1937, George Stibitz (1904–1995) of Bell Telephone Laboratories took home a couple of telephone relays and wired a 1-bit adder on his kitchen table that his wife later dubbed the K Machine (K for kitchen). This experimentation led to Bell Labs' Complex Number Computer in 1939.

Meanwhile, Harvard graduate student Howard Aiken (1900–1973) needed some way to do lots of repetitive calculations, and that led to a collaboration between Harvard and IBM that resulted in the Automated Sequence Controlled Calculator (ASCC) eventually known as the Harvard Mark I, completed in 1943. This was the first digital computer that printed tables, thus finally realizing Charles Babbage's dream. The Mark II was the largest relay-based machine, using 13,000 relays. The Harvard Computation Laboratory headed by Aiken taught the first classes in computer science.

Relays weren't perfect devices for constructing computers. Because they were mechanical and worked by bending pieces of metal, they could break after an extended workout. A relay could also fail because of a piece of dirt or paper stuck between the contacts. In one famous incident in 1947, a moth was extracted from a relay in the Harvard Mark II computer. Grace Murray Hopper (1906–1992), who had joined Aiken's staff in 1944 and who would later become quite famous in the field of computer programming languages, taped the moth to the computer logbook with the note "first actual case of bug being found."

A possible replacement for the relay is the vacuum tube, which was developed by John Ambrose Fleming (1849–1945) and Lee de Forest (1873–1961) in connection with radio. By the 1940s, vacuum tubes had long been used to amplify telephones, and virtually every home had a console radio set filled with glowing tubes that amplified radio signals to make them audible. Vacuum tubes can also be wired—much like relays—into AND, OR, NAND, and NOR gates.

It doesn't matter whether gates are built from relays or vacuum tubes. Gates can always be assembled into adders, selectors, decoders, flip-flops, and counters. Everything I explained about relay-based components in the preceding chapters remains valid when the relays are replaced by vacuum tubes.

Vacuum tubes had their own problems, though. They were expensive, required a lot of electricity, and generated a lot of heat. The big problem, however, was that they eventually burned out. This was a fact of life that people lived with. Those who owned tube radios were accustomed to replacing tubes periodically. The telephone system was designed with a lot of redundancy, so the loss of a tube now and then was no big deal. (No one expects the telephone system to work flawlessly anyway.) When a tube burns out in a computer, however, it might not be immediately detected. Moreover, a computer uses so *many* vacuum tubes, that statistically they might be burning out every few minutes.

The big advantage of using vacuum tubes over relays is that tubes can switch in about a millionth of a second—one *microsecond*. A vacuum tube changes state (switches on or off) a thousand times faster than a relay, which at its very best only manages to switch in about 1 millisecond, a thousandth of a second. Interestingly enough, the speed issue wasn't a major consideration in early computer development because overall computing speed was linked to the speed that the machine read the program from the paper or film tape. As long as computers were built in this way, it didn't matter how much faster vacuum tubes were than relays.

But beginning in the early 1940s, vacuum tubes began supplanting relays in new computers. By 1945, the transition was complete. While relay machines were known as electromechanical computers, vacuum tubes were the basis of the first *electronic* computers.

In Great Britain, the Colossus computer (first operational in 1943) was dedicated to cracking the German "Enigma" code-making machine. Contributing to this project (and to some later British computer projects) was Alan M. Turing (1912–1954), who is most famous these days for writing two influential papers. The first, published in 1937, pioneered the concept of "computability," which is an analysis of what computers can and can't do. He conceived of an abstract model of a computer that's now known as the Turing Machine. The second famous paper Turing wrote was on the subject of artificial intelligence. He introduced a test for machine intelligence that's now known as the Turing Test.

At the Moore School of Electrical Engineering (University of Pennsylvania), J. Presper Eckert (1919–1995) and John Mauchly (1907–1980) designed the ENIAC (Electronic Numerical Integrator and Computer). It used 18,000 vacuum tubes and was completed in late 1945. In sheer tonnage (about 30), the ENIAC was the largest computer that was ever (and probably will ever be) made. By 1977, you could buy a faster computer at Radio Shack. Eckert and Mauchly's attempt to patent the computer was, however, thwarted by a competing claim of John V. Atanasoff (1903–1995), who earlier designed an electronic computer that never worked quite right.

The ENIAC attracted the interest of mathematician John von Neumann (1903–1957). Since 1930, the Hungarian-born von Neumann (whose last name is pronounced *noy mahn*) had been living in the United States. A flamboyant man who had a reputation for doing complex arithmetic in his head, von Neumann was a mathematics professor at the Princeton Institute for Advanced Study, and he did research in everything from quantum mechanics to the application of game theory to economics.

John von Neumann helped design the successor to the ENIAC, the EDVAC (Electronic Discrete Variable Automatic Computer). Particularly in the 1946 paper "Preliminary Discussion of the Logical Design of an Electronic Computing Instrument," coauthored with Arthur W. Burks and Herman H. Goldstine, he described several features of a computer that made the EDVAC a considerable advance over the ENIAC. The designers of the EDVAC felt that the computer should use binary numbers internally. The ENIAC used decimal numbers. The computer should also have as much memory as possible, and this memory should be used for storing both program code and data as the program was being executed. (Again, this wasn't the case with the ENIAC. Programming the ENIAC was a matter of throwing switches and plugging in cables.) These instructions should be sequential in memory and addressed with a program counter but should also allow conditional jumps. This design came to be known as the *stored-program concept*.

These design decisions were such an important evolutionary step that today we speak of *von Neumann architecture*. The computer that we built in the last chapter was a classic von Neumann machine. But with von Neumann architecture comes the *von Neumann bottleneck*. A von Neumann machine generally spends a significant amount of time just fetching instructions from memory in preparation for executing them. You'll recall that the final design of the Chapter 17 computer required that three-quarters of the time it spent on each instruction be involved in the instruction fetch.

At the time of the EDVAC, it wasn't cost effective to build a lot of memory out of vacuum tubes. Some very odd solutions were proposed instead. One successful one was *mercury delay line memory,* which used 5-foot tubes of mercury. At one end of the tube, little pulses were sent into the mercury about 1 microsecond apart. These pulses took about a millisecond to reach the other end (where they were detected like sound waves and routed back to the beginning), and hence each tube of mercury could store about 1024 bits of information.

It wasn't until the mid-1950s that *magnetic core memory* was developed. Such memory consisted of large arrays of little magnetized metal rings strung with wires. Each little ring could store a bit of information. Long after core memory had been replaced by other technologies, it was common to hear older programmers refer to the memory that the processor accessed as *core*.

John von Neumann wasn't the only person doing some major conceptual thinking about the nature of computers in the 1940s.

Claude Shannon (born 1916) was another influential thinker. In Chapter 11, I discussed his 1938 master's thesis, which established the relationship between switches, relays, and Boolean algebra. In 1948, while working for Bell Telephone Laboratories, he published a paper in the *Bell System Technical Journal* entitled "A Mathematical Theory of Communication" that not only introduced the word *bit* in print but established a field of study today known as *information theory*. Information theory is concerned with transmitting digital information in the presence of noise (which usually prevents all the information from getting through) and how to compensate for that. In 1949, he wrote the first article about programming a computer to play chess, and in 1952 he designed a mechanical mouse controlled by relays that could learn its way around a maze. Shannon was also well known at Bell Labs for riding a unicycle and juggling simultaneously.

Norbert Wiener (1894–1964), who earned his Ph.D. in mathematics from Harvard at the age of 18, is most famous for his book *Cybernetics, or Control and Communication in the Animal and Machine* (1948). He coined the word *cybernetics* (derived from the Greek for *steersman*) to identify a theory that related biological processes in humans and animals to the mechanics of computers and robots. In popular culture, the ubiquitous *cyber-* prefix now denotes anything related to the computer. Most notably, the interconnection of millions of computers through the Internet is known as *cyberspace,* a word coined by *cyberpunk* science-fiction novelist William Gibson in his 1984 novel *Neuromancer*.

In 1948, the Eckert-Mauchly Computer Corporation (later part of Remington Rand) began work on what would become the first commercially available computer—the Universal Automatic Computer, or UNIVAC. It was completed in 1951, and the first one was delivered to the Bureau of the Census. The UNIVAC made its prime-time network debut on CBS, when it was used to predict results of the 1952 presidential election. Walter Cronkite referred to it as an "electronic brain." Also in 1952, IBM announced the company's first commercial computer system, the 701.

And thus began a long history of corporate and governmental computing. However interesting that history might be, we're going to pursue another historical track—a track that shrank the cost and size of computers and brought them into the home, and which began with an almost unnoticed electronics breakthrough in 1947.

Bell Telephone Laboratories was for many years a place where smart people could work on just about anything that interested them. Some of them, fortunately, were interested in computers. I've already mentioned George Stibitz and Claude Shannon, both of whom made significant contributions to early computing while working at Bell Labs. Later on, in the 1970s, Bell Labs was the birthplace of the influential computer operating system named Unix and a programming language named C, which I'll describe in upcoming chapters.

Bell Labs came about when American Telephone and Telegraph officially separated their scientific and technical research divisions from the rest of their business, creating the subsidiary on January 1, 1925. The primary purpose of Bell Labs was to develop technologies for improving the telephone system. That mandate was fortunately vague enough to encompass all sorts of things, but one obvious perennial goal within the telephone system was the undistorted amplification of voice signals transmitted over wires.

Since 1912, the Bell System had worked with vacuum tube amplification, and a considerable amount of research and engineering went into improving vacuum tubes for use by the telephone system. Despite this work, vacuum tubes still left much to be desired. Tubes were large, consumed a lot of power, and eventually burned out. But they were the only game in town.

All that changed December 16, 1947, when two physicists at Bell Labs named John Bardeen (1908–1991) and Walter Brattain (1902–1987) wired a different type of amplifier. This new amplifier was constructed from a slab of germanium—an element known as a *semiconductor*—and a strip of gold foil. They demonstrated it to their boss, William Shockley (1910–1989), a week later. It was the first *transistor,* a device that some people have called the most important invention of the twentieth century.

The transistor didn't come out of the blue. Eight years earlier, on December 29, 1939, Shockley had written in his notebook, "It has today occurred to me that an amplifier using semiconductors rather than vacuum is in principle possible." And after that first transistor was demonstrated, many years followed in perfecting it. It wasn't until 1956 that Shockley, Bardeen, and Brattain were awarded the Nobel Prize in physics "for their researches on semiconductors and their discovery of the transistor effect."

Earlier in this book, I talked about conductors and insulators. Conductors are so called because they're very conducive to the passage of electricity. Copper, silver, and gold are the best conductors, and it's no coincidence that all three are found in the same column of the periodic table of the elements.

As you'll recall, the electrons in an atom are distributed in shells that surround the nucleus of the atom. What characterizes these three conductors is a lone electron in the outermost shell. This electron can be easily dislodged from the rest of the atom and hence is free to move as electrical current. The opposites of conductors are insulators—like rubber and plastic—that barely conduct electricity at all.

The elements germanium and silicon (as well as some compounds) are called *semiconductors,* not because they conduct half as well as conductors, but because their conductance can be manipulated in various ways. Semiconductors have four electrons in the outermost shell, which is half the maximum number the outer shell can have. In a pure semiconductor, the atoms form very stable bonds with each other and have a crystalline structure similar to the diamond. Such semiconductors aren't good conductors.

But semiconductors can be *doped,* which means that they're combined with certain impurities. One type of impurity adds extra electrons to those needed for the bond between the atoms. These are called *N-type semiconductors* (N for *negative*). Another type of impurity results in a *P-type semiconductor.*

Semiconductors can be made into amplifiers by sandwiching a P-type semiconductor between two N-type semiconductors. This is known as an

NPN transistor, and the three pieces are known as the *collector,* the *base,* and the *emitter.*

Here's a schematic diagram of an NPN transistor:

Collector

Base

Emitter

A small voltage on the base can control a much larger voltage passing from the collector to the emitter. If there's no voltage on the base, it effectively turns off the transistor.

Transistors are usually packaged in little metal cans about a quarter-inch in diameter with three wires poking out:

The transistor inaugurated *solid-state* electronics, which means that transistors don't require vacuums and are built from solids, specifically semiconductors and most commonly (these days) silicon. Besides being much smaller than vacuum tubes, transistors require much less power, generate much less heat, and last longer. Carrying around a tube radio in your pocket was inconceivable. But a transistor radio could be powered by a small battery, and unlike tubes, it wouldn't get hot. Carrying a transistor radio in your pocket became possible for some lucky people opening presents on Christmas morning in 1954. Those first pocket radios used transistors made by Texas Instruments, an important company of the semiconductor revolution.

The *first* commercial application of the transistor was, however, a hearing aid. In commemorating the heritage of Alexander Graham Bell in his lifelong work with deaf people, AT&T allowed hearing aid manufacturers to use transistor technology without paying any royalties. The first transistor television debuted in 1960, and today tube appliances have almost disappeared. (Not entirely, however. Some audiophiles and electric guitarists continue to prefer the sound of tube amplifiers to their transistor counterparts.)

In 1956, Shockley left Bell Labs to form Shockley Semiconductor Laboratories. He moved to Palo Alto, California, where he had grown up. His was the first such company to locate in that area. In time, other semiconductor and computer companies set up business there, and the area south of San Francisco is now informally known as Silicon Valley.

Vacuum tubes were originally developed for amplification, but they could also be used for switches in logic gates. The same goes for the transistor. On the next page, you'll see a transistor-based AND gate structured much like the relay version. Only when both the A input is 1 and the B input is 1 will both transistors conduct current and hence make the output 1. The resistor prevents a short circuit when this happens.

Wiring two transistors as you see below in the diagram on the right creates an OR gate. In the AND gate, the emitter of the top transistor is connected to the collector of the bottom transistor. In the OR gate, the collectors of both transistors are connected to the voltage supply. The emitters are connected together.

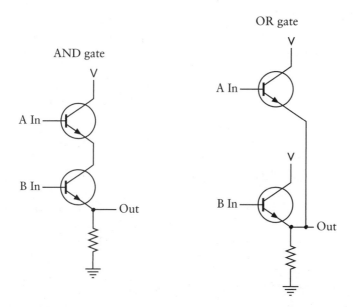

So everything we learned about constructing logic gates and other components from relays is valid for transistors. Relays, tubes, and transistors were all initially developed primarily for purposes of amplification but can be connected in similar ways to make logic gates out of which computers can be built. The first transistor computers were built in 1956, and within a few years tubes had been abandoned for the design of new computers.

Here's a question: Transistors certainly make computers more reliable, smaller, and less power hungry. But do transistors make computers any simpler to *construct*?

Not really. The transistor lets you fit more logic gates in a smaller space, of course, but you still have to worry about all the *interconnections* of these components. It's just as difficult wiring transistors to make logic gates as it is wiring relays and vacuum tubes. In some ways, it's even more difficult because the transistors are smaller and less easy to hold. If you wanted to build the Chapter 17 computer and the 64-KB RAM array out of transistors, a good part of the design work would be devoted to inventing some kind of structure in which to hold all the components. Most of your physical labor would be the tedious wiring of millions of interconnections among millions of transistors.

As we've discovered, however, there are certain combinations of transistors that show up repeatedly. Pairs of transistors are almost always wired as gates. Gates are often wired into flip-flops or adders or selectors or decoders. Flip-flops are combined into multibit latches or RAM arrays. Assembling a computer would be much easier if the transistors were prewired in common configurations.

This idea seems to have been proposed first by British physicist Geoffrey Dummer (born 1909) in a speech in May 1952. "I would like to take a peep into the future," he said.

> With the advent of the transistor and the work in semiconductors generally, it seems now possible to envisage electronic equipment in a solid block with no connecting wires. The block may consist of layers of insulating, conducting, rectifying and amplifying materials, the electrical functions being connected directly by cutting out areas of the various layers.

A working product, however, would have to wait a few years.

Without knowing about the Dummer prediction, in July 1958 it occurred to Jack Kilby (born 1923) of Texas Instruments that multiple transistors as well as resistors and other electrical components could be made from a single piece of silicon. Six months later, in January 1959, basically the same idea occurred to Robert Noyce (1927–1990). Noyce had originally worked for Shockley Semiconductor Laboratories, but in 1957 he and seven other scientists had left and started Fairchild Semiconductor Corporation.

In the history of technology, simultaneous invention is more common than one might suspect. Although Kilby had invented the device six months before Noyce, and Texas Instruments had applied for a patent before Fairchild, Noyce was issued a patent first. Legal battles ensued, and only after a decade were they finally settled to everyone's satisfaction. Although they never worked together, Kilby and Noyce are today regarded as the coinventors of the *integrated circuit,* or *IC,* commonly called the *chip.*

Integrated circuits are manufactured through a complex process that involves layering thin wafers of silicon that are precisely doped and etched in different areas to form microscopic components. Although it's expensive to develop a new integrated circuit, they benefit from mass production—the more you make, the cheaper they become.

The actual silicon chip is thin and delicate, so it must be securely packaged, both to protect the chip and to provide some way for the components in the chip to be connected to other chips. Integrated circuits are packaged in a couple of different ways, but the most common is the rectangular plastic *dual inline package* (or DIP), with 14, 16, or as many as 40 pins protruding from the side:

This is a 16-pin chip. If you hold the chip so the little indentation is at the left (as shown), the pins are numbered 1 through 16 beginning at the lower left and circling around the right side to end with pin 16 at the upper left. The pins on each side are exactly ⅒ inch apart.

Throughout the 1960s, the space program and the arms race fueled the early integrated circuits market. On the civilian side, the first commercial product that contained an integrated circuit was a hearing aid sold by Zenith in 1964. In 1971, Texas Instruments began selling the first pocket calculator, and Pulsar the first digital watch. (Obviously the IC in a digital watch is packaged much differently from the example just shown.) Many other products that incorporated integrated circuits in their design followed.

In 1965, Gordon E. Moore (then at Fairchild and later a cofounder of Intel Corporation) noticed that technology was improving in such a way that the number of transistors that could fit on a single chip had doubled every year since 1959. He predicted that this trend would continue. The actual trend was a little slower, so Moore's Law (as it was eventually called) was modified to predict a doubling of transistors on a chip every 18 months. This is still an astonishingly fast rate of progress and reveals why home computers always seem to become outdated in just a few short years. Some people believe that Moore's Law will continue to be accurate until about 2015.

In the early days, people used to speak of *small-scale integration,* or SSI, to refer to a chip that had fewer than 10 logic gates; *medium-scale integration,* or MSI (10 to 100 gates); and *large-scale integration,* or LSI (100 to 5000). Then the terms ascended to *very-large-scale integration,* or VLSI (5000 to 50,000); *super-large-scale integration,* or SLSI (50,000 to 100,000); and *ultra-large-scale integration,* (more than 100,000 gates).

For the remainder of this chapter and the next, I want to pause our time machine in the mid-1970s, an ancient age before the first *Star Wars* movie was released and with VLSI just on the horizon. At that time, several different technologies were used to fabricate the components that make up integrated circuits. Each of these technologies is sometimes called a *family* of ICs. By the mid-1970s, two families were prevalent: TTL (pronounced *tee tee ell*) and CMOS (*see moss*).

TTL stands for *transistor-transistor logic.* If in the mid-1970s you were a digital design engineer (which meant that you designed larger circuits from ICs), a 1 ¼-inch-thick book first published in 1973 by Texas Instruments called *The TTL Data Book for Design Engineers* would be a permanent fixture on your desk. This is a complete reference to the 7400 (*seventy-four hundred*) series of TTL integrated circuits sold by Texas Instruments and several other companies, so called because each IC in this family is identified by a number beginning with the digits 74.

Every integrated circuit in the 7400 series consists of logic gates that are prewired in a particular configuration. Some chips provide simple prewired gates that you can use to create larger components; other chips provide common components such as flip-flops, adders, selectors, and decoders.

The first IC in the 7400 series is number 7400 itself, which is described in the *TTL Data Book* as "Quadruple 2-Input Positive-NAND Gates." What this means is that this particular integrated circuit contains four 2-input NAND gates. They're called *positive* NAND gates because a voltage corresponds to 1 and no voltage corresponds to 0. This is a 14-pin chip, and a little diagram in the data book shows how the pins correspond to the inputs and outputs:

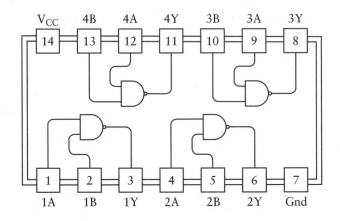

This diagram is a top view of the chip (pins on the bottom) with the little indentation (shown on page 250) at the left.

Pin 14 is labeled V_{CC} and is equivalent to the V symbol that I've been using to indicate a voltage. (By convention, any double letter subscript on a capital V indicates a power supply. The C in this subscript refers to the *collector* input of a transistor, which is internally where the voltage supply is connected.) Pin 7 is labeled GND for *ground*. Every integrated circuit that you use in a particular circuit must be connected to a power supply and a common ground.

For 7400 series TTL, V_{CC} must be between 4.75 and 5.25 volts. Another way of saying this is that the power supply voltage must be 5 volts plus or minus 5 percent. If the power supply is below 4.75 volts, the chip might not work. If it's higher than 5.25, the chip could be damaged. You generally can't use batteries with TTL; even if you were to find a 5-volt battery, the voltage wouldn't be exact enough to be adequate for these chips. TTL usually requires a power supply that you plug into the wall.

Each of the four NAND gates in the 7400 chip has two inputs and one output. They work independently of each other. In past chapters, we've been differentiating between inputs being either 1 (which is a voltage) or 0 (which is no voltage). In reality, an input to one of these NAND gates can range anywhere from 0 volts (ground) to 5 volts (V_{CC}). In TTL, anything between 0 volts and 0.8 volt is considered to be a logical 0, and anything between

2 volts and 5 volts is considered to be a logical 1. Inputs between 0.8 volt and 2 volts should be avoided.

The output of a TTL gate is typically about 0.2 volt for a logical 0 and 3.4 volts for a logical 1. Because these voltages can vary somewhat, inputs and outputs to integrated circuits are sometimes referred to as *low* and *high* rather than 0 and 1. Moreover, sometimes a low voltage can mean a logical 1 and a high voltage can mean a logical 0. This configuration is referred to as *negative logic*. When the 7400 chip is referred to as "Quadruple 2-Input Positive-NAND Gates," the word *positive* means positive logic is assumed.

If the output of a TTL gate is typically 0.2 volt for a logical 0 and 3.4 volts for a logical 1, these outputs are safely within the input ranges, which are between 0 and 0.8 volt for a logical 0 and between 2 and 5 volts for a logical 1. This is how TTL is insulated against *noise*. A 1 output can lose about 1.4 volts and still be high enough to qualify as a 1 input. A 0 output can gain 0.6 volt and still be low enough to qualify as a 0 input.

Probably the most important fact to know about a particular integrated circuit is the *propagation time*. That's the time it takes for a change in the inputs to be reflected in the output.

Propagation times for chips are generally measured in *nanoseconds,* abbreviated nsec. A nanosecond is a *very* short period of time. One thousandth of a second is a millisecond. One millionth of a second is a microsecond. One billionth of a second is a nanosecond. The propagation time for the NAND gates in the 7400 chip is guaranteed to be less than 22 nanoseconds. That's 0.000000022 seconds, or 22 billionths of a second.

If you can't get the feel of a nanosecond, you're not alone. Nobody on this planet has anything but an intellectual appreciation of the nanosecond. Nanoseconds are much shorter than anything in human experience, so they'll forever remain incomprehensible. Every explanation makes the nanosecond more elusive. For example, I can say that if you're holding this book 1 foot away from your face, a nanosecond is the time it takes the light to travel from the page to your eyes. But do you really have a better feel for the nanosecond now?

Yet the nanosecond is what makes computers possible. As we saw in Chapter 17, a computer processor does moronically simple things—it moves a byte from memory to register, adds a byte to another byte, moves the result back to memory. The only reason anything substantial gets completed (not in the Chapter 17 computer but in real ones) is that these operations occur very quickly. To quote Robert Noyce, "After you become reconciled to the nanosecond, computer operations are conceptually fairly simple."

Let's continue perusing the *TTL Data Book for Design Engineers.* You will see a lot of familiar little items in this book. The 7402 chip contains four 2-input NOR gates, the 7404 has six inverters, the 7408 has four 2-input

AND gates, the 7432 has four 2-input OR gates, and the 7430 has an 8-input NAND gate:

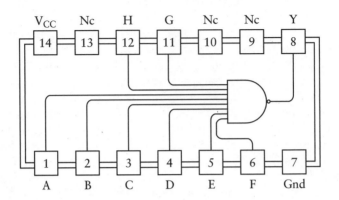

The abbreviation *NC* means *no connection*.

The 7474 chip is another that will sound very familiar. It's a "Dual D-Type Positive-Edge-Triggered Flip-Flop with Preset and Clear" and is diagrammed like this:

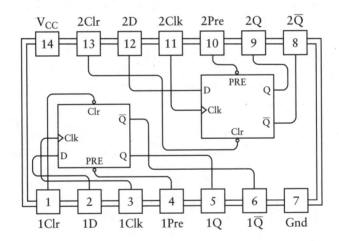

The *TTL Data Book* even includes a logic diagram for each flip-flop in this chip:

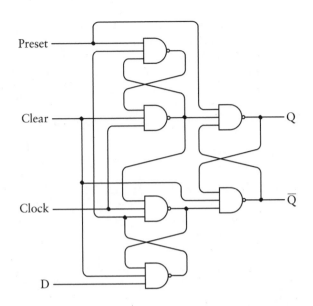

You'll recognize this as being similar to the diagram at the end of Chapter 14, except that I used NOR gates. The logic table in the *TTL Data Book* is a little different as well:

Inputs				Outputs	
Pre	Clr	Clk	D	Q	$\overline{Q}$
L	H	X	X	H	L
H	L	X	X	L	H
L	L	X	X	H*	H*
H	L	↑	H	H	L
H	H	↑	L	L	H
H	H	L	X	Q_0	$\overline{Q}_0$

In this table, the H stands for *High* and the L stands for *Low*. You can think of these as 1 and 0 if you wish. In my flip-flop, the Preset and Clear inputs were normally 0; here they're normally 1.

Moving right along in the *TTL Data Book*, you'll discover that the 7483 chip is a 4-Bit Binary Full Adder, 74151 is a 8-Line-To-1-Line Data Selector, the 74154 is a 4-line-To-16-Line Decoder, 74161 is a Synchronous 4-Bit Binary Counter, and 74175 is a Quadruple D-Type Flip-Flop with Clear. You can use two of these chips for making an 8-bit latch.

So now you know how I came up with all the various components I've been using since Chapter 11. I stole them from the *TTL Data Book for Design Engineers*.

As a digital design engineer, you would spend long hours going through the *TTL Data Book* familiarizing yourself with the types of TTL chips that were available. Once you knew all your tools, you could actually build the computer I showed in Chapter 17 out of TTL chips. Wiring the chips together is a lot easier than wiring individual transistors together. But you might want to consider *not* using TTL to make the 64-KB RAM array. In the 1973 *TTL Data Book*, the heftiest RAM chip listed is a mere 256 × 1 bits. You'd need 2048 of these chips to make 64 KB! TTL was never the best technology for memory. I'll have more to say about memory in Chapter 21.

You'd probably want to use a better oscillator as well. While you can certainly connect the output of a TTL inverter to the input, it's better to have an oscillator with a more predictable frequency. Such an oscillator can be constructed fairly easily using a quartz crystal that comes in a little flat can with two wires sticking out. These crystals vibrate at very specific frequencies, usually at least a million cycles per second. A million cycles per second is called a *megahertz* and abbreviated MHz. If the Chapter 17 computer were constructed out of TTL, it would probably run fine with a clock frequency of 10 MHz. Each instruction would execute in 400 nanoseconds. This, of course, is much faster than anything we conceived when we were working with relays.

The other popular chip family was (and still is) CMOS, which stands for *complementary metal-oxide semiconductor*. If you were a hobbyist designing circuits from CMOS ICs in the mid-1970s, you might use as a reference source a book published by National Semiconductor and available at your local Radio Shack entitled *CMOS Databook*. This book contains information about the 4000 (*four thousand*) series of CMOS ICs.

The power supply requirement for TTL is 4.75 to 5.25 volts. For CMOS, it's anything from 3 volts to 18 volts. That's quite a leeway! Moreover, CMOS requires much less power than TTL, which makes it feasible to run small CMOS circuits from batteries. The drawback of CMOS is lack of speed. For example, the CMOS 4008 4-bit full adder running at 5 volts is only guaranteed to have a propagation time of 750 nanoseconds. It gets faster as the power supply gets higher—250 nsec at 10 volts and 190 nsec at 15 volts. But the CMOS device doesn't come close to the TTL 4-bit adder, which has a propagation time of 24 nsec. (Twenty-five years ago, the trade-off between the speed of TTL and the low power requirements of CMOS was fairly clear cut. Today there are low-power versions of TTL and high-speed versions of CMOS.)

On the practical side, you would probably begin wiring chips together on a plastic *breadboard:*

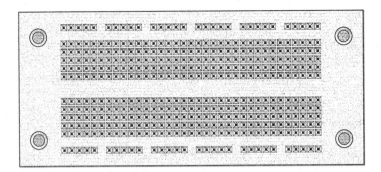

Each short row of 5 holes is electrically connected underneath the plastic base. You insert chips into the breadboard so that a chip straddles the long central groove and the pins go into the holes on either side of the groove. Each pin of the IC is then electrically connected to 4 other holes. You connect the chips with pieces of wires pushed into the other holes.

You can wire chips together more permanently using a technique called *wire-wrapping*. Each chip is inserted into a socket that has long square posts:

Each post corresponds to a pin of the chip. The sockets themselves are inserted into thin perforated boards. From the other side of the board, you use a special wire-wrap gun to tightly wrap thin pieces of insulated wire around the post. The square edges of the post break through the insulation and make an electrical connection with the wire.

If you were actually manufacturing a particular circuit using ICs, you'd probably use a *printed circuit* board. Back in the old days, this was something a hobbyist could do. Such a board has holes and is covered by a thin layer of copper foil. Basically, you cover all the areas of copper you want to preserve with an acid resistant and use acid to etch away the rest. You can then solder IC sockets (or the ICs themselves) directly to the copper on the board. But because of the very many interconnections among ICs, a single area of copper foil is usually inadequate. Commercially manufactured printed circuit boards have multiple layers of interconnections.

By the early 1970s, it became possible to use ICs to create an entire computer processor on a single circuit board. It was really only a matter of time before somebody put the whole processor on a single chip. Although Texas Instruments filed a patent for a single-chip computer in 1971, the honor of actually making one belongs to Intel, a company started in 1968 by former

Fairchild employees Robert Noyce and Gordon Moore. Intel's first major product was, in 1970, a memory chip that stored 1024 bits, which was the greatest number of bits on a chip at that time.

Intel was in the process of designing chips for a programmable calculator to be manufactured by the Japanese company Busicom when they decided to take a different approach. As Intel engineer Ted Hoff put it, "Instead of making their device act like a calculator with some programming abilities, I wanted to make it function as a general-purpose computer programmed to be a calculator." This led to the Intel 4004 (pronounced *forty oh four*), the first "computer on a chip," or *microprocessor*. The 4004 became available in November 1971 and contained 2300 transistors. (By Moore's Law, microprocessors made 18 years later should contain about 4000 times as many transistors, or about 10 million. That's a fairly accurate prediction.)

Having told you the number of its transistors, I'll now describe three other important characteristics of the 4004. These three measures are often used as standards for comparison among microprocessors since the 4004.

First, the 4004 was a *4-bit* microprocessor. This means that the data paths in the processor were only 4 bits wide. When adding or subtracting numbers, it handled only 4 bits at a shot. In contrast, the computer developed in Chapter 17 has 8-bit data paths and is thus an 8-bit processor. As we'll soon see, 4-bit microprocessors were surpassed very quickly by 8-bit microprocessors. No one stopped there. In the late 1970s, 16-bit microprocessors became available. When you think back to Chapter 17 and recall the several instruction codes necessary to add two 16-bit numbers on an 8-bit processor, you'll appreciate the advantage that a 16-bit processor gives you. In the mid-1980s, 32-bit microprocessors were introduced and have remained the standard for home computers since then.

Second, the 4004 had a maximum *clock speed* of 108,000 cycles per second, or 108 *kilohertz* (KHz). Clock speed is the maximum speed of an oscillator that you can connect to the microprocessor to make it go. Any faster and it might not work right. By 1999, microprocessors intended for home computers had hit the 500-megahertz point—about 5000 times faster than the 4004.

Third, the *addressable memory* of the 4004 was 640 bytes. This seems like an absurdly low amount; yet it was in line with the capacity of memory chips available at the time. As you'll see in the next chapter, within a couple of years microprocessors could address 64 KB of memory, which is the capability of the Chapter 17 machine. Intel microprocessors in 1999 can address 64 terabytes of memory, although that's overkill considering that most people have fewer than 256 megabytes of RAM in their home computers.

These three numbers don't affect the *capability* of a computer. A 4-bit processor can add 32-bit numbers, for example, simply by doing it in 4-bit chunks. In one sense, all digital computers are the same. If the hardware of one processor can do something another can't, the other processor can do it in software; they all end up doing the same thing. This is one of the implications of Alan Turing's 1937 paper on computability.

Where processors ultimately *do* differ, however, is in *speed*. And speed is a big reason why we're using computers to begin with.

The maximum clock speed is an obvious influence on the overall speed of a processor. That clock speed determines how fast each instruction is being executed. The processor data width affects speed as well. Although a 4-bit processor can add 32-bit numbers, it can't do it nearly as fast as a 32-bit processor. What might be confusing, however, is the effect on speed of the maximum amount of memory that a processor can address. At first, addressable memory seems to have nothing to do with speed and instead reflects a limitation on the processor's ability to perform certain functions that might require a lot of memory. But a processor can always get around the memory limitation by using some memory addresses to control some other medium for saving and retrieving information. (For example, suppose every byte written to a particular memory address is actually punched on a paper tape, and every byte read from that address is read from the tape.) What happens, however, is that this process slows down the whole computer. The issue again is speed.

Of course, these three numbers indicate only roughly how fast the microprocessor operates. These numbers tell you nothing about the internal architecture of the microprocessor or about the efficiency and capability of the machine-code instructions. As processors have become more sophisticated, many common tasks previously done in software have been built into the processor. We'll see examples of this trend in the chapters ahead.

Even though all digital computers have the same capabilities, even though they can do nothing beyond the primitive computing machine devised by Alan Turing, the speed of a processor *of course* ultimately affects the overall usefulness of a computer system. Any computer that's slower than the human brain in performing a set of calculations is useless, for example. And we can hardly expect to watch a movie on our modern computer screens if the processor needs a minute to draw a single frame.

But back to the mid-1970s. Despite the limitations of the 4004, it was a start. By April 1972, Intel had released the 8008—an 8-bit microprocessor running at 200 kHz that could address 16 KB of memory. (See how easy it is to sum up a processor with just three numbers?) And then, in a five-month period in 1974, both Intel and Motorola came out with microprocessors that were intended to improve on the 8008. These two chips changed the world.

Chapter Nineteen

Two Classic Microprocessors

T he microprocessor—a consolidation of all the components of a central processing unit (CPU) of a computer on a single chip of silicon—was born in 1971. It was a modest beginning: The first microprocessor, the Intel 4004, contained about 2300 transistors. Today, nearly three decades later, microprocessors made for home computers are approaching the 10,000,000 transistor mark.

Yet what the microprocessor actually does on a fundamental level has remained unchanged. While those millions of additional transistors in today's chips might be doing interesting things, in an initial exploration of the microprocessor they offer more distraction than enlightenment. To obtain the clearest view of what a microprocessor does, let's look at the first ready-for-prime-time microprocessors.

These microprocessors appeared in 1974, the year in which Intel introduced the 8080 (pronounced *eighty eighty*) in April and Motorola—a company that had been making semiconductors and transistor-based products since the 1950s—introduced the 6800 (*sixty-eight hundred*) in August. These weren't the only microprocessors available that year. Also in 1974, Texas Instruments introduced the 4-bit TMS 1000, which was used in many calculators, toys, and appliances; and National Semiconductor introduced the PACE, which was the first 16-bit microprocessor. In retrospect, however, the 8080 and the 6800 were certainly the two most historically significant chips.

Intel set the initial price of the 8080 at $360, a sly dig at IBM's System/360, a large mainframe system used by many large corporations that cost millions. (Today you can buy an 8080 chip for $1.95.) It's not as if the 8080 is comparable to System/360 in any way, but within a few years IBM itself would certainly be taking notice of these very small computers.

The 8080 is an 8-bit microprocessor that contains about 6000 transistors, runs at a 2 MHz clock speed, and addresses 64 kilobytes of memory. The 6800 (also selling these days for $1.95) has about 4000 transistors and also addresses 64 KB of memory. The first 6800 ran at 1 MHz, but by 1977 Motorola introduced later versions running at 1.5 and 2 MHz.

These chips are referred to as *single-chip microprocessors* and less accurately as *computers on a chip*. The processor is only one part of the whole computer. In addition to the processor, a computer at the very least requires some random access memory (RAM), some way for a person to get information into the computer (an input device), some way for a person to get information out of the computer (an output device), and several other chips that bind everything together. But I'll describe these other components in greater detail in Chapter 21.

For now, let's look at the microprocessor itself. Often a description of a microprocessor is accompanied by a block diagram that illustrates the internal components of the microprocessor and how they're connected. But we had enough of that in Chapter 17. Instead, we'll get a sense of what's inside the processor by seeing how it interacts with the outside world. In other words, we can think of the microprocessor as a black box whose internal operations we don't need to study minutely in order to understand what it does. We can instead grasp what the microprocessor does by examining the chip's input and output signals, and in particular the chip's instruction set.

Both the 8080 and 6800 are 40-pin integrated circuits. The most common IC package for these chips is about 2 inches long, about a half inch wide, and ⅛ inch thick:

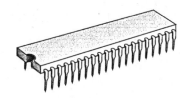

Of course, what you see is just the packaging. The actual wafer of silicon inside is much smaller—in the case of the early 8-bit microprocessors, the silicon is less than ¼ inch square. The packaging protects the silicon chip and also provides access to all of the chip's input and output points through the pins. The diagram on the following page shows the function of the 40 pins of the 8080.

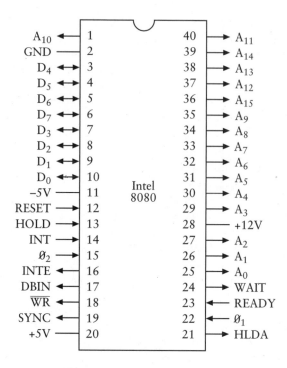

Every electrical or electronic device that we've built in this book has required some kind of electrical power supply. One of the 8080's quirks is that it requires *three* power supply voltages. Pin 20 must be connected to a 5-volt power supply, pin 11 to a −5-volt power supply, and pin 28 to a 12-volt power supply. You connect pin 2 to ground. (In 1976, Intel released the 8085 chip, which simplified these power requirements.)

All the remaining pins are drawn as arrows. An arrow *from* the chip indicates an *output* signal. This is a signal controlled by the microprocessor that other chips in the computer respond to. An arrow *into* the chip indicates an *input* signal. This is a signal that comes from another chip in the computer that the 8080 responds to. Some pins are both inputs *and* outputs.

The processor in Chapter 17 required an oscillator to make it go. The 8080 requires two different synchronized 2-MHz clock inputs labeled $\emptyset_1$ and $\emptyset_2$ on pins 22 and 15. These signals are most conveniently supplied by another chip made by Intel known as the 8224 Clock Signal Generator. You connect an 18-MHz quartz crystal to this chip, and it basically does the rest.

A microprocessor always has multiple output signals that address memory. The number of signals it has for this purpose is directly related to the amount of memory the microprocessor can address. The 8080 has 16 signals labeled A_0 through A_{15}, which give it the ability to address 2^{16}, or 65,536, bytes of memory.

The 8080 is an 8-bit microprocessor that reads data from memory and writes data to memory 8 bits at a time. The chip includes eight signals labeled D_0 through D_7. These signals are the only ones on the chip that are both inputs and outputs. When the microprocessor reads a byte of memory, the pins function as inputs; when the microprocessor writes a byte to memory, the pins function as outputs.

The other ten pins of the microprocessor are *control* signals. The *RESET* input, for example, is used to reset the microprocessor. The output signal $\overline{WR}$ indicates that the microprocessor needs to write a byte of memory into RAM. (The $\overline{WR}$ signal corresponds to the Write input of the RAM array.) In addition, other control signals appear on the D_0 through D_7 pins at a particular time while the chip reads instructions. Computer systems built around the 8080 generally use the 8228 System Controller chip to latch these additional control signals. I'll describe some control signals later on, but the 8080's control signals are notoriously messy, so unless you're going to actually design a computer based on the chip, it's best not to torture yourself with its control signals.

Let's assume that the 8080 microprocessor is connected to 64 KB of memory that we have the ability to write bytes into and read bytes from independent of the microprocessor.

After the 8080 chip is reset, it reads the byte located at memory address 0000h into the microprocessor. It does this by outputting 16 zeros on the address signals A_0 through A_{15}. The byte it reads should be an 8080 instruction, and the process of reading this byte is known as an *instruction fetch*.

In the computer we built in Chapter 17, all instructions (except *HLT*) were 3 bytes in length, consisting of an opcode and a 2-byte address. In the 8080, instructions can be 1 byte, 2 bytes, or 3 bytes in length. Some instructions cause the 8080 to read a byte from a particular location in memory into the microprocessor. Some instructions cause the 8080 to write a byte from the microprocessor into a particular location in memory. Other instructions cause the 8080 to do something internally without using any RAM. After processing the first instruction, the 8080 accesses the second instruction in memory, and so forth. Together, these instructions constitute a computer program that can do something interesting.

When the 8080 is running at its maximum speed of 2 MHz, each clock cycle is 500 nanoseconds. ($1 \div 2{,}000{,}000$ cycles per second = 0.000000500 seconds.) The instructions in the Chapter 17 computer all required 4 clock cycles. Each 8080 instruction requires anywhere from 4 to 18 clock cycles. This means that each instruction is executed in 2 to 9 microseconds (millionths of a second).

Probably the best way to understand what a particular microprocessor is capable of doing is to examine its complete instruction set in a systematic manner.

The final computer in Chapter 17 had only 12 instructions. An 8-bit microprocessor could easily have as many as 256 instructions, each opcode corresponding to a particular 8-bit value. (It could actually have more if some instructions have 2-byte opcodes.) The 8080 doesn't go quite that far, but it does have 244 opcodes. That might seem like a lot, but all in all, the 8080 doesn't really do all that much more than the computer in Chapter 17. For example, if you need to do multiplication or division using an 8080, you still need to write your own little program to do it.

As you'll recall from Chapter 17, each opcode in a processor's instruction set is usually associated with a particular mnemonic, and some of these mnemonics might have arguments. But these mnemonics are solely for convenience in referring to the opcodes. The processor reads only bytes; it knows nothing about the text that makes up the mnemonics. (For purposes of clarity, I've taken some liberty with the mnemonics as they appear in Intel's documentation of the 8080.)

The Chapter 17 computer had two important instructions that we initially called *Load* and *Store*. Each of these instructions occupied 3 bytes of memory. The first byte of a *Load* instruction was the opcode, and the 2 bytes that followed the opcode indicated a 16-bit address. The processor loaded the byte at that address into the accumulator. Similarly, the *Store* instruction saved the contents of the accumulator in the address indicated in the instruction.

Later on, we discovered that we could abbreviate these two opcodes using mnemonics:

```
LOD A,[aaaa]
STO [aaaa],A
```

where *A* stands for the accumulator (the destination in the Load instruction and the source in the *Store* instruction) and *aaaa* indicates a 32-bit memory address, usually written as 4 hexadecimal digits.

The 8-bit accumulator in the 8080 is called A, just like the accumulator in Chapter 17. And like the computer in Chapter 17, the 8080 includes two instructions that do exactly the same thing as the *Load* and *Store* instructions. The 8080 opcodes for these two instructions are 32h and 3Ah, and each opcode is followed by a 16-bit address. The 8080 mnemonics are *STA* (standing for *Store Accumulator*) and *LDA* (*Load Accumulator*):

Opcode	Instruction
32	STA [aaaa],A
3A	LDA A,[aaaa]

In addition to the accumulator, the 8080 contains six *registers* that can also hold 8-bit values inside the microprocessor. These registers are very similar to the accumulator; indeed, the accumulator is considered to be a special type of register. Like the accumulator, the other six registers are latches; the processor can move bytes from memory into registers, and from registers back into memory. The other registers, however, aren't as versatile as the accumulator. When you add two 8-bit numbers, for example, the result always goes into the accumulator rather than into one of the other registers.

The six additional registers in the 8080 are named B, C, D, E, H, and L. The first question people usually ask is, "What happened to F and G?" and the second question is, "And what about I, J, and K?" The answer is that registers H and L are so called because they're special in a certain way. H stands for *high* and L stands for *low*. Very often the 8-bit quantities in H and L are treated in tandem as a 16-bit *register pair* named HL, H being the high-order byte and L being the low-order byte. This 16-bit value is often used to address memory. We'll see how this works shortly.

Are all these registers necessary? Why didn't we need them in the Chapter 17 computer? In theory, they aren't necessary. But they turn out to be very convenient. Many computer programs juggle several numbers at the same time. It's easiest to do this if all the numbers are stored in microprocessor registers rather than memory. The program is usually faster as well: The fewer times a program needs to access memory, generally the faster it will run.

No fewer than 63 opcodes are devoted to a single 8080 instruction called *MOV*, which is short for *Move*. This instruction is just a single byte. The instruction usually moves the contents of one register into another (or the same) register. The large number of *MOV* instructions is a normal consequence of designing a microprocessor with seven registers (including the accumulator).

Here are the first 32 *MOV* instructions. Remember that the destination is the argument on the left and the source is the argument on the right:

Opcode	Instruction	Opcode	Instruction
40	MOV B,B	50	MOV D,B
41	MOV B,C	51	MOV D,C
42	MOV B,D	52	MOV D,D
43	MOV B,E	53	MOV D,E
44	MOV B,H	54	MOV D,H
45	MOV B,L	55	MOV D,L
46	MOV B,[HL]	56	MOV D,[HL]
47	MOV B,A	57	MOV D,A
48	MOV C,B	58	MOV E,B
49	MOV C,C	59	MOV E,C
4A	MOV C,D	5A	MOV E,D
4B	MOV C,E	5B	MOV E,E
4C	MOV C,H	5C	MOV E,H
4D	MOV C,L	5D	MOV E,L
4E	MOV C,[HL]	5E	MOV E,[HL]
4F	MOV C,A	5F	MOV E,A

These are handy instructions to have. Whenever you have a value in one register, you know you can move it to another register. Notice also the four instructions that use the HL register pair, such as

```
MOV B,[HL]
```

The *LDA* instruction shown earlier transfers a byte from memory into the accumulator; the 16-bit address of the byte directly follows the *LDA* opcode. This *MOV* instruction transfers a byte from memory into register B. But the address of the byte to be loaded into the register is stored in the register pair HL registers. How did HL come to hold a 16-bit memory address? Well, it could happen in a variety of ways. Maybe the address was calculated in some way.

To summarize, these two instructions

```
LDA A,[aaaa]
MOV B,[HL]
```

both load a byte from memory into the microprocessor, but they use two different methods to address memory. The first method is called *direct addressing* and the second method is called *indexed addressing*.

The second batch of 32 *MOV* instructions shows that the memory location addressed by HL can also be a destination:

Opcode	Instruction	Opcode	Instruction
40	MOV B,B	50	MOV D,B
60	MOV H,B	70	MOV [HL],B
61	MOV H,C	71	MOV [HL],C
62	MOV H,D	72	MOV [HL],D
63	MOV H,E	73	MOV [HL],E
64	MOV H,H	74	MOV [HL],H
65	MOV H,L	75	MOV [HL],L
66	MOV H,[HL]	76	HLT
67	MOV H,A	77	MOV [HL],A
68	MOV L,B	78	MOV A,B
69	MOV L,C	79	MOV A,C
6A	MOV L,D	7A	MOV A,D
6B	MOV L,E	7B	MOV A,E
6C	MOV L,H	7C	MOV A,H
6D	MOV L,L	7D	MOV A,L
6E	MOV L,[HL]	7E	MOV A,[HL]
6F	MOV L,A	7F	MOV A,A

Several of these instructions, such as

```
MOV A,A
```

don't do anything useful. But the instruction

```
MOV [HL],[HL]
```

doesn't exist. The opcode that would otherwise correspond to that instruction is actually a *HLT* (*Halt*) instruction.

A more revealing way to look at all these *MOV* opcodes is to examine the bit pattern of the opcode. The *MOV* opcode consists of the 8 bits

```
01dddsss
```

in which the letters *ddd* represent a 3-bit code that refers to a destination, and *sss* is a 3-bit code that refers to a source. These 3-bit codes are

000 = Register B
001 = Register C
010 = Register D
011 = Register E
100 = Register H
101 = Register L
110 = Contents of memory at address HL
111 = Accumulator

For example, the instruction

```
MOV L,E
```

is associated with the opcode

01101011

or 6Bh. You can check the preceding table to verify that.

So probably somewhere inside the 8080, the 3 bits labeled *sss* are used in a 8-Line-to-1-Line Data Selector, and the 3 bits labeled *ddd* are used to control a 3-Line-to-8-Line Decoder that determines which register latches a value.

It's also possible to use registers B and C as a 16-bit register pair BC, and registers D and E as a 16-bit register pair DE. If either register pair contains the address of a memory location that you want to use to load or store a byte, you can use the following instructions:

Opcode	Instruction	Opcode	Instruction
02	STAX [BC],A	0A	LDAX A,[BC]
12	STAX [DE],A	1A	LDAX A,[DE]

Another type of *Move* instruction is called *Move Immediate* and is assigned the mnemonic *MVI*. The *Move Immediate* instruction is composed of 2 bytes. The first is the opcode, and the second is a byte of data. That byte is transferred from memory into one of the registers or to the memory location addressed by the HL register pair:

Opcode	Instruction
06	MVI B,xx
0E	MVI C,xx
16	MVI D,xx
1E	MVI E,xx
26	MVI H,xx
2E	MVI L,xx
36	MVI [HL],xx
3E	MVI A,xx

For example, after the instruction

```
MVI E,37h
```

the register E contains the byte 37h. This is considered to be a third method of addressing memory, called *immediate addressing*.

A collection of 32 opcodes do the four basic arithmetical operations we're familiar with from the processor we developed in Chapter 17. These are addition (*ADD*), addition with carry (*ADC*), subtraction (*SUB*), and subtraction with borrow (*SBB*). In all cases, the accumulator is one of the two operands and is also the destination for the result:

Opcode	Instruction	Opcode	Instruction
80	ADD A,B	90	SUB A,B
81	ADD A,C	91	SUB A,C
82	ADD A,D	92	SUB A,D
83	ADD A,E	93	SUB A,E
84	ADD A,H	94	SUB A,H
85	ADD A,L	95	SUB A,L
86	ADD A,[HL]	96	SUB A,[HL]
87	ADD A,A	97	SUB A,A
88	ADC A,B	98	SBB A,B
89	ADC A,C	99	SBB A,C
8A	ADC A,D	9A	SBB A,D
8B	ADC A,E	9B	SBB A,E
8C	ADC A,H	9C	SBB A,H
8D	ADC A,L	9D	SBB A,L
8E	ADC A,[HL]	9E	SBB A,[HL]
8F	ADC A,A	9F	SBB A,A

Suppose A contains the byte 35h and register B contains the byte 22h. After executing

```
SUB A,B
```

the accumulator contains the byte 13h.

If A contains the byte 35h, and register H contains the byte 10h, and L contains the byte 7Ch, and the memory location 107Ch contains the byte 4Ah, the instruction

```
ADD A,[HL]
```

adds the byte in the accumulator (35h) and the byte addressed by the register pair HL (4Ah) and stores the result (7Fh) in the accumulator.

The *ADC* and *SBB* instructions allow the 8080 to add and subtract 16-bit, 24-bit, 32-bit, and larger numbers. For example, suppose the register pairs BC and DE both contain 16-bit numbers. You want to add them and put the result in BC. Here's how to do it:

```
MOV A,C    ; Low-order byte
ADD A,E
MOV C,A
MOV A,B    ; High-order byte
ADC A,D
MOV B,A
```

The two addition instructions are *ADD* for the low-order byte and *ADC* for the high-order byte. Any carry bit that results from the first addition is included in the second addition. But because you can add only with the accumulator, this little snippet of code requires no fewer than 4 *MOV* instructions. Lots of *MOV* instructions usually show up in 8080 code.

This is a good time to talk about the 8080 flags. In our processor in Chapter 17, we had a Carry flag and a Zero flag. The 8080 has three more, called Sign, Parity, and Auxiliary Carry. All the flags are stored in yet another 8-bit register called the *Program Status Word* (*PSW*). Instructions such as *LDA*, *STA*, or *MOV* don't affect the flags at all. The *ADD*, *SUB*, *ADC*, and *SBB* instructions do affect the flags, however, in the following way:

- The Sign flag is set to 1 if the most significant bit of the result is 1, meaning that the result is negative.
- The Zero flag is set to 1 if the result is 0.
- The Parity flag is set to 1 if the result has *even parity*, which means that the number of 1 bits in the result is even. The parity flag is 0 if the result has *odd parity*. Parity is sometimes used as a crude form of error checking. This flag isn't often used in 8080 programming.
- The Carry flag is set to 1 if an *ADD* or *ADC* operation results in a carry or if a *SUB* and *SBB* does *not* result in a carry. (This is different from the implementation of the Carry flag in the Chapter 17 computer.)
- The Auxiliary Carry flag is 1 if the operation results in a carry from the low nibble into the high nibble. This flag is used only for the *DAA* (*Decimal Adjust Accumulator*) instruction.

Two instructions affect the carry flag directly:

Opcode	Instruction	Meaning
37	STC	Set Carry flag to 1
3F	CMC	Complement Carry flag

The computer in Chapter 17 performed *ADD*, *ADC*, *SUB*, and *SBB* instructions (although not with nearly as much flexibility), but the 8080 does Boolean AND, OR, and XOR operations as well. Both arithmetic and logical operations are performed by the processor's Arithmetic Logic Unit (ALU).

Opcode	Instruction	Opcode	Instruction
A0	AND A,B	B0	OR A,B
A1	AND A,C	B1	OR A,C
A2	AND A,D	B2	OR A,D
A3	AND A,E	B3	OR A,E
A4	AND A,H	B4	OR A,H
A5	AND A,L	B5	OR A,L
A6	AND A,[HL]	B6	OR A,[HL]
A7	AND A,A	B7	OR A,A
A8	XOR A,B	B8	CMP A,B
A9	XOR A,C	B9	CMP A,C
AA	XOR A,D	BA	CMP A,D
AB	XOR A,E	BB	CMP A,E
AC	XOR A,H	BC	CMP A,H
AD	XOR A,L	BD	CMP A,L
AE	XOR A,[HL]	BE	CMP A,[HL]
AF	XOR A,A	BF	CMP A,A

The *AND, XOR,* and *OR* instructions perform *bitwise* operations. This means that the logical operation is performed on each pair of bits separately. For example,

```
MVI A,0Fh
MVI B,55h
AND A,B
```

The value in the accumulator will be 05h. If the third instruction were an *OR*, the result would be 5Fh. If the instruction were an *XOR*, the result would be 5Ah.

The *CMP* (*Compare*) instruction is just like the *SUB* instruction except that the result isn't stored in the accumulator. In other words, the *CMP* performs a subtraction and then throws away the result. What's the point? The flags! The flags tell you the relationship between the 2 bytes that you compared. For example, consider the following instructions:

```
MVI B,25h
CMP A,B
```

After this instruction, the contents of A remain unchanged. However, the Zero flag is set if the value in A equals 25h. The Carry flag is set if the value in A is less than 25h.

The eight arithmetic and logic operations also have versions that operate on an immediate byte:

Opcode	Instruction	Opcode	Instruction
C6	ADI A,xx	E6	ANI A,xx
CE	ACI A,xx	EE	XRI A,xx
D6	SUI A,xx	F6	ORI A,xx
DE	SBI A,xx	FE	CPI A,xx

For example, the two lines shown above can be replaced with

```
CPI A,25h
```

Here are two miscellaneous 8080 instructions:

Opcode	Instruction
27	DAA
2F	CMA

CMA stands for *Complement Accumulator*. It performs a ones' complement of the value in the accumulator. Every 0 becomes a 1 and every 1 becomes a 0. If the accumulator is 01100101, the *CMA* instruction causes it to be 10011010. You can also complement the accumulator using the instruction

```
XRI A,FFh
```

DAA stands for *Decimal Adjust Accumulator*, as I mentioned earlier, and it's probably the most sophisticated single instruction in the 8080. A whole little section of the microprocessor is dedicated specifically to performing this instruction.

The *DAA* instruction helps a programmer implement decimal arithmetic using a method of representing numbers known as *binary-coded decimal*, or *BCD*. In BCD, each nibble of data may range only from 0000 through 1001, corresponding to decimal digits 0 through 9. The 8 bits of a byte can store two decimal digits in BCD format.

Suppose the accumulator contains the BCD value 27h. Because this is a BCD value, it actually refers to the decimal value 27. (Normally, the hexadecimal value 27h has the decimal equivalent 39.) Suppose also that register B contains the BCD value 94h. If you execute the instruction

```
MOV A,27h
MOV B,94h
ADD A,B
```

the accumulator will contain the value BBh, which, of course, isn't a BCD value because the nibbles of BCD bytes never exceed 9. But now execute the instruction

```
DAA
```

Now the accumulator contains 21h, and the Carry flag is set. That's because the decimal sum of 27 and 94 equals 121. This can be handy if you need to do BCD arithmetic.

Very often it's necessary to add 1 to a particular value or subtract 1 from a value. In the multiplication program in Chapter 17, we needed to subtract

1 from a value, and the way we did it was to add FFh, which is the two's complement value of −1. The 8080 includes special instructions for increasing a register or memory location by 1 (this is known as an *increment*) or decreasing by 1 (*decrement*):

Opcode	Instruction	Opcode	Instruction
04	INR B	05	DCR B
0C	INR C	0D	DCR C
14	INR D	15	DCR D
1C	INR E	1D	DCR E
24	INR H	25	DCR H
2C	INR L	2D	DCR L
34	INR [HL]	35	DCR [HL]
3C	INR A	3D	DCR A

The single-byte *INR* and *DCR* instructions affect all flags except the Carry flag.

The 8080 also includes four *Rotate* instructions. These instructions shift the contents of the accumulator 1 bit to the left or right:

Opcode	Instruction	Meaning
07	RLC	Rotate accumulator left
0F	RRC	Rotate accumulator right
17	RAL	Rotate accumulator left through carry
1F	RAR	Rotate accumulator right through carry

Only the Carry flag is affected by these instructions.

Suppose the accumulator contains the value A7h, or 10100111 in binary. The *RLC* instruction shifts the bits left. The lowest bit (shifted out of the bottom) becomes the highest bit (shifted into the top) and also determines the state of the Carry flag. The result is 01001111, and the Carry flag is 1. The *RRC* instruction shifts the bits right in the same way. Beginning with 10100111, the result after an *RRC* instruction is 11010011, and the Carry flag is 1.

The *RAL* and *RAR* instructions work a little differently. The *RAL* instruction sets the Carry flag to the lowest bit of the accumulator when shifting left but sets the highest bit to the previous contents of the Carry flag. For example, if the accumulator contains 10100111 and the Carry flag is 0, *RAL* causes the accumulator to become 01001110 and the Carry flag to be 1. Similarly, under the same initial conditions *RAR* causes the accumulator to become 01010011 and the Carry flag to be set to 1.

The shift instructions come in handy when you're multiplying a number by 2 (that's a shift right) or dividing a number by 2 (a shift left).

The memory that the microprocessor addresses is called *random access memory* (RAM) for a reason: The microprocessor can access any particular memory location simply by supplying an address of that location. RAM is like a book that we can open to any page. It's *not* like a week's worth of a newspaper on microfilm. Finding something in Saturday's edition requires us to scan through most of the week. Similarly, playing the last song on a cassette tape requires us to fast forward through the whole side of the album. The term for microfilm or tape storage isn't random access but *sequential access.*

Random access memory is definitely a good thing, particularly for microprocessors, but sometimes it's advantageous to treat memory a little differently. Here's a form of storage that's neither random nor sequential: Suppose you work in an office where people come to your desk to give you jobs to do. Each job involves a file folder of some sort. Often when you're working on one job, you find that before you can continue you must do a related job using another file folder. So you leave the first folder on your desk and put the second one on top of it to work on that. Now someone comes to your desk to give you yet another job that has higher priority than the earlier one. You're handed a new file folder and you work with that one on top of the other two. That job requires yet another file folder, and soon you have a pile of four file folders on your desk.

Notice that this pile is actually a very orderly way to store and keep track of all the jobs you're doing. The topmost file folder always has the highest-priority job. After you get rid of that one, the next one on the pile must be attended to, and so on. When you finally get rid of the last file folder on your desk (the first one you started with), you can go home.

The technical term for this form of storage is a *stack.* You're stacking things from the bottom up and removing them from the top down. It's also called *last-in-first-out* storage, or *LIFO.* The last thing put on the stack is the first thing taken off the stack. The first thing put on the stack is the last thing taken off the stack.

Computers also can use a stack, not for storing jobs but for storing numbers, and it's something that turns out to be quite convenient. Putting something on the stack is called a *push,* and taking something off the stack is called a *pop.*

Suppose you were writing an assembly-language program that used registers A, B, and C. But you notice that you've reached a point where the program needs to do something else—another little calculation that also needs to use registers A, B, and C. You eventually want to come back to what you were doing before, however, and continue using A, B, and C with the values they previously had.

What you could do, of course, is simply store registers A, B, and C in various locations in memory and later load these locations back into the registers. But that requires keeping track of where you stored them. A much cleaner way to do it is to push the registers on the stack:

```
PUSH A
PUSH B
PUSH C
```

I'll explain what these instructions actually do in a moment. For now, all we need to know is that they somehow save the contents of the registers in last-in-first-out memory. Once these statements are executed, your program can use these registers for other purposes without worry. To get the earlier values back, you simply pop them from the stack in the reverse order, as shown at the top of the following page.

```
POP C
POP B
POP A
```

Remember: Last in, first out. Accidentally switching around these *POP* statements would constitute a bug.

What's particularly nice about the stack mechanism is that lots of different sections of a program can use the stack without causing problems. For example, after the program pushes A, B, and C on the stack, another section of the program could decide it needs to do the same thing with registers C, D, and E:

```
PUSH C
PUSH D
PUSH E
```

Then all that's necessary is for that section of the program to restore the registers this way:

```
POP E
POP D
POP C
```

before the first section popped C, B, and A.

How is the stack implemented? The stack is, first of all, just a section of normal RAM that isn't being used for anything else. The 8080 microprocessor contains a special 16-bit register that addresses this section of memory. That 16-bit register is called the *Stack Pointer*.

My examples of pushing and popping individual registers weren't quite accurate for the 8080. The 8080 *PUSH* instruction actually stores *16-bit* values on the stack, and the *POP* instruction retrieves them. So instead of instructions like *PUSH C* and *POP C*, we have the following 8 instructions:

Opcode	Instruction	Opcode	Instruction
C5	PUSH BC	C1	POP BC
D5	PUSH DE	D1	POP DE
E5	PUSH HL	E1	POP HL
F5	PUSH PSW	F1	POP PSW

The *PUSH BC* instruction stores registers B and C on the stack, and *POP BC* retrieves them. The abbreviation PSW in the last row refers to the *Program Status Word*, which, as you'll recall, is the 8-bit register that contains the flags. The two instructions in the bottom row actually push and pop both the accumulator *and* the PSW. If you want to save the contents of *all* the registers and flags, you can use

```
PUSH PSW
PUSH BC
PUSH DE
PUSH HL
```

When you later need to restore the contents of these registers, use the *POP* instructions in reverse order:

```
POP HL
POP DE
POP BC
POP PSW
```

How does the stack work? Let's assume the Stack Pointer is 8000h. The *PUSH BC* instruction causes the following to occur:

- The Stack Pointer is decremented to 7FFFh.
- The contents of register B are stored at the Stack Pointer address, or 7FFFh.
- The Stack Pointer is decremented to 7FFEh.
- The contents of register C are stored at the Stack Pointer address, or 7FFEh.

A *POP BC* instruction executed when the Stack Pointer is still 7FFEh undoes everything:

- The contents of register C are loaded from the Stack Pointer address, or 7FFEh.
- The Stack Pointer is incremented to 7FFFh.
- The contents of register B are loaded from the Stack Pointer address, or 7FFFh.
- The Stack Pointer is incremented to 8000h.

For every *PUSH* instruction, the stack increases 2 bytes in size. It's possible—possibly due to a bug in a program—that the stack will get so big that it will begin to overwrite some code or data needed by a program. This is a problem known as *stack overflow*. Similarly, too many *POP* instructions can prematurely exhaust the contents of the stack, a condition known as *stack underflow*.

If you have 64 KB of memory connected to your 8080, you might want to initially set the Stack Pointer to 0000h. The first *PUSH* instruction decrements that address to FFFFh. The stack then occupies the area of memory with the very highest addresses, quite a distance from your programs, which will probably be in the area of memory starting at address 0000h.

The instruction to set the value of the stack register is *LXI*, which stands for *Load Extended Immediate*. These instructions also load 16-bit register pairs with the two bytes that follow the opcode:

Opcode	Instruction
01	LXI BC,xxxx
11	LXI DE,xxxx
21	LXI HL,xxxx
31	LXI SP,xxxx

The instruction

```
LXI BC,527Ah
```

is equivalent to

```
MVI B,52
MVI C,7Ah
```

The *LXI* instruction saves a byte. In addition, the last *LXI* instruction in the preceding table is used to set the Stack Pointer to a particular value. It's not uncommon for this instruction to be one of the first instructions that a microprocessor executes after being restarted:

```
0000h:    LXI SP,0000h
```

It's also possible to increment and decrement register pairs and the Stack Pointer as if they were 16-bit registers:

Opcode	Instruction	Opcode	Instruction
03	INX BC	0B	DCX BC
13	INX DE	1B	DCX DE
23	INX HL	2B	DCX HL
33	INX SP	3B	DCX SP

While I'm on the subject of 16-bit instructions, let's look at a few more. The following instructions add the contents of 16-bit register pairs to the register pair HL:

Opcode	Instruction
09	DAD HL,BC
19	DAD HL,DE
29	DAD HL,HL
39	DAD HL,SP

These instructions could save a few bytes. For example, the first of these instructions would normally require 6 bytes:

```
MOV A,L
ADD A,C
MOV L,A
MOV A,H
ADC A,B
MOV H,A
```

The *DAD* instruction is normally used for calculating memory addresses. The only flag that the instruction affects is the Carry flag.

Next let's look at some miscellaneous instructions. These two opcodes are followed by a 2-byte address and store and load the contents of the register pair HL at that address:

Opcode	Instruction	Meaning
2h	SHLD [aaaa],HL	Store HL Direct
2Ah	LHLD HL,[aaaa]	Load HL Direct

The L register is stored at address *aaaa,* and the H register is stored at address *aaaa* + 1.

These two instructions load the Program Counter or the Stack Pointer from the register pair HL:

Opcode	Instruction	Meaning
E9h	PCHL PC,HL	Load Program Counter from HL
F9h	SPHL SP,HL	Load Stack Pointer from HL

The *PCHL* instruction is actually a type of *Jump*. The next instruction that the 8080 executes is the one located at the address stored in the HL register pair. *SPHL* is another method to set the Stack Pointer.

These two instructions exchange the contents of HL first with the two bytes located on top of the stack and second with the register pair DE:

Opcode	Instruction	Meaning
E3h	XTHL HL,[SP]	Exchange top of stack with HL
EBh	XCHG HL,DE	Exchange DE and HL

I haven't described the 8080 *Jump* instructions yet, except for *PCHL*. As you'll recall from Chapter 17, a processor includes a register called the Program Counter that contains the memory address the processor uses to retrieve the instructions that it executes. Normally the Program Counter causes the processor to execute instructions that are located sequentially in memory. But some instructions—usually named *Jump* or *Branch* or *Goto*— cause the processor to deviate from this steady course. Such instructions cause the Program Counter to be loaded with another value. The next instruction that the processor fetches is somewhere else in memory.

While a plain old ordinary *Jump* instruction is certainly useful, *conditional* jumps are even better. These instructions cause the processor to jump to another address based on the setting of a particular flag, such as the Carry flag or the Zero flag. The presence of a conditional Jump instruction is what turned the Chapter 17 automated adding machine into a general-purpose digital computer.

The 8080 has five flags, four of which are used for conditional jumps. The 8080 supports nine different Jump instructions, including the unconditional Jump and conditional jumps based on whether the Zero, Carry, Parity, and Sign flags are 1 or 0.

Before I show these instructions to you, however, I want to introduce two other types of instructions that are related to the *Jump*. The first is the *Call* instruction. A *Call* is similar to a *Jump* except that prior to loading the Program Counter with a new address, the processor saves the previous address. Where does it save that address? Why, on the stack, of course!

This strategy means that the *Call* instruction effectively saves a reminder of *where it jumped from*. The saved address allows the processor to eventually return to the original location. The returning instruction is called, appropriately, *Return*. The *Return* instruction pops 2 bytes from the stack and loads the Program Counter with that value.

The *Call* and *Return* instructions are extremely important features of any processor. They allow a programmer to implement *subroutines,* which are snippets of frequently used code. (By *frequently* I generally mean *more than once.*) Subroutines are the primary organizational elements of assembly-language programs.

Let's look at an example. Suppose you're writing an assembly-language program and you come to a point where you need to multiply 2 bytes. So you write some code that does precisely that, and you continue with the program. Now you come to another point where you need to multiply 2 bytes. Well, you already know how to multiply two numbers, so you can simply use the same instructions all over again. But do you simply enter the instructions into memory a second time? I hope not. It's a waste of time and memory. What you'd rather do is just jump to the previous code. But the normal *Jump* doesn't work either because there's no way to return to the current place in the program. That's what the *Call* and *Return* instructions let you do.

A group of instructions that multiply 2 bytes is an ideal candidate for a subroutine. Let's take a look at such a subroutine. In Chapter 17, the bytes to be multiplied (and the result) were stored in particular locations in memory. This 8080 subroutine instead multiplies the byte in register B by the byte in register C and puts the 16-bit product in register HL:

```
Multiply:    PUSH PSW        ; Save registers being altered
             PUSH BC

             SUB H,H         ; Set HL (result) to 0000h
             SUB L,L

             MOV A,B         ; The multiplier goes in A
             CPI A,00h       ; If it's 0, we're finished.
             JZ AllDone

             MVI B,00h       ; Set high byte of BC to 0

MultLoop:    DAD HL,BC       ; Add BC to HL
             DEC A           ; Decrement multiplier
             JNZ MultLoop    ; Loop if it's not 0

AllDone:     POP BC          ; Restore saved registers
             POP PSW
             RET             ; Return
```

Notice that the first line of the subroutine begins with a label, which is the word *Multiply.* This label, of course, actually corresponds to a memory address where the subroutine is located. The subroutine begins with two *PUSH* instructions. Usually a subroutine should attempt to save (and later restore) any registers that it might need to use.

The subroutine then sets the contents of the H and L registers to 0. It could have used the *MVI* (*Move Immediate*) instructions rather than *SUB* instructions for this job, but that would have required 4 instruction bytes rather than 2. The register pair HL will hold the result of the multiplication when the subroutine is completed.

Next the subroutine moves the contents of register B (the multiplier) into A and checks if it's 0. If it's 0, the multiplication subroutine is complete because the product is 0. Since registers H and L are already 0, the subroutine can just use the *JZ* (*Jump If Zero*) instruction to skip to the two *POP* instructions at the end.

Otherwise, the subroutine sets register B to 0. Now the register pair BC contains a 16-bit multiplicand and A contains the multiplier. The *DAD* instruction adds BC (the multiplicand) to HL (the result). The multiplier in A is decremented and, as long as it's not 0, the *JNZ* (*Jump If Not Zero*) instruction causes BC to be added to HL again. This little loop will continue until BC is added to HL a number of times equal to the multiplier. (It's possible to write a more efficient multiplication subroutine using the 8080 shift instructions.)

A program that wishes to make use of this subroutine to multiply (for example) 25h by 12h uses the following code:

```
MOV B,25h
MOV C,12h
CALL Multiply
```

The *CALL* instruction saves the value of the Program Counter on the stack. The value saved on the stack is the address of the next instruction *after* the *CALL* instruction. Then the *CALL* instruction causes a jump to the instruction identified by the label *Multiply*. That's the beginning of the subroutine. When the subroutine has calculated the product, it executes a *RET* (*Return*) instruction, which causes the Program Counter to be popped from the stack. The program continues with the next statement after the *CALL* instruction.

The 8080 instruction set includes conditional *Call* instructions and conditional *Return* instructions, but these are used much less than the conditional *Jump* instructions. The complete array of these instructions is shown in the following table:

Condition	Opcode	Instruction	Opcode	Instruction	Opcode	Instruction
None	C9	RET	C3	JMP aaaa	CD	CALL aaaa
Z not set	C0	RNZ	C2	JNZ aaaa	C4	CNZ aaaa
Z set	C8	RZ	CA	JZ aaaa	CC	CZ aaaa
C not set	D0	RNC	D2	JNC aaaa	D4	CNC aaaa
C set	D8	RC	DA	JC aaaa	DC	CC aaaa
Odd parity	E0	RPO	E2	JPO aaaa	E4	CPO aaaa
Even parity	E8	RPE	EA	JPE aaaa	EC	CPE aaaa
S not set	F0	RP	F2	JP aaaa	F4	CP aaaa
S set	F8	RM	FA	JM aaaa	FC	CM aaaa

As you probably know, memory isn't the only thing connected to a microprocessor. A computer system usually requires input and output (I/O) devices that make it easier for humans to communicate with the machine. These input devices usually include a keyboard and a video display.

How does the microprocessor communicate with these *peripherals* (as anything connected to a microprocessor that isn't memory is called)? Peripherals are built so that they have an interface similar to memory. A microprocessor can write into and read from a peripheral by specifying certain addresses that the peripheral responds to. In some microprocessors, peripherals actually replace some addresses that would normally be used to address memory. This configuration is known as *memory-mapped I/O*. In the 8080, however, 256 additional addresses beyond the normal 65,536 are specifically reserved for input and output devices. These are known as I/O *ports*. The I/O address signals are A_0 through A_7, but I/O accesses are distinguished from memory accesses through signals latched by the 8228 System Controller chip.

The *OUT* instruction writes the contents of the accumulator to a port addressed by the byte that follows the instruction. The *IN* instruction reads a byte into the accumulator.

Opcode	Instruction
D3	OUT pp
DB	IN pp

Peripherals sometimes need to get the attention of the microprocessor. For example, when you press a key on a keyboard, it's usually helpful if the microprocessor knows about this event right away. This is a accomplished by a mechanism called an *interrupt,* which is a signal connected from the peripheral to the INT input of the 8080.

When the 8080 is reset, however, it doesn't respond to interrupts. A program must execute the *EI* (*Enable Interrupts*) instruction to enable interrupts and can later execute *DI* (*Disable Interrupts*) to disable them:

Opcode	Instruction
F3	DI
FB	EI

The INTE output signal from the 8080 indicates when interrupts have been enabled. When a peripheral needs to interrupt the microprocessor, it sets the INT input of the 8080 to 1. The 8080 responds to that by fetching an instruction from memory, but control signals indicate that an interrupt is occurring. The peripheral usually responds by supplying one of the following instructions to the 8080:

Opcode	Instruction	Opcode	Instruction
C7	RST 0	E7	RST 4
CF	RST 1	EF	RST 5
D7	RST 2	F7	RST 6
DF	RST 3	FF	RST 7

These are called *Restart* instructions, and they're similar to *Call* instructions in that the current Program Counter is saved on the stack. But the Restart instructions then jump to specific locations: *RST 0* jumps to address 0000h, *RST 1* to address 0008h, and so forth, up to *RST 7*, which jumps to address 0038h. Located at these addresses are sections of code that deal with the interrupt. For example, an interrupt from the keyboard might cause a *RST 4* instruction to be executed. At address 0020h begins some code to read a byte from the keyboard. (I'll explain this more fully in Chapter 21.)

So far I've described 243 opcodes. The 12 bytes that aren't associated with any opcodes are 08h, 10h, 18h, 20h, 28h, 30h, 38h, CBh, D9h, DDh, EDh, and FDh. That brings the total to 255. There's one more opcode I need to mention, and that's this one:

Opcode	Instruction
00	NOP

NOP stands for (and is pronounced) *no op*, as in *no operation*. The *NOP* causes the processor to do absolutely nothing. What's it good for? Filling space. The 8080 can usually execute a bunch of *NOP* instructions without anything bad happening.

I won't go into nearly as much detail discussing the Motorola 6800 because many of the aspects of its design and functionality are quite similar to those of the 8080. Here are the 40 pins of the 6800:

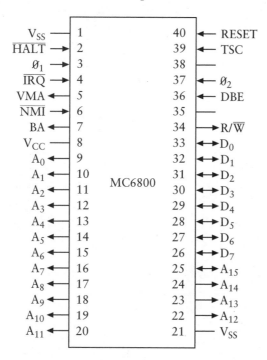

The V_{SS} indicates Ground, and V_{CC} is 5 volts. Like the 8080, the 6800 has 16 output Address signals and 8 Data signals used for both input and output. There's a RESET signal and a R/$\overline{W}$ (read/write) signal. The $\overline{IRQ}$ signal stands for *interrupt request*. The signal timing of the 6800 is considered to be much simpler than that of the 8080. What the 6800 doesn't have is the concept of I/O ports. All input and output devices must be part of the 6800 memory address space.

The 6800 has a 16-bit Program Counter, a 16-bit Stack Pointer, an 8-bit Status Register (for flags), and two 8-bit accumulators called A and B. These are both considered accumulators (rather than B being considered just a register) because there is nothing that you can do with A that you can't also do with B. There are no additional 8-bit registers, however.

The 6800 instead has a 16-bit *index register* that can be used to hold a 16-bit address, much like the register pair HL is used in the 8080. For many instructions, an address can be formed from the sum of the index register and the byte that follows the opcode.

While the 6800 does just about the same operations as the 8080—loading, storing, adding, subtracting, shifting, jumping, calling—it should be obvious that the opcodes and the mnemonics are completely different. Here, for example, are the 6800 *Branch* instructions:

Opcode	Instruction	Meaning
20h	BRA	Branch
22h	BHI	Branch If Higher
23h	BLS	Branch If Lower or Same
24h	BCC	Branch If Carry Clear
25h	BCS	Branch If Carry Set
26h	BNE	Branch If Not Equal
27h	BEQ	Branch If Equal
28h	BVC	Branch If Overflow Clear
29h	BVS	Branch If Overflow Set
2Ah	BPL	Branch If Plus
2Bh	BMI	Branch If Minus
2Ch	BGE	Branch If Greater than or Equal to Zero
2Dh	BLT	Branch If Less than Zero
2Eh	BGT	Branch If Greater than Zero
2Fh	BLE	Branch If Less than or Equal to Zero

The 6800 doesn't have a Parity flag like the 8080, but it does have a flag the 8080 doesn't have—an Overflow flag. Some of these *Branch* instructions depend on *combinations* of flags.

Of *course* the 8080 and 6800 instructions sets are different. The two chips were designed about the same time by two different groups of engineers at two different companies. What this incompatibility means is that neither chip can execute the other chip's machine codes. Nor can an assembly-language program written for one chip be translated into opcodes that run on the other chip. Writing computer programs that run on more than one processor is the subject of Chapter 24.

Here's another interesting difference between the 8080 and the 6800: In both microprocessors, the instruction *LDA* loads the accumulator from a specified memory address. In the 8080, for example, the following sequence of bytes:

3Ah	8080 LDA instruction
7Bh	
34h	

will load the accumulator with the byte stored at memory address 347Bh. Now compare that with the 6800 *LDA* instruction using the so-called 6800 extended addressing mode:

B6h	6800 LDA instruction
7Bh	
34h	

This sequence of bytes loads accumulator A with the byte stored at memory address 7B34h.

The difference is subtle. You expect the opcode to be different, of course: 3Ah for the 8080 and B6h for the 6800. But the two microprocessors treat the address that follows the opcode differently. The 8080 assumes that the low-order byte comes first, followed by the high-order byte. The 6800 assumes that the high-order byte comes first!

This fundamental difference in how Intel and Motorola microprocessors store multibyte values *has never been resolved*. To this very day, Intel microprocessors continue to store multibyte values with the least-significant byte first (that is, at the lowest memory address), and Motorola microprocessors store multibyte values with the most-significant byte first.

These two methods are known as *little-endian* (the Intel way) and *big-endian* (the Motorola way). It might be fun to argue over which method is better, but before you do so, be aware that the term *Big-Endian* comes from Jonathan Swift's *Gulliver's Travels* and refers to the war between Lilliput and Blefuscu over which end of an egg to break before eating it. Such an argument is probably purposeless. (On the other hand, I feel obliged to confess that the approach I used in the Chapter 17 computer wasn't the one I personally prefer!) Despite neither method being intrinsically "right," the difference does create an additional incompatibility problem when sharing information between systems based on little-endian and big-endian machines.

What became of these two microprocessors? The 8080 was used in what some people have called the first personal computer but which is probably more accurately the first *home* computer. This is the Altair 8800, which appeared on the cover of the January 1975 issue of *Popular Electronics*.

When you look at the Altair 8800, the lights and switches on the front panel should seem familiar. This is the same type of primitive "control panel" interface that I proposed for the 64-KB RAM array in Chapter 16.

The 8080 was followed by the Intel 8085 and, more significantly, by the Z-80 chip made by Zilog, a rival of Intel founded by former Intel employee Federico Faggin, who had done important work on the 4004. The Z-80 was entirely compatible with the 8080 but added many more very useful instructions. In 1977, the Z-80 was used in the Radio Shack TRS-80 Model 1.

Also in 1977, the Apple Computer Company, founded by Steven Jobs and Stephen Wozniak, introduced the Apple II. The Apple II, however, used neither the 8080 nor the 6800 but instead used MOS Technology's less expensive 6502 chip, which was an enhancement of the 6800.

In June 1978, Intel introduced the 8086, which was a 16-bit microprocessor that could access 1 megabyte of memory. The 8086 opcodes weren't compatible with the 8080, but I should note that they included instructions to multiply and divide. A year later, Intel introduced the 8088, which internally was identical to the 8086 but externally accessed memory in bytes, thus allowing the microprocessor to use the more-prevalent 8-bit support chips designed for the 8080. IBM used the 8088 chip in its 5150 Personal Computer—commonly called the IBM PC—introduced in the fall of 1981.

IBM's entrance into the personal computer market had a great impact, with many companies releasing machines that were compatible with the PC. (What it means to be compatible will be explored more in subsequent chapters.) Over the years "IBM PC compatible" has also implied "Intel inside," specifically Intel microprocessors of the so-called x86 family. The x86 family continued in 1985 with the 32-bit 386 chip, in 1989 with the 486, and beginning in 1993, with the Intel Pentium line of microprocessors that are currently used in PC compatibles. While these Intel microprocessors have ever-increasing instruction sets, they continue to support the opcodes of all earlier processors starting with the 8086.

The Apple Macintosh, first introduced in 1984, used the Motorola 68000, a 16-bit microprocessor that's a direct descendant of the 6800. The 68000 and its descendants (often called the 68K series) are some of the most beloved microprocessors ever made.

Since 1994, Macintosh computers have used the PowerPC microprocessor that was developed in a coalition of Motorola, IBM, and Apple. The PowerPC was designed with a type of microprocessor architecture known as RISC (Reduced Instruction Set Computing), which attempts to increase the speed of the processor by simplifying it in some respects. In a RISC computer, generally each instruction is the same length (32 bits on the PowerPC), memory accesses are restricted to just load and store instructions, and instructions do simple operations rather than complex ones. RISC processors usually have plenty of registers to avoid frequent accesses of memory.

The PowerPC can't execute 68K code because it has a whole different instruction set. But the PowerPC microprocessors currently used in the Apple Macintoshes can *emulate* the 68K. An emulator program running on the PowerPC examines each opcode of a 68K program, one by one, and performs an appropriate action. It's not as fast as native PowerPC code, but it works.

According to Moore's Law, the number of transistors in microprocessors should double every 18 months. What are those many additional transistors used for?

Some of the transistors accommodate the increase in processor data width, from 4 bits to 8 bits to 16 bits to 32 bits. Another part of the increase is due to new instructions. Most microprocessors these days have instructions to do floating-point arithmetic (as I'll explain in Chapter 23); new instructions have also been added to microprocessors to do some of the repetitive calculations required to display pictures or movies on computer screens.

Modern processors use several techniques to help improve their speed. One is pipelining. When the processor is executing one instruction, it's reading in the next instructions, even to a certain extent anticipating how *Jump* instructions will alter the execution flow. Modern processors also include a cache (pronounced *cash*). This is an array of very fast RAM inside the processor that is used to store recently executed instructions. Because computer programs often execute small loops of instructions, the cache prevents these instructions from being repetitively reloaded. All these speed-improving features require more logic and more transistors in the microprocessor.

As I mentioned earlier, the microprocessor is only one part (although the most important part) of a complete computer system. We'll build such a system in Chapter 21, but first we must learn how to encode something else in memory besides opcodes and numbers. We must go back to first grade and learn again how to read and write text.

Chapter Twenty

ASCII and a Cast of Characters

D igital computer memory stores only bits, so anything that we want to work with on the computer must be stored in the form of bits. We've already seen how bits can represent numbers and machine code. The next challenge must be text. After all, the great bulk of the accumulated information of this world is in the form of text, and our libraries are full of books and magazines and newspapers. Although we'd eventually like to use our computers to store sounds and pictures and movies, text is a much easier place to begin.

To represent text in digital form, we must develop some kind of system in which each letter corresponds to a unique code. Numbers and punctuation also occur in text, so codes for these must be developed as well. In short, we need codes for all *alphanumeric* characters. Such a system is sometimes known as a *coded character set,* and the individual codes are known as *character codes.*

The first question must be: How many bits do we need for these codes? The answer isn't an easy one!

When we think about representing text using bits, let's not get too far ahead of ourselves. We're accustomed to seeing text nicely formatted on the pages of a book or in the columns of a magazine or newspaper. Paragraphs are neatly separated into lines of a consistent width. Yet this formatting isn't essential to the text itself. When we read a short story in a magazine and years later encounter that same story in a book, we don't think the story has changed just because the text column is wider in the book than in the magazine.

In other words, don't think about text as formatted into two-dimensional columns on the printed page. Think of text instead as a one-dimensional stream of letters, numbers, and punctuation marks, with perhaps an additional code to indicate the end of one paragraph and the start of another.

Again, if you read a story in a magazine and later see it in a book and the typeface is a little different, is that a big deal? If the magazine version begins

Call me Ishmael.

and the book version begins

Call me Ishmael.

is that something we really want to be concerned with just yet? Probably not. Yes, the typeface subtly affects the tone of the text, but the story hasn't been lost with the change of typeface. The typeface can always be changed back. There's no harm done.

Here's another way we're going to simplify the problem: Let's stick to plain vanilla text. No italics, no boldface, no underlining, no colors, no outlined letters, no subscripts, no superscripts. And no accent marks. No Å or é or ñ or ö. Just the naked Latin alphabet as it's used in 99 percent of English.

In our earlier studies of Morse code and Braille, we've already seen how the letters of the alphabet can be represented in a binary form. Although these systems are fine for their specific purposes, both have their failings when it comes to computers. Morse code, for example, is a *variable-width* code: It uses shorter codes for frequently used letters and longer codes for less common ones. Such a code is suitable for telegraphy, but it might be awkward for computers. In addition, Morse code doesn't differentiate between uppercase and lowercase versions of letters.

Braille is a fixed-width code, which is much preferable for computers. Every letter is represented by 6 bits. Braille also differentiates between uppercase and lowercase letters, although it does so with the use of a special *escape* code. This code indicates that the next character is uppercase. What this really means is that every capital letter requires two codes rather than one. Numbers are represented with a *shift* code: After that special code, the codes that follow are assumed to represent numbers until another shift code signals the return to letters.

Our goal here is to develop a coded character set so that a sentence such as

I have 27 sisters.

can be represented by a series of codes, each of which is a certain number of bits. Some of the codes will represent letters, some will representation punctuation marks, and some will represent numbers. There should even be a code that represents the space between words. There are 18 characters in that sentence (including the spaces between the words). The consecutive character codes for such a sentence are often referred to as a text *string*.

That we need codes for numbers in a text string such as *27* might seem odd because we've been using bits to represent numbers for many chapters now. We may be tempted to assume that the codes for the 2 and 7 in this sentence are simply the binary numbers *10* and *111*. But that's not necessarily the case. In the context of a sentence such as this, the characters 2 and 7 can be treated like any other character found in written English. They can have character codes that are completely unrelated to the actual values of the numbers.

Perhaps the most economical code for text is a 5-bit code that originated in an 1874 printing telegraph developed by Emile Baudot (pronounced *baw-doh*), an officer in the French Telegraph Service; his code was adopted by the Service in 1877. This code was later modified by Donald Murray and standardized in 1931 by the *Comité Consultatif International Télégraphique et Téléphonique* (CCITT), which is now known as the International Telecommunication Union (ITU). The code is formally known as the International Telegraph Alphabet No. 2, or ITA-2, and it's more popularly known in the United States as Baudot, although it's more correctly called the Murray code.

In the twentieth century, Baudot was often used in *teletypewriters*. A Baudot teletypewriter has a keyboard that looks something like a typewriter, except that it has only 30 keys and a spacebar. Teletypewriter keys are actually switches that cause a binary code to be generated and sent down the teletypewriter's output cable, one bit after the other. A teletypewriter also contains a printing mechanism. Codes coming through the teletypewriter's input cable trigger electromagnets that print characters on paper.

Because Baudot is a 5-bit code, there are only 32 codes. The hexadecimal values of these codes range from 00h through 1Fh. Here's how the 32 available codes correspond to the letters of the alphabet:

Hex Code	Baudot Letter	Hex Code	Baudot Letter
00		10	E
01	T	11	Z
02	*Carriage Return*	12	D
03	O	13	B
04	*Space*	14	S
05	H	15	Y
06	N	16	F
07	M	17	X
08	*Line Feed*	18	A
09	L	19	W
0A	R	1A	J
0B	G	1B	*Figure Shift*
0C	I	1C	U
0D	P	1D	Q
0E	C	1E	K
0F	V	1F	*Letter Shift*

Code 00h isn't assigned to anything. Of the remaining 31 codes, 26 are assigned to letters of the alphabet and the other five are indicated by italicized words or phrases in the table.

Code 04h is the Space code, which is used for the space separating words. Codes 02h and 08h are labeled Carriage Return and Line Feed. This terminology comes from the typewriter. When you're typing on a typewriter and reach the end of a line, you push a lever or button that does two things. First, it causes the carriage to be moved to the right so that the next line begins at the left side of the paper. That's a carriage return. Second, the typewriter rolls the carriage so that the next line is underneath the line you just finished. That's the linefeed. In Baudot, separate keyboard keys generate these two codes. A Baudot teletypewriter printer responds to these two codes when printing.

Where are the numbers and punctuation marks in the Baudot system? That's the purpose of code 1Bh, identified in the table as Figure Shift. After the Figure Shift code, all subsequent codes are interpreted as numbers or punctuation marks until the Letter Shift code (1Fh) causes them to revert to the letters. Here are the codes for the numbers and punctuation:

Hex Code	Baudot Figure	Hex Code	Baudot Figure
00		10	3
01	5	11	+
02	*Carriage Return*	12	*Who Are You?*
03	9	13	?
04	*Space*	14	'
05	#	15	6
06	,	16	$
07	.	17	/
08	*Line Feed*	18	-
09	)	19	2
0A	4	1A	*Bell*
0B	&	1B	*Figure Shift*
0C	8	1C	7
0D	0	1D	1
0E	:	1E	(
0F	=	1F	*Letter Shift*

Actually, the code as formalized by the ITU doesn't define codes 05h, 0Bh, and 16h, and instead reserves them "for national use." The table shows how these codes were used in the United States. The same codes were often used for accented letters of some European languages. The *Bell* code is supposed to ring an audible bell on the teletypewriter. The "Who Are You?" code activates a mechanism whereby a teletypewriter can identify itself.

Like Morse code, this 5-bit code doesn't differentiate between uppercase and lowercase. The sentence

I SPENT $25 TODAY.

is represented by the following stream of hexadecimal data:

0C 04 14 0D 10 06 01 04 1B 16 19 01 1F 04 01 03 12 18 15 1B 07 02 08

Notice the three shift codes: 1Bh right before the number, 1Fh after the number, and 1Bh again before the final period. The line concludes with carriage-return and linefeed codes.

Unfortunately, if you sent this stream of data to a teletypewriter printer twice in a row, it would come out like this:

> *I SPENT $25 TODAY.*
> *8 '03,5 $25 TODAY.*

What happened? The last shift code the printer received before the second line was a Figure Shift code, so the codes at the beginning of the second line were interpreted as numbers.

Problems like this are typical nasty results of using shift codes. Although Baudot is certainly an economical code, it's probably preferable to use unique codes for numbers and punctuation, as well as separate codes for lowercase and uppercase letters.

So if we want to figure out how many bits we need for a *better* character encoding system than Baudot, just add them up: We need 52 codes just for the uppercase and lowercase letters and 10 codes for the digits 0 through 9. We're up to 62 already. Throw in a few punctuation marks, and we top 64 codes, which means we need more than 6 bits. But we seem to have lots of leeway before we exceed 128 characters, which would require 8 bits.

So the answer is 7. We need 7 bits to represent the characters of English text if we want uppercase and lowercase with no shifting.

And what are these codes? Well, the actual codes can be anything we want. If we were going to build our own computer, and we were going to build every piece of hardware required by this computer, and we were going to program this computer ourselves and never use the computer to connect to any other computer, we could make up our own codes. All we need do is assign every character we'll be using a unique code.

But since it's rarely the case that computers are built and used in isolation, it makes more sense for everyone to agree to use the same codes. That way, the computers that we build can be more compatible with one another and maybe even actually exchange textual information.

We also probably shouldn't assign codes in a haphazard manner. For example, when we work with text on the computer, certain advantages accrue if the letters of the alphabet are assigned to sequential codes. This ordering scheme makes alphabetizing and sorting easier, for example.

Fortunately, such a standard has already been developed. It's called the *American Standard Code for Information Interchange*, abbreviated ASCII, and referred to with the unlikely pronunciation *ASS-key*. It was formalized in 1967 and remains the single most important standard in the entire computer industry. With one big exception (which I'll describe later), whenever you deal with text on a computer you can be sure that ASCII is involved in some way.

ASCII is a 7-bit code using binary codes 0000000 through 1111111, which are hexadecimal codes 00h through 7Fh. Let's take a look at the ASCII codes, but let's not start at the very beginning because the first 32 codes are conceptually a bit more difficult than the rest of the codes. I'll begin with the second batch of 32 codes, which includes punctuation and the ten numeric digits. This table shows the hexadecimal code and the character that corresponds to that code:

Hex Code	ASCII Character	Hex Code	ASCII Character
20	*Space*	30	0
21	!	31	1
22	"	32	2
23	#	33	3
24	$	34	4
25	%	35	5
26	&	36	6
27	'	37	7
28	(	38	8
29	)	39	9
2A	*	3A	:
2B	+	3B	;
2C	,	3C	<
2D	-	3D	=
2E	.	3E	>
2F	/	3F	?

Notice that 20h is the space character that divides words and sentences.

The next 32 codes include the uppercase letters and some additional punctuation. Aside from the @ sign and the underscore, these punctuation symbols aren't normally found on typewriters. They're all now standard on computer keyboards.

Hex Code	Baudot Figure	Hex Code	Baudot Figure
40	@	50	P
41	A	51	Q
42	B	52	R
43	C	53	S
44	D	54	T
45	E	55	U
46	F	56	V
47	G	57	W
48	H	58	X
49	I	59	Y
4A	J	5A	Z
4B	K	5B	[
4C	L	5C	\
4D	M	5D	]
4E	N	5E	^
4F	O	5F	_

The next 32 characters include all the lowercase letters and some additional punctuation, again not often found on typewriters:

Hex Code	ASCII Character	Hex Code	ASCII Character
60	`	70	p
61	a	71	q
62	b	72	r
63	c	73	s
64	d	74	t
65	e	75	u
66	f	76	v
67	g	77	w
68	h	78	x
69	i	79	y
6A	j	7A	z
6B	k	7B	{
6C	l	7C		
6D	m	7D	}
6E	n	7E	~
6F	o		

Notice that this table is missing the last character corresponding to code 7Fh. If you're keeping count, the three tables here show a total of 95 characters. Because ASCII is a 7-bit code, 128 codes are possible, so 33 more codes should be available. I'll get to those shortly.

The text string

Hello, you!

can be represented in ASCII using the hexadecimal codes

48 65 6C 6C 6F 2C 20 79 6F 75 21

Notice the comma (code 2C), the space (code 20) and the exclamation point (code 21) as well as the codes for the letters. Here's another short sentence:

I am 12 years old.

and its ASCII representation:

49 20 61 6D 20 31 32 20 79 65 61 72 73 20 6F 6C 64 2E

Notice that the number 12 in this sentence is represented by the hexadecimal numbers 31h and 32h, which are the ASCII codes for the digits 1 and 2. When the number 12 is part of a text stream, it should *not* be represented by the hexadecimal codes 01h and 02h, or the BCD code 12h, or the hexadecimal code 0Ch. These other codes all mean something else in ASCII.

A particular uppercase letter in ASCII differs from its lowercase counterpart by 20h. This fact makes it fairly easy to write some code that (for example) capitalizes a string of text. Suppose a certain area of memory contains a text string, one character per byte. The following 8080 subroutine assumes that the address of the first character in the text string is stored in register HL. Register C contains the length of that text string, which is the number of characters:

```
Capitalize: MOV A,C       ; C = number of characters left
            CPI A,00h      ; Compare with 0
            JZ  AllDone    ; If C is 0, we're finished

            MOV A,[HL]     ; Get the next character
            CPI A,61h      ; Check if it's less than 'a'
            JC  SkipIt     ; If so, ignore it

            CPI A,7Bh      ; Check if it's greater than 'z'
            JNC SkipIt     ; If so, ignore it

            SBI A,20h      ; It's lowercase, so subtract 20h
            MOV [HL],A     ; Store the character

SkipIt:     INX HL         ; Increment the text address
            DCR C          ; Decrement the counter
            JMP Capitalize ; Go back to the top

AllDone:    RET
```

The statement that subtracts 20h from the lowercase letter to convert it to uppercase can be replaced with this:

```
ANI A,DFh
```

The *ANI* instruction is an *AND Immediate*. It performs a bitwise AND operation between the value in the accumulator and the value DFh, which is 11011111 in binary. By *bitwise*, I mean that the instruction performs an AND operation between each pair of corresponding bits that make up the two numbers. This AND operation preserves all the bits in A except the third from the left, which is set to 0. Setting that bit to 0 also effectively converts an ASCII lowercase letter to uppercase.

The 95 codes shown above are said to refer to *graphic characters* because they have a visual representation. ASCII also includes 33 *control characters* that have no visual representation but instead perform certain functions. For the sake of completeness, here are the 33 ASCII control characters, but don't worry if they seem mostly incomprehensible. At the time ASCII was developed, it was intended mostly for teletypewriters, and many of these codes are currently obscure.

Hex Code	Acronym	Control Character Name
00	NUL	Null (Nothing)
01	SOH	Start of Heading
02	STX	Start of Text
03	ETX	End of Text
04	EOT	End of Transmission
05	ENQ	Enquiry (i.e., Inquiry)
06	ACK	Acknowledge
07	BEL	Bell
08	BS	Backspace
09	HT	Horizontal Tabulation
0A	LF	Line Feed
0B	VT	Vertical Tabulation
0C	FF	Form Feed
0D	CR	Carriage Return
0E	SO	Shift-Out
0F	SI	Shift-In
10	DLE	Data Link Escape
11	DC1	Device Control 1
12	DC2	Device Control 2
13	DC3	Device Control 3
14	DC4	Device Control 4
15	NAK	Negative Acknowledge
16	SYN	Synchronous Idle
17	ETB	End of Transmission Block
18	CAN	Cancel
19	EM	End of Medium
1A	SUB	Substitute Character
1B	ESC	Escape
1C	FS	File Separator or Information Separator 4
1D	GS	Group Separator or Information Separator 3
1E	RS	Record Separator or Information Separator 2
1F	US	Unit Separator or Information Separator 1
7F	DEL	Delete

The idea here is that control characters can be intermixed with graphic characters to do some rudimentary formatting of the text. This is easiest to understand if you think of a device—such as a teletypewriter or a simple printer—that types characters on a page in response to a stream of ASCII codes. The device's printing head normally responds to character codes by printing a character and moving one space to the right. The most important control characters alter this normal behavior.

For example, consider the hexadecimal character string

41 09 42 09 43 09

The 09 character is a Horizontal Tabulation code, or *Tab* for short. If you think of all the horizontal character positions on the printer page as being numbered starting with 0, the *Tab* code usually means to print the next character at the next horizontal position that's a multiple of 8, like this:

A   B   C

This is a handy way to keep text lined up in columns.

Even today, many computer printers respond to a Form Feed code (12h) by ejecting the current page and starting a new page.

The Backspace code can be used for printing composite characters on some old printers. For example, suppose the computer controlling the teletypewriter wanted to display a lowercase *e* with a grave accent mark, like so: *è*. This could be achieved by using the hexadecimal codes 65 08 60.

By far the most important control codes are Carriage Return and Line Feed, which have the same meaning as the similar Baudot codes. On a printer, the Carriage Return code moves the printing head to the left side of the page, and the Line Feed code moves the printing head one line down. Both codes are generally required to go to a new line. A Carriage Return can be used by itself to print over an existing line, and a Line Feed can be used by itself to skip to the next line without moving to the left margin.

Although ASCII is the dominant standard in the computing world, it isn't used on many of IBM's larger computer systems. In connection with the System/360, IBM developed its own 8-bit character code known as the *Extended BCD Interchange Code*, or EBCDIC (pronounced *EBB-see-dick*), which was an extension of an earlier 6-bit code known as BCDIC, which was derived from codes used on IBM punch cards. This style of punch card—capable of storing 80 characters of text—was introduced by IBM in 1928 and used for over 50 years.

When considering the relationship between punch cards and their associated 8-bit EBCDIC character codes, keep in mind that these codes evolved over many decades under several different types of technologies. For that reason, don't expect to discover too much logic or consistency.

A character is encoded on a punch card by a combination of one or more rectangular holes punched in a single column. The character itself is often printed near the top of the card. The lower 10 rows are identified by number and are known as the 0-row, the 1-row, and so forth through the 9-row. The unnumbered row above the 0-row is called the 11-row, and the top row is called the 12-row. There is no 10-row.

More IBM punch card terminology: Rows 0 through 9 are known as the *digit rows*, or *digit punches*. Rows 11 and 12 are known as the *zone rows*, or *zone punches*. And some IBM punch card confusion: Sometimes rows 0 and 9 are considered to be zone rows rather than digit rows.

An 8-bit EBCDIC character code is composed of a high-order nibble (4-bit value) and a low-order nibble. The low-order nibble is the BCD code corresponding to the digit punches of the character. The high-order nibble is a code corresponding (in a fairly arbitrary way) to the zone punches of the character. You'll recall from Chapter 19 that BCD stands for *binary-coded decimal*—a 4-bit code for digits 0 through 9.

For the digits 0 through 9, there are no zone punches. That lack of punches corresponds to a high-order nibble of 1111. The low-order nibble is the BCD code of the digit punch. Here's a table of EBCDIC codes for the digits 0 through 9:

Hex Code	EBCDIC Character
F0	0
F1	1
F2	2
F3	3
F4	4
F5	5
F6	6
F7	7
F8	8
F9	9

For the uppercase letters, a zone punch of just the 12-row is indicated by the nibble 1100, a zone punch of just the 11-row is indicated by the nibble 1101, and a zone punch of just the 0-row is indicated by the nibble 1110. The EBCDIC codes for the uppercase letters are

Hex Code	EBCDIC Character	Hex Code	EBCDIC Character	Hex Code	EBCDIC Character
C1	A	D1	J		
C2	B	D2	K	E2	S
C3	C	D3	L	E3	T
C4	D	D4	M	E4	U
C5	E	D5	N	E5	V
C6	F	D6	O	E6	W
C7	G	D7	P	E7	X
C8	H	D8	Q	E8	Y
C9	I	D9	R	E9	Z

Notice the gaps in the numbering of these codes. In some applications, these gaps can be maddening when you're writing programs using EBCDIC text.

The lowercase letters have the same digit punches as the uppercase letters but different zone punches. For lowercase letters *a* through *i*, the 12-row and 0-row are punched, corresponding to the code 1000. For *j* through *r*, the 12-row and 11-row are punched. This is the code 1001. For the letters *s* through *z*, the 11-row and 0-row are punched—the code 1010. The EBCDIC codes for the lowercase letters are

Hex Code	EBCDIC Character	Hex Code	EBCDIC Character	Hex Code	EBCDIC Character
81	a	91	j		
82	b	92	k	A2	s
83	c	93	l	A3	t
84	d	94	m	A4	u
85	e	95	n	A5	v
86	f	96	o	A6	w
87	g	97	p	A7	x
88	h	98	q	A8	y
89	i	99	r	A9	z

Of course, there are other EBCDIC codes for punctuation and control characters, but it's hardly necessary to do a full-blown exploration of this system.

It might seem as if each column of an IBM punch card is sufficient to encode 12 bits of information. Each hole is a bit, right? So it should be possible to encode ASCII character codes on a punch card using only 7 of the 12 positions in each column. But in practice, this doesn't work very well. Too many holes get punched, threatening the physical integrity of the card.

Many of the 8-bit codes in EBCDIC aren't defined, suggesting that the use of 7 bits in ASCII makes more sense. At the time ASCII was being developed, memory was very expensive. Some people felt that ASCII should be a 6-bit code using a shift character to differentiate between lowercase and uppercase to conserve memory. Once that idea was rejected, others believed that ASCII should be an 8-bit code because even at that time it was considered more likely that computers would have 8-bit architectures than 7-bit architectures. Of course, 8-bit bytes are now the standard. Although ASCII is technically a 7-bit code, it's almost universally stored as 8-bit values.

The equivalence of bytes and characters is certainly convenient because we can get a rough sense of how much computer memory a particular text document requires simply by counting the characters. To some, the kilos and megas of computer storage are more comprehensible when expressed in terms of text.

For example, a traditional double-spaced typewritten 8½-by-11-inch page with 1-inch margins has about 27 lines of text. Each line is about 6½ inches wide with 10 characters per inch, for a total of about 1750 bytes. A single-space typewritten page has about double that, or 3.5 kilobytes.

A page in *The New Yorker* magazine has 3 columns of text with 60 lines per column and about 40 characters per line. That's 7200 characters (or bytes) per page.

The New York Times has six columns of text per page. If the entire page is covered with text without any titles or pictures (which is highly unusual), each column has 155 lines of about 35 characters each. The entire page has 32,550 characters, or 32 kilobytes.

A hardcover book has about 500 words per page. An average word is about 5 letters—actually 6 characters, counting the space between words. So a book has about 3000 characters per page. Let's say the average book has 333 pages, which may be a made-up figure but nicely implies that the average book is about 1 million bytes, or 1 megabyte.

Of course, books vary all over the place:

F. Scott Fitzgerald's *The Great Gatsby* is about 300 kilobytes.

J. D. Salinger's *Catcher in the Rye* is about 400 kilobytes.

Mark Twain's *The Adventures of Huckleberry Finn* is about 540 kilobytes.

John Steinbeck's *The Grapes of Wrath* is about a megabyte.

Herman Melville's *Moby Dick* is about 1.3 megabytes.

Henry Fielding's *The History of Tom Jones* is about 2.25 megabytes.

Margaret Mitchell's *Gone with the Wind* is about 2.5 megabytes.

Stephen King's complete and uncut *The Stand* is about 2.7 megabytes.

Leo Tolstoy's *War and Peace* is about 3.9 megabytes.

Marcel Proust's *Remembrance of Things Past* is about 7.7 megabytes.

The United States Library of Congress has about 20 million books for a total of 20 trillion characters, or 20 terabytes, of text data. (It has a bunch of photographs and sound recordings as well.)

Although ASCII is certainly the most important standard in the computer industry, it isn't perfect. The big problem with the American Standard Code for Information Interchange is that it's just too darn American! Indeed, ASCII is hardly suitable even for other nations whose principal language is English. Although ASCII includes a dollar sign, where is the British pound sign? And what about the accented letters used in many Western European languages? To say nothing of the non-Latin alphabets used in Europe, including Greek, Arabic, Hebrew, and Cyrillic. Or the Brahmi scripts of India and Southeast Asia, including Devanagari, Bengali, Thai, and Tibetan. And how can a 7-bit code possibly handle the *tens of thousands* of ideographs of Chinese, Japanese, and Korean and the ten thousand–odd Hangul syllables of Korean?

Even when ASCII was being developed, the needs of some other nations were kept in mind, although without much consideration for non-Latin alphabets. According to the published ASCII standard, ten ASCII codes (40h, 5Bh, 5Ch, 5Dh, 5Eh, 60h, 7Bh, 7Ch, 7Dh, and 7Eh) are available to be redefined for national uses. In addition, the number sign (#) can be replaced by the British pound sign (£), and the dollar sign ($) can be replaced by a generalized currency sign (¤) if necessary. Obviously, replacing symbols makes sense only when everyone involved in using a particular text document containing these redefined codes knows about the change.

Because many computer systems store characters as 8-bit values, it's possible to devise an *extended ASCII character set* that contains 256 characters rather than just 128. In such a character set, codes 00h through 7Fh are defined just as they are in ASCII; codes 80h through FFh can be something else entirely. This technique has been used to define additional character codes to accommodate accented letters and non-Latin alphabets. As an example, here's a 96-character extension of ASCII called the Latin Alphabet No. 1 that defines characters for codes A0h through FFh. In this table, the high-order nibble of the hexadecimal character code is shown in the top row; the low-order nibble is shown in the left column.

	A-	B-	C-	D-	E-	F-
-0		°	À	Ð	à	ð
-1	¡	±	Á	Ñ	á	ñ
-2	¢	²	Â	Ò	â	ò
-3	£	³	Ã	Ó	ã	ó
-4	¤	´	Ä	Ô	ä	ô
-5	¥	µ	Å	Õ	å	õ
-6	¦	¶	Æ	Ö	æ	ö
-7	§	·	Ç	×	ç	÷
-8	¨	¸	È	Ø	è	ø
-9	©	¹	É	Ù	é	ù
-A	ª	º	Ê	Ú	ê	ú
-B	«	»	Ë	Û	ë	û
-C	¬	¼	Ì	Ü	ì	ü
-D	-	½	Í	Ý	í	ý
-E	®	¾	Î	Þ	î	þ
-F	¯	¿	Ï	ß	ï	ÿ

The character for code A0h is defined as a *no-break space*. Usually when a computer program formats text into lines and paragraphs, it breaks each line at a space character, which is ASCII code 20h. Code A0h is supposed to be displayed as a space but can't be used for breaking a line. A no-break space might be used in the text "WW II," for example. Code ADh is defined as a *soft hyphen*. This is a hyphen used to separate syllables in the middle of words. It appears on the printed page only when it's necessary to break a word between two lines.

Unfortunately, many *different* extensions of ASCII have been defined over the decades, leading to much confusion and incompatibility. ASCII has been extended in a more radical way to encode the ideographs of Chinese, Japanese, and Korean. In one popular encoding—called Shift-JIS (Japanese Industrial Standard)—codes 81h through 9Fh actually represent the initial byte of a 2-byte character code. In this way, Shift-JIS allows for the encoding of about 6000 additional characters. Unfortunately, Shift-JIS isn't the only system that uses this technique. Three other standard *double-byte character sets* (DBCS) are popular in Asia.

That there are a number of incompatible double-byte character sets is only one of the problems with them. The other problem is that some characters—specifically, the normal ASCII characters—are represented by 1-byte codes, while the thousands of ideographs are represented by 2-byte codes. This makes it difficult to work with such character sets.

Under the assumption that it's preferable to have just one unambiguous character encoding system that's suitable for all the world's languages, in 1988 several major computer companies got together and began developing an alternative to ASCII known as *Unicode*. Whereas ASCII is a 7-bit code, Unicode is a 16-bit code. Each and every character in Unicode requires 2 bytes. That means that Unicode has character codes ranging from 0000h through FFFFh and can represent 65,536 different characters. That's enough for all the world's languages that are likely to be used in computer communication, with room for expansion.

Unicode doesn't start from scratch. The first 128 characters of Unicode—codes 0000h through 007Fh—are the same as the ASCII characters. Also, Unicode codes 00A0h through 00FFh are the same as the Latin Alphabet No. 1 extension of ASCII that I described earlier. Other worldwide standards are also incorporated into Unicode.

While Unicode may be an obvious improvement over existing character codes, that doesn't guarantee it instant acceptability. ASCII and the myriad flawed extensions of ASCII have become so entrenched in the computing world that it will be difficult to dislodge them.

The only real problem with Unicode is that it makes invalid the old equivalence between one character of text and 1 byte of storage. Encoded in ASCII, *The Grapes of Wrath* is about 1 megabyte in size. Encoded in Unicode, it's about 2 megabytes. But that's a small price to pay for a universal unambiguous character encoding system.

Chapter Twenty-One

Get on the Bus

T he processor is certainly the most important component of a computer, but it's not the only component. A computer also requires random access memory (RAM) that contains machine-code instructions for the processor to execute. The computer must also include some way for those instructions to get into RAM (an input device) and some way for the results of the program to be observed (an output device). As you'll also recall, RAM is volatile—it loses its contents when the power is turned off. So another useful component of a computer is a long-term storage device that can retain code and data when the computer is turned off.

All the integrated circuits that make up a complete computer must be mounted on circuit boards. In some smaller machines, all the ICs can fit on a single board. But it's more usual for the various components of the computer to be divided among two or more boards. These boards communicate with each other by means of a *bus*. A bus is simply a collection of digital signals that are provided to every board in a computer. These signals fall into four categories:

- Address signals. These are signals generated by the microprocessor and used mostly to address random access memory. But they're also used to address other devices attached to the computer.

- Data Output signals. These also are signals provided by the microprocessor. They're used to write data to RAM or to other devices. Be careful with the terms *input* and *output*. A data output signal from the microprocessor becomes a data input signal to RAM and other devices.

- Data Input signals. These are signals that are provided by other parts of the computer and are read by the microprocessor. The data input signals most often originate in RAM output; this is how the microprocessor reads the contents of memory. But other components also provide data input signals to the microprocessor.

- Control signals. These are miscellaneous signals that usually correspond to the control signals of the particular microprocessor around which the computer is built. Control signals may originate in the microprocessor or from other devices to signal the microprocessor. An example of a control signal is the signal used by the microprocessor to indicate that it needs to write some data output into a particular memory address.

In addition, the bus supplies power to the various boards that the computer comprises.

One of the earliest popular busses for home computers was the S-100 bus, which was introduced in 1975 in the first home computer, the MITS Altair. Although this bus was based on the 8080 microprocessor, it was later adapted to other processors such as the 6800. An S-100 circuit board is 5.3 inches by 10 inches. One edge of the circuit board fits into a socket that has 100 connectors (hence the name S-100).

An S-100 computer contains a larger board called a *motherboard* (or *main board*) that contains a number of S-100 sockets (perhaps 12 of them) wired to one another. These sockets are sometimes called *expansion slots*. The S-100 circuit boards (also called *expansion boards*) fit into these sockets. The 8080 microprocessor and support chips (some of which I mentioned in Chapter 19) occupy one S-100 board. Random access memory occupies one or more other boards.

Because the S-100 bus was designed for the 8080 chip, it has 16 address signals, 8 data input signals, and 8 data output signals. (As you'll recall, the 8080 itself combines the data input and data output signals. These signals are divided into separate input and output signals by other chips on the circuit board that contains the 8080.) The bus also includes 8 *interrupt* signals. These are signals generated by other devices when they need immediate attention from the CPU. For example (as we'll see later in this chapter), a keyboard might generate an interrupt signal when a key is pressed. A short program run by the 8080 can then determine what that key was and take some action. The board containing the 8080 also generally includes a chip called the Intel 8214 Priority Interrupt Control Unit to handle these interrupts. When an interrupt occurs, this chip generates an interrupt signal to the 8080. When the 8080 acknowledges the interrupt, the chip provides a *RST* (*Restart*) instruction that causes the microprocessor to save the current program counter and branch to address 0000h, 0008h, 0010h, 0018h, 0020h, 0028h, 0030h, or 0038h depending on the interrupt.

If you were designing a new computer system that included a new type of bus, you could choose whether to publish (or otherwise make available) the specifications of the bus or to keep them secret.

If the specifications of a particular bus are made public, other manufacturers—so-called *third-party* manufacturers—can design and sell expansion boards that work with that bus. The availability of these additional expansion boards makes the computer more useful and hence more desirable. More sales of the computer create more of a market for more expansion boards. This phenomenon is the incentive for designers of most small computer systems that adhere to the principle of *open architecture,* which allows other manufacturers to create peripherals for the computer. Eventually, a bus might be considered an industry-wide *standard.* Standards have been an important part of the personal computer industry.

The most famous open architecture personal computer was the original IBM PC introduced in the fall of 1981. IBM published a *Technical Reference* manual for the PC that contained complete circuit diagrams of the entire computer, including all the expansion boards that IBM manufactured for it. This manual was an essential tool that enabled many manufacturers to make their own expansion boards for the PC and, in fact, to create entire *clones* of the PC—computers that were nearly identical to IBM's and ran all the same software.

The descendants of that original IBM PC now account for about 90 percent of the market in the desktop computers. Although IBM itself has only a small share of this market, it could very well be that IBM's share is larger than if the original PC had a *closed architecture* with a *proprietary* design. The Apple Macintosh was originally designed with a closed architecture, and despite occasional flirtations with open architecture, that original decision possibly explains why the Macintosh currently accounts for less than 10 percent of the desktop market. (Keep in mind that whether a computer system is designed under the principle of open architecture or closed architecture doesn't affect the ability of other companies to write *software* that runs on the computer. Only the manufacturers of certain video games have restricted other companies from writing software for their systems.)

The original IBM PC used the Intel 8088 microprocessor, which can address 1 megabyte of memory. Although internally the 8088 is a 16-bit microprocessor, externally it addresses memory in 8-bit chunks. The bus that IBM designed for the original PC is now called the ISA (Industry Standard Architecture) bus. The expansion boards have 62 connectors. The signals include 20 address signals, 8 combined data input and output signals, 6 interrupt requests, and 3 *direct memory access* (DMA) requests. DMA allows storage devices (which I'll describe toward the end of this chapter) to perform more quickly than would otherwise be possible. Normally, the microprocessor handles all reading from and writing to memory. But using DMA, another device can bypass the microprocessor by taking over the bus and reading from or writing to memory directly.

In an S-100 system, all components are mounted on expansion boards. In the IBM PC, the microprocessor, some support chips, and some RAM are located on what IBM called the *system board* but which is also often called a motherboard or a main board.

In 1984, IBM introduced the Personal Computer AT, which used the 16-bit Intel 80286 microprocessor that can address 16 megabytes of memory. IBM retained the existing bus but added another 36-connector socket that included

7 more address signals (although only 4 more were needed), 8 more data input and output signals, 5 more interrupt requests, and 4 more DMA requests.

Busses need to be upgraded or replaced when microprocessors outgrow them, either in data width (from 8 to 16 to 32 bits) or in the number of address signals they output. But microprocessors also outgrow busses when they achieve faster speeds. Early busses were designed for microprocessors operating at a clock speed of several megahertz rather than several hundred megahertz. When a bus isn't properly designed for high speeds, it can give off radio frequency interference (RFI) that causes static or other noise on nearby radios and television sets.

In 1987, IBM introduced the Micro Channel Architecture (MCA) bus. Some aspects of this bus had been patented by IBM, so IBM was able to collect licensing fees from other companies that used the bus. Perhaps for this reason, the MCA bus did *not* become an industry standard. Instead, in 1988 a consortium of nine companies (not including IBM) countered with the 32-bit EISA (Extended Industry Standard Architecture) bus. More recently, the Intel-designed Peripheral Component Interconnect (PCI) bus has become common in PC-compatibles.

To understand how the various components of the computer work, it's again helpful to return to that earlier and simpler era of the mid-1970s. We might imagine that we're designing boards for the Altair, or perhaps for an 8080 or 6800 computer of our own design. We probably want to design some memory for the computer and to have a keyboard for input, a TV set for output, and perhaps some way to save the contents of memory when we turn off the computer. Let's look at the various *interfaces* we can design to add these components to our computer.

You'll recall from Chapter 16 that RAM arrays have address inputs, data inputs, data outputs, and a signal used to write data into memory. The number of address inputs indicates the number of separate values that can be stored in the RAM array:

$$\text{Number of values in RAM array} = 2^{\text{Number of address inputs}}$$

The number of data input and output signals indicates the size of the stored values.

One popular memory chip for home computers in the mid-1970s was the 2102:

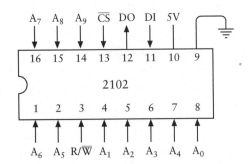

The 2102 is a member of the MOS (metal-oxide semiconductor) family of semiconductors, which is the same technology used for the 8080 and 6800 microprocessors themselves. MOS semiconductors can be easily connected to TTL chips; they generally have a higher density of transistors than TTL but aren't as fast.

As you can probably figure out by counting the address signals (A_0 through A_9) and noting the single data output (DO) and data input (DI) signals, this chip stores 1024 bits. Depending on the type of 2102 chip you're using, the *read access time*—the time it takes for the data output to be valid after a particular address has been applied to the chip—ranges from 350 to 1000 nanoseconds. The R/$\overline{\text{W}}$ (*read/write*) signal is normally 1 when you're reading memory. When you want to write data into the chip, this signal must be 0 for a period of at least 170 to 550 nsec, again depending on the type of 2102 chip you're using.

Of particular interest is the $\overline{\text{CS}}$ signal, which stands for *chip select*. When this signal is 1, the chip is *deselected*, which means that it doesn't respond to the R/$\overline{\text{W}}$ signal. The $\overline{\text{CS}}$ signal has another profound effect on the chip, however, that I'll describe shortly.

Of course, if you're putting together memory for an 8-bit microprocessor, you want to organize this memory so that it stores 8-bit values rather than 1-bit values. At the very least, you'll need to wire 8 of these 2102 chips together to store entire bytes. You can do this by connecting all the corresponding address signals, the R/$\overline{\text{W}}$ signals, and the $\overline{\text{CS}}$ signals of eight 2102 chips. The result can be drawn like this:

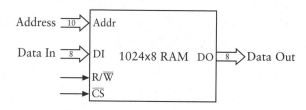

This is a 1024 × 8 RAM array, or 1 KB of RAM.

From a practical perspective, you need to put the memory chips on a circuit board. How many can you fit on one board? Well, if you really cram them close together, you can fit 64 of these chips on a single S-100 board. That will give you 8 KB of memory. But let's go for a more modest 4 KB using just 32 chips. Each set of chips that are wired together to store a whole byte (as illustrated above) is known as a *bank*. A 4-KB memory board contains four banks of 8 chips each.

Eight-bit microprocessors such as the 8080 and 6800 have 16-bit addresses that can address a total of 64 KB of memory. When you wire a 4-KB memory board containing four banks of chips, the memory board's 16 address signals perform the following functions:

$$A_{15}\ A_{14}\ A_{13}\ A_{12}\ \underbrace{A_{11}\ A_{10}}\ \underbrace{A_9\ A_8\ A_7\ A_6\ A_5\ A_4\ A_3\ A_2\ A_1\ A_0}$$

Select   Select   Address the RAM
the board   the bank

The 10 address signals A_0 through A_9 are directly wired to the RAM chips. The address signals A_{10} and A_{11} select which of the four banks is being addressed. The address signals A_{12} through A_{15} determine which addresses apply to this particular board—in other words, the addresses that the board responds to. The 4-KB memory board we're designing can occupy one of 16 different 4-KB ranges in the entire 64-KB memory space of the microprocessor:

0000h through 0FFFh, or
1000h through 1FFFh, or
2000h through 2FFFh, or
⋮
F000h through FFFFh.

For example, suppose we decide that this 4-KB memory board will apply to addresses A000h through AFFFh. This means that addresses A000h through A3FFh will apply to the first bank of 1-KB chips, addresses A400h through A7FFh to the second bank, addresses A800h through ABFFh to the third bank, and addresses AC00h through AFFFh to the fourth bank.

It's common to wire a 4-KB memory board so that you can flexibly specify at a later time what range of addresses it responds to. To achieve this flexibility, you use something called a *DIP switch*. This is a series of tiny switches (anywhere from 2 through 12) in a dual inline package (DIP) that can be inserted in a normal IC socket:

You can wire this switch with the high 4 address bits from the bus in a circuit called a *comparator*.

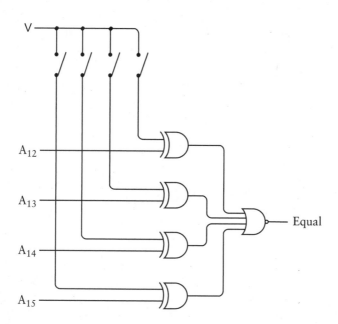

As you'll recall, the output of an XOR gate is 1 if either of the two inputs is 1 but not both. Another way to think of this is that the output of an XOR gate is 0 if the two inputs are the same—either both 0 or both 1.

For example, if we close the switches corresponding to A_{13} and A_{15}, that means we want the memory board to respond to memory addresses A000h through AFFFh. When the address signals A_{12}, A_{13}, A_{14}, and A_{15} from the bus are equal to the values set on the switches, the outputs of all four XOR gates are 0, which means the output from the NOR gate is 1:

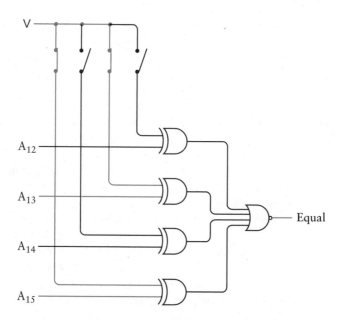

You can then combine that Equal signal with a 2-Line-to-4-Line Decoder to generate $\overline{CS}$ signals for each of the four banks of memory:

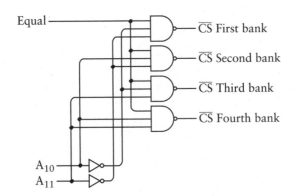

For example, when A_{10} is 0 and A_{11} is 1, that's the third bank.

If you recall the messy details of combining RAM arrays in Chapter 16, you might assume that we also need eight 4-to-1 Selectors to select the correct data output signals from the four banks of memory. But we don't, and here's why.

Normally, the output signals of TTL-compatible integrated circuits are either greater than 2.2 volts (for a logical 1) or less than 0.4 volts (for a logical 0). But what happens if you try connecting outputs? If one integrated circuit has a 1 output and another has a 0 output, and these two outputs are connected, what will result? You can't really tell, and that's why outputs of integrated circuits aren't normally connected together.

The data output signal of the 2102 chip is known as a *3-state*, or *tri-state*, output. Besides a logical 0 and a logical 1, this data output signal can also be a third state. This state is—lo and behold—nothing at all! It's as if nothing is connected to the pin of the chip. The data output signal of the 2102 chip goes into this third state when the $\overline{CS}$ input is 0. This means that we *can* connect the corresponding data output signals of all four banks and use those eight combined outputs as the eight data input signals of the bus.

I'm emphasizing the concept of the tri-state output because it's essential to the operation of a bus. Just about everything that's connected to the bus uses the data input signals of the bus. At any time, only one board connected to the bus should be determining what those data input signals are. The other boards must be connected to the bus with deselected tri-state outputs.

The 2102 chip is known as *static* random access memory, or SRAM (pronounced *ess ram*), to differentiate it from *dynamic* random access memory, or DRAM (pronounced *dee ram*). SRAM generally requires 4 transistors per bit of memory (not quite as many transistors as the flip-flops I used for memory in Chapter 16). DRAM, however, requires only 1 transistor per bit. The drawback of DRAM is that it requires more complex support circuitry.

An SRAM chip such as the 2102 will retain its contents as long as the chip has power. If the power goes off, the chip loses its contents. The DRAM is also similar in that respect, but a DRAM chip requires also that the contents of the memory be periodically accessed, even if the contents aren't needed. This is called a *refresh* cycle, and it must occur several hundred times per second. It's like periodically nudging someone so that the person doesn't fall asleep.

Despite the hassle of using DRAM, the ever-increasing capacity of DRAM chips over the years has made DRAM the standard. In 1975, Intel introduced a DRAM chip that stored 16,384 bits. In accordance with Moore's Law, DRAM chips have quadrupled in capacity roughly every three years. Today's computers usually have sockets for memory right on the system board. The sockets take small boards called *single inline memory modules* (SIMMs) or *dual inline memory modules* (DIMMs) that contain several DRAM chips. Today you can buy a DIMM containing 128 megabytes of memory for under $300.

Now that you know how to make memory boards, you don't want to fill up the entire memory space of your microprocessor with memory. You want to leave some memory space for your output device.

The *cathode-ray tube* (CRT)—a familiar sight in homes for the last half century in its guise as the television set—has become the most common output device for computers. A CRT attached to a computer is usually known as the *video display,* or *monitor.* The electronic components that provide the signal to the video display are usually known as the *video display adapter.* Often the video display adapter occupies its own board in the computer, which is known as the *video board.*

While the two-dimensional image of a video display or a television might seem complex, the image is actually composed of a single continuous beam of light that sweeps across the screen very rapidly. The beam begins in the upper left corner and moves across the screen to the right, whereupon it zips back to the left to begin the second line. Each horizontal line is known as a *scan line.* The movement back to the beginning of each of these lines is known as the *horizontal retrace.* When the beam finishes the bottom line, it zips from the lower right corner of the screen to the upper left corner (the *vertical retrace*) and the process begins again. For American television signals, this happens 60 times a second, which is known as the *field rate.* It's fast enough so that the image doesn't appear to be flickering.

Television is complicated somewhat by the use of an *interlaced* display. Two fields are required to make up a single *frame,* which is a complete still video image. Each field contributes half the scan lines of the entire frame— the first field has the even scan lines, and the second field has the odd scan lines. The *horizontal scan rate,* which is the rate at which each horizontal scan line is drawn, is 15,750 Hertz. If you divide that number by 60 Hertz, you get 262.5 lines. That's the number of scan lines in one field. An entire frame is double that, or 525 scan lines.

Regardless of the mechanics of interlaced displays, the continuous beam of light that makes up the video image is controlled by a single continuous signal. Although the audio and video components of a television program are combined when they're broadcast or transmitted through a cable television system, they're eventually separated. The *video signal* that I'll describe here is identical to the signal that's input to or output from those jacks labeled *Video* found on VCRs, camcorders, and some television sets.

For black and white television, this video signal is quite straightforward and easy to comprehend. (Color gets a bit messier.) Sixty times per second, the signal contains a *vertical sync pulse* that indicates the beginning of a field. This pulse is 0 volts (ground) for about 400 microseconds. A *horizontal sync pulse* indicates the beginning of each scan line: The video signal is 0 volts for 5 microseconds 15,750 times per second. Between the horizontal sync pulses, the signal varies from 0.5 volt for black to 2 volts for white, with voltages between 0.5 volt and 2 volts to indicate shades of gray.

The image of a television is thus partially digital and partially analog. The image is divided into 525 lines vertically, but each scan line is a continuous variation of voltages—an analog of the visual intensity of the image. But the voltage can't vary indiscriminately. There's an upper limit to how quickly the television set can respond to the varying signal. This is known as the television's *bandwidth*.

Bandwidth is an extremely important concept in communication, and it relates to the amount of information that can be transferred over a particular communication medium. In the case of television, bandwidth is the limit to the speed with which the video signal can change from black to white and back to black again. For American broadcast television, this is about 4.2 MHz.

If we want to connect a video display to a computer, it's awkward to think of the display as a hybrid analog and digital device. It's easier to treat it as a completely digital device. From the perspective of a computer, it's most convenient to conceive of the video image as being divided into a rectangular grid of discrete dots known as *pixels*. (The term comes from the phrase *picture element*.)

The video bandwidth enforces a limit to the number of pixels that can fit in a horizontal scan line. I defined the bandwidth as the speed with which the video signal can change from black to white and back to black again. A bandwidth of 4.2 MHz for television sets allows two pixels 4.2 million times a second, or—dividing 2 × 4,200,000 by the horizontal scan rate of 15,750—533 pixels in each horizontal scan line. But about a third of these pixels aren't available because they're hidden from view—either at the far ends of the image or while the light beam is in the horizontal retrace. That leaves about 320 useful pixels horizontally.

Likewise, we don't get 525 pixels vertically. Instead, some are lost at the top and bottom of the screen and during the vertical retrace. Also, it's most convenient to *not* rely upon interlace when computers use television sets. A reasonable number of pixels in the vertical dimension is 200.

We can thus say that the *resolution* of a primitive video display adapter attached to a conventional television set is 320 pixels across by 200 pixels down, or 320 pixels horizontally by 200 pixels vertically, commonly referred to as 320 by 200 or 320 × 200:

To determine the total number of pixels in this grid, you can count them or simply multiply 320 by 200 to get 64,000 pixels. Depending on how you've configured your video adapter (as I'll explain shortly), each pixel can be either black or white, or each pixel can be a particular color.

Suppose we wanted to display some text on this display. How much can we fit?

Well, that obviously depends on how many pixels are used for each text character. Here's one possible approach that uses an 8 × 8 grid (64 pixels) for each character:

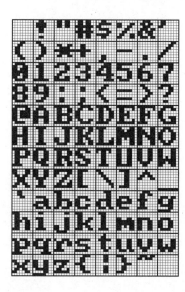

These are the characters corresponding to ASCII codes 20h through 7Fh. (No visible characters are associated with ASCII codes 00h through 1Fh.)

Each character is identified by a 7-bit ASCII code, but each character is also associated with 64 bits that determine the visual appearance of the character. You can also think of these 64 bits of information as codes.

Using these character definitions, you can fit 25 lines of 40 characters each on the 320 × 200 video display, which (for example) is enough to fit an entire short poem by Amy Lowell:

A video display adapter must contain some RAM to store the contents of the display, and the microprocessor must be able to write data into this RAM to change the display's appearance. Most conveniently, this RAM is part of the microprocessor's normal memory space. How much RAM is required for a display adapter like the one I'm describing?

This isn't a simple question! The possible answers can range from 1 kilobyte to 192 kilobytes!

Let's start with the low estimate. One way to reduce the memory requirements of a video display adapter is to restrict the adapter to text only. We've already established that we can display 25 rows of 40 characters each, or a total of 1000 characters. The RAM on the video board need only store the 7-bit ASCII codes of those 1000 characters. That's 1000 7-bit values, which is approximately 1024 bytes, or 1 kilobyte.

Such a video adapter board must also include a *character generator* that contains the pixel patterns of all the ASCII characters, such as I illustrated earlier. This character generator is generally *read-only memory,* or ROM (pronounced *rahm*). A ROM is an integrated circuit manufactured so that a particular address always results in a particular data output. Unlike RAM, a ROM doesn't have any data input signals.

You can think of ROM as a circuit that converts one code to another. A ROM that stores 8 × 8 pixel patterns of 128 ASCII characters could have 7 address signals (for the ASCII codes) and 64 data output signals. The ROM thus converts a 7-bit ASCII code to a 64-bit code that defines the character's appearance. But 64 data output signals would make the chip quite large! It's more convenient to have 10 address signals and 8 output signals. Seven of the address signals specify the particular ASCII character. (These 7 address bits come from the data output of the RAM on the video board.) The other 3 address signals indicate the row. For example, address bits 000 indicate the top row and 111 indicate the bottom row. The 8 output bits are the eight pixels of each row.

For example, suppose the ASCII code is 41h. That's a capital A. There are eight rows of 8 bits each. This table shows the 10-bit address (a space separates the ASCII code from the row code) and the data output signals for a capital A:

Address	Data Output
1000001 000	00110000
1000001 001	01111000
1000001 010	11001100
1000001 011	11001100
1000001 100	11111100
1000001 101	11001100
1000001 110	11001100
1000001 111	00000000

Do you see the A drawn with 1s against a background of 0s?

A video display adapter that displays text only must also have logic for a *cursor*. The cursor is the little underline that indicates where the next character you type on the keyboard will appear on the display. The character row and column position of the cursor is usually stored in two 8-bit registers on the video board that the microprocessor can write values into.

If the video adapter board is *not* restricted to text only, it's referred to as a *graphics* board. By writing into the RAM on a graphics video board, a microprocessor can draw pictures, including text in a multitude of sizes and styles. Graphics video boards require more memory than text-only boards. A graphics video board that displays 320 pixels across by 200 pixels down has 64,000 pixels. If each pixel corresponds to one bit of RAM, such a board requires 64,000 bits of RAM, or 8000 bytes. This, however, is the rock-bottom minimum. A correspondence of 1 bit to 1 pixel allows the use of only two colors—for instance, black and white. A 0 bit might correspond to a black pixel, and a 1 bit might correspond to a white pixel.

Black-and-white televisions display more than just black and white, of course. They're also capable of displaying many shades of gray. To display shades of gray from a graphics board, it's common for each pixel to correspond to an entire *byte* of RAM, where 00h is black and FFh is white, and all the values in between correspond to shades of gray. A 320-by-200 video board that displays 256 gray shades requires 64,000 *bytes* of RAM. That's very nearly the entire address space of one of the 8-bit microprocessors I've been talking about!

Moving up to full gorgeous color requires 3 bytes per pixel. If you use a magnifying glass to examine a color television or a computer video display, you'll discover that each color is represented by various combinations of the primary colors red, green, and blue. To get the full range of color, a byte is required to indicate the intensity of each of the three primaries. That means 192,000 bytes of RAM. (I'll have more to say about color graphics in the last chapter of this book.)

The number of different colors that a video adapter is capable of is related to the number of bits used for each pixel. The relationship might look famil- iar because like many codes in this book, it once again involves a power of 2:

$$\text{Number of Colors} = 2^{\text{Number of bits per pixel}}$$

The 320-by-200 resolution is just about the best you can do on a standard television set. That's why monitors made specifically for computers have a much higher bandwidth than television sets. The first monitors sold with the IBM Personal Computer in 1981 could display 25 lines of 80 characters each. This is the number of characters found on the CRT displays used with IBM's large and expensive mainframe computers. To IBM, 80 characters is a very special number. And why? *Because that's the number of characters on an IBM punch card!* Indeed, in the early days the CRT displays attached to mainframes were often used for viewing the contents of punch cards. Occasionally, you'll hear an old-timer refer to the lines of a text-only video display as *cards*.

Over the years, video display adapters have been characterized by increas- ing resolution and color capability. An important milestone was reached in 1987 when IBM's Personal System/2 series of personal computers and Apple's Macintosh II both introduced video adapters that did 640 pixels horizon- tally by 480 pixels vertically. This has remained the minimum-standard video resolution ever since.

The 640-by-480 resolution was a significant milestone, but you might not believe that the reason for its importance goes back to Thomas Edison! Around 1889, when Edison and his engineer William Kennedy Laurie Dickson were working on the Kinetograph motion picture camera and the Kinetoscope projector, they decided to make the motion picture image one-third wider than it was high. The ratio of the width of the image to its height is called the *aspect ratio*. The ratio that Edison and Dickson established is commonly ex- pressed as 1.33 to 1, or 1.33:1, or, to avoid fractions, 4:3. This aspect ratio was used for most movies for over 60 years, and it was also used for televi- sion. Only in the early 1950s did the Hollywood studios introduce some *wide- screen* techniques that competed against television by going beyond the 4:3 aspect ratio.

The aspect ratio of most computer monitors is (like television) also 4:3, which you can easily prove to yourself using a ruler. The resolution 640 by 480 is also in the ratio 4:3. This means that (for example) a 100-pixel hori- zontal line is the same physical length as a 100-pixel vertical line. This is considered a desirable feature for computer graphics and is known as *square pixels*.

Today's video adapters and monitors almost always do 640 by 480 but are also capable of various additional video *modes*, often including resolu- tions of 800 by 600, 1024 by 768, 1280 by 960, and 1600 by 1200.

Although we normally think of the computer display and the keyboard as connected in some way—what you type on the keyboard is displayed on the screen—they're usually physically distinct.

Each key on the keyboard is a simple switch. The switch is closed when the key is pressed. A keyboard that resembles a typewriter might have as few as 48 keys; keyboards for today's personal computers often have over 100 keys.

A keyboard attached to a computer must include some hardware that provides a unique code for each key that's pressed. It's tempting to assume that this code is the ASCII code for the key. But it's not practical nor desirable to design hardware that figures out the ASCII code. For example, the A key on the keyboard could correspond to the ASCII code 41h or 61h depending on whether a user also pressed the Shift key. Also, today's computer keyboards have many keys that don't correspond to ASCII characters. The code provided by the keyboard hardware is instead referred to as a *scan code*. A short computer program can figure out what ASCII code (if any) corresponds to a particular key being pressed on the keyboard.

To prevent my diagram of the keyboard hardware from becoming unwieldy, I'm going to assume that our keyboard has a mere 16 keys. Whenever a key is pressed, the keyboard hardware should generate a 4-bit code with binary values ranging from 0000 through 1111.

The keyboard hardware contains components that we've seen before:

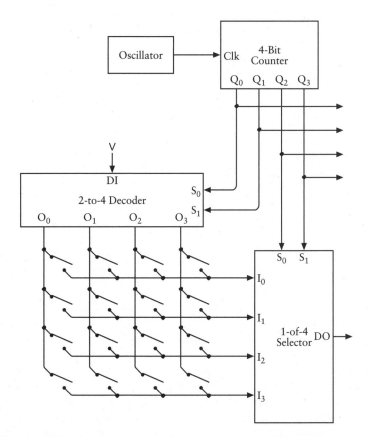

The 16 keys of the keyboard are shown as simple switches in the lower left area of this diagram. A 4-bit counter repetitively and very quickly cycles through the 16 codes corresponding to the keys. It must be fast enough to cycle through all the codes faster than a person can press and release a key.

The outputs of the 4-bit counter are the select inputs of both a 2-Line-to-4-Line Decoder and a 4-Line-to-1-Line Data Selector. If no keys are pressed, none of the inputs to the selector can be 1. Therefore the output of the selector isn't 1. But if a particular key is pressed, at a particular 4-bit counter output the output from the selector will be 1. For example, if the switch second from the top and right is pressed, and if the counter output is 0110, the output from the selector becomes 1:

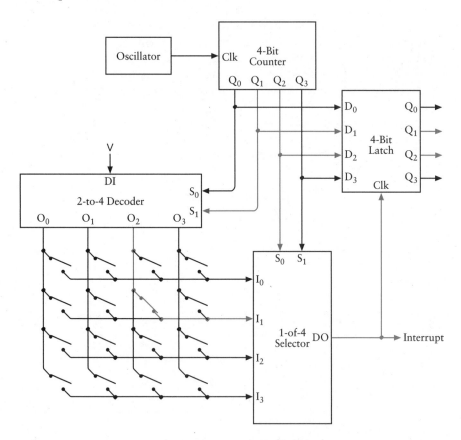

That's the code corresponding to that key. When that key is pressed, no other counter output will cause the output of the selector to be 1. Each key has its own code.

If your keyboard has 64 keys, you need a 6-bit scan code. That would involve a 6-bit counter. You could arrange the keys in an 8×8 array, using a 3-to-8 Decoder and a 1-of-8 Selector. If your keyboard has between 65 and 128 keys, you need a 7-bit code. You could arrange the keys in an 8×16 array and use a 4-to-16 Decoder and an 8-to-1 Selector (or a 3-to-8 Decoder and a 16-to-1 Selector).

What happens next in this circuit depends on the sophistication of the keyboard interface. The keyboard hardware could include 1 bit of RAM for each key. The RAM would be addressed by the counter, and the contents of the RAM could be 0 if the key is up and 1 if the key is down. This RAM could also be read by the microprocessor to determine the status of each key.

One useful part of a keyboard interface is an interrupt signal. As you'll recall, the 8080 microprocessor has an input signal that allows an external device to interrupt what the microprocessor is doing. The microprocessor responds by reading an instruction from memory. This is usually a *RST* instruction and causes the microprocessor to branch to a specific area of memory where a program to handle the interrupt is located.

The final peripheral I'll describe in this chapter is a long-term storage device. As you'll recall, random access memory—whether constructed from relays, tubes, or transistors—loses its contents when the electrical power is shut off. For this reason, a complete computer also needs something for long-term storage. One time-honored approach involves punching holes in paper or cardboard, such as IBM punch cards. In the early days of small computers, rolls of paper tape were punched with holes to save programs and data and to later reload them into memory.

One problem with punch cards and paper tape is that the medium isn't reusable. Once a hole is punched it can't easily be unpunched. Another problem is that it's not particularly efficient. These days, if you can actually *see* a bit, it's probably safe to say that the bit is taking up entirely too much space!

For these reasons, the type of long-term storage that has become much more prevalent is *magnetic storage*. The origins of magnetic storage date back to 1878, when the principles were described by American engineer Oberlin Smith (1840–1926). The first *working* device, however, came 20 years later in 1898 and was built by Danish inventor Valdemar Poulsen (1869–1942). Poulsen's *telegraphone* was originally intended as a device to record telephone messages when the person receiving the call wasn't at home. He employed an electromagnet—that ubiquitous device we've already encountered in the telegraph—to record sound along a moving length of steel wire. The electromagnet magnetizes the wire proportional to the ups and downs of the waveform of the sound. The magnetized wire can then induce a current to the same degree as it's moved along the coils of wire in the electromagnet. The electromagnet used for storing and reading is known as a *head,* regardless of the type of magnetic medium it's used with.

In 1928, Austrian inventor Fritz Pfleumer patented a magnetic recording device based on long lengths of paper tape that had been coated with iron particles using a technology originally designed for creating metallic bands on cigarettes. The paper was soon replaced with a stronger cellulose acetate base, and one of the most enduring and well-known of all recording media was born. Reels of magnetic tape—now conveniently packaged in plastic cassettes—still provide an extremely popular medium for recording and playing back music and video.

The first commercial tape system for recording digital computer data was introduced by Remington Rand in 1950. At the time, a reel of half-inch tape could store a few megabytes of data. In the early days of home computers, people adapted common cassette tape recorders to save information. Small programs stored the contents of a block of memory to tape and later read it back from tape into memory. The first IBM PCs had a connector for cassette tape storage. Tape remains a popular medium today, particularly for long-term archiving. Tape, however, isn't an ideal medium because moving quickly to an arbitrary spot on the tape isn't possible. It's usually necessary to fast-forward or rewind, and that takes time.

A medium geometrically more conducive to fast access is the disk. The disk itself is spun around its center while one or more heads attached to arms can be moved from the outside of the disk to the inside. Any area on the disk can be accessed very quickly.

For recording sounds, the magnetic disk actually predates the magnetic tape. For storing computer data, however, the first disk drive was invented at IBM in 1956. The Random Access Method of Accounting and Control (RAMAC) contained 50 metal disks 2 feet in diameter and could store 5 megabytes of data.

Since then, disks have become much smaller and of higher capacity. Disks are generally categorized as *floppy disks* (also called *diskettes*) or *hard disks* (also called *fixed disks*). Floppy disks are single sheets of coated plastic inside a protective casing made of cardboard or (more recently) plastic. (A plastic casing prevents the diskette from bending, so the diskette is no longer quite as floppy as the older ones, but it's still referred to as a floppy disk.) Floppy disks must be physically inserted by a person into a floppy disk *drive,* which is the component attached to the computer that writes to and reads from the floppy disk. Early floppy disks were 8 inches in diameter. The first IBM PC used 5 ¼-inch floppy disks; today the most common format is 3.5 inches in diameter. That floppy disks can be removed from the disk drive allows them to be used for transferring data from one computer to another. Diskettes are also still an important distribution medium of commercial software.

A hard disk usually contains multiple metal disks permanently built into the drive. Hard disks are generally faster than floppy disks and can store more data. But the disks themselves can't be removed.

The surface of a disk is divided into concentric rings called *tracks*. Each track is divided like slices of a pie into *sectors*. Each sector stores a certain number of bytes, usually 512 bytes. The floppy disk drive on the first IBM PC used only one side of the 5 ¼-inch disk and divided it into 40 tracks with 8 sectors per track and 512 bytes per sector. Each floppy disk thus stored 163,840 bytes, or 160 kilobytes. The 3.5-inch floppy disks used in PC compatibles today have two sides, 80 tracks per side, 18 sectors per track, and 512 bytes per sector for a total of 1,474,560 bytes, or 1440 kilobytes.

The first hard disk drive introduced by IBM for the Personal Computer-XT in 1983 stored ten megabytes. Today, in 1999, a 20-gigabyte hard disk drive (that's 20 *billion* bytes of storage) can be purchased for under $400.

A floppy disk or hard disk usually comes with its own electrical interface and also requires an additional interface between that and the microprocessor. Several standard interfaces are popular for hard drives, including SCSI (Small Computer System Interface, pronounced *scuzzy*), ESDI (Enhanced Small Device Interface, pronounced *ez dee*), and IDE (Integrated Device Electronics). All these interfaces make use of direct memory access (DMA) to take over the bus and transfer data directly between random access memory and the disk, bypassing the microprocessor. These transfers are in increments of the disk sector size, which is usually 512 bytes.

Many newcomers to home computers hear too much technical talk about megabytes of this and gigabytes of that, and they get confused about the difference between semiconductor random access memory and disk storage. In recent years, a rule of sorts has emerged to help alleviate some confusion about terminology. The rule is that the word *memory* is to be used to refer only to semiconductor random access memory, while the word *storage* is to be used for everything else—usually floppy disks, hard disks, and tape. I've tried to follow that rule (even though we've encountered microprocessor machine-code instructions named *Store* that store bytes in RAM).

The most obvious difference between memory and storage is that memory is volatile; it loses its contents when the power is shut off. Storage is non-volatile; data stays on the floppy disk or hard disk until it's deliberately erased or written over. Yet there's another significant difference that you can appreciate only by understanding what a microprocessor does. When the microprocessor outputs an address signal, it's always addressing memory, not storage.

Getting something from disk storage into memory so that it *can* be accessed by the microprocessor requires extra steps. It requires that the microprocessor run a short program that accesses the disk drive so that the disk drive transfers data from the disk into memory.

The difference between memory and storage can also be understood in a common analogy: Memory is like the top of your desk. Anything that's on your desk you can work with directly. Storage is like a file cabinet. If you need to use something from the file cabinet, you have to get up, walk over to the file cabinet, pull out the file you need, and bring it back to your desk. If your desk gets too crowded, you need to take something from your desk back over to the file cabinet.

This analogy is particularly apt because data stored on disks is actually stored in entities called *files*. Storing files and retrieving them is the province of an extremely important piece of software known as the *operating system*.

Chapter Twenty-Two

The Operating System

We have, at long last, assembled—at least in our imaginations— what seems to be a complete computer. This computer has a microprocessor, some random access memory, a keyboard, a video display, and a disk drive. All the hardware is in place, and we eye with excitement the on/off switch that will power it up and bring it to life. Perhaps this project has evoked in your mind the labors of Victor Frankenstein as he assembled his monster, or Geppetto as he built the wooden puppet that he will name Pinocchio.

But still we're missing something, and it's neither the power of a lightning bolt nor the purity of a wish upon a star. Go ahead: Turn on this new computer and tell me what you see.

As the cathode-ray tube warms up, the screen displays an array of perfectly formed—but totally random—ASCII characters. This is as we expect. Semiconductor memory loses its contents when the power is off and begins in a random and unpredictable state when it first gets power. Likewise, all the RAM that we've constructed for the microprocessor contains random bytes. The microprocessor begins executing these random bytes as if they were machine code. This won't cause anything *bad* to happen—the computer won't blow up, for instance—but it won't be very productive either.

What we're missing here is software. When a microprocessor is first turned on or reset, it begins executing machine code at a particular memory address. In the case of the Intel 8080, that address is 0000h. In a properly designed computer, that memory address should contain a machine-code instruction (most likely the first of many) when the computer is turned on.

How does that machine-code instruction get there? The process of getting software into a newly designed computer is possibly one of the most confusing aspects of the project. One way to do it is with a control panel similar to the one in Chapter 16 used for writing bytes into random access memory and later reading them:

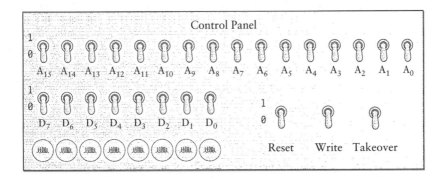

Unlike the earlier control panel, this one has a switch labeled Reset. The Reset switch is connected to the Reset input of the microprocessor. As long as that switch is on, the microprocessor doesn't do anything. When you turn off the switch, the microprocessor begins executing machine code.

To use this control panel, you turn the Reset switch on to reset the microprocessor and to stop it from executing machine code. You turn on the Takeover switch to take over the address signals and data signals on the bus. At this time, you can use the switches labeled A_0 through A_{15} to specify a 16-bit memory address. The lightbulbs labeled D_0 through D_7 show you the 8-bit contents of that memory address. To write a new byte into that address, you set the byte up on switches D_0 through D_7 and flip the Write switch on and then off again. After you're finished inserting bytes into memory, turn the Takeover switch off and the Reset switch off, and the microprocessor will execute the program.

This is how you enter your first machine-code programs into a computer that you've just built from scratch. That it's laborious goes without saying. That you will make little mistakes now and then is a given. That your fingers will get blisters and your brain will turn to mush is an occupational hazard.

But what makes it all worthwhile happens when you start to use the video display to show the results of your programs. The text-only video display we built in the last chapter has 1 kilobyte of random access memory that's used to store the ASCII codes of 25 lines of 40 characters each. A program writes to this memory the same way that it writes to any other memory in the computer.

But getting program output to the video display isn't as simple as it might first seem. If, for example, a program that you write does a particular calculation that results in the value 4Bh, you can't simply write that value to the video display memory. What you'll see in the screen in that case is the letter K because that's the letter that corresponds to the ASCII code 4Bh. Instead, you need to write *two* ASCII characters to the display: 34h, which is the ASCII code for 4, and 42h, which is the ASCII code for B. Each nibble of the 8-bit result is a hexadecimal digit, which must be displayed by the ASCII code for that digit.

Of course, you'll probably write little subroutines that perform this conversion. Here's one in 8080 assembly language that converts a nibble in the accumulator (assumed to be a value between 00h and 0Fh inclusive) to its ASCII equivalent:

```
NibbleToAscii: CMP A,0Ah ; Check if it's a letter or number
               JC Number
               ADD A,37h ; A to F converted to 41h to 46h
               RET
Number:        ADD A,30h ; 0 to 9 converted to 30h to 39h
               RET
```

This subroutine calls *NibbleToAscii* twice to convert a byte in accumulator A to two ASCII digits in registers B and C:

```
ByteToAscii: PUSH PSW               ; Save accumulator
             RRC                    ; Rotate A right 4 times...
             RRC
             RRC
             RRC                    ; ...to get high-order nibble
             CALL NibbleToAscii     ; Convert to ASCII code
             MOV B,A                ; Move result to register B
             POP PSW                ; Get original A back
             AND A,0Fh              ; Get low-order nibble
             CALL NibbleToAscii     ; Convert to ASCII code
             MOV C,A                ; Move result to register C
             RET
```

These subroutines now let you display a byte in hexadecimal on the video display. If you want to convert to decimal, it's a bit more work. The process is actually quite similar to the way a person converts hexadecimal to decimal—by several divisions by 10.

Remember that you're not actually entering these assembly-language programs into memory. Instead, you're probably writing them on paper and then converting them to machine code that you then enter into memory. This "hand assembling" is something that we'll continue doing until Chapter 24.

Although the control panel doesn't require a lot of hardware, what it also lacks is ease of use. The control panel has to be the absolute worst form of input and output ever devised. It's downright embarrassing that we're clever enough to build our own computer from scratch, yet we're still keying in numbers in 0s and 1s. The first priority has to be to get rid of the control panel.

The key, of course, is the keyboard. We've constructed the computer keyboard so that every time a key is pressed, an interrupt to the microprocessor occurs. The interrupt controller chip that we've used in our computer causes the microprocessor to respond to this interrupt by executing a *RST* (*Restart*) instruction. Let's suppose that this is a *RST 1* instruction. This instruction causes the microprocessor to save the current program counter on the stack and to jump to address 0008h. Beginning at that address, you'll enter some code (using the control panel) that we'll call the *keyboard handler*.

To get this all working right, you'll need some code that's executed when the microprocessor is reset. This is called *initialization* code. The initialization code first sets the stack pointer so that the stack is located in a valid area of memory. The code then sets every byte in the video display memory to the hexadecimal value 20h, which is the ASCII space character. This procedure gets rid of all the random characters on the screen. The initialization code uses the *OUT* (*Output*) instruction to set the position of the cursor—the underline on the video display that shows you where the next character you type will be entered—to the first column of the first row. The next instruction is *EI* to enable interrupts so that the microprocessor can respond to the keyboard interrupt. That instruction is followed by a *HLT* to halt the microprocessor.

And that's it for the initialization code. From now on, the computer will mostly be in a halted state resulting from executing the *HLT* instruction. The only event that can nudge the computer from the halted state is a Reset from the control panel or an interrupt from the keyboard.

The keyboard handler is much longer than the initialization code. Here's where all the really useful stuff takes place.

Whenever a key is pressed on the keyboard, the interrupt signal causes the microprocessor to jump from the *HLT* statement at the end of the initialization code to the keyboard handler. The keyboard handler uses the *IN* (*Input*) instruction to determine the key that has been pressed. The keyboard handler then does something based on which key has been pressed (that is, the keyboard handler *processes* each key) and then executes a *RET* (*Return*) instruction to go back to the *HLT* statement to await another keyboard interrupt.

If the pressed key is a letter or a number or a punctuation mark, the keyboard handler uses the keyboard scan code, taking into account whether the Shift key is up or down, to determine the appropriate ASCII code. It then writes this ASCII code into the video display memory at the cursor position. This procedure is called *echoing* the key to the display. The cursor position is then incremented so that the cursor appears in the space after the character just displayed. In this way, someone can type a bunch of characters on the keyboard and they'll be displayed on the screen.

If the key pressed is the Backspace key (corresponding to ASCII code 08h), the keyboard handler erases the character that was last written to the video display memory. (Erasing the character is simply a matter of writing ASCII code 20h—the space character—in that memory location.) It then moves the cursor backward one space.

Usually a person typing at the keyboard types in a line of characters—using the Backspace key when necessary to correct mistakes—and then presses the Return key, often labeled Enter on computer keyboards. In the same way that pressing the Return key on an electric typewriter indicates that the typist is ready to go to the beginning of the next line, pressing the Enter key indicates that the typist is finished typing a line of text.

When the keyboard handler processes the Return or Enter key (corresponding to ASCII code 0Dh), the line of text in the video display memory is interpreted as a *command* to the computer, that is, something for the keyboard handler to do. The keyboard handler includes a *command processor* that understands (for example) three commands: W, D, and R.

If the line of text begins with a *W*, the command means *Write* some bytes into memory. The line you type on the screen looks something like this:

```
W 1020 35 4F 78 23 9B AC 67
```

This command instructs the command processor to write the hexadecimal bytes 35, 4F, and so on into the memory addresses beginning at address 1020h. For this job, the keyboard handler needs to convert ASCII codes to bytes—a reversal of the conversion I demonstrated earlier.

If the line of text begins with a *D*, the command means *Display* some bytes in memory. The line you type on the screen looks like this:

```
D 1030
```

The command processor responds by displaying the 11 bytes stored beginning at location 1030h. (I say *11 bytes* because that's how many will fit on a 40-character-wide display on the same line following the address.) You can use the *Display* command to examine the contents of memory.

If the line of text begins with an *R*, the command means *Run*. Such a command looks like this:

```
R 1000
```

and means "Run the program that's stored beginning at address 1000h." The command processor stores 1000h in the register pair HL and then executes the instruction *PCHL*, which loads the program counter from register pair HL, effectively jumping to that address.

Getting this keyboard handler and command processor working is an important milestone. Once you have it, you no longer need suffer the indignity of the control panel. Typing bytes in from the keyboard is easier, faster, and classier.

Of course, you still have the problem of all the code you've entered disappearing when you turn off the power. For that reason, you'll probably want to store all this new code in read-only memory, or ROM. In the last chapter, we obtained a ROM chip that contained all the dot patterns necessary for displaying ASCII characters on the video display. We assumed our chip was configured with this data during manufacture. You can also program ROM chips in the privacy of your home. *Programmable read-only memory* (PROM) chips are programmable only once. *Erasable programmable read-only memory* (EPROM) chips can be programmed and reprogrammed after being entirely erased by exposure to ultraviolet light.

As you'll recall, we wired our RAM boards with a DIP switch that allows us to specify the starting address of the board. If you're working with an 8080 system, initially one of your RAM boards will be set for address 0000h. After you create a ROM, that ROM will occupy address 0000h and the RAM board can be switched to a higher address.

The creation of the command processor is an important milestone not only because it provides a faster means to enter bytes into memory but also because the computer is now *interactive*. When you type something on the keyboard, the computer responds by displaying something on the screen.

Once you have the command processor in ROM, you can start experimenting with writing data from memory to the disk drive (probably in chunks that correspond to the sector size of the disk) and reading the data back into memory. Storing programs and data on the disk is much safer than storing them in RAM (where they'll disappear if the power fails) and much more flexible than storing them in ROM.

Eventually you might want to add some new commands to the command processor. For example, the *S* command stands for *Store*:

```
S 2080 2 15 3
```

This command indicates that the block of memory beginning at address 2080h is to be stored on the disk on side 2, track 15, and sector 3. (The size of this memory block is dependent on the sector size of the disk.) Similarly, you can add a *Load* command:

```
L 2080 2 15 3
```

to load the sector from the disk back into memory.

Of course, you'll have to keep track of what you're storing where. You'll probably keep a pad and pencil handy for this purpose. Be careful: You can't just store some code located at one address and then later load it back into memory at another address and expect it to work. All the *Jump* and *Call* instructions will be wrong because they indicate the old addresses. Also, you might have a program that's longer than the sector size of your disk, so you need to store it in several sectors. Because some sectors on the disk might be occupied by other programs or data and some sectors might be free, the sectors in which you store a long program might not be consecutive on the disk.

Eventually, you could decide that the manual clerical work involved in keeping track of where everything is stored on the disk is just too much. At this point, you're ready for a *file system*.

A file system is a method of disk storage in which data is organized into *files*. A file is simply a collection of related data that occupies one or more sectors on the disk. Most important, each file is identified by a *name* that helps you remember what the file contains. You can think of the disk as resembling a file cabinet in which each file has a little tab that indicates the name of the file.

A file system is almost always part of a larger collection of software known as an *operating system*. The keyboard handler and command processor we've been building in this chapter could certainly evolve into an operating system. But instead of trudging through that long evolutionary process, let's take a look instead at a real operating system and get a feel for what it does and how it works.

Historically, the most important operating system for 8-bit microprocessors was CP/M (Control Program for Micros), written in the mid-1970s for the Intel 8080 microprocessor by Gary Kildall (born 1942), who later founded Digital Research Incorporated (DRI).

CP/M is stored on a disk. In the early days of CP/M, the most common medium for CP/M was a single-sided 8-inch diskette with 77 tracks, 26 sectors per track, and 128 bytes per sector. (That's a total of 256,256 bytes.) The first two tracks of the disk contain CP/M itself. I'll describe shortly how CP/M gets from the disk into the computer memory.

The remaining 75 tracks on the CP/M disk are used for storing files. The CP/M file system is fairly simple, but it satisfies the two major requirements: First, each file on the disk is identified by a name. This name is also stored on the disk; indeed, all the information that CP/M needs to read these files is stored on the disk along with the files themselves. Second, files don't have to occupy consecutive sectors on a disk. It often happens that as files of various sizes are created and deleted, free space on the disk becomes fragmented. The ability of a file system to store a large file in nonconsecutive sectors is very useful.

The sectors in the 75 tracks used for storing files are grouped into *allocation blocks*. Each allocation block contains 8 sectors, or 1024 bytes. There are 243 allocation blocks on the disk, numbered 0 through 242.

The first two allocation blocks (a total of 2048 bytes) are used for the *directory*. The directory is the area of the disk that contains the names and some crucial information about every file stored on the disk. Each file stored on the disk requires a *directory entry* 32 bytes long. Because the total directory is just 2048 bytes, the diskette is limited to 2048 ÷ 32, or 64, files.

Each 32-byte directory entry contains the following information:

Bytes	Meaning
0	Usually set to 0
1–8	Filename
9–11	File type
12	File extent
13–14	Reserved (set to 0)
15	Sectors in last block
16–31	Disk map

The first byte in the directory entry is used only when the file system can be shared by two or more people at the same time. Under CP/M, this byte is normally set to 0, as are bytes 13 and 14.

Under CP/M, each file is identified with a two-part name. The first part is known as the *filename* and can have up to eight characters stored in bytes 1 through 8 of the directory entry; the second part is known as the *file type* and can have up to three characters stored in bytes 9 through 11. There are several standard file types. For example, *TXT* indicates a text file (that is, a file containing only ASCII codes), and *COM* (which is short for *command*) indicates a file containing 8080 machine-code instructions—a program. When specifying a file, the two parts are separated by a period, like this:

```
MYLETTER.TXT
CALC.COM
```

This file-naming convention has come to be known as 8.3 (pronounced *eight dot three*), indicating the maximum eight letters before the period and the three letters after.

The disk map of the directory entry indicates the allocation blocks in which the file is stored. Suppose the first four entries in the disk map are 14h, 15h, 07h, and 23h, and the rest are zeros. This means that the file occupies four allocation blocks, or 4 KB of space. The file might actually be a bit shorter. Byte 15 in the directory entry indicates how many 128-byte sectors are actually used in the last allocation block.

The disk map is 16 bytes long; that length accommodates a file up to 16,384 bytes. A file longer than 16 KB must use multiple directory entries, which are called *extents*. In that case, byte 12 is set to 0 in the first directory entry, 1 in the second directory entry, and so forth.

I mentioned text files. Text files are also called *ASCII files,* or *text-only files,* or *pure-ASCII files,* or something along those lines. A text file contains ASCII codes (including carriage return and linefeed codes) that correspond to text readable by human beings. A file that isn't a text file is called a *binary* file. A CP/M COM file is a binary file because it contains 8080 machine code.

Suppose a file (a very small file) must contain three 16-bit numbers—for example, 5A48h, 78BFh, and F510h. A binary file with these three numbers is just 6 bytes long:

```
48 5A BF 78 10 F5
```

Of course, that's the Intel format for storing multibyte numbers. The least-significant byte comes first. A program written for Motorola processors might be more inclined to create the file this way:

```
5A 48 78 BF F5 10
```

An ASCII text file storing these same four 16-bit values contains the bytes

```
35 41 34 38 68 0D 0A 37 38 42 46 68 0D 0A 46 35 31 30 68 0D 0A
```

These bytes are ASCII codes for numbers and letters, where each number is terminated by a carriage return (0Dh) and a linefeed (0A) character. The text file is more conveniently displayed not as a string of bytes that happen to be ASCII codes, but as the characters themselves:

```
5A48h
78BFh
F510h
```

An ASCII text file that stores these three numbers could also contain these bytes:

```
32 33 31 31 32 0D 0A 33 30 39 31 31 0D 0A 36 32 37 33 36 0D 0A
```

These bytes are the ASCII codes for the decimal equivalents of the three numbers:

```
23112
30911
62736
```

Since the intent of using text files is to make the files easier for humans to read, there's really no reason not to use decimal rather than hexadecimal numbers.

As I mentioned, CP/M itself is stored on the first two tracks of a disk. To run, CP/M must be loaded from the disk into memory. The ROM in a computer that uses CP/M need not be extensive. All the ROM needs to contain is a small piece of code known as a *bootstrap loader* (because that code effectively pulls the rest of the operating system up by its bootstraps). The bootstrap loader loads the very first 128-byte sector from the diskette into memory and runs it. This sector contains code to load the rest of CP/M into memory. The entire process is called *booting* the operating system.

Eventually, CP/M arranges itself to occupy the area of RAM with the highest memory addresses. The entire organization of memory after CP/M has loaded looks like this:

0000h:	System Parameters
0100h:	Transient Program Area (TPA)
	Console Command Processor (CCP)
	Basic Disk Operating System (BDOS)
Highest Address:	Basic Input/Output System (BIOS)

This diagram isn't to scale. The three components of CP/M—the Basic Input/Output System (BIOS), the Basic Disk Operating System (BDOS), and the Console Command Processor (CCP)—occupy only about 6 KB of memory in total. The Transient Program Area (TPA)—about 58 KB of memory in a 64-KB computer—initially contains nothing.

The Console Command Processor is equivalent to the command processor that we were building earlier. The word *console* refers to a combination of a keyboard and a display. The CCP displays a *prompt* on the display, which looks like this:

```
A>
```

The prompt is your signal to type something in. In computers that have more than one disk drive, the A refers to the first disk drive, the one from which CP/M was loaded. You type in commands following the prompt and press the Enter key. The CCP then executes these commands, which usually produces information displayed on the screen. When the command has finished, the CCP displays the prompt again.

The CPP recognizes just a few commands. Possibly the most important is this one:

```
DIR
```

which displays the directory of the disk—that is, a list of all the files stored on the disk. You can use the special characters ? and * to limit this list to files of a particular name or type. For example,

```
DIR *.TXT
```

displays all text files, while

```
DIR A???B.*
```

displays a list of all files that have a five-character name where the first letter is A and the last letter is B.

Another command is *ERA*, which is short for *Erase*. You use this to erase a file from the disk. For example,

```
ERA MYLETTER.TXT
```

erases the file with that name, while

```
ERA *.TXT
```

erases all text files. Erasing a file means freeing the directory entry and the disk space occupied by the file.

Another command is *REN*, which is short for *Rename*. You use this command to change the name of a file. The *TYPE* command displays the contents of a text file. Because a text file contains only ASCII codes, this command allows you to read a file right on the screen, like this:

```
TYPE MYLETTER.TXT
```

The *SAVE* command saves one or more 256-byte memory blocks located in the Transient Program Area to a disk file with a specified name.

If you type in a command that CP/M doesn't recognize, it assumes you're specifying the name of a program that's stored as a file on the disk. Programs always have the file type *COM*, which stands for Command. The CCP searches for a file of that name on the disk. If one exists, CP/M loads the file from disk into the Transient Program Area, which begins at memory address 0100h. This is how you run programs that are located on the disk. For example, if you type

```
CALC
```

following the CP/M prompt, and if a file named *CALC.COM* exists on the disk, the CCP loads that file into memory starting at address 0100h and then executes the program by jumping to the machine-code instruction located at address 0100h.

Earlier I explained how you can insert machine-code instructions anywhere into memory and execute them, but in CP/M programs that are stored in disk files must be designed to be loaded into memory beginning at a specific memory location, which is 0100h.

CP/M comes with several useful programs, including *PIP,* the Peripheral Interchange Program, which allows you to copy files. The *ED* program is a text editor that allows you to create and modify text files. Programs such as PIP and ED, which are small and designed to do simple chores, are often known as *utility* programs. If you were running a CP/M system, you would probably purchase larger *application* programs, such as word processors or computer spreadsheets. Or you might write such programs yourself. All these programs are also stored in files of the *COM* type.

So far we've seen how CP/M (like most operating systems) provides commands and utilities that let you perform rudimentary housekeeping regarding files. We've also seen how CP/M loads program files into memory and executes them. An operating system also has a third major function.

A program running under CP/M often needs to write some output to the video display. Or the program might need to read something that you've typed on the keyboard. Or the program might need to read a file from the disk or to write a file to the disk. But in most cases, the CP/M program does *not* write its output directly into video display memory. Likewise, the CP/M program does *not* access the hardware of the keyboard to see what you've typed. And the CP/M program definitely does *not* access the disk drive hardware to read and write disk sectors.

Instead, a program running under CP/M makes use of a collection of subroutines built into CP/M for performing these common chores. These subroutines have been specifically designed so that programs can get easy access to all the hardware of the computer—including the video display, keyboard, and disk—without worrying programmers about how these peripherals are actually connected. Most important, a program running under CP/M doesn't *need* to know about disk sectors and tracks. That's CP/M's job. It can instead store whole files on the disk and later read them.

Providing a program with easy access to the hardware of the computer is the third major function of an operating system. The access that the operating system provides is called the *application programming interface,* or API.

A program running under CP/M uses the API by setting register C to a particular value (called the *function* value) and executing the instruction

```
CALL 5
```

For example, a program obtains the ASCII code of a key typed on the keyboard by executing

```
MOV C,01h
CALL 5
```

On return, accumulator A contains the ASCII code of the key that was pressed. Similarly,

```
MOV C,02h
CALL 5
```

writes the ASCII character in accumulator A to the video display at the cursor position and then increments the cursor.

If a program needs to create a file, it sets register pair DE to an area of memory that basically contains the name of the file. Then it executes the code:

```
MOV C,16h
CALL 5
```

In this case, the *CALL 5* instruction causes CP/M to create an empty file on the disk. The program can then use other functions to write to the file and eventually *close* the file, which means it has finished using the file for now. The same program or another program can later *open* the file and read its contents.

What does *CALL 5* actually do? The memory location at 0005h is set up by CP/M to contain a *JMP* (*Jump*) instruction, which jumps to a location in the Basic Disk Operating System (BDOS) of CP/M. This area contains a bunch of subroutines that execute each of the CP/M functions. The BDOS— as its name implies—is primarily responsible for maintaining the file system on the disk. Frequently, the BDOS has to make use of subroutines in the Basic Input/Output System (BIOS) of CP/M, which is the area that actually accesses the hardware of the keyboard, the video display, and the disk drives. In fact, the BIOS is the only section of CP/M that needs to know about the hardware of the computer. The CCP does everything it needs to do using BDOS functions, and so do the utilities that come with CP/M.

The API is a *device-independent* interface to the hardware of the computer. What this means is that a program written for CP/M doesn't need to know the actual mechanics of how the keyboard works on a particular machine, or how the video display works, or how to read and write disk sectors. It simply uses the CP/M functions to perform tasks that involve the keyboard, display, and disk. The bonus is that a CP/M program can run on many different computers that might use very different hardware to access these peripherals. (All CP/M programs must have an Intel 8080 microprocessor, however, or a processor that executes 8080 instructions, such as the Intel 8085 or the Zilog Z-80.) Just as long as the computer is running CP/M, the program uses the CP/M functions to indirectly access this hardware. Without standard APIs, programs would have to be specifically tailored to run on different types of computers.

CP/M was once a very popular operating system for the 8080 and remains historically important. CP/M was the major influence behind a 16-bit operating system named QDOS (Quick and Dirty Operating System) written by Tim Paterson of Seattle Computer Products for Intel's 16-bit 8086 and 8088 chips. QDOS was eventually renamed 86-DOS and licensed by Microsoft Corporation. Under the name MS-DOS (Microsoft Disk Operating System, pronounced *em ess dahs,* like the German article *das*), the operating system was licensed to IBM for the first IBM Personal Computer, introduced in 1981. Although a 16-bit version of CP/M (called CP/M-86) was also available for the IBM PC, MS-DOS quickly became the standard. MS-DOS (called PC-DOS on IBM's computers) was also licensed to other manufacturers who created computers compatible with the IBM PC.

MS-DOS didn't retain CP/M's file system. The file system in MS-DOS instead used a scheme called the File Allocation Table, or FAT, which had been originally invented at Microsoft in 1977. The disk space is divided into clusters, which—depending on the size of the disk—can range in size from 512 bytes to 16,384 bytes. Each file is a collection of clusters. The directory entry for a file indicates only that file's *starting* cluster. The FAT itself indicates for each cluster on the disk what the next cluster is.

The directory entries on an MS-DOS disk are 32 bytes long and use the same 8.3 filenaming convention as CP/M. The terminology is a little different, however: The last three letters are called the filename *extension* rather than the file type. The MS-DOS directory entry need not contain a list of allocation blocks. Instead, the directory includes such useful information as the date and time the file was last modified, and the size of the file.

The early versions of MS-DOS were structured much like CP/M. But the BIOS wasn't required in MS-DOS because the IBM PC itself included a complete BIOS in ROM. The command processor in MS-DOS is a file named COMMAND.COM. MS-DOS programs come in two flavors. Programs with the filename extension COM are limited to 64 KB in size. Larger programs have the filename extension EXE (pronounced *eks-ee,* for executable).

Although MS-DOS initially supported the *CALL 5* interface for API functions, a newer interface was recommended for new programs. The newer interface used a feature of the 8086 called the *software interrupt,* which is similar to a subroutine call except that the program doesn't need to know the actual address that it's calling. A program calls an MS-DOS API function by executing the instruction *INT 21h* (pronounced *int twenty-one,* even though it's hexadecimal).

In theory, application programs are supposed to access the hardware of the computer only through the interfaces provided by the operating system. But many application programmers who dealt with small computer operating systems of the 1970s and early 1980s often bypassed the operating system, particularly in dealing with the video display. Programs that directly wrote bytes into video display memory ran faster than programs that didn't. Indeed, for some applications—such as those that needed to display graphics on the video display—the operating system was totally inadequate. What many programmers liked most about MS-DOS was that it "stayed out of the way" and let programmers write programs as fast as the hardware allowed.

For this reason, popular software that ran on the IBM PC often relied upon idiosyncrasies of the IBM PC hardware. Manufacturers of machines intended to be competitive with the IBM PC were often forced to duplicate these idiosyncrasies; not doing so would cause popular programs to run poorly, if at all. Such software often included the hardware requirement "IBM Personal Computer or 100 percent compatible" or something similar.

MS-DOS version 2.0, released in March 1983, was enhanced to accommodate hard disk drives, which at the time were small (by today's standards) but which would soon get much larger. The larger a disk drive, of course, the more files it can store. And the more files a disk can store, the more confusing it becomes to find a particular file or to impose any type of organization on the files.

The solution in MS-DOS 2.0 is called a *hierarchical file system*. This was added to the existing MS-DOS file system with a minimum number of changes. As you'll recall, a disk contains an area called a directory, which is a list of files that includes information about where the files are stored on the disk. In a hierarchical file system, some of these files might *themselves* be directories—that is, they're files that contain a list of other files. Some of these files might also be directories. The normal directory on the disk is called the *root directory*. Directories contained in other directories are called *subdirectories*. The directories (sometimes called *folders*) become a way to group related files.

The hierarchical file system—and some other features of MS-DOS 2.0— were borrowed from an operating system named UNIX, which was developed in the early 1970s at Bell Telephone Laboratories largely by Ken Thompson (born 1943) and Dennis Ritchie (born 1941). The funny name of the operating system is a play on words: UNIX was originally written as a less hardy version of an earlier operating system named Multics (which stands for Multiplexed Information and Computing Services) that Bell Labs had been codeveloping with MIT and GE.

Among hard-core computer programmers, UNIX is the most beloved operating system of all time. While most operating systems are written for specific computers, UNIX was designed to be *portable*, which means that it can be adapted to run on a variety of computers.

Bell Labs was, of course, a subsidiary of American Telephone & Telegraph at the time UNIX was developed, and therefore subject to court decrees intended to curb AT&T's monopoly position in the telephone industry. Originally, AT&T was prohibited from marketing UNIX; the company was obliged to license it to others. So beginning in 1973, UNIX was extensively licensed to universities, corporations, and the government. In 1983, AT&T was allowed back into the computer business and released its own version of UNIX.

The result is that there's no single version of UNIX. There are, instead, a variety of different versions known under different names running on different computers sold by different vendors. Lots of people have put their fingers into UNIX and left their fingerprints behind. Still, however, a prevalent "UNIX philosophy" seems to guide people as they add pieces to UNIX. Part of that philosophy is using text files as a common denominator. Many UNIX utilities read text files, do something with them, and then write another text file. UNIX utilities can be strung together in chains that do different types of processing on these text files.

UNIX was originally written for computers that were too large and too expensive for just one person to use. Such computers allow multiple users to interact with them simultaneously through a technique known as *time-sharing*. The computer is connected to multiple displays and keyboards called *terminals*. By quickly switching attention among all the terminals, an operating system can make it seem as if the computer is servicing everyone at the same time.

An operating system that runs multiple programs concurrently is known as a *multitasking* operating system, and obviously such an operating system is more complex than single-tasking operating systems such as CP/M and MS-DOS. Multitasking complicates the file system because multiple users might try to use the same files at the same time. It also affects how the computer allocates memory to the different programs, so some kind of *memory management* is required. As the multiple programs running concurrently need more memory, it's likely that the computer won't have enough memory to go around. The operating system might need to implement a technique called *virtual memory,* in which blocks of memory are stored in temporary files during periods when the memory blocks aren't needed and then read back into memory when they are needed.

The most interesting development for UNIX in recent years has been the Free Software Foundation (FSF) and the GNU project, both founded by Richard Stallman. GNU (pronounced not like the animal but instead with a distinct G at the beginning) stands for "GNU's Not UNIX," which, of course, it's not. Instead, GNU is intended to be compatible with UNIX but distributed in a manner that prevents the software from becoming proprietary. The GNU project has resulted in many UNIX-compatible utilities and tools, and also Linux, which is the core (or *kernel*) of a UNIX-compatible operating system. Written largely by Linus Torvalds of Finland, Linux has become quite popular in recent years.

The most significant trend in operating systems since the mid-1980s, however, has been the development of large and sophisticated systems, such as the Apple Macintosh and Microsoft Windows, that incorporate graphics and a visually rich video display intended to make applications easier to use. I'll describe this trend in the last chapter of this book.

Chapter Twenty-Three

Fixed Point, Floating Point

N umbers are numbers, and in most of our daily lives we drift casually between whole numbers, fractions, and percentages. We buy half a carton of eggs and pay 8 ¼ percent sales tax with money earned getting time-and-a-half for working 2 ¾ hours overtime. Most people are fairly comfortable—if not necessarily proficient—with numbers such as these. We can even hear a statistic like "the average American household has 2.6 people" without gasping in horror at the widespread mutilation that must have occurred to achieve this.

Yet this interchange between whole numbers and fractions isn't so casual when it comes to computer memory. Yes, everything is stored in computers in the form of bits, which means that everything is stored as binary numbers. But some kinds of numbers are definitely easier to express in terms of bits than others.

We began using bits to represent what mathematicians call the positive *whole numbers* and what computer programmers call the positive *integers*. We've also seen how two's complements allow us to represent *negative* integers in a way that eases the addition of positive and negative numbers. The table on the following page shows the range of positive integers and two's-complement integers for 8, 16, and 32 bits of storage.

Number of Bits	Range of Positive Integers	Range of Two's-Complement Integers
8	0 through 255	−128 through 127
16	0 through 65,535	−32,768 through 32,767
32	0 through 4,294,967,295	−2,147,483,648 through 2,147,483,647

But that's where we stopped. Beyond whole numbers, mathematicians also define *rational* numbers as those numbers that can be represented as a *ratio* of two whole numbers. This ratio is also referred to as a *fraction*. For example, ¾ is a rational number because it's the ratio of 3 and 4. We can also write this number in *decimal fraction,* or just *decimal,* form: 0.75. When we write it as a decimal, it really indicates a fraction, in this case $^{75}/_{100}$.

You'll recall from Chapter 7 that in a decimal number system, digits to the left of the decimal point are multiples of integral powers of ten. Similarly, digits to the right of the decimal point are multiples of *negative* powers of ten. In Chapter 7, I used the example 42,705.684, showing first that it's equal to

$$4 \times 10,000 +$$
$$2 \times 1000 +$$
$$7 \times 100 +$$
$$0 \times 10 +$$
$$5 \times 1 +$$
$$6 \div 10 +$$
$$8 \div 100 +$$
$$4 \div 1000$$

Notice the division signs. Then I showed how you can write this sequence without any division:

$$4 \times 10,000 +$$
$$2 \times 1000 +$$
$$7 \times 100 +$$
$$0 \times 10 +$$
$$5 \times 1 +$$
$$6 \times 0.1 +$$
$$8 \times 0.01 +$$
$$4 \times 0.001$$

And finally here's the number using powers of ten:

$$4 \times 10^4 +$$
$$2 \times 10^3 +$$
$$7 \times 10^2 +$$
$$0 \times 10^1 +$$
$$5 \times 10^0 +$$
$$6 \times 10^{-1} +$$
$$8 \times 10^{-2} +$$
$$4 \times 10^{-3}$$

Some rational numbers aren't so easily represented as decimals, the most obvious being ⅓. If you divide 3 into 1, you'll find that ⅓ is equal to

0.333333333333333333333333333333333333333333333333333333...

and on and on and on. It's common to write this more concisely with a little bar over the 3 to indicate that the digit repeats forever:

$$0.\overline{3}$$

Even though writing ⅓ as a decimal fraction is a bit awkward, it's still a rational number because it's the ratio of two integers. Similarly, ⅐ is

0.142857142857142857142857142857142857142857142857142857...

or

$$0.\overline{142857}$$

Irrational numbers are monsters such as the square root of 2. This number can't be expressed as the ratio of two integers, which means that the decimal fraction continues indefinitely without any repetition or pattern:

$$\sqrt{2} \approx 1.4142135623730950488016887242096980785696718753769 5...$$

The square root of 2 is a solution of the following algebraic equation:

$$x^2 - 2 = 0$$

If a number is *not* a solution of any algebraic equation with whole number coefficients, it's called a *transcendental*. (All transcendental numbers are irrational, but not all irrational numbers are transcendental.) Transcendental numbers include π, which is the ratio of the circumference of a circle to its diameter and which is approximately

3.14159265358979328462643383279502884197169399375 11...

Another transcendental number is *e*, which is the number that this expression approaches:

$$\left(1 + \frac{1}{n}\right)^n$$

as *n* gets very large, or approximately

2.7182818284590452353602874713526624977572470936 9996...

All the numbers we've been talking about so far—rational numbers and irrational numbers—are called *real* numbers. This designation distinguishes them from the *imaginary* numbers, which are square roots of negative numbers. *Complex* numbers are combinations of imaginary numbers and real numbers. Despite their name, imaginary numbers *do* show up in the real world and are used (for example) in solving some advanced problems in electronics.

We're accustomed to thinking of numbers as *continuous*. If you give me two rational numbers, I can give you a number between those two numbers. In practice, all I have to do is take an average. But digital computers can't deal with continuums. Bits are either 0 or 1, with nothing in between. So by their very nature, digital computers must deal with *discrete* values. The number of discrete values you can represent is directly related to the number of bits you have available. For example, if you choose to store positive integers using 32 bits, the values that you can store are the whole numbers from 0 through 4,294,967,295. If you need to store the value 4.5, you must rethink your approach and do something different.

Can fractional values be represented in binary? Yes they can. The easiest approach is probably binary-coded decimal (BCD). As you might remember from Chapter 19, BCD is a binary coding of decimal numbers. Each decimal digit (0, 1, 2, 3, 4, 5, 6, 7, 8, and 9) requires 4 bits, as shown in the following table:

Decimal Digit	Binary Value
0	0000
1	0001
2	0010
3	0011
4	0100
5	0101
6	0110
7	0111
8	1000
9	1001

BCD is particularly useful in computer programs that work with money amounts in dollars and cents. Banks and insurance companies are just two obvious industries that deal with money a lot; in computer programs used by these sorts of companies, many of the fractional numbers require just two decimal places.

It's common to store two BCD digits in 1 byte, a system that's sometimes called *packed BCD*. Two's complements aren't used with BCD. For this reason, packed BCD also usually requires an extra bit to indicate whether the number is positive or negative. This is called the *sign bit*. Because it's convenient to have a particular BCD number stored in a whole number of bytes, that one little sign bit usually involves sacrificing 4 bits or 8 bits of storage.

Let's look at an example. Suppose the amounts of money that your computer program needs to work with never get as high as $10 million in either the positive or negative direction. In other words, you only need to represent money values ranging from –9,999,999.99 through 9,999,999.99. You can do that by using 5 bytes for every dollar amount you need to store in memory. For example, the amount –4,325,120.25 is represented by the 5 bytes

   00010100   00110010   01010001   00100000   00100101

or, in hexadecimal:

    14h   32h   51h   20h   25h

Notice the nibble at the far left is 1 to indicate a negative value. That's the sign bit. It would be 0 if the number were positive. All the digits in the number require 4 bits each, and you can read them directly from the hexadecimal values.

If you needed instead to represent values from –99,999,999.99 through 99,999,999.99, you'd need 6 bytes—5 bytes for the 10 digits and a whole byte just for the sign bit.

This type of storage and notation is also called *fixed-point* format because the decimal point is always fixed at a particular number of places—in our example, at two decimal places. Notice that there's nothing actually stored along with the number that indicates the position of the decimal point. Programs that work with numbers in fixed-point format must know where the decimal point is. You can create fixed-point numbers with any number of decimal places, and you can mix and match these numbers in the same computer program. But any part of the program that does arithmetic on the numbers has to know where the decimal points are.

Fixed-point format works well only if you know that numbers aren't going to get too large for the memory location that you've mapped out and that you won't need more decimal places. Where fixed-point format utterly fails is in situations in which numbers can get very large or very small. Suppose you need to reserve an area of memory where you can store certain distances in units of feet. The problem is that these distances can range all over the place. The distance from the earth to the sun is 490,000,000,000 feet, and the radius of the hydrogen atom is 0.00000000026 feet. You'd need 12 bytes of fixed-point storage to accommodate values that can get as large and as small as these.

We can probably work out a better way of storing numbers such as these if we recall that scientists and engineers enjoy specifying numbers using a system called *scientific notation*. Scientific notation is particularly useful for representing very large and very small numbers because it incorporates a power of ten that allows us to avoid writing out long strings of zeros. In scientific notation, the number

                490,000,000,000

is written

$$4.9 \times 10^{11}$$

and the number

$$0.00000000026$$

is written

$$2.6 \times 10^{-10}$$

In these two examples, the numbers 4.9 and 2.6 are called the *fraction part,* or the *characteristic,* or sometimes (although this word is more properly used in conjunction with logarithms) the *mantissa.* But to be more in tune with the terminology used with computers, I'm going to call this part of scientific notation the *significand.*

The *exponent* part is the power to which 10 is raised. In the first example, the exponent is 11; and in the second example, the exponent is −10. The exponent tells you how many places the decimal point has been moved in the significand.

By convention, the significand is always greater than or equal to 1 and less than 10. Although the following numbers are the same,

$$4.9 \times 10^{11} = 49 \times 10^{10} = 490 \times 10^{9} = 0.49 \times 10^{12} = 0.049 \times 10^{13}$$

the first is preferred. That's sometimes called the *normalized* form of scientific notation.

Notice that the sign of the exponent indicates only the magnitude of the number and not whether the number itself is negative or positive. Here are two examples of negative numbers in scientific notation:

$$-5.8125 \times 10^{7}$$

is equal to

$$-58,125,000$$

and

$$-5.8125 \times 10^{-7}$$

is equal to

$$-0.00000058125$$

In computers, the alternative to fixed-point notation is called *floating-point* notation, and the floating-point format is ideal for storing small and large numbers because it's based on scientific notation. But the floating-point format as used in computers employs *binary* numbers written in scientific notation. The first thing we have to figure out is what fractional numbers look like in binary.

This is actually easier than it might first seem. In decimal notation, digits to the right of the decimal point represent negative powers of ten. In binary notation, digits to the right of the *binary point* (which is simply a period and looks just like a decimal point) represent negative powers of two. For example, this binary number

$$101.1101$$

can be converted to decimal using this formula:

$$1 \times 4 +$$
$$0 \times 2 +$$
$$1 \times 1 +$$
$$1 \div 2 +$$
$$1 \div 4 +$$
$$0 \div 8 +$$
$$1 \div 16$$

The division signs can be replaced with negative powers of two:

$$1 \times 2^2 +$$
$$0 \times 2^1 +$$
$$1 \times 2^0 +$$
$$1 \times 2^{-1} +$$
$$1 \times 2^{-2} +$$
$$0 \times 2^{-3} +$$
$$1 \times 2^{-4}$$

Or the negative powers of two can be calculated by starting at 1 and repeatedly dividing by 2:

$$1 \times 4 +$$
$$0 \times 2 +$$
$$1 \times 1 +$$
$$1 \times 0.5 +$$
$$1 \times 0.25 +$$
$$0 \times 0.125 +$$
$$1 \times 0.0625$$

By this calculation, the decimal equivalent of 101.1101 is 5.8125.

In decimal scientific notation, the normalized significand should be greater than or equal to 1 but less than 10. Similarly, the normalized significand of numbers in binary scientific notation is always greater than or equal to 1 but less than binary 10, which is 2 in decimal. So in binary scientific notation, the number

$$101.1101$$

is expressed as

$$1.011101 \times 2^2$$

One interesting implication of this rule is that a normalized binary floating-point number always has a 1 and nothing else at the left of the binary point.

Most contemporary computers and computer programs that deal with floating-point numbers use a standard established by the IEEE (the Institute of Electrical and Electronics Engineers) in 1985, a standard also recognized by ANSI (the American National Standards Institute). ANSI/IEEE Std 754-1985 is called the *IEEE Standard for Binary Floating-Point Arithmetic*. It's not very lengthy as standards go—just 18 pages—but gives the basics of encoding binary floating-point numbers in a convenient manner.

The IEEE floating-point standard defines two basic formats: single precision, which requires 4 bytes, and double precision, which requires 8 bytes.

Let's look at the single-precision format first. It has three parts: a 1-bit sign (0 for positive and 1 for negative), an 8-bit exponent, and a 23-bit significand fraction arranged like this, with the least-significant bits on the right:

s = 1-Bit Sign	e = 8-Bit Exponent	f = 23-Bit Significand Fraction

That's a total of 32 bits, or 4 bytes. Because the significand of a normalized binary floating-point number always has a 1 to the left of the binary point, that bit is *not* included in the storage of floating-point numbers in the IEEE format. The 23-bit *fractional* part of the significand is the only part stored. So even though only 23 bits are used to store the significand, the *precision* is said to be 24 bits. We'll get a feel for what 24-bit precision means in a moment.

The 8-bit exponent part can range from 0 through 255. This is called a *biased* exponent, which means that you must subtract a number—called the *bias*—from the exponent in order to determine the signed exponent that actually applies. For single-precision floating-point numbers, this bias is 127.

The exponents 0 and 255 are used for special purposes that I'll describe shortly. If the exponent ranges from 1 through 254, the number represented by particular values of s (the sign bit), e (the exponent), and f (the significand fraction) is

$$(-1)^s \times 1.f \times 2^{e-127}$$

That negative 1 to the s power is a mathematician's annoyingly clever way of saying, "If s is 0, the number is positive (because anything to the 0 power equals 1); and if s is 1, the number is negative (because -1 to the 1 power is -1)."

The next part of the expression is *1.f*, which means a 1 followed by a binary point, followed by the 23 bits of the significand fraction. This is multiplied by 2 to a power. The exponent is the 8-bit biased exponent stored in memory minus 127.

Notice that I haven't mentioned any way to express a very common number that we seem to have forgotten about, namely 0. That's one of the special cases, which are these:

- If e equals 0, and f equals 0, the number is 0. Generally, all 32 bits are set to 0 to signify 0. But the sign bit can be 1, in which case the number is interpreted as a *negative 0*. A negative 0 can indicate a very small number that can't be represented with the available digits and exponents in single-precision format but which is still less than 0.

- If e equals 0 and f doesn't equal 0, the number is valid, but it's not normalized. The number equals

$$(-1)^s \times 0.f \times 2^{-127}$$

Notice that the significand has a 0 to the left of the binary point.

- If e equals 255 and f equals 0, the number is positive or negative infinity, depending on the sign s.

- If e equals 255 and f doesn't equal 0, the value is considered to be *not a number,* which is abbreviated *NaN*. A NaN could indicate an unknown number or the result of an invalid operation.

The smallest normalized positive or negative binary number that can be represented in single-precision floating-point format is

$$1.00000000000000000000000_{TWO} \times 2^{-126}$$

That's 23 binary zeros following the binary point. The largest normalized positive or negative number is that can be represented in single-precision floating-point format is this:

$$1.11111111111111111111111_{TWO} \times 2^{127}$$

In decimal, these two numbers are approximately $1.175494351 \times 10^{-38}$ and $3.402823466 \times 10^{38}$. That's the effective range of single-precision floating-point notation.

You might recall that 10 binary digits are approximately the same as 3 decimal digits. By that I mean that 10 bits set to 1, which is 3FFh in hexadecimal and 1023 in decimal, is approximately equal to 3 decimal digits set to 9, or 999. Or

$$2^{10} \approx 10^3$$

This relationship implies that the 24-bit binary number stored in single-precision floating-point format is roughly the equivalent of 7 decimal digits. For this reason, it's said that the single-precision floating-point format offers a *precision* of 24 bits, or about 7 decimal digits. What does this mean?

When we were looking at fixed-point numbers, it was obvious how accurate the numbers were. For amounts of money, for example, a fixed-point number with two decimal places is obviously accurate to the nearest penny. But with floating-point numbers, we can't say something like that. Depending on the value of the exponent, sometimes a floating-point number can be accurate to a tiny fraction of a penny, and sometimes it's not even accurate to the nearest dollar.

It's more appropriate to say that a single-precision floating-point number is accurate to 1 part in 2^{24}, or 1 part in 16,777,216, or about 6 parts in a million. But what does this *really* mean?

For one thing, it means that if you try to represent both 16,777,216 and 16,777,217 as single-precision floating-point numbers, they'll end up being identical! Moreover, any number between those two (such as 16,777,216.5) is also considered to be identical. All three of these decimal numbers are stored as the 32-bit single-precision floating-point value

4B800000h

which, divided into the sign, exponent, and significand bits, looks like this:

0 10010111 00000000000000000000000

which is the number

$$1.00000000000000000000000_{\text{TWO}} \times 2^{24}.$$

The next-highest significand is the binary floating-point number that represents 16,777,218 or

$$1.00000000000000000000001_{\text{TWO}} \times 2^{24}$$

It might or might not be a problem that two different decimal numbers end up being stored as identical floating-point values.

But if you were writing a program for a bank, and you were using single-precision floating-point arithmetic to store dollars and cents, you probably would be deeply disturbed to discover that $262,144.00 is the same as $262,144.01. Both these numbers are

$$1.00000000000000000000000_{\text{TWO}} \times 2^{18}.$$

That's one reason why fixed-point is preferred when dealing with dollars and cents. When you work with floating-point numbers, you could also discover other little quirks that can drive you mad. Your program will do a calculation that should yield the result 3.50 and instead you get 3.499999999999. This type of thing tends to happen in floating-point calculations, and there isn't a whole lot you can do about it.

If floating-point notation is what you want to use but single-precision doesn't quite hack it, you'll probably want to use *double-precision* floating-point format. These numbers require 8 bytes of storage, arranged like this:

s = 1-Bit Sign	e = 11-Bit Exponent	f = 52-Bit Significand Fraction

The exponent bias is 1023, or 3FFh, so the number stored in such a format is

$$(-1)^s \times 1.f \times 2^{e-1023}$$

Similar rules as those we encountered with single-precision format apply for 0, infinity, and NaN.

The smallest positive or negative double-precision floating-point number is

$$1.0000000000000000000000000000000000000000000000000000_{TWO} \times 2^{-1022}$$

That's 52 zeros following the binary point. The largest is

$$1.1111111111111111111111111111111111111111111111111111_{TWO} \times 2^{1023}$$

The range is decimal in approximately $2.2250738585072014 \times 10^{-308}$ to $1.7976931348623158 \times 10^{308}$. Ten to the 308th power is a very big number. It's 1 followed by 308 decimal zeros.

The 53 bits of the significand (including the 1 bit that's not included) is a resolution approximately equivalent to 16 decimal digits. This is much better than single-precision floating-point format, but it still means that eventually some number will equal some other number. For example, 140,737,488,355,328.00 is the same as 140,737,488,355,328.01. These two numbers are both stored as the 64-bit double-precision floating-point value

$$42E0000000000000h$$

which decodes as

$$1.0000000000000000000000000000000000000000000000000000_{TWO} \times 2^{47}$$

Of course, developing a format for storing floating-point numbers in memory is only a small part of actually using these numbers in your assembly-language programs. If you were indeed developing a desert-island computer, you would now be faced with the job of writing a collection of functions that add, subtract, multiply, and divide floating-point numbers. Fortunately, these jobs can be broken down into smaller jobs that involve adding, subtracting, multiplying, and dividing *integers,* which you already know how to do.

For example, floating-point addition basically requires that you add two significands; the tricky part is using the two exponents to figure out how the two significands mesh. Suppose you needed to perform the following addition:

$$(1.1101 \times 2^5) + (1.0010 \times 2^2)$$

You need to add 11101 and 10010, but not exactly like that. The difference in exponents indicates that the second number must be offset from the first.

The integer addition really requires that you use 11101000 and 10010. The final sum is

$$1.1111010 \times 2^5$$

Sometimes the exponents will be so far apart that one of the two numbers won't even affect the sum. This would be the case if you were adding the distance to the sun and the radius of the hydrogen atom.

Multiplying two floating-point numbers means multiplying the two significands as if they were integers and adding the two integer exponents. Normalizing the significand could result in your decrementing the new exponent once or twice.

Another layer of complexity in floating-point arithmetic involves the calculation of fun stuff such as roots and exponents and logarithms and trigonometric functions. But all of these jobs can be done with the four basic floating-point operations: addition, subtraction, multiplication, and division.

For example, the sine function in trigonometry can be calculated with a series expansion, like this:

$$\sin(x) = x - \frac{x^3}{3!} + \frac{x^5}{5!} - \frac{x^7}{7!} + \ldots$$

The x argument must be in *radians*. There are 2π radians in 360 degrees. The exclamation point is a *factorial* sign. It means to multiply together all the integers from 1 through the indicated number. For example, 5! equals $1 \times 2 \times 3 \times 4 \times 5$. That's just a multiplication. The exponent in each term is also a multiplication. The rest is just division, addition, and subtraction. The only really scary part is the ellipsis at the end, which means to continue the calculations *forever*. In reality, however, if you restrict yourself to the range 0 through $\pi/2$ (from which all other sine values can be derived), you don't have to go anywhere close to forever. After about a dozen terms, you're accurate to the 53-bit resolution of double-precision numbers.

Of course, computers are supposed to make things easy for people, so the chore of writing a bunch of routines to do floating-point arithmetic seems at odds with the goal. That's the beauty of software, though. Once somebody writes the floating-point routines for a particular machine, other people can use them. Floating-point arithmetic is so important to scientific and engineering applications that it's traditionally been given a very high priority. In the early days of computers, writing floating-point routines was always one of the first software jobs when a new type of computer was built.

In fact, it even makes sense to implement computer machine-code instructions that perform floating-point arithmetic directly! Obviously, that's easier to say than to do. But that's how important floating-point calculations are. If you can implement floating-point arithmetic in hardware—similar to the multiply and divide instructions in 16-bit microprocessors—all floating-point calculations done on the machine will be faster.

The first commercial computer that included floating-point hardware as an option was the IBM 704 in 1954. The 704 stored all numbers as 36-bit values. For floating-point numbers, that broke down to a 27-bit significand, an 8-bit exponent, and a sign bit. The floating-point hardware could do addition, subtraction, multiplication, and division. Other floating-point functions had to be implemented in software.

Hardware floating-point arithmetic came to the desktop in 1980, when Intel released the 8087 Numeric Data Coprocessor chip, a type of integrated circuit usually referred to these days as a *math coprocessor* or a *floating-point unit* (FPU). The 8087 is called a *co*processor because it couldn't be used by itself. It could be used only in conjunction with the 8086 and 8088, Intel's first 16-bit microprocessors.

The 8087 is a 40-pin chip that uses many of the same signals as the 8086 and 8087 chips. The microprocessor and the math coprocessor are connected by means of these signals. When the CPU reads a special instruction—called *ESC* for *Escape*—the coprocessor takes over and executes the next machine code, which indicates one of 68 instructions that include trigonometry, exponents, and logarithms. Data types are based on the IEEE standard. At the time, the 8087 was considered to be the most sophisticated integrated circuit ever made.

You can think of the coprocessor as a little self-contained computer. In response to a particular floating-point machine code instruction (for example, *FSQRT* to calculate a square root), the coprocessor internally executes its own series of instructions coded in ROM. These internal instructions are called *microcode*. The instructions generally loop, so the result of the calculation isn't immediately available. Still, however, the math coprocessor is usually at least 10 times faster than the equivalent routines done in software.

The motherboard of the original IBM PC had a 40-pin socket for an 8087 chip right next to the 8088 chip. Unfortunately, this socket was empty. Users who needed the extra floating-point speed had to buy an 8087 separately and install it themselves. Even after installation of the math coprocessor, not all applications could be expected to run faster. Some applications—such as word processors—have very little need for floating-point arithmetic. Others, such as spreadsheet programs, can use floating-point calculation much more, and these programs should run faster, but not all of them did.

You see, programmers had to write specific code for the coprocessor that used the coprocessor's machine-code instructions. Because a math coprocessor wasn't a standard piece of hardware, many programmers didn't bother to do so. After all, they had to write their own floating-point subroutines anyway (because most people didn't have a math coprocessor installed), so it became extra work—not less work—to support the 8087 chip. Eventually, programmers learned to write their applications to use the math coprocessor if it was present on the machine their programs were running on and to emulate it if it wasn't there.

Over the years, Intel also released a 287 math coprocessor for the 286 chip, and a 387 for the 386. But with the release of the Intel 486DX in 1989, the FPU was built right into the CPU itself. No longer was it an option! Unfortunately, in 1991 Intel released a lower-cost 486SX that did *not* have the built-in FPU and instead offered a 487SX math coprocessor as an option. With the 1993 release of the Pentium, however, the built-in FPU became standard again, perhaps for all time. Motorola integrated an FPU with its 68040 microprocessor, which was released in 1990. Previously Motorola sold 68881 and 68882 math coprocessors to support the earlier microprocessors in the 68000 family. The PowerPC chips also have built-in floating-point hardware.

Although hardware for floating-point arithmetic is a nice gift for the beleaguered assembly-language programmer, it's a rather minor historical advance when compared with some other work that began in the early 1950s. Our next stop: computer languages.

Chapter Twenty-Four

Languages
High and Low

Programming in machine code is like eating with a toothpick. The bites are so small and the process so laborious that dinner takes forever. Likewise, the bytes of machine code perform the tiniest and simplest of imaginable computing tasks—loading a number from memory into the processor, adding it to another, storing the result back to memory—so that it's difficult to imagine how they contribute to an entire meal.

We have at least progressed from that primitive era at the beginning of Chapter 22, in which we were using switches on a control panel to enter binary data into memory. In that chapter, we discovered how we could write simple programs that let us use the keyboard and the video display to enter and examine hexadecimal bytes of machine code. This was certainly better, but it's not the last word in improvements.

As you know, the bytes of machine code are associated with certain short mnemonics, such as *MOV*, *ADD*, *CALL*, and *HLT,* that let us refer to the machine code in something vaguely resembling English. These mnemonics are often written with operands that further indicate what the machine-code instruction does. For example, the 8080 machine-code byte 46h causes the microprocessor to move into register B the byte stored at the memory address referenced by the 16-bit value in the register pair HL. This is more concisely written as

```
MOV B,[HL]
```

Of course, it's much easier to write programs in assembly language than in machine code, but the microprocessor can't understand assembly language.

I've explained how you'd write assembly-language programs on paper. Only when you thought you were ready to run an assembly-language program on the microprocessor would you hand-assemble it, which means that you'd convert the assembly-language statements to machine-code bytes and enter them into memory.

What's even better is for the computer to do this conversion for you. If you were running the CP/M operating system on your 8080 computer, you'd already have all the tools you need. Here's how it works.

First you create a text file to contain your program written in assembly language. You can use the CP/M program ED.COM for this job. This program is a text editor, which means that it allows you to create and modify text files. Let's suppose you create a text file with the name PROGRAM1.ASM. The ASM file type indicates that this file contains an assembly-language program. The file might look something like this:

```
      ORG 0100h
      LXI DE, Text
      MVI C,9
      CALL 5
      RET
Text: DB 'Hello!$'
      END
```

This file has a couple of statements we haven't seen before. The first one is an *ORG* (for *origin*) statement. This statement does *not* correspond to an 8080 instruction. Instead, it indicates that the address of the next statement is to begin at address 0100h, which you'll recall is the address where CP/M loads programs into memory.

The next statement is an *LXI* (*Load Extended Immediate*) instruction, which loads a 16-bit value into the register pair DE. In this case, that 16-bit value is given as the label *Text*. That label is located near the bottom of the program in front of a *DB* (*Data Byte*) statement, something else we haven't seen before. The *DB* statement can be followed by several bytes separated by commas or (as I do here) by some text in single quotation marks.

The *MVI* (*Move Immediate*) statement moves the value 9 into register C. The *CALL 5* statement makes a CP/M function call. Function 9 means to display a string of characters beginning at the address given by the DE register pair and stop when a dollar sign is encountered. (You'll notice that the text in the last line of the program ends with a dollar sign. The use of a dollar sign to signify the end of a character string is quite odd, but that's the way CP/M happens to work.) The final *RET* statement ends the program and returns control to CP/M. (That's actually one of several ways to end a CP/M program.) The *END* statement indicates the end of the assembly-language file.

So we have a text file containing seven lines of text. The next step is to assemble it, which means to convert it to machine code. Previously we've done this by hand. But since we're running CP/M, we can use a program included with CP/M named ASM.COM. This is the CP/M *assembler*. We run ASM.COM from the CP/M command line this way:

```
ASM PROGRAM1.ASM
```

The ASM program looks at the file PROGRAM1.ASM and creates a new file named PROGRAM1.COM that contains the machine code corresponding to the assembly-language statements that we wrote. (Actually there's another step in the process, but it's not important in this account of what happens.) Now you can run PROGRAM1.COM from the CP/M command line. It displays the text "Hello!" and then ends.

The PROGRAM1.COM file contains the following 16 bytes:

```
11 09 01 0E 09 CD 05 00 C9 48 65 6C 6C 6F 21 24
```

The first 3 bytes are the *LXI* instruction, the next 2 the *MVI* instruction, the next 3 the *CALL* instruction, and the next the *RET* instruction. The last 7 bytes are the ASCII characters for the five letters of "Hello," the exclamation point, and the dollar sign.

What an assembler such as ASM.COM does is read an assembly-language program (often called a *source-code* file) and write out a file containing machine code—an *executable* file. In the grand scheme of things, assemblers are fairly simple programs because there's a one-to-one correspondence between the assembly-language mnemonics and machine code. The assembler works by separating each line of text into mnemonics and arguments and then comparing these small words and letters with a list that the assembler contains of *all* the possible mnemonics and arguments. These comparisons reveal which machine-code instructions correspond to each statement.

Notice how the assembler figures out that the *LXI* instruction must set the register pair DE to the address 0109h. If the *LXI* instruction itself is located at 0100h (as it is when CP/M loads the program into memory to run), address 0109h is where the text string begins. Generally a programmer using an assembler doesn't need to worry about the specific addresses associated with different parts of the program.

The first person to write the first assembler had to hand-assemble the program, of course. A person who writes a new (perhaps improved) assembler for the same computer can write it in assembly language and then use the first assembler to assemble it. Once the new assembler is assembled, it can assemble itself.

Every time a new microprocessor comes out, a new assembler is needed. The new assembler, however, can first be written on an existing computer using that computer's assembler. This is called a *cross-assembler*. The assembler runs on Computer A but creates code that runs on Computer B.

Although an assembler eliminates the less-creative aspects of assembly-language programming (the hand-assembling part), assembly language still has two major problems. The first problem (which you've perhaps already surmised) is that it can be very tedious. You're working down on the level of the microprocessor chip, and you have to worry about every little thing.

The second problem is that assembly language isn't *portable*. If you write an assembly-language program for the Intel 8080, it's not suitable for the Motorola 6800. You must rewrite the program in 6800 assembly language. This probably won't be as difficult as writing the original program because you've already solved the major organizational and algorithmic problems. But it's still a lot of work.

I explained in the last chapter how modern microprocessors have built-in machine-code instructions that do floating-point arithmetic. This is certainly convenient, but it doesn't go quite far enough. It would be preferable to abandon entirely those processor-dependent machine-code instructions that perform individual rudimentary arithmetic operations, and instead express multiple mathematical operations using a time-honored algebraic notation. Here's an example:

$$A \times Sin\ (2 \times PI + B)\ /\ C$$

where A, B, and C are numbers and PI is equal to 3.14159.

Well, why not? If such a statement were in a text file, it should be possible to write an assembly-language program that reads the text file and converts the algebraic expression to machine code.

If you needed to calculate such an algebraic expression only once, you could do it by hand or with a calculator. It's likely you're considering a computer solution because you need to calculate that expression with many different values of A, B, and C. For this reason, the algebraic expression will probably not appear in isolation. You should also consider some kind of context for the expression that allows it to be evaluated for different values.

What you're on the verge of creating here is known as a *high-level* programming language. Assembly language is considered a *low-level* language because it's very close to the hardware of the computer. Although the term *high-level* is used to describe any programming language other than assembly language, some languages are considered to be higher level than others. If you were the president of a company and you could sit at your computer and type in (or better yet, just prop your feet up and dictate), "Calculate all the profits and losses for this year, write up an annual report, print off a couple thousand copies, and send them to all our stockholders," you would be working with a very high-level language indeed! In the real world, programming languages don't come anywhere close to that ideal.

Human languages are usually the result of hundreds and thousands of years of complex influences, random changes, and adaptations. Even artificial languages such as Esperanto betray their origins in real language. High-level computer languages are, however, more deliberate conceptions. The challenge of inventing a programming language is quite appealing to some people because the language defines how a person conveys instructions to the computer. It was estimated in 1993 that there had been over 1000 high-level languages invented and implemented since the beginning of the 1950s.

Of course, it's not enough to simply *define* a high-level language (which involves developing a *syntax* to express all the things you want to do with the language); you must also write a *compiler*, which is the program that converts the statements of your high-level language to machine code. Like an assembler, a compiler must read through a source-code file character by character and break it down into short words and symbols and numbers. A compiler, however, is much more complex than an assembler. An assembler is simplified somewhat because of the one-to-one correspondence between assembly-language statements and machine code. A compiler usually must translate a single statement of a high-level language into many machine-code instructions. Compilers aren't easy to write. Whole books are devoted to their design and construction.

High-level languages have advantages and disadvantages. A primary advantage is that high-level languages are usually easier to learn and to program in than assembly languages. Programs written in high-level languages are often clearer and more concise. High-level languages are often portable—that is, they aren't dependent on a particular processor as are assembly languages. Thus, they let a programmer work without knowing about the underlying structure of the machine on which the program will be running. Of course, if you need to run the program on more than one processor, you need compilers that generate machine code for those processors. The actual executable files are still specific to individual processors.

On the other hand, it's almost always the case that a good assembly-language programmer can write better code than a compiler can. What this means is that an executable produced from a program written in a high-level language will be larger and slower than a functionally identical program written in assembly language. (In recent years, however, this has become less obvious as microprocessors have become more complex and compilers have also become more sophisticated in optimizing code.)

Also, although a high-level language might make a processor easy to use, it doesn't make it more powerful. Anything that a processor is capable of you can exploit in assembly language. Because a high-level language must be translated into machine code, a high-level language can only reduce the capabilities of a processor. Indeed, if a high-level language is truly portable, it can't use features specific to certain processors.

An example: Many processors have bit-shifting instructions. As you'll recall, these instructions shift the bits of the accumulator to the right or left. But almost no high-level programming languages include such operations. If you have a programming job that could use bit shifting, you'll have to mimic it by multiplying or dividing by 2. (Not that this is bad: Indeed, many modern compilers use a processor's bit-shifting instructions to implement multiplication or division by powers of two.) Many languages also don't include Boolean operations on bits.

In the early days of home computers, most application programs were written in assembly language. These days, however, assembly language is rarely used except for special purposes. As hardware has been added to processors that implements pipelining—the progressive execution of several instruction codes simultaneously—assembly language has become trickier and more difficult. At the same time, compilers have become more sophisticated. The larger storage and memory capacity of today's computers has also played a role in this trend: Programmers no longer feel the need to create code that runs in a small amount of memory and fits on a small diskette.

Although designers of many early computers attempted to formulate problems for them in algebraic notation, the first real working compiler is generally considered to be the A-0 for the UNIVAC created by Grace Murray Hopper (1906–1992) at Remington-Rand in 1952. Dr. Hopper got an early start with computers when she worked for Howard Aiken on the Mark I in 1944. In her eighties, she was still working in the computer industry doing public relations for Digital Equipment Corporation (DEC).

The oldest high-level language still in use today (although extensively revised over the years) is FORTRAN. Many computer languages have made-up names that are written in uppercase because they're acronyms of sorts. FORTRAN is a combination of the first three letters of FORmula and the first four letters of TRANslation. It was developed at IBM for the 704 series of computers in the mid-1950s. For many years, FORTRAN was considered the language of choice for scientists and engineers. It has very extensive floating-point support and even supports complex numbers (which, as I explained in the last chapter, are combinations of real and imaginary numbers).

All programming languages have their defenders and detractors, and people can get passionate about their favorites. In an attempt to assume a neutral position, I've chosen a language to serve as an archetype for this account of programming concepts that almost no one uses anymore. Its name is ALGOL (which stands for ALGOrithmic Language, but ALGOL the language also shares its name with the second brightest star in the constellation Perseus). ALGOL is also appropriate for this exploration into the nature of high-level programming languages because it's in many ways a seminal language, the direct ancestor of many popular general-purpose languages of the past 40 years. Even today, people refer to "ALGOL-like" programming languages.

The first version of the language, known as ALGOL 58, was designed by an international committee in 1957 and 1958. It was improved two years later in 1960, and the revised version was named ALGOL 60. Eventually, there was an ALGOL 68, but for this chapter I'll be using the version of ALGOL as described by the document "Revised Report on the Algorithmic Language ALGOL 60" finalized in 1962 and first published in 1963.

Let's write some ALGOL code. We'll assume we have an ALGOL compiler named ALGOL.COM that runs under CP/M or perhaps MS-DOS. Our first ALGOL program is a text file named FIRST.ALG. Notice the ALG file type.

An ALGOL program must be enclosed within the words *begin* and *end*. Here's a program that displays a line of text:

```
begin
    print ('This is my fist ALGOL program!');
ende
```

You can run the ALGOL compiler by specifying the FIRST.ALG program like this:

```
ALGOL FIRST.ALG
```

The ALGOL compiler will probably respond by displaying something similar to the following:

```
Line 3: Unrecognized keyword 'ende'.
```

A compiler is pickier about spelling than an old-fashioned English teacher. I misspelled the word *end* when I was typing the program, so the compiler tells me that the program has a *syntax error.* At the time it encountered *ende,* it expected to find a *keyword,* which is a word that it recognizes.

After fixing the problem, you can run the ALGOL compiler again. Sometimes a compiler will create an executable directly (named FIRST.COM, or perhaps FIRST.EXE under MS-DOS); sometimes you need to perform another step. Regardless, you'll soon be able to run the FIRST program from the command line:

```
FIRST
```

The FIRST program responds by displaying

```
This is my fist ALGOL program!
```

Oops! Another spelling error. This is one that the compiler could *not* be expected to find. For that reason it's called a *run-time error*—an error that's apparent only when you run the program.

As is probably obvious, the *print* statement in our first ALGOL program displays something on the screen, in this case a line of text. (The program is thus the ALGOL equivalent of the CP/M assembly-language program shown earlier in this chapter.) The *print* statement isn't actually part of the official specification of the ALGOL language, but I'm assuming that the particular ALGOL compiler we're using includes such a facility, sometimes called a *built-in function.* The *print* statement—like many ALGOL statements (but not *begin* and *end*)—must be followed by a semicolon. The indenting of the *print* statement isn't required, but indenting is often used to make the structure of the program clearer.

Let's assume now that you want to write a program that multiplies two numbers. Every programming language includes the concepts of *variables.* In a program, a variable's name is a letter, a short sequence of letters, or even a short word. In reality, the variable corresponds to a memory location, but in the program it's referenced by means of a name, not a numeric memory address. This program has three variables named *a, b,* and *c*:

```
begin
    real a, b, c;

    a := 535.43;
    b := 289.771;
    c := a × b;

    print ('The product of ', a, ' and ', b, ' is ', c);
end
```

The *real* statement is called a *declaration* statement. It indicates that you want to declare the presence of variables in your program. In this case, the variables are named *a, b,* and *c* and are real or floating-point numbers. (ALGOL also supports the keyword *integer* to declare integer variables.) Usually programming languages require that variable names begin with a letter. Variable names can also contain numbers, just as long as the first character is a letter, but they must not contain spaces or most other characters. Often compilers place limits on the length of a variable name. I'll just use single letters in the example in this chapter.

If the particular ALGOL compiler we happen to be using supports the IEEE floating-point standard, the three variables in the program each require 4 bytes of storage (for single-precision numbers) or 8 bytes of storage (for double-precision numbers).

The next three statements are *assignment* statements. In ALGOL, you can always recognize an assignment statement because it's designated by a colon followed by the equal sign. (In most computer languages, only the equal sign is required for an assignment statement.) On the left is a variable. On the right is an expression. The variable is set to the number that results from an evaluation of the expression. The first two assignment statements indicate that both *a* and *b* are assigned particular values. The third assignment statement in the program assigns the variable *c* to the product of variables *a* and *b*.

These days, the familiar × multiplication symbol is usually not allowed in programming languages because it's not part of the ASCII and EBCDIC character sets. Most programming languages use an asterisk to indicate multiplication. While ALGOL uses a slash (/) for multiplication, the language also includes a division sign (÷) for integer division, which indicates how many times the divisor is contained in the dividend. ALGOL also defines an arrow (↑), another non-ASCII character, for exponentiation.

Finally the *print* statement displays everything. It combines text and variables separated by commas. Displaying ASCII characters is probably not a major chore for the *print* statement, but here the function must also convert the floating-point numbers to ASCII:

```
The product of 535.43 and 289.771 is 155152.08653
```

The program then terminates and returns control to the operating system.

If you want to multiply a couple of other numbers, you'll need to edit the program, change the numbers, recompile it, and run it again. You can avoid this frequent recompiling by taking advantage of another built-in function named *read*.

```
begin
    real a, b, c;

    print ('Enter the first number: ');
    read (a);

    print ('Enter the second number: ');
    read (b);

    c := a × b;

    print ('The product of ', a, ' and ', b, ' is ', c);
end
```

The *read* statements read ASCII characters that you type at the keyboard and convert them to floating-point values.

A very important construction in high-level languages is the *loop*. The loop allows you to write a program that does the same thing for many different values of a variable. Suppose you want to write a program that calculates the cubes of 3, 5, 7, and 9. You can do it like this:

```
begin
    real a, b;

    for a := 3, 5, 7, 9 do
    begin
        b := a × a × a;
        print ('The cube of ', a, ' is ', b);
    end
end
```

The *for* statement sets the variable *a* first to the value 3 and then executes the statement that follows the *do* keyword. If there's more than one statement that must be executed (as is the case here), the multiple statements must be included between *begin* and *end* statements. These two keywords define a *block* of statements. The *for* statement then executes those same statements for the variable *a* set to 5, 7, and 9.

Here's another version of the *for* statement. This one calculates the cubes of odd numbers from 3 through 99:

```
begin
    real a, b;

    for a := 3 step 2 until 99 do
    begin
        b := a × a × a;
        print ('The cube of ', a, ' is ', b);
    end
end
```

The *for* statement initially sets the variable *a* to 3 and executes the block following the *for* statement. Then *a* is increased by the number following the *step* keyword, which is 2. The new value of *a*, which is 5, is used to execute the block. The variable *a* will continue to be increased by 2. When it exceeds 99, the *for* loop is completed.

Programming languages usually have a very strict syntax. In Algol 60, for example, the keyword *for* can be followed by only one type of thing—a variable name. In English, however, the word *for* can be followed by all sorts of different words, such as *example* in the previous sentence. While compilers aren't simple programs to write, they're obviously much easier than programs that must interpret human languages.

Another important feature of most programming languages is the *conditional*. This is a statement that causes another statement to execute only if a particular condition is true. Here's an example that uses the ALGOL built-in function *sqrt*, which calculates a square root. The *sqrt* function doesn't work for negative numbers, so this program avoids that occurrence:

```
begin
    real a, b;

    print ('Enter a number: ');
    read (a);

    if a < 0 then
        print ('Sorry, the number was negative.');
    else
        begin
            b = sqrt(a);
            print ('The square root of ', a, ' is ', b);
        end
end
```

The left angle bracket (<) is a *less than* sign. If the user of this program types in a number that is less than 0, the first *print* statement is executed. If not—that is, if the number is greater than or equal to 0—the block containing the other *print* statement is executed.

So far, the variables shown in the programs in this chapter store only one value each. Often it's convenient for the same variable to store many values. This is known as an *array*. An array is declared in an ALGOL program like this:

```
real array a[1:100];
```

In this case, we've indicated that we want to use this variable to store 100 different floating-point values, called *elements* of the array. The first one is referenced by *a[1]*, the second by *a[2]*, and the last by *a[100]*. The number in brackets is called the *index* of the array.

This program calculates all the square roots of 1 through 100 and stores them in an array. Then it prints them out:

```
begin
    real array a[1:100];
    integer i;

    for i := 1 step 1 until 100 do
        a[i] := sqrt(i);

    for i := 1 step 1 until 100 do
        print ('The square root of ', i, ' is ', a[i]);
end
```

This program also shows an *integer* variable named *i* (which is a traditional name for an *integer* variable because it's the first letter of the word). In the first *for* loop, each element of the array is assigned the square root of its index. In the second *for* loop, these are printed out.

In addition to *real* and *integer*, variables can also be declared as *Boolean*. (Remember George Boole from Chapter 10?) A *Boolean* variable has only two possible values, which are *true* and *false*. I make use of a *Boolean* array (and almost every other feature we've learned about so far) in the final program of this chapter—a program that implements a famous algorithm for finding prime numbers called the Sieve of Eratosthenes. Eratosthenes (circa 276–196 BCE) was the librarian of the legendary library at Alexandria and is best remembered today for accurately calculating the circumference of the earth.

Prime numbers are those whole numbers that are divisible without a remainder only by themselves and 1. The first prime number is 2 (the only even prime number), and the primes continue with 3, 5, 7, 11, 13, 17, and so forth.

Eratosthenes' technique begins with a list of the positive whole numbers beginning with 2. Because 2 is a prime number, cross out all the numbers that are multiples of 2. (That's all the even numbers except 2.) Those numbers aren't primes. Because 3 is a prime number, cross out all the numbers that are multiples of 3. We already know 4 isn't a prime number because it has been crossed out. The next prime is 5, so cross out all the multiples of 5. Continue in this way. What you have left are the prime numbers.

An ALGOL program to determine all the prime numbers through 10,000 can implement this algorithm by declaring a *Boolean* array with indices from 2 through 10,000:

```
begin
    Boolean array a[2:10000];
    integer i, j;

    for i := 2 step 1 until 10000 do
        a[i] := true;

    for i := 2 step 1 until 100 do
        if a[i] then
            for j := 2 step 1 until 10000 ÷ i do
                a[i × j] := false;

    for i := 2 step 1 until 10000 do
        if a[i] then
            print (i);
end
```

The first *for* loop sets all the array elements to the Boolean value *true*. Thus, the program starts by assuming that all the numbers are prime. The second *for* loop goes from 1 through 100 (the square root of 10,000). If the number is prime, which means that *a[i]* is true, another *for* loop sets all the multiples of that number to *false*. Those numbers aren't prime. The final *for* loop prints out all the prime numbers, which are the values of *i* where *a[i]* is true.

Sometimes people squabble over whether programming is an art or a science. On the one hand, you have college curricula in Computer *Science,* and on the other hand, you have books such as Donald Knuth's famous *The Art of Computer Programming* series. "Rather," wrote physicist Richard Feynman, "computer science is like engineering—it is all about getting something to do something."

If you ask 100 different people to write a program that prints out prime numbers, you'll get 100 different solutions. Even those programmers who use the Sieve of Eratosthenes won't implement it in precisely the same way that I did. If programming truly were a science, there wouldn't be so many possible solutions, and incorrect solutions would be more obvious. Occasionally, a programming problem incites flashes of creativity and insight, and that's the "art" part. But programming is mostly a designing and building process not unlike erecting a bridge.

Many of the early programmers were scientists and engineers who could be expected to formulate their problems in the mathematical algorithms required by FORTRAN and ALGOL. Throughout the history of programming languages, however, people have tried creating languages that could be used by a wider range of people.

One of the first successful languages designed for businesspeople and business problems was COBOL (the COmmon Business Oriented Language), still widely used today. A committee that combined American industries and the defense department created COBOL beginning in 1959, influenced by Grace Hopper's early compilers. In part, COBOL was designed so that managers, while probably not doing the actual coding, could at least *read* the program code and check that it was doing what it was supposed to be doing. (In real life, however, this rarely occurs.)

COBOL has extensive support for reading *records* and generating *reports*. Records are collections of information organized in a consistent manner. For example, an insurance company might maintain large files containing information on all the policies it has sold. Each policy would be a separate record. The record would include the person's name, a birth date, and other information. Many early COBOL programs were written to deal with 80-column records stored on IBM punch cards. To use as little space as possible on these cards, calendar years were often coded as two digits rather than four, leading to the most common (but least publicized) instances of the infamous "millennium bug" as the year 2000 approached.

In the mid-1960s, IBM, in connection with its System/360 project, developed a language named PL/I. (The I is actually a Roman numeral and pronounced *one*, so PL/I really stands for Programming Language Number One.) PL/I was intended to incorporate the block structure of ALGOL, the scientific and mathematics functions of FORTRAN, and the record and report capabilities of COBOL. But the language never quite achieved the popularity of FORTRAN and COBOL.

Although versions of FORTRAN, ALGOL, COBOL, and PL/I were available for home computers, none of them had quite the impact on small machines that BASIC had.

BASIC (Beginner's All-purpose Symbolic Instruction Code) was developed in 1964 by John Kemeny and Thomas Kurtz, of the Dartmouth Mathematics Department, in connection with Dartmouth's time-sharing system. Most students at Dartmouth weren't math or engineering majors and hence couldn't be expected to mess around with punch cards and difficult program syntax. A Dartmouth student sitting at a terminal could create a BASIC program by simply typing BASIC statements preceded by numbers. The numbers indicated the order of the statements in the program. Statements not preceded by numbers were commands to the system such as *SAVE* (save the BASIC program to disk), *LIST* (display the lines in order), and *RUN* (compile and run the program). The first BASIC program in the first published BASIC instruction manual was

```
10 LET X = (7 + 8) / 3
20 PRINT X
30 END
```

Unlike ALGOL, BASIC didn't require the programmer to specify whether a variable was to be stored as an integer or a floating-point value. Most numbers were stored as floating-point values without the programmer needing to worry about it.

Many subsequent implementations of BASIC have been in the form of *interpreters* rather than *compilers*. As I explained earlier, a compiler reads a source-code file and creates an executable file. An interpreter, however, reads source code and executes it directly as it's reading it without creating an executable file. Interpreters are easier to write than compilers, but the execution time of the interpreted program tends to be slower than that of a compiled program. On home computers, BASIC got an early start when buddies Bill Gates (born 1955) and Paul Allen (born 1953) wrote a BASIC interpreter for the Altair 8800 in 1975 and jump-started their company, Microsoft Corporation.

The Pascal programming language, which inherited much of its structure from ALGOL but included record handling from COBOL, was designed in the late 1960s by Swiss computer science professor Niklaus Wirth (born 1934). Pascal was quite popular for IBM PC programmers, but in a very specific form—the product Turbo Pascal, introduced by Borland International in 1983 for the bargain price of $49.95. Turbo Pascal (written by Danish student Anders Hejlsberg, born in 1960) was a version of Pascal that came complete with an *integrated development environment*. The text editor and the compiler were combined in a single program that facilitated very fast programming. Integrated development environments had been popular on large mainframe computers, but Turbo Pascal heralded their arrival on small machines.

Pascal was also a major influence on Ada, a language developed for use by the United States Department of Defense. The language was named after Augusta Ada Byron, who I mentioned in Chapter 18 as the chronicler of Charles Babbage's Analytical Engine.

And then there's C, a much-beloved programming language created between 1969 and 1973 largely by Dennis M. Ritchie at Bell Telephone Laboratories. People often ask why the language is called C. The simple answer is that it was derived from an early language called B, which was a simplified version of BCPL (Basic CPL), which was derived from CPL (Combined Programming Language).

I mentioned in Chapter 22 that the UNIX operating system was designed to be portable. Most operating systems at the time were written in assembly language for a specific processor. In 1973, UNIX was written (or rather, rewritten) in C, and since then the operating system and the language have been closely identified.

C is generally a very terse language. For example, instead of the words *begin* and *end* used in ALGOL and Pascal to delimit blocks, C uses the curly braces { and }. Here's another example. It's very common for a programmer to add a constant amount to a variable:

```
i = i + 5;
```

In C, you can shorten this to

```
i += 5;
```

If you only need to add 1 to the variable (that is, to increment it), you can shorten the statement even further:

```
i++;
```

On 16-bit or 32-bit microprocessors, such a statement can be carried out by a single machine-code instruction.

I mentioned earlier that most high-level languages don't include bit-shifting operations or Boolean operations on bits, which are features supported by many processors. C is the exception to this rule. In addition, an important feature of C is its support of *pointers,* which are essentially numeric memory addresses. Because C has operations that parallel many common processor instructions, C is sometimes categorized as a *high-level assembly language.* More than any ALGOL-like language, C closely mimics common processor instruction sets.

Yet *all* ALGOL-like languages—which really means *most* commonly used programming languages—were designed based on von Neumann architecture computers. Breaking out of the von Neumann mind-set when designing a computer language isn't easy, and getting other people to use such a language is even harder. One such non–von Neumann language is LISP (which stands for List Processing), which was designed by John McCarthy in the late 1950s and is useful for work in the field of artificial intelligence. Another language that's just as unusual but nothing like LISP is APL (A Programming Language), developed in the late 1950s by Kenneth Iverson. APL uses a collection of odd symbols that perform operations on whole arrays of numbers at once.

While ALGOL-like languages have retained their dominance, in recent years they've picked up certain enhancements that have resulted in what are called *object-oriented* languages. These languages are useful for working with the graphical operating systems that I'll describe in the next (and last) chapter.

Chapter Twenty-Five

The Graphical Revolution

R eaders of the September 10, 1945, issue of *Life* magazine encountered mostly the usual eclectic mix of articles and photographs:
stories about the end of the Second World War, an account of dancer
Vaslav Nijinsky's life in Vienna, a photo essay on the United Auto Workers.
Also included in that issue was something unexpected: a provocative article
by Vannevar Bush (1890–1974) about the future of scientific research. Van
Bush (as he was called) had already made his mark in the history of computing by designing one of the most significant analog computers—the dif-
ferential analyzer—between 1927 and 1931 while an engineering professor
at MIT. At the time of the *Life* article in 1945, Bush was serving as Direc-
tor of the Office of Scientific Research and Development, which had been
responsible for coordinating U.S. scientific activities during the war, including
the Manhattan Project.

Condensed somewhat from its first appearance two months earlier in *The
Atlantic Monthly*, Bush's *Life* article "As We May Think" described some
hypothetical inventions of the future ostensibly for the scientist and re-
searcher who must deal with an ever-increasing number of technical jour-
nals and articles. Bush saw microfilm as the solution and imagined a device
he called the *Memex* to store books, articles, records, and pictures inside a
desk. The Memex also allowed the user to establish thematic connections
among these works, according to the associations normally made by the human mind. He even imagined a new professional group of people who would
forge these trails of association through massive bodies of information.

Although articles about the delights of the future have been common throughout the twentieth century, "As We May Think" is different. This isn't a story about household laborsaving devices or futuristic transportation or robots. This is a story about *information* and how new technology can help us successfully deal with it.

Through the six and a half decades since the first relay calculators were built, computers have become smaller, faster, and cheaper all at the same time. This trend has changed the very nature of computing. As computers get cheaper, each person can have his or her own. As computers get smaller and faster, software can become more sophisticated and the machines can assume more and more work.

One way in which this extra power and speed can be put to good use is in improving the most crucial part of the computer system, which is the *user interface*—the point at which human and computer meet. People and computers are very different animals, and unfortunately it's easier to persuade people to make adjustments to accommodate the peculiarities of computers than the other way around.

In the early days, digital computers weren't interactive at all. Some of them were programmed using switches and cables, while others used punched paper tape or film. By the 1950s and 1960s (and even continuing into the 1970s), computers had evolved to the point where *batch processing* was the norm: Programs and data were punched on cards, which were then read into computer memory. The program analyzed the data, drew some conclusions, and printed the results on paper.

The earliest interactive computers used teletypewriters. Setups such as the Dartmouth time-sharing system (dating from the early 1960s) that I described in the preceding chapter supported multiple teletypewriters that could be used at the same time. In such a system, a user types a line at the teletypewriter, and the computer replies with one or more lines in response. The exchange of information between teletypewriter and computer consists entirely of streams of ASCII (or another character set), which are almost entirely character codes with some simple control codes, such as the carriage return and linefeed. The transaction proceeds only in one direction down the roll of paper.

The cathode-ray tube (which became more common during the 1970s) shouldn't have such restrictions, however. Software can instead treat the entire screen in a more flexible manner—as a two-dimensional platform for information. Yet, possibly in an attempt to keep the display output logic of an operating system generalized, much early software written for small computers continued to treat the CRT as a "glass teletypewriter"—displaying output line by line going down the screen and scrolling the contents of the screen up when the text reached the bottom. All the utilities in CP/M and most utilities in MS-DOS used the video display in a teletypewriter mode. Perhaps the archetypal teletypewriter operating system is UNIX, which still proudly upholds that tradition.

Interestingly enough, the ASCII character set isn't entirely inadequate in dealing with the cathode-ray tube. When ASCII was originally designed, the code *1Bh* was labeled Escape and was specifically intended for handling extensions of the character set. In 1979, the American National Standards Institute (ANSI) published a standard entitled "Additional Controls for Use with American National Standard Code for Information Interchange." The purpose of this standard was "to accommodate the foreseeable needs for input/output control of two-dimensional character-imaging devices, including interactive terminals of both the cathode ray tube and printer types…"

Of course, the Escape code *1Bh* is just 1 byte and can mean only one thing. The Escape code works by prefacing variable-length sequences that perform a variety of functions. For example, the sequence

    1Bh 5Bh 32h 4Ah

which is the Escape code followed by the characters *[2J*, is defined to erase the entire screen and move the cursor to the upper left corner. This isn't something that can be done on a teletypewriter. The sequence

    1Bh 5Bh 35h 3Bh 32h 39h 48h

which is the Escape code followed by the characters *[5;29H*, moves the cursor to row 5 and column 29.

A combined keyboard and CRT that responds to ASCII codes (and possibly to a collection of Escape sequences) coming from a remote computer is sometimes called a *dumb terminal*. Such terminals are faster than teletypewriters and somewhat more flexible, but they're not quite fast enough for real innovations in the user interface. Such innovations came with small computers in the 1970s that—like the hypothetical computer we built in Chapter 21—included the video display memory as part of the microprocessor's address space.

The first indication that home computers were going to be much different from their larger and more expensive cousins was probably the application VisiCalc. Designed and programmed by Dan Bricklin (born 1951) and Bob Frankston (born 1949) and introduced in 1979 for the Apple II, VisiCalc used the screen to give the user a two-dimensional view of a spreadsheet. Prior to VisiCalc, a spreadsheet (or worksheet) was a piece of paper with rows and columns generally used for doing series of calculations. VisiCalc replaced the paper with the video display, allowing the user to move around the spreadsheet, enter numbers and formulas, and recalculate everything after a change.

What was amazing about VisiCalc is that it was an application that *could not be duplicated on larger computers*. A program such as VisiCalc needs to update the screen very quickly. For this reason, it wrote directly to the random access memory used for the Apple II's video display. This memory is part of the address space of the microprocessor. The interface between a large time-shared computer and a dumb terminal is simply not fast enough to make a spreadsheet program usable.

The faster a computer can respond to the keyboard and alter the video display, the tighter the potential interaction between user and computer. Most of the software written in the first decade of the IBM Personal Computer (through the 1980s) wrote directly to video display memory. Because IBM set a hardware standard that other computer manufacturers adhered to, software manufacturers could bypass the operating system and use the hardware directly without fear that their programs wouldn't run right (or at all) on some machines. If all the PC clones had different hardware interfaces to their video displays, it would have been too difficult for software manufacturers to accommodate all the different designs.

For the most part, early applications for the IBM PC used only text output and not graphics. The use of text output also helped the applications run as fast as possible. When a video display is designed like the one described in Chapter 21, a program can display a particular character on the screen by simply writing the character's ASCII code into memory. A program using a graphical video display usually needs to write 8 or more bytes into memory to draw the image of the text character.

The move from character displays to graphics was, however, an extremely important step in the evolution of computers. Yet the development of computer hardware and software that work with graphical images rather than just text and numbers evolved very slowly. As early as 1945, John von Neumann envisioned an oscilloscope-like display that could graph pictorial information. But it wasn't until the early 1950s that computer graphics were ready to become a reality when MIT (with help from IBM) set up the Lincoln Laboratory to develop computers for the Air Force's air defense system. This project was known as SAGE (Semi-Automatic Ground Environment) and included graphics display screens to help the operators analyze large amounts of data.

The early video displays used in systems such as SAGE weren't like those we use today on personal computers. Today's common PC displays are known as *raster* displays. Much like a TV, the total image is composed of a series of horizontal raster lines drawn by an electron gun shooting a beam that moves very rapidly back and forth across the screen. The screen can be visualized as a large rectangular array of dots called *pixels* (*picture elements*). Within the computer, a block of memory is devoted to the video display and contains 1 or more bits for each pixel on the screen. The values of these bits determine whether pixels are illuminated and what color they are.

For example, most computer displays nowadays have a resolution of at least 640 pixels horizontally and 480 pixels vertically. The total number of pixels is the product of these two numbers: 307,200. If only 1 bit of memory is devoted to each pixel, each pixel is limited to just two colors, usually black and white. A 0 pixel could be black and a 1 pixel could be white, for example. Such a video display requires 307,200 *bits* of memory, or 38,400 bytes.

Increasing the number of possible colors necessitates more bits per pixel and increases the memory requirements of the display adapter. For example, a byte could be used for each pixel to encode gray shades. In such an arrangement, the byte 00h is black, FFh is white, and the values in between are shades of gray.

Color on a CRT is achieved by means of three electron guns, one for each of the three additive primary colors, red, green, and blue. (You can examine a television or color computer screen with a magnifying glass to convince yourself that this is true. Printing uses a different set of primaries.) The combination of red and green is yellow, the combination of red and blue is magenta, the combination of green and blue is cyan, and the combination of all three primary colors is white.

The simplest type of color graphics display adapter requires 3 bits per pixel. The pixels could be encoded like this with 1 bit per primary color:

Bits	Color
000	Black
001	Blue
010	Green
011	Cyan
100	Red
101	Magenta
110	Yellow
111	White

But such a scheme would be suitable only for simple cartoonlike images. Most real-world colors are combinations of various *levels* of red, green, and blue. If you were willing to devote 2 bytes per pixel, you could allocate 5 bits for each primary color (with 1 bit left over). That gives you 32 levels of red, green, and blue and a total of 32,768 different colors. This scheme is often referred to as *high color* or *thousands of colors*.

The next step is to use 3 bytes per pixel, or 1 byte for each primary. This encoding scheme results in 256 levels of red, green, and blue for a total of 16,777,216 different colors, often referred to as *full color* or *millions of colors*. If the resolution of the video display is 640 pixels horizontally by 480 pixels vertically, the total amount of memory required is 921,600 bytes, or nearly a megabyte.

The number of bits per pixel is sometimes referred to as the *color depth* or *color resolution*. The number of different colors is related to the number of bits per pixel in this way:

$$\text{Number of colors} = 2^{\text{Number of bits per pixel}}$$

A video adapter board has only a certain amount of memory, so it's limited in the combinations of resolutions and color depths that are possible. For example, a video adapter board that has a megabyte of memory can do a 640-by-480 resolution with 3 bytes per pixel. But if you want to use a resolution of 800 by 600, there's not enough memory for 3 bytes per pixel. Instead, you'll need to use 2 bytes per pixel.

Although raster displays seem very natural to us now, in the early days they were not quite practical because they required what was then a great deal of memory. Instead, the SAGE video displays were *vector* displays, more like an oscilloscope than a TV. The electron gun could be electrically positioned to point to any part of the display and draw lines and curves directly. The persistence of the image on the screen allowed assembling these lines and curves into rudimentary pictures.

The SAGE computers also supported *light pens* that let the operators alter images on the display. Light pens are peculiar devices that look like a stylus with a wire attached to one end. If the proper software is running, the computer can detect where the light pen is pointing on the screen and alter an image in response to the pen's movements.

How does this work? Even technological sophisticates are sometimes puzzled when they first encounter a light pen. The key is that a light pen doesn't *emit* light—it *detects* light. The circuitry that controls the movements of the electron gun in the CRT (regardless of whether a raster or vector display is used) can also determine when the light from the electron gun hits the light pen and hence where the light pen is pointing on the screen.

One of the first people to envision a new era of interactive computing was Ivan Sutherland (born 1938), who in 1963 demonstrated a revolutionary graphics program he had developed for the SAGE computers named Sketchpad. Sketchpad could store image descriptions in memory and display the images on the video display. In addition, you could use the light pen to draw images on the display and change them, and the computer would keep track of it all.

Another early visionary of interactive computing was Douglas Engelbart (born 1925), who read Vannevar Bush's article "As We May Think" when it was published in 1945 and five years later began a lifetime of work developing new ideas in computer interfaces. In the mid-1960s, while at the Sanford Research Institute, Engelbart completely rethought input devices and came up with a five-pronged keyboard for entering commands (which never caught on) and a smaller device with wheels and a button that he called a *mouse*. The mouse is now almost universally accepted for moving a pointer around the screen to select on-screen objects.

Many of the early enthusiasts of interactive graphical computing (although not Engelbart) came together at Xerox, fortunately at a time when raster displays became economically feasible. Xerox had founded the Palo Alto Research Center (PARC) in 1970 in part to help develop products that would allow the company to enter the computer industry. Perhaps the most famous visionary at PARC was Alan Kay (born 1940), who encountered Van Bush's microfilm library (in a short story by Robert Heinlein) when he was 14, and who had already conceived of a portable computer he called the Dynabook.

The first big project at PARC was the Alto, designed and built between 1972 and 1973. By the standards of those years, it was an impressive piece of work. The floor-standing system unit had 16-bit processing, two 3-MB disk drives, 128 KB of memory (expandable to 512 KB), and a mouse with three buttons. Because the Alto preceded the availability of 16-bit single-chip microprocessors, the Alto processor had to be built from about 200 integrated circuits.

The video display was one of the several unusual aspects of the Alto. The screen was approximately the size and shape of a sheet of paper—8 inches wide and 10 inches high. It ran in a raster graphics mode with 606 pixels horizontally by 808 pixels vertically, for a total of 489,648 pixels. One bit of memory was devoted to each pixel, which meant that each pixel could be either black or white. The total amount of memory devoted to the video display was 64 KB, which was part of the address space of the processor.

By writing into this video display memory, software could draw pictures on the screen or display text in different fonts and sizes. By rolling the mouse on the desk, the user of the Alto could position a pointer on the screen and interact with on-screen objects. Rather than treating the video display in the same way as the teletypewriter—linearly echoing user input and writing out program output—the screen became a two-dimensional high-density array of information and a more direct source of user input.

Over the remainder of the 1970s, programs written for the Alto developed some very interesting characteristics. Multiple programs were put into windows and displayed on the same screen simultaneously. The video graphics of the Alto allowed software to go beyond text and truly mirror the user's imagination. Graphical objects (such as buttons and menus and little pictures called *icons*) became part of the user interface. The mouse was used for selecting windows or triggering the graphical objects to perform program functions.

This was software that went beyond the user interface into user intimacy, software that facilitated the extension of the computer into realms beyond those of simple number crunching. This was software that was designed— to quote the title of a legendary paper written by Douglas Engelbart in 1963—"for the Augmentation of Man's Intellect."

What PARC developed in the Alto was the beginnings of the *graphical user interface*, or GUI (pronounced *gooey*). But Xerox didn't sell the Alto (one would have cost over $30,000 if they had), and over a decade passed before the ideas in the Alto would be embodied in a successful consumer product.

In 1979, Steve Jobs and a contingent from Apple Computer visited PARC and were quite impressed with what they saw. But it took them over three years to introduce a computer that had a graphical interface. This was the ill-fated Apple Lisa in January 1983. A year later, however, Apple introduced the much more successful Macintosh.

The original Macintosh had a Motorola 68000 microprocessor, 64 KB of ROM, 128 KB of RAM, a 3½-inch diskette drive (storing 400 KB per diskette), a keyboard, a mouse, and a video display capable of displaying 512 pixels horizontally by 342 pixels vertically. (The CRT itself measured only 9 inches diagonally.) That's a total of 175,104 pixels. Each pixel was associated with 1 bit of memory and could be colored either black or white, so about 22 KB were required for the video display RAM.

The hardware of the original Macintosh was elegant but hardly revolutionary. What made the Mac so different from other computers available in 1984 was the Macintosh operating system, generally referred to as the *system software* at the time and later known as the *Mac OS*.

A text-based single-user operating system such as CP/M or MS-DOS isn't very large and doesn't have an extensive application programming interface (API). As I explained in Chapter 22, mostly what's required in these text-based operating systems is a way for applications to use the file system. A graphical operating system such as the Mac OS, however, is much larger and has hundreds of API functions. Each of them is identified by a name that describes what the function does.

While a text-based operating system such as MS-DOS provides a couple of simple API functions to let application programs display text on the screen in a teletypewriter manner, a graphical operating system such as the Mac OS must provide a way for programs to display *graphics* on the screen. In theory, this can be accomplished by implementing a single API function that lets an application set the color of a pixel at a particular horizontal and vertical coordinate. But it turns out that this is inefficient and results in very slow graphics.

It makes more sense for the operating system to provide a complete graphics programming system, which means that the operating system includes API functions to draw lines, rectangles, and ellipses (including circles) as well as text. Lines can be either solid or composed of dashes or dots. Rectangles and ellipses can be filled with various patterns. Text can be displayed in various fonts and sizes and with effects such as boldfacing and underlining. The graphics system is responsible for determining how to render these graphical objects as a collection of dots on the display.

Programs running under a graphical operating system use the same APIs to draw graphics on both the computer's video display and the printer. A word processing application can thus display a document on the screen so that it looks very similar to the document later printed, a feature known as WYSIWYG (pronounced *wizzy wig*). This is an acronym for "What you see is what you get," the contribution to computer lingo of the comedian Flip Wilson in his Geraldine persona.

Part of the appeal of a graphical user interface is that different applications work roughly the same and leverage a user's experience. This means that the operating system must also support API functions that let applications implement the various components of the user interface, such as buttons and menus. Although the GUI is generally viewed as an easy environment for users, it's also just as importantly an environment for programmers. Programmers can implement a modern user interface without re-inventing the wheel.

Even before the introduction of the Macintosh, several companies had begun to create a graphical operating system for the IBM PC and compatibles. In one sense, the Apple developers had an easier job because they were designing the hardware and software together. The Macintosh system software had to support only one type of diskette drive, one type of video display, and two printers. Implementing a graphical operating system for the PC, however, required supporting many different pieces of hardware.

Moreover, although the IBM PC had been introduced just a few years earlier (in 1981), many people had grown accustomed to using their favorite MS-DOS applications and weren't ready to give them up. It was considered very important for a graphical operating system for the PC to run MS-DOS applications as well as applications designed expressly for the new operating system. (The Macintosh didn't run Apple II software primarily because it used a different microprocessor.)

In 1985, Digital Research (the company behind CP/M) introduced GEM (the Graphical Environment Manager), VisiCorp (the company marketing VisiCalc) introduced VisiOn, and Microsoft released Windows version 1.0, which was quickly perceived as being the probable winner in the "windows wars." It wasn't until the May 1990 release of Windows 3.0, however, that Windows began to attract a lot of users. Its popularity has increased since then, and today Windows is the operating system used on about 90 percent of small computers. Despite the similar appearances of the Macintosh and Windows, the APIs for the two systems are very different.

In theory, aside from the graphics display, a graphical operating system doesn't require much more in the way of hardware than a text-based operating system. In theory, not even a hard disk drive is required: The original Macintosh didn't have one, and Windows 1.0 didn't require one. Windows 1.0 didn't even require a mouse, although everyone agreed that it was much easier to use with a mouse.

Still, however, it's not surprising that graphical user interfaces have become more popular as microprocessors have grown faster and as memory and storage have become more plentiful. As more and more features are added to graphical operating systems, they have grown large. Today's graphical operating systems generally require a couple hundred megabytes of hard disk space and upwards of 32 megabytes of memory.

Applications for graphical operating systems are almost never written in assembly language. In the early days, the popular language for Macintosh applications was Pascal. For Windows applications, it was C. But once again, PARC had demonstrated a different approach. Beginning about 1972, the researchers at PARC were developing a language named Smalltalk that embodied the concept of *object-oriented programming*, or OOP (pronounced *oop*).

Traditionally, high-level programming languages differentiate between code (which is statements generally beginning with a keyword such as *set* or *for* or *if*) and data, which is numbers represented by variables. This distinction no doubt originates from the architecture of von Neumann computers, in which something is either machine code or is data acted upon by machine code.

In object-oriented programming, however, an *object* is a combination of code and data. The actual way in which the data in an object is stored is understood only by code associated with the object. Objects communicate with one another by sending and receiving *messages,* which give instructions to an object or ask for information from it.

Object-oriented languages are often helpful for programming applications for graphical operating systems because the programmer can treat objects on the screen (such as windows and buttons) in much the same way that a user perceives them. A button is an example of an object in an object-oriented language. A button has a certain dimension and position on the screen and displays some text or a little picture, all of which is data associated with the object. Code associated with the object determines when the user "presses" the button with the keyboard or the mouse and sends a message indicating the button has been triggered.

The most popular object-oriented languages for small computers, however, are extensions of traditional ALGOL-like languages, such as C and Pascal. The most popular object-oriented extension of C is called C++. (As you might recall, two plus signs in C is an increment operator.) Largely the brainchild of Bjarne Stroustrup (born 1950) of Bell Telephone Laboratories, C++ was implemented first as a translator that converted a program written in C++ to one written in C (although very ugly and virtually unreadable C). The C program could then be compiled normally.

Object-oriented languages can't do anything more than traditional languages can do, of course. But programming is a problem-solving activity, and object-oriented languages allow the programmer to consider different solutions that are often structurally superior. It's also possible—although not exactly easy—to write a single program using an object-oriented language that can be compiled to run either on the Macintosh or under Windows. Such a program doesn't refer to the APIs directly but rather uses objects that in turn call the API functions. Two different object definitions are used to compile the program for the Macintosh or Windows API.

Most programmers working on small computers no longer run a compiler from a command line. Instead, programmers use an *integrated development environment* (IDE), which combines all the tools they need in one convenient program that runs like other graphical applications. Programmers also take advantage of a technique called *visual programming,* in which windows are designed interactively by using the mouse to assemble buttons and other components.

In Chapter 22, I described text files, which are files that contain only ASCII characters and which are readable by human beings like you and me. Back in the days of text-based operating systems, text files were ideal to exchange information among applications. One big advantage of text files is that they're searchable—that is, a program can look at many text files and determine which of them contains a particular text string. But once you have a facility in the operating system to display text using various fonts and sizes and effects such as italics, boldfacing, and underlining, the text file suddenly seems woefully inadequate. Indeed, most word processing programs save documents in a proprietary binary format. Text files are also not suitable for pictorial information.

But it's possible to encode information (such as font specifications and paragraph layout) along with text and still have a readable text file. The key is to choose an escape character to denote this information. In the Rich Text Format (RTF) designed by Microsoft as a means to exchange formatted text among applications, the curly brackets { and } and the backslash character \ are used to enclose information that indicates how the text is to be formatted.

PostScript is a text file format that takes this concept to extremes. Designed by John Warnock (born 1940), cofounder of Adobe Systems, PostScript is an entire general-purpose graphics programming language used today mostly to draw text and graphics on high-end computer printers.

The incorporation of graphical images into the personal computing environment is the direct result of better and cheaper hardware. As microprocessors have become faster, as memory has become cheaper, as video displays and printers have increased in resolution and blossomed in full color, that power has been exploited through computer graphics.

Computer graphics comes in two flavors, which are referred to by the same words I used earlier to differentiate graphical video displays: vector and raster.

Vector graphics involves creating images algorithmically using straight lines, curves, and filled areas. This is the province of the *computer-assisted drawing* (or CAD) program. Vector graphics finds its most important application in engineering and architectural design. A vector graphics image can be stored in a file in a format referred to as a *metafile*. A metafile is simply a collection of vector graphics drawing commands usually encoded in binary form.

The use of lines, curves, and filled areas of vector graphics is entirely appropriate when you're designing a bridge but hopelessly inadequate when you want to show what the actual constructed bridge looks like. That bridge is a real-world image. It's simply too complex to be represented by vector graphics.

Raster graphics (also known as *bitmap graphics*) comes to the rescue. A bitmap encodes an image as a rectangular array of bits that correspond to the pixels of an output device. Just like a video display, a bitmap has a spatial dimension (or resolution), which is the width and height of the image in pixels. Bitmaps also have a color dimension (or color resolution, or color depth), which is the number of bits associated with each pixel. Each pixel in a bitmap has the same number of bits.

Although a bitmap image is two dimensional, the bitmap itself is just a single stream of bytes—usually the top row of pixels, followed by the second row, followed by the third row, and so on.

Some bitmap images are created "manually" by someone using a paint program designed for a graphical operating system. Other bitmap images are created algorithmically by computer code. These days, however, bitmaps are very often used for images from the real world (such as photographs), and there are several different pieces of hardware that allow you to move images from the real world into the computer. These devices generally use something called a *charge-coupled device* (CCD), which is a semiconductor that releases an electrical charge when exposed to light. One CCD cell is required for each pixel to be sampled.

The *scanner* is the oldest of these devices. Much like a photocopy machine, it uses a row of CCDs that sweep along the surface of a printed image, such as a photograph. The CCDs generate electrical charges based on the intensity of light. Software that works with the scanner translates the image into a bitmap that's stored in a file.

Video camcorders use a two-dimensional array of CCD cells to capture images. Generally these images are recorded on videotape. But the video output might be fed directly into a *video frame grabber*, which is a board that converts an analog video signal to an array of pixel values. These frame grabbers can be used with any common video source, such as that from a VCR or a laser disc player, or even directly from a cable television box.

Most recently, digital cameras have become financially viable for the home user. These often look very much like normal cameras. But instead of film, an array of CCDs is used to capture an image that's stored directly in memory within the camera and later transferred into the computer.

A graphical operating system often supports the storage of bitmaps in files in a particular format. The Macintosh uses the Paint format, the name of which is a reference to the MacPaint program that inaugurated the format. (The Macintosh PICT format that combines bitmaps and vector graphics is actually the preferred format.) In Windows, the native format is referred to as BMP, which is the filename extension used for bitmaps.

Bitmaps can be quite large, and it's beneficial to figure out some way to make them smaller. This effort falls under an area of computer science known as *data compression*.

Suppose we were dealing with an image with 3 bits per pixel such as I described earlier. You have a picture of sky and a house and a lawn. This picture probably has large patches of blue and green. Maybe the very top row of the bitmap has 72 blue pixels in a row. The bitmap file could be made smaller if there were some way to actually encode the number 72 in the file to mean that the blue pixel repeats 72 times. This type of compression is known as *run-length encoding,* or RLE.

The common office fax machine uses RLE compression to reduce the size of an image before sending it over the telephone line. Because a fax interprets an image as black and white with no gray shades or colors, there are generally long stretches of white pixels.

A bitmap file format that's been popular for over a decade is the Graphics Interchange Format, or GIF (pronounced *jif* like the peanut butter), developed by CompuServe in 1987. GIF files use a compression technique called LZW, which stands for its creators, Lempel, Ziv, and Welch. LZW is more powerful than RLE because it detects *patterns* of differently valued pixels rather than just consecutive strings of same-value pixels.

Both RLE and LZW are referred to as *lossless* compression techniques because the original file can be entirely re-created from the compressed data. In other words, the compression is *reversible*. It's fairly easy to prove that reversible compression doesn't work for every type of file. In some cases, the "compressed" file is actually larger than the original file!

In recent years, *lossy* compression techniques have become popular. A lossy compression isn't reversible because some of the original data is effectively discarded. You wouldn't want to use lossy compression on your spreadsheets or word processing documents. Presumably every number and word is important. But you probably wouldn't mind lossy compression for images, just as long as the data that's discarded doesn't make much of a difference in the overall picture. That's why lossy compression techniques are based on psychovisual research that investigates human vision to determine what's important and what's not.

The most significant lossy compression techniques used for bitmaps are collectively referred to as JPEG (pronounced *jay peg*). JPEG stands for the Joint Photography Experts Group and actually describes several compression techniques, some lossless and some lossy.

It's fairly straightforward to convert a metafile to a bitmap. Because video display memory and bitmaps are conceptually identical, if a program knows how to draw a metafile in video display memory, it knows how to draw a metafile on a bitmap.

But converting a bitmap to a metafile isn't so easy, and for some complex images might well be impossible. One technique related to this job is *optical character recognition,* or OCR. OCR is used when you have a bitmap of some text (from a fax machine, perhaps, or scanned from typed pages) and need to convert it to ASCII character codes. The OCR software needs to analyze the patterns of bits and determine what characters they represent. Due to the algorithmic complexity of this job, OCR software is usually not 100 percent accurate. Even less accurate is software that attempts to convert handwriting to ASCII text.

Bitmaps and metafiles are the digital representations of visual information. Audio information can also be converted to bits and bytes.

Digitized sound made a big consumer splash in 1983 with the compact disc, which became the biggest consumer electronics success story ever. The CD was developed by Philips and Sony to store 74 minutes of digitized sound on one side of a disk 12 centimeters in diameter. The length of 74 minutes was chosen so that Beethoven's Ninth Symphony could fit on one CD.

Sound is encoded on a CD using a technique called *pulse code modulation,* or PCM. Despite the fancy name, PCM is conceptually a fairly simple process.

Sound is vibration. Human vocal cords vibrate, a tuba vibrates, a tree falling in a forest vibrates, and these objects cause air molecules to move. The air alternately pushes and pulls, compresses and thins, back and forth some hundreds of times or thousands of times a second. The air in turn vibrates our eardrums, and we sense sound.

Analogous to these waves of sound are the little hills and valleys in the surface of the tin foil cylinder used to record and play back sound in Thomas Edison's first phonograph in 1877. Until the compact disc, this technique of recording sound barely changed, although cylinders were replaced by disks, and tin foil by wax and eventually plastic. Early phonographs were entirely mechanical, but eventually electrical amplification was used to strengthen the sound. The variable resistor in a microphone converts sound to electricity, and the electromagnet in a loudspeaker converts electricity back to sound.

An electrical current that represents sound isn't like the on-off digital signals that we've encountered throughout this book. Sound waves vary continuously, and so does the voltage of such a current. The electrical current is an *analog* of the sound waves. A device known as an *analog-to-digital converter* (ADC)—generally implemented in a chip—converts an analog voltage to a binary number. The output of an ADC is a certain number of digital signals—usually 8, 12, or 16—that together indicate the relative level of the voltage. A 12-bit ADC, for example, converts a voltage to a number between 000h and FFFh and can differentiate 4096 different voltage levels.

In the technique known as *pulse code modulation*, the voltage representing a sound wave is converted to digital values at a constant rate. These numbers are stored on the CD in the form of little holes carved into the surface of the disc. They're read with a laser light reflected from the surface of the CD. During playback, the numbers are converted to an electrical current again using a *digital-to-analog converter*, or DAC. (A DAC is also used in color graphics boards to convert a pixel value to analog color signals that go to the monitor.)

The voltage of the sound wave is converted to numbers at a constant rate, known as the *sampling rate*. In 1928, Harry Nyquist of Bell Telephone Laboratories showed that a sampling rate must be at least twice the maximum frequency that needs to be recorded and played back. It's commonly assumed that humans hear sounds ranging from 20 Hz to 20,000 Hz. The sampling frequency used for CDs is a bit more than double that maximum, specifically 44,100 samples per second.

The number of bits per sample determines the dynamic range of the CD, which is the difference between the loudest and the softest sound that can be recorded and played back. This is somewhat complicated: As the electrical current varies back and forth as an analog of the sound waves, the peaks it hits represent the waveform's *amplitude*. What we perceive as the *intensity* of the sound is proportional to twice the amplitude. A *bel* (which is three-quarters of Alexander Graham Bell's last name) is a tenfold increase in intensity; a *decibel* is one-tenth of a bel. One decibel represents approximately the smallest increase in loudness that a person can perceive.

It turns out that the use of 16 bits per sample allows a dynamic range of 96 decibels, which is approximately the difference between the threshold of hearing (below which we can't hear anything) and the threshold of pain. The compact disk uses 16 bits per sample.

So for each second of sound, a compact disk contains 44,100 samples of 2 bytes each. But you probably want stereo as well. So double that for a total of 176,400 bytes per second. That's 10,584,000 bytes per minute of sound. (Now you know why digital recording of sound wasn't common before the 1980s.) The full 74 minutes of stereo sound on the CD requires 783,216,000 bytes.

Digitized sound has many well-known advantages over analog sound. In particular, whenever analog sound is copied (for example, when a phonograph record is created from a master recording tape) some fidelity is lost. Digitized sound is numbers, however, and numbers can always be faithfully transcribed and copied. It used to be that the longer a telephone signal had to travel in a wire, the worse it would sound. This is no longer the case. Because much of the telephone system is now digital, calls from across the country sound as clear as those from across the street.

CDs can store data as well as sound. When used exclusively for data, they're called CD-ROM (CD Read-Only Memory). A CD-ROM is generally limited to about 660 megabytes. Most computers these days have CD-ROM drives installed, and much application and game software is distributed on CD-ROM.

The introduction of sound, music, and video into the personal computer was known as *multimedia* just a decade ago and is now so common that it doesn't need a special name. Most home computers sold these days have a sound board that includes an ADC for digitally recording sound through a microphone and a DAC for playing back recorded sound through speakers. Sounds can be stored on a disk in *waveform files*.

Because you don't always need CD quality sound when recording and playing back sound on home computers, the Macintosh and Windows offer lower sampling rates, specifically 22,050 Hz, 11,025 Hz, and 8000 Hz; a lower sample size of 8 bits; and monophonic recording. Sound can be recorded using as few as 8000 bytes per second, which is 480,000 bytes per minute.

Everybody knows from science fiction movies and television shows that computers of the future converse with their users in spoken English. Once a computer is equipped with hardware to digitally record and play back sound, everything else involved in this goal is a software problem.

There are a couple of ways that computers can be made to talk in recognizable words and sentences. One approach is to have a human being record sentence fragments, phrases, words, and numbers that can then be stored in files and strung together in different ways. This approach is often used for information systems accessed over the telephone, and it works fine when there are only a limited number of combinations of words and numbers that must be played back.

A more general form of voice synthesis involves a process that converts arbitrary ASCII text to waveform data. Because English spelling, for example, isn't always consistent, such a software system uses a dictionary or complex algorithms to determine the actual pronunciation of words. Basic vocal sounds (called phonemes) are combined to form whole words. Often the software must make other adjustments. For example, if a sentence is followed by a question mark, the sound of the last word must be increased in frequency.

Voice recognition—the conversion of waveform data to ASCII text—is a much more complex problem. Indeed, many humans have problems understanding regional variations in spoken language. While dictation software for the personal computer is available, it usually requires some training so that it can reasonably transcribe what a particular person is saying. Far beyond the conversion to ASCII text is the problem of programming the computer so that it actually "understands" what is said. Such a problem is in the realm of the field of *artificial intelligence*.

The sound boards in today's computers are also supplied with small electronic music synthesizers that can imitate the sounds of 128 different musical instruments and 47 different percussion instruments. These are referred to as MIDI (pronounced *middy*) synthesizers. MIDI is the Musical Instrument Digital Interface, a specification developed in the early 1980s by a consortium of manufacturers of electronic music synthesizers to connect these electronic instruments to one another and to computers.

Various types of MIDI synthesizers use a variety of methods for synthesizing instrument sounds, some of which are more realistic than others. The overall quality of a particular MIDI synthesizer is quite outside the province of the MIDI specification. All that's required is that the synthesizer respond to short messages—usually 1, 2, or 3 bytes in length—by playing sounds. MIDI messages mostly indicate what instrument is desired, that a particular note should begin playing, or that a note currently playing should stop playing.

A MIDI file is a collection of MIDI messages with timing information. A MIDI file usually contains an entire musical composition that can be played back on the computer's MIDI synthesizer. A MIDI file is usually much smaller than a waveform file containing the same music. In terms of relative size, if a waveform file is like a bitmap file, a MIDI file is like a vector graphics metafile. The downside is that the music encoded in a MIDI file could sound great on one MIDI synthesizer and quite horrid on another.

Another feature of multimedia is digitized movies. The apparent motion of movie and television images is achieved by quickly displaying a sequence of individual still images. These individual images are called *frames*. Movies proceed at the rate of 24 frames per second, North American television at 30 frames per second, and television in most other places in the world at 25 frames per second.

A movie file on a computer is simply a series of bitmaps with sound. But without compression, a movie file requires a huge amount of data. For example, consider a movie with each frame the size of a 640-by-480-pixel computer screen with 24-bit color. That's 921,600 bytes per frame. At 30 frames per second, we're up to 27,648,000 bytes per second. Keep multiplying and you get 1,658,880,000 bytes per minute, and 199,065,600,000 bytes—just about 200 gigabytes—for a two-hour movie. This is why most movies displayed on the personal computer are short, small, and jumpy.

Just as JPEG compression is used to reduce the amount of data required to store still images, MPEG compression is used for movies. MPEG (pronounced *em peg*) stands for Moving Pictures Expert Group. Compression techniques for moving images take advantage of the fact that a particular frame usually contains much information that's duplicated from the previous frame.

There are different MPEG standards for different media. MPEG-2 is for high-definition television (HDTV) and for *digital video discs* (DVDs), also called *digital versatile discs*. DVDs are the same size as CDs, but they can be recorded on both sides and in two layers per side. On DVDs, video is compressed by a factor of about 50, so a two-hour movie requires only 4 gigabytes, which can fit on one layer of one side. The use of both layers and both sides increases the capacity of DVDs to about 16 gigabytes, which is about 25 times the capacity of a CD. It's expected that DVD-ROM will eventually replace CD-ROM for the distribution of software.

Are CD-ROM and DVD-ROM the modern day realization of Vannevar Bush's Memex? He originally conceived of Memex as using microfilm, but CD-ROM and DVD-ROM make much more sense for such a device. Electronic media have an advantage over physical media by being easily searchable. Unfortunately, few people have simultaneous access to multiple CD or DVD drives. The closest that we've come to Bush's concept doesn't involve storing all the information you'll need at your desk. It involves *interconnecting* computers to give them the ability to share information and use storage much more efficiently.

The first person to publicly operate a computer from a remote location was George Stibitz, the same man who designed the Bell Labs relay computer in the 1930s. The remote operation of a relay computer occurred at a demonstration at Dartmouth in 1940.

The telephone system is built to transmit sound, not bits, over wires. Sending bits over telephone wires requires that the bits be converted to sound and then back again. A continuous sound wave of a single frequency and a single amplitude (called a *carrier*) doesn't convey any substantial information at all. But change something about that sound wave—in other words, *modulate* that sound wave between two different states—and you can represent 0s and 1s. The conversion between bits and sound occurs in a device called the *modem* (which stands for modulator/demodulator). The modem is a form of *serial* interface because the individual bits in a byte are sent one after another rather than all at once. (Printers are often connected to computers with a parallel interface: Eight wires allow an entire byte to be transmitted at the same time.)

In early modems, a technique called *frequency-shift keying* (FSK) was used. A modem operating at 300 bits per second (for example) might convert a 0 bit to a frequency of 1070 Hz and a 1 bit to a frequency of 1270 Hz. Each byte is prefaced by a start bit and concluded with a stop bit, so each byte requires 10 bits. At 300 bits per second, the transmission speed is only 30 bytes per second. More modern modems use more sophisticated techniques to achieve speeds over 100 times that.

An early home computer enthusiast could set up a computer and a modem as a *bulletin board system* (BBS), to which other computers could call in and *download* files, which means transferring files from a remote computer to one's own computer. This concept was extended into large information services such as CompuServe. In most cases, communication was entirely in the form of ASCII text.

The Internet is qualitatively different from these early efforts because it's decentralized. The Internet really exists as a collection of protocols for computers to talk to one another. Of major importance is TCP/IP, which consists of the *Transmission Control Protocol* and the *Internet Protocol*. Rather than just sending ASCII characters through the wires, TCP/IP-based transmitters divide larger blocks of data into smaller *packets,* which are sent separately over the transmission line (often a telephone line) and reassembled on the other end.

The popular graphical part of the Internet is the World Wide Web, which makes use of HTTP, the *Hypertext Transfer Protocol.* The actual data viewed on Web pages is defined by a text format called HTML, or *Hypertext Markup Language.* The *hypertext* part of these names is a word used to describe the linking of associated information, much like that proposed by Vannevar Bush for the Memex. An HTML file can contain links to other Web pages that can be easily invoked.

HTML is similar to the Rich Text Format that I described earlier, in that it contains ASCII text with formatting information. HTML also allows referencing pictures in the form of GIF files, PNG (Portable Network Graphics) files, and JFIF (JPEG File Interchange Format) files. Most World Wide Web browsers allow you to look at the HTML files, which is an advantage of their text format. Another advantage of defining HTML as a text file is that it's more easily searchable. Despite its name, HTML isn't really a *programming* language such as we've explored in Chapters 19 and 24. The Web browser reads the HTML file and formats the text and graphics accordingly.

It's sometimes helpful if some special program code runs while you are viewing and working with particular Web pages. Such code can run on either the *server* (which is the computer on which the original Web pages are stored) or the *client,* which is your computer. On the server side, usually all necessary work (such as interpreting online forms that a client fills out) can be handled with Common Gateway Interface (CGI) scripts. On the client side, HTML files can contain a simple programming language known as *JavaScript.* Your Web browser interprets the JavaScript statements just as it interprets HTML text.

Why can't a Web site simply provide an executable program that can run on your computer? Well, for one thing, what is your computer? If it's a Macintosh, it needs an executable that contains PowerPC machine code and uses the Mac OS API. A PC-compatible needs an executable that contains Intel Pentium machine code and probably uses the Windows API. But there are other computers and other graphical operating systems as well. Moreover, you don't want to be indiscriminately downloading executable files. They could originate from an untrustworthy source and might be malicious in some way.

An answer to these problems was provided by Sun Microsystems in the language Java (not to be confused with JavaScript). Java is a full-fledged object-oriented programming language much like C++. In the preceding chapter, I explained the difference between compiled languages (which result in an executable that contains machine code), and interpreted languages (which don't). Java is somewhere in between. Java programs must be compiled, but the result of the compilation isn't machine code. It's instead *Java byte codes*. These are similar in structure to machine code, but they're for an imaginary computer called the *Java virtual machine* (JVM). A computer running the compiled Java program emulates the JVM by interpreting the Java byte codes. The Java program uses whatever graphical operating system is on the machine, thus allowing *platform-independent* programming.

While much of this book has focused on using electricity to send signals and information through a wire, a more efficient medium is light transmitted through optical fiber—thin tubes made of glass or polymer that guide the light around corners. Light passing through such optical fibers can achieve data transmission rates in the gigahertz region—some billion of bits per second.

So it seems that photons, not electrons, will be responsible for delivering much of the information of the future into our homes and offices; they'll be like faster dots and dashes of Morse code and those careful pulses of blinking light we once used to communicate late-night wisdom to our best friend across the way.

❧ Acknowledgments ❧

Code was conceived in 1987. It rattled around in my head for nearly a decade and was finally committed to a Microsoft Word file between January 1996 and July 1999. I offer many thanks:

to the readers of early drafts of *Code* who contributed comments, criticisms, and suggestions: Sheryl Canter, Jan Eastlund, Peter Goldeman, Lynn Magalska, and Deirdre Sinnott;

to my agent, Claudette Moore of Moore Literary Agency, and to everyone at Microsoft Press who helped make *Code* a reality, particularly those whose names are listed on the copyright page of this book and on the colophon, following the index;

to my mother, who never held me back;

to Little Cat, who shared my apartment with me from 1982 through May 1999, and who inspired many cat references in my writing;

to Web sites such as Bibliofind (*www.bibliofind.com*) and Advanced Book Exchange (*www.abebooks.com*) that offer convenient access to used books, and to the staff of the Science, Industry, and Business Library (SIBL) branch of the New York Public Library (*www.nypl.org*);

to my friends in the rooms, without whose support none of this would be possible;

and again to Deirdre, my ideal reader and so much more.

Charles Petzold
July 15, 1999

❧ Bibliography ❧

An annotated bibliography for this book is available on the World Wide Web site *www.charlespetzold.com/code*.

≈ Index ≈

Note: Page numbers in italics refer to illustrations.

V

vacuum tubes, 37–38, 142, 243,
  247, 249
variables, 355–56
video displays, 311–15, 321, 324, 332,
  334, 349, 366–70, 372
virtual memory, 334
VisiCalc, 366–67
voltage, 27–30, 37–39, 43
  flip-flops and, 157, 159
  logic gates and, 107–9, 113–14, 120
Volto, Count Alessandro, 28
von Neumann architecture, 245
von Neumann bottleneck, 245

W

Warnock, John, 374
Watson, Thomas J., 242
Watt, James, 31
white space, 234
Wiener, Norbert, 246
Wilson, Flip, 371
Windows (Microsoft). *See* Microsoft
  Corporation, Windows
  operating system
Wirth, Niklaus, 362
Wozniak, Stephen, 284
WYSIWYG (What You See Is What
  You Get), 371

X

Xerox PARC, 369, 370, 372

Z

Zenith, 251
Zuse, Conrad, 243

➤ About the Author ➤

Donal Holway

Charles Petzold has been writing about personal computers and programming for more than 15 years, and his classic book *Programming Windows,* now in its fifth edition, has influenced an entire generation of programmers. *Code* shares this gifted teacher and communicator with every reader interested in understanding how computers work— no matter what their level of technological savvy. He resides in New York City.

❧ Colophon ❧

The manuscript for this book was prepared using Microsoft Word 2000. Pages were composed using Adobe PageMaker 6.52, with text and display type in Sabon and math fonts in Syntax. Composed pages were delivered to the printer as electronic prepress files.

Dust Jacket and Cover Graphic Designer
Greg Hickman

Interior Book Design
Jimmie Young and Sally Slevin

Illustrator
Joel Panchot

Compositor
Elizabeth Hansford

Principal Proofreader/Copy Editor
Shawn Peck

Indexer
Liz Cunningham